Miss Peggy Lee

ALSO BY ROBERT STROM

*Lady of Burlesque: The Career of
Gypsy Rose Lee* (McFarland, 2011)

Miss Peggy Lee
A Career Chronicle

ROBERT STROM
Foreword by Keely Smith

McFarland & Company, Inc., Publishers
Jefferson, North Carolina

Grateful acknowledgement is made for permission to reprint the following:

"I See You" by Benny Carter. Copyright © 2000 Bee Cee Music.
All rights reserved. Used by permission.

"Postscript: Peggy Lee" by Nancy Franklin.
Copyright © 2002 Conde Nast Publications Inc.
Originally published in the February 4, 2002, issue of *The New Yorker*.
Reprinted by permission. All rights reserved.

"Still Here" by Whitney Balliet.
Copyright © 1988.
Originally published in *American Singers — 27 Portraits in Song*.
Reprinted by permission.

"Always True in Her Fashion" by Gary Giddins.
Originally published in the August 18, 1992,
issue of *The Village Voice*.
Reprinted by permission.

All excerpts from *Down Beat* magazine
are reprinted by permission.

The present work is a reprint of the illustrated casebound edition of Miss Peggy Lee: A Career Chronicle, *first published in 2005 by McFarland.*

LIBRARY OF CONGRESS CATALOGUING-IN-PUBLICATION DATA

Strom, Robert, 1961–
Miss Peggy Lee : a career chronicle / Robert Strom ; foreword by Keely Smith.
p.   cm.
Includes bibliographical references and index.

ISBN 978-0-7864-9568-9 (softcover : acid free paper) ∞

1. Lee, Peggy, 1920–[2002].   2. Women jazz singers—
United States— Biography.   I. Title.
ML420.L294S77   2014   782.42165'092 — dc22   2004028958

BRITISH LIBRARY CATALOGUING DATA ARE AVAILABLE

© 2005 Robert Strom. All rights reserved

No part of this book may be reproduced or transmitted in any form or by any means, electronic or mechanical, including photocopying or recording, or by any information storage and retrieval system, without permission in writing from the publisher.

Cover photograph: Peggy Lee singing "Lover" in *The Jazz Singer*

Printed in the United States of America

*McFarland & Company, Inc., Publishers
Box 611, Jefferson, North Carolina 28640
www.mcfarlandpub.com*

To the memory of Ronald Towe

My love and thanks to
Lana Strom

and to the memory of
Miss Peggy Lee

Acknowledgments

Anyone who has created books, paintings, plays or music will tell you that it is a lonely process. However, it is not done alone. Every artist needs support. The ability to create also depends on "how close the muse is," as Miss Lee once said. In my case I was fortunate to have numerous muses nearby. Each person listed below is a loyal friend. Without them this book would not have been possible. They are my angels on Earth. I am blessed to know them. My heartfelt gratitude goes to each and every one.

Miss Peggy Lee — Teacher. One of my soulmates. I remember every kind, giving gesture with great clarity. The greatest compliment I ever received was when she said to me, "I always knew you were a gentleman." She also told me, "You're in tune with the infinite." Her music will play in my heart forever.

Elmer and Mildred Birchland — Maternal grandparents. Thank you for all the unconditional love. I miss you.

Dr. Claire Borkert — Hero. Gentle, compassionate, wise. A doctor who treats with love rather than with medicine.

Rosemary Clooney — Friend. Her heart was as warm as her voice. Her voice was as warm as the sun. I think of her every day.

Sean Connors — Friend. Devoted to the art of Miss Peggy Lee. Strong and honest. Lover of America's very best music. His generosity knows no bounds. A gentleman.

Larry Dunlap — Friend. Loves life, music and good jokes. The most talented pianist I know. Music from the heart.

John Fricke — Mentor. Always encouraging. An extraordinary author who needs to write more! His book, *Judy Garland — World's Greatest Entertainer*, is the finest tribute to her artistic achievements that you'll ever read.

Arnold Goodpasture — Friend. He deals with each situation with great care, attention to detail and heart. That's why he's "The Incredible One." Also the funniest person I know!

Linda Goppert—Aunt. A spiritual soulmate. My love and admiration for the true stars of Hollywood comes from her. There is great strength in her tenderness. A humanitarian. I send you love.

Ted Goppert—Uncle. He cares more than he lets on. Quiet, firm support. I send you love.

Jenny Goppert—Cousin. Tremendous passion. Dedicated to truth. Unconditional love.

Jeff Goppert—Cousin. An artist who doesn't see his true talent. Paint, draw, and create!

Ian Harries—Friend. Total love and support. What a great sense of humor you have, dear Sir Ian.

Marti Hicks—Friend. My "Lady." My second "Mom." She gives of herself totally. She makes me laugh till I cry!

Duke, Marsha and Eugenia Hill—Friends. Support and love without hesitation.

Ellie Hoffman—Friend. Honest. She makes me think carefully before acting rashly. Her own well being comes second to that of her friends. I adore you.

Ray Holt—Uncle Devil Ray. A loyal and caring friend. A talented actor whose star is destined to shine.

Renate Kohlman—Friend. Your loving guidance played a tremendous part in the creation of this book. Thank you.

Jim Lange—Friend. "Gentleman Jim" is not just a title, it is the truth. Music lover.

Bernice Mills—Friend. Gentle, gentle, gentle. A Sinatra fan who dubbed me "Young Blue Eyes." That's an honor!

Bobbe Norris—Friend. Her kindness overwhelms me, as does her musical gift. One of the finest jazz singers I know. A majestic voice filled with pure love and total honesty.

Trina Oliver—Friend. Dedicated to the arts and the beauty of the human spirit. A creative, compassionate force. More talented than she'll ever know. More tender than she reveals.

Penny Peck—Friend. Trustworthy, knowledgeable, supportive. Her total belief in her friends never falters. The queen of Hollywood trivia!

Phyllis Plate—A wonderful new friend. She is intelligent, witty and very supportive. A fellow dog lover.

Luanne Prima—Friend. Great humor and genuine warmth. A beauty like her Mom.

Toni Prima—Friend. Trusting, open, honest. Great spiritual wisdom from a caring heart. Our marathon phone calls give me great strength and joy!

Barb Rayboy— Friend. She is honest, loyal and has a great sense of humor. A dedicated musician.

Dr. Janell Routh— Friend. Intelligent, loyal and giving. Her enthusiasm and belief in my abilities is inspiring. A genuine free spirit. I adore you.

Sal Russo— Friend. So quiet you hardly know he's there. A kindness that touches the heart.

Keely Smith— Friend. Brave and honest. When you need her she is there. Her kindness brings tears of gratitude. A soul as big as her glorious, pure voice. Our most underrated singer. The best!

Kay Starr— Friend. Giving of her time and talent. Wickedly funny and very real.

Erik Strom— Brother. Deeply caring of everyone he loves. Committed to every cause he believes in. Quiet strength and intelligence. A dry, original sense of humor!

Lana Strom— Mom. Loving, giving, caring, encouraging. Simply — The World's Greatest Mom. She listens and finds balance in an unbalanced world. Her children come first. Honesty is her creed. All of my friends adore her and so do I!

Gus and Signe Strom— Paternal grandparents. I love you and I miss you.

Craig Wolf— Friend. Ask and he was there. Unequaled kindness. A gentle soul who loved beauty in music, art and people. He was a sensitive, gentle man. Farewell.

Bella Wiener— Niece. I adore you and I know that like Peggy you will make beautiful music with your life. Love to your family, Sara Wiener and Joanne Richter. You three girls are the best!

Mark Vieira— Friend. His glorious books keep real Hollywood glamour alive. His work is inspiring.

    I would also like to thank each of the following people for their genuine love and unwavering support: Lisa Anderson, Lynn Anderson, Gene Arceri, Joan Arthur, Gerry Atkinson, Martyne Bachmen, Ron and Jeanne Bloomfield, Daniel Clemson, Raymond Daum, Dino Donikian, Pat Dees, Giuliano Fournier, Marne and Ron Garriety and family, Jarl Ingves, Cinny Green, Lynn Hicks, Anthony Houben, Rae Ann Inniello, Wilfred Johnson, Vivian Kellner, Erik and Valerie Kellner and family, Juanita Kirby, Dennis Kohles, Camille Larrea, Carlos Lopez, Malcolm Macfarlane, Michel Macaire, Ramona McMaster, Shawna Martin and family, Betty Mayo and family, Jeannie Moran, Richard Morrison, Birgitta Nilsson, Emilio Palame and family, Ray Purslow, James O. Rugland, Steve Sandos, Jimmy Scalia, Tom Schluckebier, Roger Schram, Liz Smith, Sally Strom and family, Patrick Tracy, Lars-Anders Westlin and Peggy Williams.

    Many thanks to the trinity of great American jazz writers: Whitney Balliett, Will Friedwald and Gary Giddins. Also Jason Koransky editor of *Down Beat* magazine.

Table of Contents

Acknowledgments	vii
Foreword by Keely Smith	1
Preface	3
One • If I Could Swing with a Band: 1920 to 1940	5
Two • The Benny Goodman Years and the First Capitol Period: 1940 to 1951	17
Three • Decca: 1952 to 1957	53
Four • Return to Capitol: 1957 to 1967	77
Five • Grammy Winner: 1968 to 1972	129
Six • Becoming a Legend: 1972 to 1982	157
Seven • There'll Be Another Spring: 1982 to 1988	193
Eight • Peggy Sings the Blues: 1988 to 1995	219
Epilogue (Nancy Franklin)	242
Closing Comments	244
Appendix A. Miss Peggy Lee on CD	247
Appendix B. Songs Written by Miss Peggy Lee	281
Bibliography	285
Index	287

Foreword
by Keely Smith

The 1950s were a golden time for popular American singers. This was especially true for those of us at Capitol Records. Capitol was *the* label for singers.

Imagine working in the same studio where Frank Sinatra, Nat "King" Cole, Ella Fitzgerald, Kay Starr and Peggy Lee recorded their hits. Well, that's where I found myself.

In those days I did whatever my husband, Louis Prima, told me to do. We had a job, I showed up and I performed. Now, as I look back, I realize how blessed I was to be in the Capitol Tower during that magic time. I was in the best school a young singer could ever hope for. I was a very lucky kid. And I still to this day make my recordings at Capitol Records!

It wasn't just the singers at Capitol who made great music. We did not do it alone. We had top-notch producers, superb musicians and the world's greatest arrangers. I was fortunate enough to work with both Nelson Riddle and Billy May. Nelson with his glorious strings and Billy with his swinging horn section.

Peggy worked with Nelson on her *Jump for Joy* album. Billy May arranged and conducted the *Pretty Eyes* LP for her. On *Blues Cross Country* and *If You Go*, Peggy brought a young arranger-conductor to the Capitol label, Quincy Jones. Yes, it was Peggy who gave the legendary Quincy his start as an arranger. She also worked with Benny Carter on her *Mink Jazz* album. In short, we worked with the very best.

Incidentally, my favorite Peggy Lee recording is "The Man I Love." This appears on the album of the same name and is conducted by our mutual friend Frank Sinatra.

Of course Peggy also brought her tremendous talent to each recording session. She had the ability to swing hard on one tune and then give you a sultry reading on a slow ballad. I admire her wonderful diction and her unique phrasing. Peggy also had a great ear. She knew, instinctively it seemed, if the arrangement was right for her. She was a true original, and she was at her peak at Capitol in the 1950s and 1960s.

Years later Peggy and I appeared at Capitol's anniversary concert in September of 1982. It was a great reunion for many of the Capitol stars. The show was in a high school auditorium in Hackensack, New Jersey.

In spite of an awful blizzard we had a packed house. I closed the first half of the show. Everyone stayed there until 2 A.M. when Peggy came on to close the show. I stayed too, just to see her.

She came on stage with that "Miss Peggy Lee" charm. Her charisma and regal presence filled the theater. She was magnetic. She looked great and sang wonderfully. I'm glad I stayed up that late. Peggy made it worthwhile.

Now, about this book—Robert Strom has put together an impressive reference book. I've known Robert for a decade, and I can tell you that this book is the perfect blend of author and subject. Robert has an intense passion for and extensive knowledge of the great American singers.

This is a book that no music fan should be without. In a sense it is a diary of Peggy's career as a singer, songwriter and spellbinding performer.

Peggy Lee fans won't have to look any further for the definitive book on the facts and milestones of Peggy's fabled career. It is all here, lovingly gathered in these pages.

This book is a tribute to an American Icon, and rightfully so. We all love Peggy. I know I do.

I Wish You Love,
Keely Smith
Palm Springs, California
February 2005

Preface

One of the clearest ways to become acquainted with the life history of an artist is to study his or her art. When you examine artistic accomplishment you unearth many facets of the artist's personality. The body of work reflects the artist's environment and influences. Here, too, you will find the artist's political, emotional and spiritual truths.

What sources influenced the growth of Peggy Lee's exceptional talent? What nurtured the blossom we knew as Miss Peggy Lee?

By looking chronologically at her artistic achievements, this book hopes to provide biographical insight. Lee's private life is not discussed; instead her public life is examined. In such an examination, that which is most private about Peggy Lee is revealed. She knew, as we do, that through her music she revealed her soul.

Miss Peggy Lee's many artistic achievements included triumphant success in radio, recordings, television, film, and live concerts. As a singer and songwriter, she displayed tremendous creative talent and virtuosity. The lyrics of the songs she wrote are not merely entertaining; they also reveal Peggy's growth as a human being. Her compositions tell her life story. I recommend that the reader listen to the songs discussed in this book. Lee's songs provide an aural biography.

Peggy Lee had a near perfect career; ultimately she would want to be remembered for the many musical gifts she gave us. For this reason, this book concentrates largely on her professional life. Important life events are included, but the focus is principally on her illustrious career.

This book looks at that career in a chronological format. There are entries for her songwriting; her recordings (both albums and individual songs); her radio, television, and concert appearances; and her work in films. Interviews and reviews are quoted throughout.

The book also includes a list of the songs that Lee performed and recorded, a selective CD discography and an index.

My thanks to Gary Giddins of the *Village Voice* for allowing me to quote his article "Always True in Her Fashion"; to Whitney Balliett for quotes from *American Singers: 27 Portraits in Song*; and the Jason Koransky, editor of *DownBeat*, for permission to quote articles from the magazine.

I am indebted to the authors who acted as my mentors on this project, and to the journalists and fans who documented Peggy Lee's professional life. Thank you.

Peggy Lee holds a special place in the history of American jazz and popular music. I hope this book will illustrate just how wonderful, unique and influential were her gifts—the gifts she shared so generously with the world.

Enjoy!

• ONE •

If I Could Swing with a Band: 1920 to 1940

"I was a strange child."

Peggy Lee's audiences laughed along with her when she described herself that way. Actually, however, she had a fairly normal childhood up until age four. When she was four her beloved Mama, Selma Egstrom, died. That event, and those that followed, would shape the emotional and spiritual landscape of the young child who would grow up to be Peggy Lee.

In his liner notes for the two CD set *Peggy Lee — Black Coffee & Other Delights — the Decca Anthology*, author Jim Lowe begins by saying, "Peggy Lee is different. But then Peggy Lee has always been different." Lowe's feeling that she is "different," and her own view of herself as "strange," are interesting observations. However, the most accurate word to describe her would be "unique." Peggy Lee has always been one of a kind.

The majority of our great American vocalists were born between 1900 and 1940. Their ethnic heritage generally falls into four groups: African American (Louis Armstrong, Nat "King" Cole, Ella Fitzgerald, Billie Holiday, Lena Horne and Joe Williams), Irish American (Rosemary Clooney, Bing Crosby and Judy Garland), Italian American (Perry Como, Dean Martin and Frank Sinatra) and American Indian (Mildred Bailey, Keely Smith, Kay Starr and Lee Wiley). Most were born in or near large cities, and all were raised by their mothers. In the cases of Sinatra, Garland and Holiday their mothers played integral roles in their careers.

Peggy Lee is the only artist in this league to be born of Scandinavian parents.

***May 26, 1920*— Norma Deloris Egstrom is born.** She was born Norma Deloris Egstrom on May 26, 1920.

This rare baby photograph shows Norma Egstrom just before her second birthday.

Her birthplace of Jamestown, North Dakota, could hardly be called a large city. In 1920 the population was only 6,000. North Dakota is a prairie state, peopled with hard-working farmers. These are sturdy, determined people. They have to be to survive the winter temperatures that can drop to 60 below, and summer highs of up to 120 degrees Fahrenheit. Young Norma Egstrom survived the harsh climate and back-breaking chores. That she made it without the love and guidance of her mother is a testament to her strength.

1925— Marvin Egstrom marries Min Schaumberg. She also survived Min. In 1925 her father, Marvin Egstrom, married Min Schaumberg. Norma was five. Min was the quintessential wicked stepmother. For the next eleven years Norma was mentally and physically abused. In her Broadway show *Peg*, the adult Peggy Lee turned the horror of her childhood into a humorous song entitled "One Beating a Day." Set to a calypso tune, Peggy's lyrics described how she was beaten with willow switches, a frying pan, a two-by-four and the metal end of a razor strap. The razor strap left a scar on her face. The refrain of "One Beating a Day" offers great insight. She sings that Min's beatings could not make her hate anyone. She only made Lee love everybody. The joke is on Min.

Still, Min's beatings left emotional scars. These wounds could not be seen, but they would surface in later years when Peggy sang the blues. Her quest for her mother would also influence her art, adding layers of sadness and hope to her singing.

She recalled her early search for her "Mama" in her autobiography *Miss Peggy Lee*. When she asked about her mother's whereabouts she received conflicting information. Some adults told her she was in the ground. Others pointed skyward and said Selma was with God.

Norma seemed to take comfort in the idea that her mother was with God. She would lie on her back and study the huge thunderclouds that drifted across the North Dakota sky. She was certain that one day she would see her mother behind a cloud. Then the clouds were swept away, taking Norma's hopes with them. She would continue to search for the rest of her life.

Norma's days were filled with more than sadness and searching. Although his job as a station agent for the Midland Railroad kept him away from home, Norma had the love of her father. She also had six brothers and sisters: Milford, Della, Leonard, Marianne, Clair and Jean. She was especially close to Marianne. And there was always music.

One of Peggy's earliest memories took place before her mother died. Norma was only three. She was singing during dinner when her mother reminded her there was "no singing at the table." Little Norma replied, "I'm not singing at the table, Mama. I'm singing at the floor." She also remembered her mother playing the household's prized possession, a Circassian piano.

Opposite: Jamestown, North Dakota, as it looked in the 1920s and 1930s. At bottom, the Gladstone Hotel, home of radio station KRMC. Young Norma Egstrom had one of her first jobs as a professional singer on the Jamestown station.

Fifth Avenue, Jamestown, N.D.

Music was her solace. Through music she entered a quiet, internal world that was hers alone. She told author and jazz historian Gene Lees that she was creating lyrics at age five. The following excerpt is from his liner notes for Capitol's four CD box set *Miss Peggy Lee*:

> Everything that was happening was so traumatic that I remember it vividly. I made up a lyric to that song called "Melody of Love." "Mama's gone to dreamland on the train." That was my first lyric. Something inside made me feel not only sad but comforted, in a releasing kind of way.

Another early source of music was the player piano at Grandpa and Grandma Schaumberg's house. It clearly left a lasting impression. Some fifty years later she wrote a song called "That Old Piano." Her lyrics recalled how she got down on her knees and pumped the pedals of the player piano with her hands.

1926—Norma's family moves to Nortonville, North Dakota. When Norma was six the Egstroms moved to the small town of Nortonville. They had no electricity. Kerosene lamps lighted the house. Nortonville, located twenty-eight miles south of Jamestown, had a population of one hundred and twenty-five. Norma's chores included milking the cows, separating the milk and washing the separator. On Sundays, after she finished her chores, she would put a roast in the oven and then hurry down to church. She liked to get there early so she could play the piano. Ever shy, she would stop playing when someone came in.

1928—Norma decides that she will be a singer. By age eight she knew for certain that she would be a singer. While on vacation at Spiritwood Lake she announced to a playmate, "I'm going to be in show business someday." When the little girl asked her what she was going to do in show business Norma promptly broke into song. Just two years later she would write her first song. Its prophetic title was "If I Could Swing with a Band." It seems the ten-year-old Norma Egstrom had a very clear sense of what her future held.

At this same time she had to have an emergency appendectomy. Before anyone realized what was happening to the child her appendix burst and peritonitis set in. Min refused to help. Norma's brother, Clair, had to threaten their stepmother with a shotgun. He forced Min to drive them to the nearby town of Edgeley, where Norma remained in the hospital for ten days.

1934—Norma is confirmed at St. John's Lutheran Church. Upon her return home, Min made Norma scrub the floor. As she was working, Min began to kick her in the stomach. She continued kicking until the incision broke open. Norma escaped and bandaged herself back together. When her father tried to protect her from Min he was beaten too. Later, to add insult to injury, Min burned many of the Egstrom family photos. Fortunately, a copy of her confirmation photo was located at St. John's Lutheran Church.

Norma Deloris Egstrom's confirmation photograph still hangs on the wall of St. John's Lutheran Church in Jamestown. The photograph was taken in 1934. Norma (front, third from right) is fourteen. *Back row:* Leslie Clemens, Darrell Fairfeld, Ferdinand Clemens, Dayle Flegel, Herbert Maas, Earl Weber, Ervin Carlson, Alfred Carlson, Edward Kratzke. *Middle row:* Leonard Clemens, Willmar Wolff, Russell Krueger, Leona Thom, Marge Krueger, Florence Enzminger, Violet Dalton, Mildred Schaller. *Front row:* Caroline Weenke Clemens, Sarah Boelter, Dorothy Rath, Eileen Peterson, Reverend W.W.A. Keller, Violet Buckholz, Norma Egstrom, Lorraine Lusk, Elga Wooddell.

1934— Norma is influenced by Count Basie. In 1934, when Norma was fourteen, the family moved again to the slightly larger town of Wimbledon. They had electricity now and a five-dial Atwater Kent radio. It was here that she first heard one of her early musical heroes, Count Basie. Basie was born William James Basie in Red Bank, New Jersey, on August 21, 1904. He got his start in the early 1920s playing piano and organ for vaudeville acts. In 1931 he joined the band of his idol, Bennie Moten. When Moten died in 1935, Basie took over as leader of the band.

In their book *Jazz Portraits— The Lives and Music of the Jazz Masters*, authors Len Lyons and Don Perlo write of Basie's first radio show:

> Count Basie and the Barons of Rhythm were a hit in Kansas City. A radio announcer at the Reno club suggested Basie adopt the title "Count" in imitation of the regal

nicknames "Earl" and "Duke" that had stuck to Hines and Ellington. In December 1935 John Hammond heard the band in Chicago on a shortwave radio broadcast. He later flew to Kansas City to hear them in person, subsequently writing enthusiastic reviews of the group for *DownBeat* magazine.

John Hammond was not the only one listening to Basie on the radio. Somewhere on the neverending plains of North Dakota, Norma Egstrom was listening too. Very soon the fifteen year old would be on the radio herself.

1935— **Norma sings with Doc Haines and on radio station KOVC.** She had been singing regularly with a local band headed by Doc Haines. Haines' college band played for local dances. As the girl singer, Norma sang popular tunes like "I Never Had a Chance," "In My Solitude," and "Moonglow" through a megaphone. Her job with Haines led to a sponsored radio program at KOVC in Valley City. She had to hitchhike to get there. Norma had her first paying jobs as a singer while with Haines and KOVC.

Circa 1935 to 1936— **The Gladstone Hotel and radio station KRMC.** Doc Haines knew his singer was going places. He called her "our little Hollywood girl." Norma couldn't wait to "get out into the world."

She packed her belongings and left Wimbledon for Jamestown. There she found her first private residence, the corner of a basement. Her furniture was a bed and an orange crate. She worked as a relief girl in the Gladstone Hotel coffee shop. Radio station KRMC was in the Gladstone as well, and soon Norma was on the air again. A young baseball player named Bill Sawyer heard her on KRMC.

Circa 1937 to 1938— **Peggy auditions for WDAY Fargo.** In her autobiography, Peggy remembers Bill Sawyer as a big brother, someone who gave her good advice and looked out for her interests. He did more than that. His belief in her dreams and her talent was so great he drove her all the way to Fargo. There he arranged for her to audition at WDAY, the biggest radio station in Fargo. As she waited to audition for WDAY's head man, Ken Kennedy, Norma was frozen with fear. Bill Sawyer literally gave her the push that started it all.

Kennedy brought in a piano. Norma sang "These Foolish Things" and was hired on the spot. However, Ken Kennedy told the young singer she would have to change her name. Norma Egstrom didn't sound right. "Ladies and gentlemen, Miss Norma Egstrom." He looked at her for awhile and decided that she looked like a "Peggy." At first he said Peggy Lynn. Then he concluded that she should become Peggy Lee. All that mattered to Norma was that he liked her singing.

WDAY's newest radio star played "Freckled Face Gertie" on the *Hayloft Jamboree*. She sang with Lem Hawkins and his swinging group, the Georgie Porgie Breakfast Food Boys.

Life was far from glamorous. The newly christened Miss Peggy Lee also worked at Regan's Bakery slicing bread from 4 P.M. to 4 A.M. She doubled production, because she did everything in rhythm! Her pay at the bakery was thirty-five cents an hour.

Judging from her hairstyle this photograph is probably circa 1938–1939. It appears to have been taken during an early radio appearance. (Courtesy of Richrd Morrison.)

1938 — **Peggy travels to Hollywood.** She didn't stay at WDAY for long. A letter from her childhood friend, Gladys Rasmussen, encouraged her to go to California. Soon she was telling friends in Fargo she was thinking of going to Hollywood. Those innocent words seemed to take on a life of their own. Before she knew it, her friends were throwing a farewell party for her. Now she felt she had to leave. She sold her graduation present, a watch, for thirty dollars. Her father gave her a railroad pass. By the

Also circa 1938–1939, here we see Peggy departing by train. This may have been taken when she was leaving for her trip to Hollywood. (Courtesy of Richard Morrison.)

time she arrived in California she had eighteen dollars. Her friend Gladys had even less.

In the midst of the Great Depression jobs were hard to come by. Gladys had been working as a cashier at the Circus Café. Then the Café flooded, leaving Gladys out of work and broke. The two friends had hit an all-time low. They were unemployed, with a loaf of bread and a jar of peanut butter between them. Peggy went to the employment agency. She told the clerk she could do any job they had. The one job left was in Balboa. She took it.

1938— Peggy works as a carnival barker. She hitchhiked to Balboa where she worked as a cook and waitress at Harry's Café. The job lasted until Easter break ended. By now she was living in a little yellow cabin near the beach.

Her landlord, Mr. Anderson, was the owner of a carnival called the FunZone. He hired Peggy as a barker. She was probably the shyest barker in the history of the carnival world.

One of the concessionaires at the FunZone had a couple of nephews. They struck up a friendship with the pretty, young barker. Both boys played the guitar, and when Peggy told them she had sung on the radio in North Dakota, they asked her to sing.

They assumed she would sing something like "Bury Me Not on the Lone Prairie," but she surprised them. She asked for "The Man I Love" in 'A flat. They were amazed that she knew the key. The boys encouraged her to return to Hollywood and audition at the Jade.

1938— Peggy works at the Jade in Hollywood. As she walked to the Jade her well-worn beach shoes fell apart. She auditioned barefoot and landed the job. Peggy remembered the Jade as dark and mysterious. Other performers there included Hal March (of *The $64,000 Question*) and a redheaded, bumping and grinding female trumpet player named Jabuti. Louis DeProng led the house band. DeProng would play an extra dance set late at night, giving the young singer a chance to eat some Chinese food before the long walk home.

1938— Peggy returns to North Dakota. Overwork and poor diet brought on throat problems for the young singer. A doctor in Los Angeles told her she would have to go home for an operation, and to recuperate.

She returned to Hillsboro, North Dakota. There she found her beloved sister Marianne struggling to keep her family together. With her fragile health, Peggy wasn't able to help her family. All she could do was dream of the day when she'd drive up in a big car filled with gifts for everyone. One day those dreams would come true. Now she was faced with throat surgery. A local physician, Dr. Cuthbert, performed the surgery in his office. When clamps failed to stop the hemorrhaging he nearly lost her. With her sister, Della, they raced to the hospital in Grand Forks.

1938 *and* 1939— Peggy and Lloyd Collins perform at the Powers Hotel. As soon as she felt well enough, she visited her old friend, Ken Kennedy, at WDAY. He introduced her to the owners of the Powers Hotel. Up until then, the Powers Coffee Shop never had live entertainment. It wasn't long before Peggy and organist Lloyd Collins had the place "jammed to the rafters."

Her salary for seven shows a week was fifteen dollars. It was enough to move her family into the nearby Hogan Apartments. Peggy and Lloyd were so popular that the Le Chateau Hotel hired another singer named Jane Leslie Larrabee. Jane came all the way from Minneapolis. The two singers were supposed to be rivals, but in fact they became great friends. Jane even loaned Peggy some dresses for her to wear while performing. Later Peggy introduced Jane to jazz critic Leonard Feather. Jane and Leonard were married for over fifty years.

1939— **Peggy sings with the Sev Olson Orchestra.** Jane returned to Minneapolis. Peggy missed her friend, but not for long. Ken Kennedy helped his favorite singer again, arranging for an audition with his cousin's band. The Sev Olson Orchestra was headquartered in Minneapolis. Peggy sang "Body and Soul" for Sev and landed the job. However, her stint with Olson was short-lived. She and Sev developed a strong crush on each other; it was her first serious romance. However, Olson was married, and Peggy knew the best thing to do was leave the band.

1939— **Peggy sings with the Will Osborne Orchestra.** When the Will Osborne Orchestra came into town Peggy signed with them. She was not with the group for more than a few weeks when her throat started acting up again. One morning she awoke to find a lump in her throat. The doctor she went to tried to excise it. He failed and she was asked to return for surgery the next day.

Her operating room troubles continued to haunt her. This time the hostile anesthesiologist refused to listen to her when she requested gas instead of ether (ether made her sick). Then, when she was under the ether, he dropped her while moving her from the table to the gurney. When she struck the floor her tongue was cut and her upper teeth went through her lower lip. Some of her teeth were damaged and would have to be capped. By the time she recovered, the Osborne orchestra had split up.

1940— **Peggy returns to California to sing at the Doll House.** With Osborne's manager, Max Schall, and pianist, Hank, she headed Peggy for California. Her friends at the Jade were happy to see her. Jack Brooks, the songwriter responsible for "Old Buttermilk Sky" and "That's Amore," was a regular at the Jade. He encouraged her to audition at the Doll House in Palm Springs. At the Doll House she entertained movie stars like Franchot Tone, Peter Lorre, James Cagney, Jack Benny and Dennis Day.

The Peggy Lee style was born during this time. Rather than try to sing above the din of the waiters and patrons, Peggy began to sing softly. As she dropped her volume to what has been called "a quiet intensity," people stopped talking and began to listen. Her newfound style offered other benefits as well. Now she seemed to be confiding in her audience. Listeners felt that she was singing directly to them.

This style of conversational singing has always been very flattering to the listener. Peggy's earliest vocal inspirations—Mildred Bailey, Maxine Sullivan and Lee Wiley—employed it.

Two other singers whose careers were blossoming at this time used conversational singing: Billie Holiday and Frank Sinatra. All three singers listened to, and

Top: Peggy and organist Lloyd Collins were an extremely popular attraction at the Powers Hotel in Jamestown, circa 1938–1939. *Right:* This autographed photograph of Jane Leslie was given to Charlotte Brunner. Charlotte, Jane and Peggy were roommates in Minneapolis prior to Peggy's departure for her second trip to Hollywood. This photograph appears courtesy of Charlotte's daughter, Martyne Bachmen. (Circa 1940)

learned from, each other in the early forties. However, two things set Peggy apart from the others. Where most singers used bright hues in their vocal palette, Peggy sang in pastels. She also understood the power of silence. She used silence and pauses more effectively than any other singer before or since.

All of these stylistic elements were in place in 1941. In just a few short months the American public would hear them for the first time when Peggy signed with one of the greatest big bands of all time.

People were soon talking about the great new singer at the Doll House. One night a prominent couple from Chicago came to hear her. Freddie and Lois Mandel owned the Detroit Tigers and Mandel's Department store in Chicago. One evening the Mandels brought Frank Bering with them. Bering, along with Ernie Byfield, owned the Ambassador East and West in Chicago. The Mandels arranged for Peggy to audition for Frank Bering. However, they arrived at the Doll House at closing time and there was no one to accompany Peggy. She suggested they all go over to Claridge's. A group called The Four of Us was performing there. They accompanied Peggy, and Bering hired her because of her enthusiasm.

• Two •

The Benny Goodman Years and the First Capitol Period 1940 to 1951

1940 to 1941— Peggy sings at Chicago's Ambassador West hotel. Peggy and The Four of Us headed for Chicago and the Ambassador West, one of the city's finest hotels. They would be performing there in a room called the Buttery. Peggy's friend Jane Leslie Larrabee met her there and both enjoyed the luxury of living in a grand hotel. However, unaccustomed to hotel life, the two almost went hungry. Peggy discussed her early days at the Ambassador West with record producer Dave Dexter. Dexter wrote the following anecdote in his book *Playback*:

> "I had no money," she recalls. "For three days and nights I had nothing to eat. One of the hotel maids learned I was hungry and brought me scraps from room service trays."
>
> Peggy laughs. How did the maid know she was hungry? "I never saw you leave your room," the woman explained to Peggy, "and I didn't see no grub coming in nor any bones going out."
>
> The Ambassador's Ernie Byfield was informed of the singer's predicament.
>
> "My God, girl," Byfield exclaimed, "don't you know you can have anything you want any time? You simply sign your name to the tabs."

Peggy's salary was seventy-five dollars a week. She was gowned by the hotel's own Mlle. Oppenheimer. After her own show Peggy would hurry down to the clubs on Rush Street. There she would absorb the sounds of jazz and blues greats like Laura Rucker and Baby Dodds. It was truly a Cinderella time for the young singer.

One night the King of Swing, Benny Goodman, came into the Buttery. His fiancée, Lady Alice Duckworth, had been in the room earlier. She knew the bandleader would have to replace his singer. Helen Forrest was leaving Goodman to join Artie Shaw. Upon Alice's suggestion, Benny went to listen to the unknown blonde vocalist. Goodman was famous for what his musicians called "the ray." The ray was Goodman's stare. Usually it meant he was preoccupied, but if he was angry it could melt you to the floor. Peggy caught a bit of the ray that night: "I was sure he didn't like me; he just stared at me and chewed his tongue." Goodman's great pianist, Mel Powell, was at Benny's table, and as Peggy sang "These Foolish Things," he remembered Goodman mumbling, "I guess we've got to get someone for Helen."

Jane Larrabee took Benny's call the next day. When Peggy returned to her room she refused to believe that Goodman had called. She told Jane someone was playing a joke. Jane assured her that it was Goodman's voice on the phone. When Peggy returned the call, he simply asked her if she'd like to join the band. He told her where to report for work.

While Peggy and Benny Goodman got along well, there were times when he could be difficult. He has been called everything from "task master" to "tyrant." There was a time when Goodman was unhappy with Peggy's phrasing, yet he couldn't articulate exactly what he wanted her to do about it. At one point he became so frustrated that he blasted a high note right in her ear.

This upset her deeply. She turned to visiting bandleader Harry James for help. James advised her to tell Benny she understood what he wanted, and then just go on singing as she always had. Harry's ploy worked, and Goodman smiled at Peggy as she finished her next song.

In truth, Benny Goodman probably didn't mean to be cruel to his singers and musicians. Like most creative geniuses he was sometimes lost in his own world, listening to the music in his head. Mel Powell's wife has been quoted as saying, "The question with Benny is whether the plug is *in* or out." In George T. Simon's *The Big Bands Songbook*, Peggy fondly recalls Benny's legendary absentmindedness:

> I'll never forget the night he asked me to have dinner with him. We got into a cab and we just sat there. Finally the driver turned around to find out where we wanted to go. But Benny just kept sitting there in a sort of fog. Finally I nudged him, and he looked up and saw the driver looking back at him. "Oh," he said, "I'm sorry. Er-er-how much do I owe you?"

The Goodman band was currently appearing at the College Inn. Peggy arrived wearing "something pretty" as instructed. She was up against some tough odds; there was no rehearsal, she had a cold and she was singing songs in Helen Forrest's keys. The critics were harsh. A photo of her in *DownBeat* was captioned "Sweet sixteen and will never be missed." She told Goodman she wanted to quit. He simply said, "I won't let you." The seasoned bandleader must have known that her talent would emerge after this initial phase of nervousness.

August 15, 1941—Peggy Lee makes her first recording. Benny Goodman was under contract with the Columbia record label. Producer John Hammond came to Chicago during the College Inn engagement to record the band.

On August 15, 1941, Peggy Lee went into a recording studio for the first time. Mel Powell tried to help her overcome her nerves. The song she would be singing was the popular "Elmer's Tune." Mel took Peggy aside. He told her he'd cue her when it was time for her to sing. Still, she was so nervous that the engineer picked up the rattling sound of the sheet music she held in her shaking hands.

Author Will Friedwald discusses Peggy's early days with Goodman in his liner notes for the two CD set *Peggy Lee & Benny Goodman — The Complete Recordings*:

> From the very beginning, Lee worked at bringing her own personality to the band, and eventually a distinct "Peggy Lee" style would emerge. On Lee's first session, she took the bull by the horns by tackling a tune — "Elmer's Tune," in fact — that was already identified with two other bands, Dick Jurgens (who introduced it as an instrumental in April) and Glenn Miller (who recorded the hit vocal version a few days earlier).
>
> As engineer Bill Savory later related to Goodman biographer Russ Firestone, Lee was understandably nervous at this, her first record date. Even Goodman admitted, "Unfortunately, when she came with the band she was so scared for about three or four months I don't think she got half the songs out of her mouth."

With Benny Goodman's band Peggy began to serve in an apprenticeship that proved typical for most band singers. There were more recordings and radio work. She also went on tour with the band. The tour schedule, made up mostly of one-nighters, was grueling. Touring was especially difficult for the girl singers, who had to worry about their hair and wardrobes. Peggy frequently found herself running for the bus with wet hair and a suitcase full of damp clothes.

On the bus she and her friend, Mel Powell, would sing the band's charts. They would take turns singing the brass and reed parts. Her friendship with Powell helped her gain confidence onstage. Still, the critics were uncertain about the talents of Goodman's new singer.

It would be several months before Goodman would write new arrangements for Peggy. Once she had songs she liked, set in keys suitable to her range, Peggy began to blossom. Now she could use the conversational style of singing she established at the Doll House in her recordings and performances. One critic dubbed her "the girl with the electric-blue voice." In the meantime, the Goodman band had numerous radio, recording and live performances to fulfill.

August 20, 1941—"I See a Million People." Recorded by Peggy Lee on this date, this R. Sour and U.M. Carlisle song was Peggy's second studio recording. She also recorded "My Old Flame" on this date; however, this recording was not released until 1999 (with the release of the two CD set *Peggy Lee & Benny Goodman — The Complete Recordings*).

August 20, 1941—"How Deep Is the Ocean." Peggy recorded "How Deep Is the Ocean" for the first time on this date. Like the aforementioned "My Old Flame," this particular rendition was not heard until 1999.

August 24, 1941— Peggy Lee's first radio broadcast. The network was NBC. Peggy's songs included "Daddy."

August 25, 1941—"That's the Way It Goes." Peggy recorded her first Alec Wilder song. The arrangement was by Eddie Sauter.

***September 11, 1941*—** Radio broadcast. Peggy's second radio broadcast was on the Mutual network. She sang "When the Sun Comes Out."

***September 13, 1941*—** *Matinee at the Meadowbrook.* For this CBS radio show Peggy sang "It's So Peaceful in the Country." The Alec Wilder tune is a staple for jazz singers. It was popularized by one of Peggy Lee's early musical heroes, Mildred Bailey. Bailey sang with the legendary Paul Whiteman.

Another *Matinee at the Meadowbrook* appearance came at this time. The exact broadcast date is unknown. It was either September 13 or September 20, 1941. Peggy sang "I Don't Want to Set the World on Fire."

***September 16, 1941*—** Radio broadcast. Peggy sang the classic "Smoke Gets in Your Eyes" for this show on the Mutual network.

***September 17, 1941*—** Radio broadcast. CBS was the host for Benny Goodman and Peggy Lee, who performed "I See a Million People."

***September 20, 1941*—** *Matinee at the Meadowbrook.* Once again Lee sang Wilder's "It's So Peaceful in the Country." This show was broadcast on CBS.

Matinee at the Meadowbrook also had broadcasts on September 27 and October 4, 1941. For the September 27 broadcast Peggy sang "That's the Way It Goes." On October 4 she performed "Soft as Spring."

***September 25, 1941*—** "How Deep Is the Ocean" and "Let's Do It." On this date Peggy and Benny Goodman recorded these songs for the first time. They would revisit the tunes in October of 1941. This rendition of "Let's Do It" was released. The recording of "How Deep Is the Ocean" was first heard in 1999 on *Peggy Lee & Benny Goodman — The Complete Recordings.*

***October 2, 1941*—** "I Got It Bad and That Ain't Good." Peggy recorded what would become a Duke Ellington classic. This rendition was arranged by Eddie Sauter. The song would remain in her repertoire for the rest of her life.

At the same recording session she recorded the A. Johnston and S. Coslow song "My Old Flame." The song was written for the Mae West film *The Belle of the Nineties.*

***October 8, 1941*—** "How Deep Is the Ocean." Re-recorded on this date, Irving Berlin's "How Deep Is the Ocean" was Peggy's seventh recording with Benny Goodman. Her eighth, recorded on the same date, was "Shady Lady Bird."

***October 21, 1941*—** "Let's Do It." Cole Porter wrote "Let's Do It" for the Broadway musical *Paris.* Peggy recorded it on October 21, 1941.

***October 26, 1941*—** *The Fitch Bandwagon.* For this NBC radio program Goodman and Lee performed "The Shrine of St. Cecilia."

This was followed by a radio broadcast on October 27, 1941, that featured Peggy singing "The Man I Love" and "I Got It Bad and That Ain't Good." The network for this broadcast is unknown.

***November 1, 1941*— Radio Broadcast.** Peggy sang "That Did It, Marie" for the Mutual network.

This was followed by Mutual broadcasts on November 7 and November 13, 1941. "More Than You Know" and "Why Don't We Do This More Often?" were Peggy's songs on November 7. For the November 13 program she sang "Somebody Else Is Taking My Place." This song became Peggy Lee's first number-one record.

***November 13, 1941*— Recording session.** November 13, 1941, marked Peggy's most productive recording session. Four songs, as opposed to the usual one or two, were recorded. Peggy recorded "Somebody Else Is Taking My Place," "Somebody Nobody Knows" and "That Did It, Marie." The classic Gershwin tune "How Long Has This Been Going On" was the fourth song recorded at this session.

***November 14, 1941*—*Spotlight Bands*.** Benny Goodman's band was in the spotlight for this Mutual network show. Peggy sang Cole Porter's "Let's Do It."

***November 15, 1941*—"I Got It Bad and That Ain't Good."** Peggy Lee's interpretation of the Duke Ellington classic charted on this date. It remained on the charts for one week, peaking at number 25.

***November 22, 1941*— Radio broadcast.** Benny Goodman's male vocalist was Art Lund. For this CBS program Lee and Lund sang their duet of "Winter Weather." The song would soon make the charts. The duo would record it within five days of this broadcast.

***November 27, 1941*—"Winter Weather."** Art Lund and Peggy recorded the T. Shapiro tune on this date. Peggy also recorded Cole Porter's "Ev'rything I Love." The Porter song was written for the Broadway musical *Let's Face It*.

***November 29, 1941*— Radio broadcast.** Lee performed "Ev'rything I Love."

This broadcast was followed by another on CBS. The radio audience heard Peggy Lee and Art Lund sing the popular "Winter Weather." The exact airdate is unknown. In all likelihood it took place in December of 1941. On another December broadcast Peggy sang "On the Sunny Side of the Street."

***December 10, 1941*—"Not Mine" and "Not a Care in the World."** These two songs were recorded by Peggy on this date. Johnny Mercer wrote "Not Mine" for the Paramount movie *The Fleet's In*. Vernon Duke's composition "Not a Care in the World" was written for Eddie Cantor's Broadway musical *Banjo Eyes*.

Winter 1941 — **Terrace Room, Hotel New Yorker, New York.** Benny's next important gig was at the Terrace Room of the Hotel New Yorker. It would be Peggy's first time in New York. The young singer stared in awe as well-known stars danced by the bandstand every night. Her musical hero, Count Basie, was there one night. As she sang "That Did It Marie," Basie winked up at her, asking, "Are you sure you don't have a little spade in you, Peggy?" Louis Armstrong and Duke Ellington also came to hear her. The Duke would later nickname her "the Queen." Clearly, she was accepted among musical royalty. Author and jazz historian George T. Simon wrote the following review during Goodman's run at the Terrace Room:

> Peggy Lee, who wasn't too impressive till she got over the shock of finding herself with Benny's band, is slowly turning into one of the great singers in the field. The lass has a great flair for phrasing — listen to her on those last sets at night, when the band is just noodling behind her.... That she gets a fine beat, that she sings in tune, and that she's awfully good-looking are self-evident.

Simon also recalled Peggy visiting him on Christmas Eve. He observed that while her appearance was sensuous and sophisticated, her true nature leaned toward someone who was "rather insecure, extremely sensitive and terribly sentimental." That evening he put on the Teddy Wilson recording of "Just the Blues."

He sat amazed as Peggy made up spontaneous lyrics to the instrumental tune. She sang about "a little girl who plays with dolls and such, a little girl who wished she'd never had that touch..." It seemed that "Peggy Lee" was an image she could put on to protect Norma Egstrom, the shy little girl who still lived inside her.

The lyrics she made up while listening to "Just the Blues" were only a hint of the material Peggy would produce as a songwriter. In 1941 her first composition was published. Peggy's composition, "Little Fool," was not recorded, and in later years Peggy would say in interviews that she was glad no one heard her fledgling tune.

December 2, 1941 — **Radio broadcast.** Peggy sang "How Long Has This Been Going On?" for this CBS broadcast.

December 5, 1941 — ***Spotlight Bands.*** "Ev'rything I Love" was Peggy's solo for this Mutual network program.

December 9, 1941 — **Radio broadcast.** Peggy sang her first Goodman hit "Somebody Else Is Taking My Place" for this CBS show.

December 24, 1941 — **"Blues in the Night."** The legendary team of Johnny Mercer and Harold Arlen wrote "Blues in the Night." Peggy's rendition was recorded on this date.

Also recorded were Peggy's classic rendition of Rodgers and Hart's "Where or When," and the Fields and McHugh hit "On the Sunny Side of the Street."

Winter 1941 — **Peggy's sense of humor.** In spite of Benny's "no fraternizing with the girl singer" policy, Peggy had a good time with her fellow musicians. Most of them treated her like a little sister. They took great pleasure in teasing the gullible farm girl from North Dakota. However, Peggy was not as innocent as she seemed. She had a fantastic, wild sense of humor. She could dish it out as well as take it.

Following their successful run at the Terrace Room the band went on the road again. This time they were traveling by train. Goodman was so popular that he had two railroad cars with "Benny Goodman" painted on the side. The band had just finished a show in Pittsburgh and was headed for St. Louis. The show had ended early, and Mel Powell, along with sax player George Berg, decided to head out to the train.

The two men found the Goodman cars in the deserted railroad yard. They had planned on enjoying a couple of drinks and some spareribs. As they sat in their pajamas, dining on the ribs, there was a sudden knock on the door.

A startled Mel Powell opened the door to find Peggy, trembling and weeping. It seems she too had come out to the train for some peace and quiet, but when she went to her compartment, she discovered a body. Now she was hysterical.

Powell tried to comfort her, saying he would escort her back to her compartment. When he got there the first thing he saw was a head covered with blood, but no body. Peggy explained that the body was in her closet. Powell felt that they should tell the police. A sobbing Peggy said she just wanted the body out of her room.

While they were discussing the situation, Goodman's brother and band manager, Freddy, arrived. Goodman's trombonist, Lou McGarrity, accompanied Freddy. Soon they were all crowded into Peggy's compartment. Much to his horror, Mel found himself in front of the closet door.

When Freddy opened the door the corpse fell out, landing on Powell and knocking him to the floor. Suddenly, the body laying on top of him began to shake with laughter. The "corpse" was Goodman's bassist, Sid Weiss. This whole prank had been planned and staged by Peggy. In later years she would say that her only vice was her "macabre sense of humor."

January 1, 1942—Spotlight Bands. Benny and Peggy were in the spotlight again. For the Mutual network program Peggy performed "Blues in the Night."

January 10, 1942— "Winter Weather." The Peggy Lee and Art Lund duet charted on this date. It reached number 24 and stayed on the charts for one week.

1942—Paramount Theatre, New York. When the band returned to New York, it was to play an engagement at the Paramount Theatre. Aside from Benny Goodman and Peggy Lee, there was a young singer billed as an "Extra Added Attraction." His name was Frank Sinatra. Young Sinatra had recently launched his solo career, having left the Tommy Dorsey Orchestra. The Paramount was packed with Sinatra's fans, the famous Bobby Soxers. Of course, Peggy and Benny generated some excitement, but it was Sinatra they came to see. When Sinatra was announced, the roar was so deafening that Goodman was heard to exclaim, "What the hell was that?"

At the Paramount, Peggy and Frank started a close friendship that lasted until his death. Back then even Peggy was caught up in the thrill of Sinatra's rise to fame. She remembered leaning out of the window of her dressing room watching Sinatra's fans swarming in the street below. They were waiting for a glimpse of the skinny, blue-eyed heartthrob.

The two singers had a great deal in common. Both loved music passionately, and both had always dreamed of a singing career. When Peggy came down with the flu during the Paramount job, it was Sinatra who acted as a nurse. He brought her blankets and tea. Their friendship would produce one of Peggy's finest albums. As it did with so many close friends, Sinatra's influence would change her life.

January 15, 1942 — "The Lamp of Memory." Peggy recorded three songs during her January 15, 1942, session. First came "The Lamp of Memory" (also known as "Incertidumbre"). Pianist Mel Powell was the arranger on this tune.

Next came "If You Build a Better Mousetrap" by J. Mercer and V. Schertzinger. This was a duet with Art London (also known as Art Lund). Finally, there was "When the Roses Bloom Again."

January 20, 1942 — Radio broadcast. Lee and Goodman performed "Blues in the Night" and "How Do You Do with Me?" for this CBS airdate. This was followed by a January 24 broadcast on which Peggy sang "Blues in the Night" again.

February 3, 1942 — Radio broadcast. Peggy's songs for this CBS show included "Somebody Nobody Loves."

February 5, 1942 — "My Little Cousin." "My Little Cousin" was written by H. Lewis, S. Braverman and C. Coben. Goodman and Lee recorded it on February 5, 1942.

February 6, 1942 — Mutual network broadcast. For this radio program Peggy sang the freshly recorded "My Little Cousin."

February 14, 1942 — "Blues in the Night." Peggy's version of Harold Arlen's "Blues in the Night" hit the charts. It remained on the charts for one week and peaked at number 20.

Peggy also appeared on two Valentine's Day radio broadcasts. On CBS she and Benny performed her favorite "Blues in the Night." The Mutual network found her singing "How Long Has This Been Going On?"

February 17, 1942 — Radio broadcast. The network for this appearance is unknown. Peggy sang "Skylark" and "Ev'rything I Love."

March 2, 1942 — Radio broadcast. Peggy sang "We'll Meet Again" for this Mutual network show.

March 5, 1942— **Radio broadcast.** Benny was finally giving his girl singer more to do. Peggy sang "My Little Cousin," "The Lamp of Memory (Incertidumbre)" and "Mandy Is Two." The network for this broadcast is unknown.

On additional broadcasts between January and March of 1942 Peggy performed "Blues in the Night," "Not Mine," "Somebody Nobody Loves" and "That Did It, Marie."

March 7, 1942—"Somebody Else Is Taking My Place." Peggy had her first number one record. "Somebody Else Is Taking My Place" hit the charts on this date and remained there for 15 weeks.

March 10, 1942—"The Way You Look Tonight." This American classic was written by the team of Dorothy Fields and Jerome Kern for the Fred Astaire and Ginger Rogers film *Swing Time*. Peggy gave the song a very tender rendition.

March 12, 1942—"I Threw a Kiss in the Ocean." Goodman and Lee recorded this underrated Irving Berlin tune on March 12, 1942. Mel Powell acted as the arranger. Additional songs recorded on this date were "We'll Meet Again," "Full Moon (Noche de Luna)" and "There Won't Be a Shortage of Love." This last tune was not heard until the 1999 release of *Peggy Lee & Benny Goodman — The Complete Recordings*.

April 11, 1942—"My Little Cousin." "My Little Cousin" made the charts. It would remain on the charts for three weeks, peaking at number 14.

May 11, 1942— **Radio broadcast.** Peggy sang "We'll Meet Again." The network is unknown.

May 14, 1942—"You're Easy to Dance With." Peggy's lightly swinging version of this tune written for the Fred Astaire–Bing Crosby film *Holiday Inn* went unheard until the release of *Peggy Lee & Benny Goodman — The Complete Recordings*. Another song recorded at this same session was "All I Need Is You."

May 23, 1942—"Full Moon (Noche de Luna)." Peggy made the charts again with "Full Moon (Noche de Luna)." The song was on the charts for one week and peaked at number 22.

June 27, 1942—"The Way You Look Tonight." Peggy's rendition of this Oscar-winning song made the charts on this date. It remained there for one week, peaking at number 21.

July 27, 1942—"Why Don't You Do Right?" Unquestionably the biggest Goodman and Lee hit, "Why Don't You Do Right?" was recorded on this date.

Peggy always traveled with a portable record player. She had an eclectic record collection that included 78s by Ravel, Debussy and several "race records." Race records were blues and jazz songs recorded by African-American artists. As with so many things in the 1930s and 1940s, the records featuring black musicians were kept separate from those recorded by white entertainers. Black artists had their own labels, frequently owned and operated by white producers who gave the performers a small recording fee and no royalties. These records were not readily available to white consumers. Only certain music stores would have them in stock. However, Peggy Lee was truly colorblind. Her criterion was not based on ethnicity; it was based on whether or not the music was good.

Peggy had a favorite among these 78s; it was Lil Green's recording of "Why Don't You Do Right?" In a 1984 interview conducted for *Andy Warhol's Interview* magazine, Peggy told writer George Christy how her recording of "Why Don't You Do Right?" came to be:

> I was and am a fan of Lil Green, a great old blues singer, and Lil recorded it. I used to play that record over and over in my dressing room, which was next door to Benny's. Finally he said, "You obviously like that song." I said, "Oh, I love it." He said, "Would you like me to have an arrangement made of it?" I said, "I'd love that," and he did.

To this day her recording of "Why Don't You Do Right?" remains one of her most popular songs. It is the song that made her a star. She performed the song with Goodman in her second movie, *Stage Door Canteen*. By the time the film was released the record was a smash hit, selling in the millions. The song was heard everywhere. One of Peggy's brothers recalled hearing it blasted over his ship's PA system as they headed off to war.

This recording is also significant because it is the first Peggy Lee recording to list Dave Barbour as the guitarist. While the band was in Detroit, Goodman hired a new guitarist. The talented musician was a handsome, dark-haired man named David Barbour. In her autobiography, Peggy's chapter about David is titled "The Man I Love." It was a bittersweet romance from the start. The first time Peggy heard David's guitar she was heading toward her dressing room. The sound stopped her in her tracks. She found herself in the wings, listening to every note.

World War II had broken out. Suddenly there were rallies to play for the war effort. They began playing at hospitals. Goodman took the band to Hollywood to make a movie. *The Powers Girl* was filmed in late 1941. It starred Anne Shirley, Carole Landis and George Murphy. The Benny Goodman band appeared, and while Peggy went unbilled, her beauty did not go unnoticed. In a typical bandstand setting she sang "The Lady Who Didn't Believe in Love."

While in California the band was faced with the possibility of a recording strike. Goodman wanted to record as much as possible in the event the strike became a reality. With Goodman's sextet, Peggy recorded "Where or When" on December 24, 1941. The song and the small combo suited Peggy's style. The intimate recording became a hit. Another song recorded in this style was her tender reading of "The Way You

Shortly after joining Benny Goodman's band, Peggy made her debut in the 1942 film *The Powers Girl*. The movie also starred Anne Shirley, George Murphy, Dennis Day and Carol Landis. Peggy performed "The Lady Who Didn't Believe in Love" with the Goodman band.

Look Tonight," recorded on March 10, 1942. Soon she would record the song that would catapult her to national stardom.

July 30, 1942 — "Let's Say a Prayer." Recorded on this date, this song by C. Farrow was not released until 1999, when it was found in the collection *Peggy Lee & Benny Goodman — The Complete Recordings*. This was Peggy Lee's final recording as Benny Goodman's singer. Goodman and Lee would be reunited for three recordings in 1947.

Peggy Lee's childhood dreams had come true. She had a number one song with the nation's most popular band. Yet there was another dream she was chasing — the dream of love, marriage and raising a family. Her romance with Dave Barbour had grown. They were in love. When Goodman found out he gave Barbour his notice. Realizing he couldn't stand to be separated from Peggy, David finally proposed marriage. Peggy left Benny Goodman's band, married David Barbour, and announced her retirement from show business.

October 1942 — **Radio broadcast.** Peggy sang "Blues in the Night" and "Cow-Cow Boogie." The network is unknown.

October 19, 1942 — **Radio broadcast.** For this CBS program Peggy sang "Cow-Cow Boogie" and "Praise the Lord and Pass the Ammunition."

November 12, 1942 — **Radio broadcast.** This was another CBS broadcast. Peggy performed "Mr. Five by Five" and "I Had the Craziest Dream."

December 3, 1942 — **Radio Broadcast.** Network unknown. Peggy's songs included "Why Don't You Do Right?"

1942 to 1943 — **Various performances.** Between late 1942 and early 1943 Peggy made several radio broadcasts on the various networks. Some of the songs she sang included "Why Don't You Do Right?," "Don't Get Around Much Anymore," "I Lost My Sugar in Salt Lake City" and "That Soldier of Mine."

Peggy and singer Jane Leslie were roommates, beginning in Minneapolis and then moving on to New York. *Click* magazine featured a four-page photograph spread on the young singers. As these photographs appeared in the April 1943 issue, they must have been taken just prior to Peggy's departure from the Goodman band. Although he is not mentioned in the original caption, Dave Barbour is seated to the right of Peggy. According to the *Click* photograph spread, roommates Peggy and Jane shared just about everything, including their wardrobe.

Left: Peggy and Jane take their cocker spaniel "Torchy" for a walk in this *Click* magazine photograph. *Right:* The girls listen "professionally to new music" in this publicity photograph for for four-page *Click* magazine spread.

January 2, 1943—"Why Don't You Do Right?" Goodman and Lee's greatest hit premiered on the charts on this date, peaking at number four and remaining on the charts for a record 19 weeks.

February 13, 1943— **Radio broadcast.** This program was broadcast on the Blue network. Peggy's songs included "As Time Goes By."

Above: Peggy rehearses with Benny Goodman. *Right, top:* Benny, David Barbour, and Peggy: This photograph appeared in the April 1943 issue of *Metronome* magazine. *Right, bottom:* Peggy and Benny in performance.

This was followed by a February 28, 1943, broadcast (network unknown), for which Peggy sang "I Love a Piano."

February and March 1943 — **Various radio broadcasts.** Between February and March of 1943 Peggy made various radio appearances, singing such tunes as "I Don't Believe in Rumors," "Why Don't You Do Right?" and "I Love a Piano."

March 3, 1943 — **Radio broadcast.** For this CBS broadcast Peggy performed "Don't Get Around Much Anymore."

March 8, 1943 — **Peggy marries David Barbour.** David Barbour and Peggy Lee were married on March 8, 1943. They moved into an apartment near Los Angeles City College. Peggy had no idea just how huge a hit "Why Don't You Do Right?" had become until the phone started to ring off the hook. Suddenly she was swamped with offers. Since she was now happily married and retired, she turned the offers down. She enjoyed being a housewife.

March 20, 1943 — **Radio broadcast.** "Slender, Tender and Tall" was Peggy's song for this CBS show.

***November 11, 1943*—Nicki Lee Barbour is born.** When the news came that Peggy was pregnant, David responded by saying, "Why Peg, I hardly know you." Their daughter, Nicki Lee Barbour, was born on November 11, 1943, one month premature. It was a difficult birth. Peggy's blood pressure rose dramatically and she developed pneumonia. In her autobiography she says her chances "seemed alarmingly slim." She may not have known just how slim. Rumor has it that she was pronounced dead at one point. Nicki was to be her only child.

Soon mother and daughter were able to go home. Peggy remembered Nicki as a beautiful, intelligent baby who learned to laugh early. During her pregnancy, and after Nicki was born, Peggy would frequently write down lyrics. She was filled with ideas for songs; music seemed to flow from her soul. When David would come home after performing or recording, he would ask, "Is dinner ready?" Peggy would reply, "No, but the song is!"

One day several good things seemed to happen right in a row. A friend brought them a pheasant, another arrived with a bottle of wine, and others called just to express their love. Suddenly, Peggy said to herself, "Well, it's a good day!" She realized it was a good song title, and started to write lyrics based on that theme. When she finished, she ran down to her sister's apartment. She sang her new song while Marianne stood in the window. Her sister was the first person to hear "It's a Good Day." When Peggy and David recorded the song on the Capitol label it sold 650,000 copies upon its first release. During this time Peggy also wrote "What More Can a Woman Do?" based on her love for David.

Among those calling to offer Peggy work (based on the sales of "Why Don't You Do Right?") were Johnny Mercer and Glenn Wallichs. Mercer, one of America's greatest songwriters, would act as Peggy's mentor in that field. Wallichs was a businessman who, along with Buddy De Sylva and Mercer, was founding Capitol Records. They worked out of a small office above Sy Devore's tailor shop located near Sunset and Vine. Eventually the famous Capi-

Peggy holds her newborn daughter Nicki Lee Barbour. This photograph appeared in the July 1944 issue of *Band Leaders* magazine.

tol Records building, designed to resemble a stack of records, would stand on that spot. The Capitol building has often been referred to as "the house that Peggy built" or "the house that Nat built." Peggy Lee and Nat "King" Cole were there from the beginning. They were also two of Capitol's biggest selling artists.

Mercer, Wallichs and De Sylva had hired an impressive line-up of stars to launch their new label. Among the founding artists were Margaret Whiting, Ella Mae Morse and the Nat "King" Cole Trio. A housewife named Peggy Lee would join their ranks, but it took a considerable amount of coaxing. The Capitol team hired Dave Dexter to produce for them. It was Dexter who talked Peggy into recording for his collection of songs entitled *New American Jazz*.

In his autobiography, *Playback*, Dave Dexter described how Peggy's first recording session with Capitol came about:

> Peggy underwent surgery while carrying her daughter, Nicki Barbour, the only child she ever was to conceive. Nicki was born by Caesarian surgery on Armistice Day. Barbour, unemployed for the first time in a decade, scurried about Los Angeles seeking work. Peggy was still recuperating when I telephoned her in January.
>
> "It's nice to hear from you," she said, "but I'm retired. I want to devote all my time to my husband and baby. I've had enough singing."
>
> I couldn't budge her. For two days I called around, trying to find someone like Ivie Anderson, Helen Humes, or Lee Wiley to make my session, but no one was available. I called Peggy a second time.
>
> "You don't give up, do you?" she kidded. "Why me?"
>
> I considered her the best singer for the job, I explained, but I didn't tell her I felt I owed her something.

Dexter felt he "owed" her because he had been among the harsh critics when she started her career with Goodman. Now he offered her one hundred dollars for two songs, telling her she'd be back home for Nicki within two hours. Peggy finally agreed. Dexter continued:

> She showed up on time. Her husband had driven her to the MacGregor studios in a rickety, sputtering, pre-war Ford two-seater. Peggy was chubby, but she was smartly dressed and enthusiastically welcomed by the musicians I had assembled.
>
> I invited Peg into the booth and asked that the old standard "Sugar" lead off the session. It gave Peg 30 or 40 minutes to get the feel of the studio and the musicians. She enjoyed every solo, particularly Eddie Miller's tenor saxing and Pete Johnson's raunchy, two-fisted piano contributions.
>
> And then Peggy officially emerged from retirement, taking over the mike to shout "Ain't Goin' No Place," a raucous, up-tempo blues that reminded me of her bawdy vocal on the Goodman "Why Don't You Do Right?" Columbia smash hit a year or so previously. All of us stood around enjoying the playback and one of the men said aloud what we were all thinking: "This chick sounds like a drunken old whore with the hots."

The versatile singer took a completely different approach for the second song recorded that day. Next up was a romantic tune that had been popular in the thirties, "That Old Feeling." Peggy sang the seldom-heard verse with great tenderness. Suddenly the blues shouter was gone. Dexter found the chorus to be "ethereal, delicate.... Her sound had become pure Angel Food. It was a stunning reading." He told a pleased Peggy she could go home. Dexter's *New American Jazz* sold well, but what pleased him most was that "many radio jocks pulled Peggy's 'That Old Feeling' and gave it heavy air-play."

Peggy's fans welcomed the new recordings. After all, they hadn't heard any new material from her since the Goodman days. Everyone thought she should go out on the road again. It took David Barbour to convince his wife to return to her greatest love, singing. David told her she should use the talent given her rather than resent not using it.

The Barbours decided to hire Carlos Gastel as their manager. Carlos represented stars like Perry Como, Dinah Shore and the Mills Brothers. Peggy liked Gastel because he treated each star like "a jewel for which he provided the setting." Unfortunately for Peggy, Gastel was also one of David's drinking buddies. Their drinking almost caused a financial disaster with the rights to one of Lee and Barbour's greatest songs.

July 30, 1945—**Peggy's first official Capitol recording.** In the meantime, Peggy and David signed with Capitol. In liner notes written for the CD *Peggy Lee—Capitol Collectors Series*, author Robin Callot describes Lee's first official Capitol date:

> Peggy's first recording session for Capitol on July 30, 1945, produced two soon-to-be-popular tunes, both featuring guitar solos by David Barbour. Peggy was very tense prior to recording "Waiting for the Train to Come In"; Johnny Mercer came to her rescue and calmed the nervous singer, urging her to relax her voice and "just bend the notes." The resulting effort, written by Martin Block and Sunny Skylar, does indeed feature many "bent" notes. The first tune charted in November 1945, reaching number four.

November 10, 1945—"**Waitin' for the Train to Come In.**" Peggy's first official recording for Capitol. It remained on the charts for 14 weeks, peaking at number four.

Soon their friend Johnny Mercer suggested Peggy and David record some of the songs they had written together. Their first recording featuring their songwriting efforts was "You Was Right, Baby," backed by "What More Can a Woman Do?" both sporting lyrics by Peggy Lee and music by David Barbour. With this release, Peggy Lee officially became a singer-songwriter, one of the first women in American music to achieve that title. This record sold 750,000 copies. Peggy Lee's retirement was a thing of the past.

Their next record was another Lee-Barbour tune called "I Don't Know Enough About You," a song that didn't come easy to Peggy. The basic idea was good, but on some level the song wasn't working. Johnny Mercer advised her to tear the whole thing apart and start all over. She rose to the challenge, creating a song that sold 500,000 platters. Given this incredible artistic success, it is not surprising that Peggy received both the *DownBeat* and *Metronome* awards for "Best Female Singer" in 1946. Peggy Lee and Dave Barbour were dubbed "Mr. and Mrs. Melody."

A striking portrait from 1946. This photograph was taken to promote Peggy's appearance in the fifteen-minute 1946 Universal Pictures release *Banquet of Melody*.

March 30, 1946—"I'm Glad I Waited for You." "I'm Glad I Waited for You" was on the charts for two weeks, peaking at number 24.

May 2, 1946—*Bing Crosby Kraft Music Hall*. Peggy made her first appearance on Bing Crosby's radio show. She would be Bing's "girl singer" until 1954. For this program Peggy sang "I Don't Know Enough About You." Bing's other guests for this NBC broadcast were Bob Hope and Eddie Duchin.

Peggy's first *DownBeat* cover, June 1945.

One would have thought that with all her years of radio work, not to mention her time with Benny Goodman, Peggy would have been at ease performing before studio audiences. It spite of her experience, the twenty-five year-old singer was still painfully shy and insecure. Bing was aware of her stage fright.

In an interview taped on October 3, 1991, Peggy discussed Bing's great sensitivity:

> He saw me standing outside the door at NBC, too frightened to go out. He said, "Can I do anything for you, Peg?" I said, "I don't think so." He said, "Would you like a drink?" I said, "No, don't drink." Bing said, "What is it, are you afraid?" I said, "Yes!" By now it was airtime and I said, "Please, when you introduce me would you stay on the stage? Stay where I can see your feet, and then I think I'll be alright." And that's what he did.

Peggy went on to tell the interviewer that she didn't feel that many stars would be willing to do that. She also loved his sense of humor. She'd arrive before the show and play the piano; Crosby would enter and ask, "Who are you today, Chopin or Stravinsky?" She also remembered Bing's great concern during David's illness:

> He did so many things when David was ill. When David was in the hospital he was seriously ill. In fact, nine times they gave him up. Bing was very attentive about everything.
> He called every morning to see how he was. He offered me blood, he offered money, offered his car, offered to be a nurse-maid for my daughter, Nicki. He was a total friend.

Peggy would never forget Bing's kindness. His admiration for her talent was obvious. On one memorable broadcast he introduced her by saying, "When Peggy sings the blues, you're gonna hear the truth." No small praise from a singer of Crosby's caliber. Bing recognized an important part of Peggy's magic. Whatever emotion the lyrics called for, she conveyed them with pure honesty. Their friendship remained strong through the years. They sang duets on records, in one film and on television.

Another established star who helped Peggy overcome her on-stage fears was Jimmy Durante. (Peggy was also a semi-regular on Durante's radio show.) Before his wild courtroom visit, during the "Mañana" trial, Durante assured his young songstress, "One day you'll feel the love flow back from the audience!" This seemed to put her at ease. In his book *Simon Says*, George T. Simon tells how Peggy overcame her shyness:

> When Peggy's boss, Benny Goodman, took on a guitarist named Dave Barbour, Peggy started coming out of her shell. It was a gradual transition until now "when I get out on a stage I feel as if I know people so well that I can say to any one of them, 'How's your family?' and I wouldn't feel foolish. And that attitude comes from being around Durante and Crosby. Jimmy is so wonderful.
> He's interested in big things and little things. And he's interested in people.... I can't say enough fine things about him as a person," a rave, by the way, which appears to be shared by just about everybody else in show business.

***May 9, 1946*—Peggy Lee's first television appearance.** Peggy appeared on the NBC program *Hour Glass*. In their book *Complete Directory to Prime-Time Network and Cable TV Shows*, authors Tim Brooks and Earl Marsh describe *Hour Glass* as follows:

> "Hour Glass was one of the most important pioneers in the early history of television.... It was the first hour-long entertainment series of any kind produced for network television, the first show to develop its own star, the first big variety series, and the most ambitious production ever attempted up to its time.

It is possible that Peggy made additional appearances on *Hour Glass*.

***May 25, 1946*—"I Don't Know Enough About You."** The Lee-Barbour composition made the charts in time for Peggy's twenty-sixth birthday (May 26, 1946). It stayed on the charts for six weeks and peaked at number seven.

***July 12, 1946*— Capitol recording session.** Lee and Barbour recorded two more of their compositions on a Capitol disc. "Everything's Movin' Too Fast" was Peggy's comment on new-fangled inventions and progress. Recorded on July 12, 1946, the song was a fine example of her ability to write clever, witty lyrics. On the flip side was "Just an Old Love of Mine," which appealed to Peggy's more romantic listeners.

***September 28, 1946*—"Linger in My Arms a Little Longer, Baby."** Lee's sexy "Linger in My Arms a Little Longer, Baby" made number 16. It would remain on the charts for two weeks.

***November 23, 1946*—"It's All Over Now."** "It's All Over Now" hit the charts. It would remain for six weeks and peaked at number 10.

***December 11, 1946*—*Bing Crosby Philco Radio Time*.** Crosby moved from NBC to ABC, and his show was now sponsored by Philco radios. Peggy sang "Linger in My Arms a Little Longer, Baby." She and Bing joined forces on "It's a Good Day."

***December 18, 1946*—*Bing Crosby Philco Radio Time*.** Bing and Peggy sang the Lee-Barbour song "Everything's Movin' Too Fast." Peggy sang solo on "It's All Over Now."

***January 1, 1947*—*Bing Crosby Philco Radio Time*.** Peggy performed "He's Just My Kind." She joined Bing for a duet of "Baby, You Can Count on Me."

***January 18, 1947*—"It's a Good Day."** Peggy and David's classic "It's a Good Day" charted for two weeks and peaked at number 16.

***February 5, 1947*—*Bing Crosby Philco Radio Time*.** Bing's guest was the legendary British stage personality Beatrice Lillie. Peggy's songs included "It's Loving Time."

February 8, 1947—"Everything's Movin' Too Fast." Another Peggy Lee and David Barbour song became a hit when "Everything's Movin' Too Fast" reached number 21. It would be on the charts for two weeks.

March 12, 1947—*Bing Crosby Philco Radio Time.* Peggy sang "Happiness Is a Thing Called Joe" and joined Bing for "The Best Man."

March 19, 1947—*Bing Crosby Philco Radio Time.* Bing's guest was Danny Kaye. Peggy performed "Squeeze Me." She and Bing sang "It's a Good Day."

March 26, 1947—*Bing Crosby Philco Radio Time.* Jack Benny was Bing's guest for this broadcast. Peggy sang "For Sentimental Reasons."₁

April 9, 1947—*Bing Crosby Philco Radio Time.* Peggy's songs included "Speaking of Angels."

April 16, 1947—*Bing Crosby Philco Radio Time.* Jimmy Durante joined Peggy and Bing. Lee and Crosby sang a duet of "It Still Suits Me." Peggy soloed on "A Nightingale Can Sing the Blues."

April 23, 1947—*Bing Crosby Philco Radio Time.* Bing's guests were jazz guitar legend Les Paul and folk singer Burl Ives. Peggy sang "I Close My Eyes." She and Crosby sang "It's a Good Day."

June 28, 1947—"Chi-baba, Chi-baba (My Bambino, Go to Sleep)." Peggy charted with the novelty tune "Chi-baba, Chi-baba (My Bambino, Go to Sleep)." The song remained on the charts for four weeks, peaking at number 10.

October 1, 1947—*Bing Crosby Philco Radio Time.* Gary Cooper was Bing's guest. Peggy, Bing and Gary joined forces for "Alla en el Rancho Grande." Peggy also sang "It Takes a Long, Long Train with a Red Caboose."

October 8, 1947—*Jimmy Durante Show.* Peggy soloed on the classic "All of Me."

October 8, 1947—*Bing Crosby Philco Radio Time.* Jimmy Durante was back for this October broadcast. Peggy sang the Lee-Barbour song "Just an Old Love of Mine."

November 15, 1947—"Golden Earrings." Peggy's sultry rendition of "Golden Earrings" hit the charts. It would remain there for 18 weeks, peaking at number two.
    While many of her earlier recordings eventually rose to the million-seller mark, "Golden Earrings" was her first instant million-seller. The team of Victor Young, Jay Livingston and Ray Evans wrote the song. Victor and Peggy shared a deep friendship. As a team they would write some of her finest compositions.

"Golden Earrings," written for the Marlene Dietrich movie of the same name, had an easy Latin tempo. This led to a new trend in music. Soon there would be several hits written and arranged in this style, but none as big as the next Lee-Barbour tune.

Early in 1948 David Barbour had to undergo an operation for bleeding duodenal ulcers. The doctors had to remove a large portion of his stomach. His condition was serious. When Peggy asked the doctors if he would live, she was told they had done all they could. David was in God's hands now. Her prayers and his sense of humor saw them through. As he was being wheeled into a second surgery, Peggy ran alongside the gurney, saying, "I love you, David. I love you." His response was "Stop nagging me."

The second operation did not go well. Peggy knew from the doctor's faces that David was probably going to die. Down the hall she saw them wheeling a resuscitator into David's room. The nurses tried to comfort her. Then, according to her autobiography, the following event occurred:

> I shall never forget this: as I walked down the corridor crying out to God in silence, I suddenly saw a shaft of light coming from my own eyes down the length of the hall, and I knew David was alive and would live. I felt as though I'd been lifted from the floor.

Shortly before David's illness, Peggy was chatting with a neighbor named Estelle "Honey" Frombach one afternoon, and the topic of spiritual beliefs came up. Estelle asked Peggy if she had ever heard of Dr. Ernest Holmes and then told Peggy the tenets of Dr. Holmes' Science of Mind Institute. Peggy became interested in the theory that we "live in a universe that is primarily spiritual, and that it is possible to get everything we need — health, money, happiness — through the scientific application of prayer and meditation."

With Estelle watching Nicki at home (Estelle was concerned that the young housewife never seemed to go out and offered to baby-sit Nicki), Peggy felt comfortable enough to attend one of Dr. Holmes' lectures. She had always been a positive thinker; now she began to see the physical benefits of positive thought and daily affirmations. In the May 1987 edition of *Science of Mind Magazine*, Peggy told journalist Elaine St. Johns about her first visit to the Institute:

> I was the first to arrive and as I sat in the lecture hall I noticed a small brass plaque on the chair in front of me. Curious, I circled around to see whose name was on the back of the chair I had selected and I could hardly believe it was Estelle Frombach! I felt a frisson of excitement and then, as I listened to Dr. Holmes, I thought with a deep thrill, "This is it. This is what I've been looking for."

Peggy attended Dr. Holmes' lectures and Sunday services as often as she could, and began to apply Holmes' teachings in her daily life. The difficulties of her personal life and career seemed to ease. Then, on a trip to New York, where she was to substitute for Jo Stafford on Stafford's popular radio show, Peggy would face a challenge that required Dr. Ernest Holmes' strength.

It began when Peggy arrived in New York by air feeling ill. Her condition worsened during the night, and the doctor (called by Peggy's manager) informed her that she would be unable to appear on the show. "He couldn't understand that I had to," Peggy recalled in the *Science of the Mind Magazine* article, "and my thoughts went immediately to Dr. Holmes. Today, long distance calls to London, Paris, Istanbul, are casual. In 1945 they were Very Important. So I put through a person-to-person call, New York to Los Angeles, to Dr. Holmes and got him right away. I heard his calm voice say, 'You'll be all right. Come and see me when you get back. I'll continue working for you. You'll be fine.'

"By air time, I was fine," continued Peggy. "My first experience of spiritual mind healing! When I got back to the coast I went to see him at once. From then on Ernest and Hazel adopted me as one of those daughters they 'didn't have.' Now I began consciously to apply principles he taught, and to experience their effect in my life. They even reached back into my childhood, for Ernest taught me to forgive what happened to me there."

As soon as David was well enough to leave the hospital, the Barbours went on a vacation. Peggy's idea was to head to a quiet setting where her husband could recuperate. They drove to the Rosarita Beach Hotel near Ensenada. The relaxed atmosphere not only helped David get better, it also inspired them to write "Mañana."

When Peggy and David returned to Los Angeles, Peggy received a phone call from Carmen Miranda. Peggy had worked with Carmen on Jimmy Durante's radio show. Carmen had simply called to ask if Peggy would like to record with her group the Brazilians.

Carmen had no idea Peggy and Dave had just written "Mañana." The Brazilians would provide the perfect backing for "Mañana." Carmen also suggested guitarist Laurindo Almeida. With this group, Peggy would become the first American artist to record with authentic Latin musicians.

"Mañana" proved to be Capitol's biggest single to date. It sold 2,500,000 copies in 1948. It would hold its "best-selling" title until the arrival of the Beatles. Fans have noted — with a smile — that it took four men from England to knock Peggy's record out of the top spot. "Mañana" displayed Peggy's many talents as singer and songwriter. It showed that she had developed into a lyricist of the highest caliber. And, her talent for dialects was heard for the first time. She was a remarkable mimic, and over the years we would hear her sing with Mexican, Italian, British, German and Siamese accents.

Sales for "Mañana" were so great that a washed-up vaudevillian named Hats McKay decided to try and cash in. McKay sued for three million dollars, claiming that he wrote "Mañana" in 1919. McKay's version of the song was called the "Laughing Song." Experts were called in on both sides. Albert Osbourne, the handwriting expert from the famous Hauptmann-Lindergh trial, testified that McKay's manuscript was freshly written. The president of ASCAP (American Society of Composers, Artists and Publishers), Deems Taylor, pointed out that when Hats demonstrated his song he never played the same melody twice.

One day the judge told Peggy she had a phone call in his chambers. When she picked up the phone she heard a familiar voice ask, "What did dey do to my goil?" It was Jimmy Durante! Before she knew it, Durante arrived in court, pushing an upright piano. Durante proceeded to demonstrate his "Laughing Song."

In vaudeville it was common for comedians—Durante included—to tell a joke and then play a vamp on the piano while the audience laughed. Laughing songs were usually marked with "ha ha ha" in place of lyrics. This was exactly the case with McKay's song. Durante's musical testimony proved that laughing songs were in the public domain. Jimmy also gave those assembled a much needed laugh.

Peggy and David's last witness was a musical historian, Dr. Sigmund Spaeth. Dr. Spaeth's testimony clinched the case. He showed that McKay's song was marked to be played as a samba. The date on the sheet music was 1919. The samba did not exist in 1919. Many years later, in her Broadway show *Peg*, Peggy would salute her devoted friend Jimmy Durante. She wrote "What Did Dey Do to My Goil?" based on Jimmy's courtroom antics, and performed the song à la Durante.

Before the advent of television in the 1950s, radio was America's greatest entertainment medium. Millions of listeners tuned in daily to hear soap operas and quiz shows. After dinner the entire family was entertained by a wide range of programs; comedies (such as *Fibber McGee and Molly*), westerns (*Gunsmoke*), and thrillers (*Lights Out*) were all great favorites. Among the most popular were variety programs hosted by stars like Bob Hope, Jimmy Durante and Bing Crosby.

Recording stars like Peggy Lee and David Barbour were very much in demand for appearances on variety shows. Peggy and Dave began to work in radio on a weekly basis as early as 1946, appearing on shows hosted by Bob Crosby (Bing's brother headed up his own popular band, "Bob Crosby and His Bobcats") and their fellow Capitol Records mate Dinah Shore. Along with Woody Herman, Peggy and Dave acted as hosts of *The Electric Hour*. Later, Peggy would serve as hostess of her own show, *The Chesterfield Supper Club*.

Summer 1947—*The Electric Hour*. *The Electric Hour* was broadcast during the summer months of 1947. During that time Peggy and Woody Herman sang duets of "When the Red, Red Robin Comes Bob-Bob-Bobbin' Along," "Pancho Maximillian Hernandez," "The Lady from 29 Palms," "On the Sunny Side of the Street" and "Up a Lazy River."

Peggy's solos during the run of *The Electric Hour* included "Somebody Loves Me," "As Long as I'm Dreaming," "Aintcha Ever Comin' Back?" "It Takes a Long, Long Train with a Red Caboose to Carry My Blues Away," "I Don't Know Enough About You," "You and I Passing By" and "It's a Good Day."

The team of "Mr. and Mrs. Melody" also found time for some film work between 1946 and 1947. In 1946 Universal Pictures made a fifteen-minute short entitled *Banquet of Melody* (in the '40s it was not uncommon to see a newsreel, a cartoon and a short, like *Banquet of Melody*, before the feature film). For *Banquet of Melody* the Barbours performed their composition "I Don't Know Enough About You."

They also did the wonderful Jimmy McHugh and Dorothy Fields tune "Don't Blame Me."

That same year Peggy's voice was featured in a George Pal Puppetoon. The eight-minute animated film was called *Jasper's in a Jam*. For the Pal film Peggy sang "Old Man Mose."

George Pal was clearly impressed with Peggy's talents as singer and songwriter. He hired Peggy and David to write the score for a project he was working on. Pal wanted to film the fairytale *The Adventures of Tom Thumb*. Peggy and Dave went to work and created five new songs. Unfortunately, *Tom Thumb* would not be completed until 1958. None of the Lee-Barbour songs were used in the final product. Peggy did write three entirely new songs for the 1958 feature, this time acting as both composer and lyricist.

Next came another short film. Paramount Pictures' *Midnight Serenade* was filmed in 1947, but not released until 1952. It would mark the first time that Peggy appeared in a movie as someone other than herself. Unfortunately, the nineteen-minute "Musical Parade Featurette" has not been seen since its release, and the name of Peggy's

In 1947 Peggy and Dave Barbour starred in the Paramount Musical Parade featurette *Midnight Serenade*. The nineteen-minute film was not released until 1952 and has not been seen since then. Lee sang "It's a Good Day," and two other unknown songs.

character remains unknown. "It's a Good Day" was one of the songs she performed in *Midnight Serenade*. The footage of "It's a Good Day," set in a recording studio, would later surface in a compilation film named *Jazz Ball*.

October 8, 1947 — *Jimmy Durante Show.* Lee performed "All of Me."

October 22, 1947 — *Jimmy Durante Show.* Peggy was unable to appear with Durante. Jo Stafford took her place.

December 3, 1947 — *Jimmy Durante Show.* Peggy sang her hit "I'll Dance at Your Wedding."

December 10, 1947 — *Jimmy Durante Show.* Peggy soloed on "There'll Be Some Changes Made."

December 17, 1947 — *Jimmy Durante Show.* Peggy sang her latest hit, "Golden Earrings."

December 24, 1947 — *Jimmy Durante Show.* For this Christmas broadcast Peggy sang the Mel Tormé–Bob Wells classic "The Christmas Song."

December 31, 1947 — *Jimmy Durante Show.* Peggy sang the Lee-Barbour smash hit "Mañana."

January 7, 1948 — *Jimmy Durante Show.* Lee sang "I'll Dance at Your Wedding Again," and added "The Gentleman Is a Dope."

January 24, 1948 — "Mañana." The Lee-Barbour tune hit the charts. It would stay for a record 21 weeks, peaking at number one.

January 21, 1948 — *Jimmy Durante Show.* Peggy reprised the popular "Golden Earrings."

January 28, 1948 — *Jimmy Durante Show.* Lee's solo for this broadcast was "I Can't Give You Anything but Love, Baby."

January 31, 1948 — "All Dressed Up with a Broken Heart." Peggy had another charting hit on this date. "All Dressed Up with a Broken Heart" was on the charts for one week. It peaked at number 21.

February 2, 1948 — *Jimmy Durante Show.* Peggy sang "You Don't Have to Know the Language" from the Bob Hope–Bing Crosby hit film *The Road to Rio*. She also performed "Lone Star Moon."

February 4, 1948 — Jimmy Durante Show. Peggy performed "I'm-a Comin' a-Courtin' Corabelle" with Victor Moore and Candy Candido. This date is listed on the CD *Jimmy Durante — I Say It with Music*, but it is possible this performance actually occurred during the February 2, 1948, broadcast.

February 11, 1948 — Bing Crosby Philco Radio Time. Bing and Peggy were joined by guests Oscar Levant and Joe Venuti. The stars performed various duets, trios and quartets. The songs included "'S Wonderful" (with Crosby, Levant and Venuti), "I've Got a Crush on You" (with Crosby), "They Can't Take That Away from Me" (with Crosby), "I Got Rhythm" (with Crosby and Venuti) and "Summertime" (with Crosby).

February 11, 1948 — Jimmy Durante Show. The Lee-Barbour hit "Mañana" was Peggy's solo for this Durante outing.

This 1948 glamour shot was taken to promote Peggy's appearance on Jimmy Durante's radio show.

February 18, 1948 — Jimmy Durante Show. Peggy performed the Johnny Burke and James Van Heusen tune "But Beautiful." The song had debuted in the film *Road to Rio*. The *Jimmy Durante — I Say It with Music* CD also lists April 7, 1948, as a broadcast date for this program.

February 25, 1948 — Bing Crosby Philco Radio Time. Peggy's solo for this Crosby show was "Golden Earrings." She and Bing joined forces on "It's About Time I Wrote the Folks in Terre Haute," "Boise, Idaho," and "These Lush Moments."

February 28, 1948 — "For Every Man There's a Woman." "For Every Man There's a Woman" hit the charts on this date, to remain for two weeks. It peaked at number 25.

March 3, 1948 — Jimmy Durante Show. Peggy sang "How Lucky You Are" for Durante's audience.

March 10, 1948 — Jimmy Durante Show. Peggy performs "The Secretary Song."

March 10, 1948—Heart of Gold award presented to Durante. Peggy gave Jimmy the nickname "Mr. Love." As a musical and comic foil to Crosby and Durante she held her own in sketches and songs. She worked with Hollywood's top film stars, including Gary Cooper, Tallulah Bankhead, Charles Boyer, Greer Garson and Van Johnson. Peggy also rode on a float with Durante in the 1947 Santa Claus Parade. On March 10, 1948, she presented her beloved friend Jimmy Durante with the Heart of Gold award.

March 24, 1948—*Bing Crosby Philco Radio Time.* Bing and Peggy joined in song for "Mañana" and Irving Berlin's "Easter Parade."

March 24, 1948—*Jimmy Durante Show.* "Laroo, Laroo, Lilli Bolero" was Peggy latest hit. She sang it for this broadcast.

March 29, 1948—*Life* magazine. A photograph of Peggy and Jimmy appeared in the March 29, 1948, issue of *Life* magazine. The caption quotes Durante as saying, "If I'm going to sleep, here is the girl I'll dream about."

The three-page spread, entitled "Busy Singer," also featured a photo of Peggy leaning on a stack of the best-selling "Mañana." It was estimated that the song brought in $75,000 in royalties in 1948. Peggy almost didn't see a penny of those royalties. During a drinking binge, David and manager Carlos Gastel tried to sell the rights to "Mañana" for two tickets to the Rose Bowl game!

Another photograph in the *Life* photo-essay showed Peggy and David in the garden. There is a beautiful collie named Banjo on the lawn behind Peggy. The dog came to the Barbours as a stray. She showed up at their house dragging her hind legs behind her, and suffering from malnutrition and an eye infection that nearly blinded her. Peggy nursed the dog back to health.

The renowned dog trainer and owner of Lassie, Frank Weatherwax, saw the photograph. He recognized Banjo as one of Lassie's offspring. Weatherwax set the legal wheels in motion. The story was big news, making the front page. In Chicago, where Peggy was performing, she was horrified to see the headline "PEGGY LEE STEALS DOG!" The phone rang and she had to defend herself, telling reporters that the story was not true.

When she returned home the saga continued. It seems that the dog's trainer came to the house one day while Peggy was still in Chicago and took Banjo. Peggy's gardener assured her that Banjo was frightened and did not want to go with the man. Not surprisingly, Peggy decided to fight for her dog. It was established that Weatherwax had given Banjo to a trainer who abused her, and Banjo had run away from that trainer. The judge felt the dog was happier and safer with Peggy. Banjo remained Peggy's loyal, loving pet for many years.

The words "busy singer" were an understatement. Since the end of her retirement, Peggy had recorded over one hundred songs for Capitol. Between 1945 and 1951, no less than thirty-four of her compositions had been published. With Dave and his quartet she also filmed ten of their biggest hits, including "I Don't Know Enough About You," "What More Can a Woman Do?," "Mañana" and "It's a Good Day." These filmed versions of their songs were made for the Snader Telescriptions company.

The Snader Telescriptions, precursors to today's music videos, were shown in movie houses around the country, and were also broadcast on television in the 1950s. These snippets (including one segment in which, dressed in an off-the-shoulder, form-fitting, sequined gown, she wriggled her way through the Lee-Barbour tune "You Was Right, Baby") demonstrate that Peggy's beauty matched her talent. In the parlance of the era, Peggy was a "looker" who "cooked on all four burners" when she sang.

April 3, 1948—"**Laroo, Laroo, Lili Bolero.**" "Laroo, Laroo, Lili Bolero" hit the charts at number 13. It stayed on the charts for four weeks.

April 7, 1948—*Bing Crosby Philco Radio Time.* The legendary Fred Astaire was Bing's guest. Peggy's solo was "Smoke Gets in Your Eyes." She and Bing sang duets on "Cheek to Cheek," "They Can't Take That Away from Me," "Dearly Beloved" and "White Christmas." Astaire joined Lee and Crosby on renditions of "A Fine Romance," "Catalog Day" and "Kamehameha Day." Lee and Astaire performed "Isn't This a Lovely Day."

April 7, 1948—*Jimmy Durante Show.* The Johnny Burke and Jimmy Van Heusen classic "But Beautiful" was introduced by Bing Crosby in *The Road to Rio*. Peggy sang it on this April broadcast.

April 14, 1948—*Jimmy Durante Show.* Peggy sang "You Turned the Tables on Me."

April 17, 1948—"**Talking to Myself About You.**" This tune charted for one week, peaking at number 23.

April 21, 1948—*Jimmy Durante Show.* Peggy sang the Harry Ruskin–Henry Sullivan tune "I May Be Wrong (but I Think You're Wonderful)."

April 28, 1948—*Jimmy Durante Show.* Peggy soloed on "It's the Sentimental Thing to Do." Peggy and Lucille Ball performed Jimmy Durante's composition "Any State in the Forty-Eight Is Great."

May 5, 1948—*Jimmy Durante Show.* Peggy performed the Dave Mann and Redd Evans song "I Went Down to Virginia."

May 12, 1948—*Jimmy Durante Show.* Nat "King" Cole had the hit version of "Nature Boy." Peggy sang her own tender version on the Durante show.

May 15, 1948—"Don't Smoke in Bed." "Don't Smoke in Bed" arrived on the charts at number 22 and remained on the charts for two weeks.

May 19, 1948—*Jimmy Durante Show.* Peggy performed "Why Don't You Do Right?"

May 26, 1948—*Jimmy Durante Show.* Peggy sang "Baby, Don't Be Mad at Me."

June 5, 1948—"Caramba! It's the Samba!" "Caramba! It's the Samba" began a chart run of five weeks, peaking at number 13. "Baby, Don't Be Mad at Me" also charted on this date, remaining there for three weeks at number 21.

June 19, 1948—"Somebody Else Is Taking My Place." This reissue of Peggy's first hit proved the song's staying power. It hit the charts for one week, peaking at number 30.

July 3, 1948—"Bubble Loo, Bubble Loo." "Bubble Loo, Bubble Loo" arrived at number 23 (its peak) and remained on the charts for four weeks.

October 27, 1948—*Bing Crosby Philco Radio Time.* This ABC program was broadcast from San Francisco. Peggy's songs included "Love, Your Spell Is Everywhere" and "You Came a Long Way from St. Louis."

November 10, 1948—*Bing Crosby Philco Radio Time.* Several top-notch musicians appear as Bing's guests, including Oscar Levant (piano), Ziggy Elman (trumpet), Red Nichols (cornet) and Joe Venuti (violin). Peggy's solo number was "What Is This Thing Called Love?" She and Bing sang "Exactly Like You" and "They Can't Take That Away from Me." Venuti, Nichols and Elman joined Lee and Crosby for "I Got Rhythm."

December 1, 1948—*Bing Crosby Philco Radio Time.* Bing's brother Bob Crosby was the guest. Peggy, Bob and Bing performed "A Little Bird Told Me." Bing and Peggy sang a duet of "On a Slow Boat to China."

December 15, 1948—*Bing Crosby Philco Radio Time.* Bob Hope joined Peggy and Bing for this show. Peggy and Bing sang "A Little Bird Told Me" again. Peggy performed "(I Want to Go Where You Go) Then I'll Be Happy."

December 17, 1948—*Jimmy Durante Show.* Peggy sang her current hit "Golden Earrings" from the Ray Milland and Marlene Dietrich film of the same name.

December 29, 1948—*Bing Crosby Philco Radio Time.* The Mills Brothers were Crosby's guests. Lee and Crosby sang "Cuanta la Gusta" and "Maybe You'll Be There." Lee soloed on the delightful "I Got Lucky in the Rain."

January 26, 1949—*Bing Crosby Philco Radio Time.* Abe Burrows was Bing's guest. This time Bing joined Peggy for "I Got Lucky in the Rain." The team also sang duets on "When You're in Love with the Lover You Love." Burrows joined them for "California" while Peggy went solo on "So Dear to My Heart."

February 23, 1949—*Bing Crosby Philco Radio Time.* Abe Burrows returned for this broadcast, singing "Happy, Happy Days" with Crosby and Lee. Peggy sang three duets with Bing: "It Means That We Are," "So in Love" and "(I Want to Go Where You Go) Then I'll Be Happy."

March 9, 1949—*Bing Crosby Philco Radio Time.* Broadcast from San Francisco, this program found Peggy and Bing singing "So in Love" and "Once and for Always."

March 12, 1949—"Blum Blum, I Wonder Who I Am." This Lee-Barbour novelty tune allowed Peggy to share her unique sense of humor. The song charted for one week at number 27.

March 16, 1949—*Bing Crosby Philco Radio Time.* This was another broadcast from San Francisco. Peggy's songs included a duet with Crosby on "You Was."

April 13, 1949—*Bing Crosby Philco Radio Time.* For this Easter broadcast Peggy and Bing sang "Down the Old Ox Road" and "Easter Parade."

April 23, 1949—"Similau." "Similau" reached the charts at number 17 and was on the charts for one week.

April 27, 1949—*Bing Crosby Philco Radio Time.* Peggy soloed on "Bali Ha'i." She and Bing sang "Be-Bop Spoken Here."

May 11, 1949—*Bing Crosby Philco Radio Time.* Alec Templeton was Bing's guest for this San Francisco broadcast. Templeton joined Lee and Crosby for "Faraway Places" and "Blue Hawaii." Peggy and Bing sang "How It Lies, How It Lies, How It Lies." Once again Peggy performed "Bali Ha'i."

May 14, 1949—"Bali Ha'i." This theme from the Broadway hit show *South Pacific* made the charts on this date and stayed for 16 weeks, peaking at number 13.

May 28, 1949—"Riders in the Sky (A Cowboy Legend)." "Riders in the Sky" arrived on the charts at number two (its peak); it would remain a chart hit for nine weeks.

September 21, 1949—*Chesterfield Presents the Bing Crosby Show.* Bing's sponsor changed from Philco radios to Chesterfield cigarettes and the show moved from

ABC to CBS. Abe Burrows was Bing's guest for this outing. Abe, Bing and Peggy joined forces on "We Love the Canadian Rockies." Peggy and Bing sang "Maybe It's Because." Lee's solo was the humorous "Louisa from Lake Louise."

September 28, 1949—Chesterfield Presents the Bing Crosby Show. Peggy and Bing welcomed Abe Burrows back to the show. Lee's solo was another very funny song, "I'm Sweet, Shy Ophelia." Lee and Crosby sang "Okay, Denmark, Okay," and joined Burrows to make a trio on "You're in Love with Someone."

October 12, 1949—Chesterfield Presents the Bing Crosby Show. "A Wonderful Guy" was Peggy's solo turn. She and Bing joined forces for "I've Got a Crush on You" and "How It Lies, How It Lies, How It Lies."

October 19, 1949—Chesterfield Presents the Bing Crosby Show. Peggy sang "I've Got a Right to Sing the Blues." She and Bing sang "It's More Fun Than a Picnic."

November 23, 1949—Chesterfield Presents the Bing Crosby Show. Violinist Joe Venuti was back. Joe, Bing and Peggy performed "A Thousand Violins." Peggy's duet with Bing was "Way Back Home."

December 7, 1949—Chesterfield Presents the Bing Crosby Show. For this Christmastime show Peggy and Bing sang "Here Comes Santa Claus," "Mañana" and "Stay Well."

January 7, 1950—"The Old Master Painter." This duet with Mel Tormé hit and peaked at number nine, remaining on the charts for seven weeks.

January 11, 1950—Chesterfield Presents the Bing Crosby Show. The legendary Groucho Marx joined Peggy and Bing. Lee and Crosby sang "Little Jack Frost, Get Lost," while Peggy's solo was the Barbour-Lee song "When You Speak with Your Eyes."

February 8, 1950—Chesterfield Presents the Bing Crosby Show. Radio comedian Fred Allen was Bing's guest. Peggy sang "A Dream Is a Wish Your Heart Makes" and her duet with Crosby was "Sunshine Cake."

August 26, 1950—"Show Me the Way to Get Out of This World." On the charts for one week, "Show Me the Way to Get Out of This World" entered and peaked on this date at number 28.

December 13, 1950—Chesterfield Presents the Bing Crosby Show. Crosby and Lee sang "A Bushel and a Peck" from the Broadway show *Guys and Dolls.* They also performed "Orange Colored Sky" and "Silver Bells."

Left, top: Arrow points to Peggy in a reception parade which preceded her performance at the Valley City auditorium. Parade was led by the American Legion Drum and Bugle corps. The *Valley City Times-Record* bannered the event. *Left, bottom:* Peggy Lee's brother, Milford Egstrom of Jamestown, joined her in song during a reception at the home of Herman Stern, the Valley City merchant who was largely responsible for Peggy's appearance at the Winter show. After her performance in Valley City, Peggy visited her sick father, a former railroad man, at Millerton. A blizzard forced her to make the trip by farm truck. Peggy had a brother, Leonard, at Grand Forks, and two sisters and a brother in Hollywood. *Above:* Right back where she started from: Peggy Lee was heard on Valley City's KOVO between performances at the North Dakota Winter show. She was a guest disc jockey on a record program called *The Peggy Lee Show*. Station manager Robert Ingstad, who gave Peggy her first radio job in 1937, is at left. Watching through the window are Mrs. Richard Stern, who used to play Peggy's piano accompaniment, and Gladys Thompson, who had a program on the station when Peggy was there.

February 21, 1951— Chesterfield Presents the Bing Crosby Show. Tallulah Bankhead joined Bing and Peggy. The Crosby-Lee duet was "Just the Way You Are"; the Lee solo was "For Just the Chance to Love You."

September 8, 1951— "(When I Dance with You) I Get Ideas." "I Get Ideas" hit the charts for an eight-week stay, reaching its peak at number 14. This was Peggy's

Left, top: Peggy and her husband are pictured during one of their four performances at the Winter show. They made two afternoon and two evening performances. A blizzard cut attendance some the second day. Audiences enjoyed Peggy's framed "soft-as-silk" style. *Right, top:* After a performance Peggy signed autographs for Valley City Boy Scouts. *Left, middle:* Peggy looked over livestock entered in the agricultural show. Here she inspects closely a prize Hereford calf owned by Douglas Richman, Tower City. Peggy, who was born in Jamestown, finished Wimbledon High School at 16. Even then she had a dream of a singing career. *Left, bottom:* During her 1950 homecoming, Peggy is reunited with Lloyd Collins. Lee and Collins performed together at the Powers Coffee Shop.

last charting song for her first stint with Capitol Records. Her next hit would be on the Decca label.

The pressures on the team of Lee and Barbour were great. In addition to their radio and recording commitments they also had nightclub contracts to fulfill. They were a big draw at Ciro's in Hollywood. It became clear at this time that Peggy's star was outshining David's. In 1949 *Billboard* magazine named her "America's No. One Female Singer of the Year." That same year she was Capitol's "Top Money-Making Female Artist."

David's drinking started to affect his ability to work. Rumors had it that he resented

standing in his famous wife's shadow. In truth, his health was fragile, and he was fearful of any lasting impression his drunkenness might have on Nicki. He asked Peggy for a divorce. Peggy was devastated. At first she refused; then, realizing David probably was right in his concern for their daughter's welfare, she finally agreed.

The team of Lee and Barbour would appear together one final time. In 1950 they

Left: This studio portrait was taken when Peggy appeared in Bing Crosby's 1950 film *Mr. Music*. Peggy was a guest among the film's galaxy of stars, including Charles Coburn, Ruth Hussey, Robert Stack, Marge and Gower Champion, Dorothy Kirsten and Groucho Marx.

Peggy and Bing Crosby sing "Life Is So Peculiar" from *Mr. Music*.

played themselves in the Bing Crosby movie *Mr. Music*. During a party sequence in the film Peggy sings a duet of "Life Is So Peculiar" with Bing. David Barbour is all but lost in the background.

May 17, 1951— **Lee and Barbour divorce.** Life was, in fact, very peculiar. During their divorce the couple was so loving toward each other that the judge questioned whether they should divorce at all. Shortly after the divorce became final on May 17, 1951, David Barbour joined Alcoholics Anonymous. He would remain sober until his untimely death in 1965. Peggy's former boss, Benny Goodman, broke the news of David's sudden death to Peggy at a Christmas party. Sadly, just days before he passed away, David and Peggy had discussed the possibility of marrying again.

July 15, 1951—*Peggy Lee Show.* Peggy welcomed Benny Goodman as her guest. Goodman soloed on "Clarinade" and his closing theme "Goodbye." Peggy and Benny joined forces for "Toodle-Lee-Oo-Doo." Peggy's solos were "If I Could Be with You," "Too Young," "Make the Man Love Me," "It Never Happened to Me" and "Shanghai."

At the end of 1951, Peggy Lee faced more than the end of her marriage. Her father had died in April. Now her contract with Capitol was about to expire. Her years with Capitol had been very profitable for all concerned. While Peggy enjoyed the comforts money brought, she cherished artistic excellence above all else. She approached Capitol with an idea for a recording that was years ahead of its time on many levels.

Unfortunately, the Capitol recording artist Les Paul (of the great team of Les Paul and Mary Ford) already had a huge hit with the song Peggy wanted to record. Fearful that the public would not buy two versions of the same song, the producers at Capitol said no to Peggy's idea. That "no" was a mistake that would cost Capitol millions of dollars.

Peggy's belief in her artistic vision was so strong that she left Capitol Records and signed with the Decca label. Decca recorded her dream project, and her vision proved to be right on the money. The song was a monster hit and launched Peggy Lee into the next decade. It established her as a singer and musical innovator with few peers.

• THREE •

Decca: 1952 to 1957

Peggy Lee entered the early 1950s as a top-notch nightclub entertainer. She was the creative force behind one of the most polished acts on the club circuit. Nothing was left to chance; her musicians, gowns, hairstyle, songs, the order of the program and her lighting cues were all carefully planned.

January 13, 1952—Ed Sullivan's Toast of the Town. Peggy joined Ed Sullivan and Rudy Vallee for this tribute to Broadway showman George White. The program was broadcast on CBS. Songs included "Thank Your Mother," "This Is the Mrs.," "My Song" and "Life Is Just a Bowl of Cherries" (a duet with Rudy Vallee).

> Topping the listing was Peggy Lee, one of the more expressive song-chicks around. Miss Lee negotiated one of the top White tunes, "Are You Having Any Fun?" and participated in a well-presented finale.—*Variety*, 1/16/52

March 30, 1952—The Paul Whiteman Revue. *The Paul Whiteman Revue* was broadcast on ABC.

> Miss Lee, who concentrated heavily on ballads rather than the current novelty pops, registered solidly with her dramatic rendition of two oldies.—*Variety*, 4/2/52

May 1952—Peggy Lee Show. On this radio broadcast Peggy played hostess to the legendary Tommy Dorsey. Peggy sang "A Guy Is a Guy," "These Foolish Things," "Just One More Chance" and "The Lady Is a Tramp" with the Sonny Burke Orchestra. Dorsey and Lee joined forces for a medley of his hits, including "Marie," "I'll Never Smile Again," "Song of India" and "This Love of Mine."

May 1, 1952—"Lover." Peggy recorded "Lover" on this date at Liederkranz Hall in New York. It was her first recording for the Decca label. Lee's rendition of "Lover" had been a part of her act for a couple of seasons, and was a showstopper from the very beginning.

The song was written by the team of Richard Rodgers and Lorenz Hart. They wrote it as a waltz for the 1932 film *Love Me Tonight*. By 1950 it was all but forgotten. Peggy's bold reading of "Lover" literally breathed new life into the song.

Lee had seen a French film starring Jean Gabin. The film told the story of a man who joined the French Foreign Legion after his lover spurned him. In one memorable scene, Gabin was shown leading his men on horseback out into the desert. As he raised his banner, the horses went from a trot to a canter to a gallop, and finally to a full gallop. Peggy, struck by the idea that each gait felt like a new tempo, was reminded of Latin rhythms, and "Lover" was born anew.

Peggy worked out the arrangement of "Lover" with her musicians. She gave them specific instructions: The bongos were to play straight eighths, congas six-eight and the drummer would play a fast four. Once the piece was perfected, Peggy tried it out in clubs.

The response was incredible. Audiences went wild, screaming for more. The new Latin sound excited musicians and arrangers as well, and provided them with new musical frontiers to explore.

In spite of the public's obvious enthusiasm, Capitol was hesitant to record "Lover." They couldn't see how vastly different Lee's version was from the hit rendition Les Paul had recently recorded for Capitol. Then Peggy's friend Sonny Burke brought Decca's Milt Gabler to see her perform. Gabler wanted to record "Lover" and Peggy left Capitol and signed with Decca for five years. "Lover" was her first recording on her new label.

Gordon Jenkins was brought in to write the orchestration for Peggy's arrangement of "Lover." On April 30, 1952, a thirty-seven-piece orchestra assembled in Liederkranz Hall, augmented by eight percussionists and back-up singers.

Peggy was overwhelmed, figuratively and literally. The sheer volume of the orchestra, coupled with the "live" acoustics of the hall, all but drowned out her vocals.

Sound engineer Morty Palitz solved the problem. Palitz worked all night building an isolation booth. The booth would separate Peggy from the musicians, allowing the technicians to better record her vocals.

"Lover" was successfully recorded on May 1, 1952. Within weeks of its release, it sold over 250,000 units.

Before the song was ever recorded it had already won Peggy a film role. Michael Curtiz, who was planning a remake of *The Jazz Singer*, had gone to see Peggy's act at Ciro's in Hollywood. When she brought the house down with her "Lover," he knew he had found the right actress for the role of Judy Lane.

When Curtiz offered to include Peggy's rendition of "Lover" in the film the deal was sealed. Peggy reported for work at the Warner Bros. lot.

Peggy discussed her thoughts on acting in the pressbook that Warners created to promote the movie:

> When I first considered the idea of playing a dramatic role and ... my first time out, I was mildly terrified. Then I gave myself a good talking to. After all, I told myself, acting is just story telling with the voice and features. That's what I've been doing for years, telling stories with my songs.... I took the script of "The Jazz Singer," ... studied my lines as if they were lyrics to a song. Then when I went before the camera I made myself imagine that I was singing to an audience.... I used everything I had learned in singing to transmit the proper feeling to tell the story.

In 1953 Peggy starred opposite Danny Thomas (left) in the Warner Bros. remake of *The Jazz Singer*. Veteran character actress Mildred Dunnock (center) plays Thomas' mother.

"Lover" was set in a New York nightclub. Wearing an off-the-shoulder white gown, Lee stands in the curve of a grand piano. Curtiz proved successful in capturing the excitement of Lee's performances. In fact, there were those who found "Lover" a bit overwhelming on film. The Catholic League of Decency labeled the segment "too suggestive."*

Peggy opens *The Jazz Singer* with her one-of-a-kind rendition of Cole Porter's "Just One of Those Things." As a songwriter, Peggy contributed "This Is a Very Special Day" to the film. She also joined forces with Danny Thomas on "I Hear the Music Now."

May 24, 1952—"Be Anything (But Be Mine)." The single of "Be Anything (But Be Mine)" made the charts on this date, remaining on the charts for three weeks and peaking at number 21.

May 25, 1952—*Colgate Comedy Hour*. Peggy's songs included "The Lady Is a Tramp" and "Where or When." The *Colgate Comedy Hour* was seen on NBC.

---

*From the collection of Ronald Towe. Exact source unknown (possibly *DownBeat*).

Danny Thomas and Peggy share a playful moment on the set of *The Jazz Singer*.

Songstress Peggy Lee, spotted midway in the show, was wasted in a bit which called for her to warble only two numbers. — *Variety*, 5/28/52

May 28, 1952 — *The Dinah Shore Show*. Peggy joined Dinah, Peter Lind Hayes and Nat "King" Cole for this radio show. Together the quartet sang "I Ain't Mad at You." Peggy's solo was "Baby, Won't You Please Come Home."

A glamorous portrait of Peggy in the dress she wore while singing "Lover" in *The Jazz Singer*.

Spring 1952 — ***The Jazz Singer* Premiere, Los Angeles.** Peggy surprised everyone when she attended the Los Angeles premiere of *The Jazz Singer* on the arm of actor Brad Dexter. During filming, Peggy's name had been linked romantically with actor Robert Preston, with whom she was often seen dancing at Hollywood nightspots. But Peggy and Brad had been dating for nearly a year. The two met when Dr. Ernest Holmes, Peggy's spiritual mentor, brought Brad to an informal dinner at Peggy's home.

Dexter, a Yugoslavian, was born Boris Milanovitch. He had some success on Broadway before entering the Air Corps during World War II. After the war he acted in several films, including *The Asphalt Jungle*, *Las Vegas*, and *Macao*.

June 7, 1952 — **"Lover."** The single of "Lover" made the charts on this date. It remained on the charts for 13 weeks and peaked at number three.

June 16, 1952 — ***Time* magazine.** The venerable magazine featured an article entitled "Singer with Instinct." The uncredited author focused on Peggy's new hit record:

> Songstress Peggy Lee has always liked the old (1932) Rodgers and Hart waltz "Lover" ("Lover, when I'm near you," etc.). She gets a picture in her head when she hears it: "The French Foreign Legion is riding out into the desert. They start off at a moderate speed. Then the leader raises his whip and swings it in the air, and they start to go faster and faster." Decca was impressed, agreed to let her record the old waltz as a triple-gaited mambo with a 37-piece accompaniment. In its first two weeks, Peggy Lee's "Lover" has sold 250,000 copies.

The article concluded with an overview of Peggy's current and upcoming projects:

> Songstress Lee has no immediate plans to make another "sound" record like "Lover," but she has irons in the fire. She has a contract to work on the score of a new Walt Disney, is opening at Ciro's Hollywood nightclub, and is planning her own TV film series.... Peggy says she's "just gardening" on the West Coast. She wants to go to New York, where "the tempo of show business is really up."

***June 18, 1952**—Chesterfield Presents the Bing Crosby Show.* Peggy appeared on Crosby's CBS radio show singing "Lover." She joined Bing for a duet of "Watermelon Weather."

***June 25, 1952**—Chesterfield Presents the Bing Crosby Show.* Peggy's solo for this CBS radio show was "You Go to My Head." She sang two duets with Crosby, "Zing a Little Zong" and "The Moon Came Up with a Great Idea Last Night."

***July 26, 1952**—*"Watermelon Weather." The single of "Watermelon Weather" made the charts on this date, remaining on the charts for two weeks and peaking at number 28. This was a duet with Bing Crosby.

***August 2, 1952**—*"Just One of Those Things." The single of "Just One of Those Things" charted on this date. It remained on the charts for four weeks and peaked at number 14.

***August 13, 1952**—DownBeat magazine.* Hal Holly's article was titled "Peggy Lee Gets Big Film Role Nixed by Doris Day." When Day turned down the role of Judy Lane in the Warner Brothers remake of *The Jazz Singer*, the part went to Peggy:

> Hollywood — Warner Brothers' forthcoming remake of *The Jazz Singer*, starring Danny Thomas ... takes on new interest for music-conscious moviegoers with the signing of Peggy Lee for what, at this stage of the operation, would appear to be virtually a costarring role with Thomas.
> The part for which Peggy was signed had been planned for Doris Day; and though Doris withdrew from the assignment because she — and her studio bosses — decided the part was not up to Doris' present standing as an attraction, it nevertheless may mark a major milestone for Peggy, who has done very little in pictures to date.

The *DownBeat* article concluded with a mention of Peggy's upcoming work on "a set of songs for a forthcoming Disney feature."

October 12, 1952—*New York Post.* Peggy was featured as Sidney Skolsky's tintype in the article "Tintyped: Peggy Lee":

> She sang a triple-gaited mambo version of Rodgers and Hart waltz, "Lover." It sold more records faster than any other recording she had ever made. It smacked the Hit Parade real hard. She was signed to play the feminine lead in *The Jazz Singer*.
>
> She was singing at Ciro's when director Michael Curtiz saw her. He wanted her for the movie, saying: "If she can put into acting the emotions that she puts into singing, she'll be terrific."

November 22, 1952—"River, River." The single of "River, River" made the charts on this date, remaining there for two weeks and peaking at number 23.

December 1952—*Theatre Arts* magazine. Sigmund Spaeth wrote "Song Stylists: The Triumph of Malady over Melody," an article that focused on how various singers interpret songs. Apparently, composer Richard Rodgers was not in favor of Peggy's rendition of "Lover." Spaeth wrote:

> The last word in this direction seems to have been uttered by the charming and successful Peggy Lee in her Decca recording of Richard Rodgers' "Lover," reputedly the biggest seller of all her flying discs. Now what Mr. Rodgers composed was a lilting waltz melody, effectively syncopated, following the pattern of the chromatic scale downward. It is an immensely clever composition, worthy of such a master of the waltz as Franz Lehar or even Johann Strauss himself.
>
> Peggy Lee sings the lovely and logical waltz in a top-speed duple time (it has been described as a "three-way mambo"), completely removing every trace of its original character. The fact that it is done with fiendish skill makes it all the more objectionable. Peggy's "Lover" may be something unrestrainably Latin-American, but it is certainly not Richard Rodgers. The worst of it is that the composer cannot possibly object if such a fantastic interpretation sells a lot of records, which it unquestionably does.

December 27, 1952—*New York World Telegram.* Muriel Fischer covered many aspects of Peggy's early life, hobbies and talents in her article "Now They Call Her Actress Peggy Lee":

> The pretty, blond North Dakota lass, who spent her growing-up years acquiring a working knowledge of farms and railroads, then skipped to fame as a singer and later cut another niche as lyricist, now makes her debut as an actress.
>
> In her first film, *The Jazz Singer*, which premieres here January 13, Miss Lee costars with Danny Thomas in the Technicolor musical remake of the screen's first talkie.

Fischer also mentioned Peggy's forthcoming book of poetry.

> While at work in *The Jazz Singer* ... Peggy spent her rare spare moments on the set compiling a poetry book.
>
> The poems, soon to be published, are Peggy's own, naturally. "Some new—but mostly old ones that just stepped back into my memory. Some sonnets, mostly lyrical, with a few short humorous rhymes mixed in," the poems come under the collective title of *Softly, with Feeling*.
>
> Peggy published *Softly, with Feeling* privately for her friends.

***January 4, 1953*—Peggy marries Brad Dexter.** Photographs from the wedding appeared in numerous movie magazines. The "Star Parade" section of *TV Magazine* included the following write-up:

> The ceremony was held in the garden of Peggy's home in Westwood Hills, Los Angeles. More than two hundred guests gathered as Mike Curtiz, who directed Peggy's new movie, escorted her to the flower-bedecked altar. Decca's blonde thrush wore an off-the-shoulder pink taffeta ballet-length gown, with a single strand of pearls at her throat.
> She carried a bouquet of orchids and lilies of the valley. Nicki, eight, daughter of Peg's first marriage to bandleader-musician Dave Barbour (which ended in divorce in 1951), proudly served as Junior Bridesmaid.

***January 13, 1953*—East Coast Premiere of *The Jazz Singer*.** The East Coast premiere of *The Jazz Singer* was held at New York's Paramount Theatre. The gala event was a benefit for the March of Dimes, with proceeds going to the National Foundation for Infantile Paralysis.

***January 28, 1953*—*DownBeat* magazine.** Don Freeman wrote of Peggy's new relationship with actor and director Mel Ferrer. Freeman's article was entitled "Peggy Lee's Progress Shows Flair of Ferrer."

> La Jolla, California — It seems that Peggy Lee, always a very capable singer, has developed into an extraordinarily appealing entertainer. And an assist for the transformation should go to a versatile fellow named Mel Ferrer, an actor, also a director, a producer, guiding hand at La Jolla Playhouse here and a jazz enthusiast.
> It was Ferrer who staged Peggy's appearance at Ciro's some time back, emphasizing dramatic as well as musical values, showmanship as well as songs.

***February 2, 1953*—Bing Crosby radio appearances.** Peggy and Bing recorded material for some of Crosby's upcoming radio shows.

***February 13, 1953*—Decca studios, Los Angeles.** On this date Peggy recorded one of her best-loved songs, "Where Can I Go Without You." The romantic ballad was a collaboration between Peggy and her friend Victor Young. Peggy recorded several songs at Decca with Victor Young and His Singing Strings.

The team of Lee and Young would go on to write three motion picture themes together: "I Love You So," for the film *About Mrs. Leslie*; "How Strange," for *The Bullfighter and the Lady*; and their greatest composition, the haunting "Johnny Guitar," written for the Joan Crawford film of the same name.

***February 18, 1953*—Peggy and David Barbour Reunite.** The team recorded a hard-driving bluesy song by Jessie Mae Robinson called "You Let My Love Get Cold."

The flip side of the single was another Peggy Lee composition. For the delightful "Who's Gonna Pay the Check," Peggy wrote both the words and music. She sang the novelty tune in a Neapolitan dialect, a fine display of her talent for mimicry.

February 26, 1953—*Bing Crosby General Electric Show.* Bing's CBS radio program was broadcast from Palm Springs. Lee and Crosby joined forces on "That's a Plenty."

Spring 1953—*La Vie en Rose, New York.* Leonard Feather, of *DownBeat* magazine, caught Peggy's act at La Vie en Rose:

> What a phenomenal quota of great tunes she managed to pack into that half hour! The ballad medley, ranging from excerpts of "What's New," "All Too Soon" and "Good Morning Heartache" to a full chorus of "Easy Living," was a superb example of how to build and sustain a mood.

April 30 and May 4, 1953—*Black Coffee.* Peggy reached a new artistic high. With her top-notch musicians she entered Decca's New York studios to create what was possibly her finest album. *Black Coffee* proved to be a hallmark not only for Peggy Lee, but for the recording industry as well. It was the first concept LP, a record with a specific mood and theme (in later years Frank Sinatra would make numerous concept albums, such as *Only the Lonely* and *In the Wee Small Hours*).

Prior to the release of *Black Coffee*, all of Peggy's recordings were in the 78-rpm format. A new recording speed, 33⅓, was introduced in 1948, giving record producers the opportunity to develop the 10-inch LP (Long Play).

At first, popular singers did not record on the new format. In his liner notes for the MCA Records CD *Peggy Lee Black Coffee and Sea Shells*, producer Ken Barnes, who worked with Peggy later in her career, explains the history behind the LP and the impact of *Black Coffee*:

> The original 1953 10 inch 8-song album "Black Coffee" occupies a special place in the history of popular music if only for the fact that it was Peggy Lee's very first album — or LP as they were often called in those days. But there are numerous other reasons for its continued prominence in the canon of recorded music. Not the least is Miss Lee's vocal uniqueness ... the felicitous choice of songs ... the excellence of the accompaniment. All of these factors have contributed to making it an all-time classic.
>
> At its commercial inception in 1948, the LP was seen as being more suited to presenting complete symphonic and operatic works, the appeal of which was diminished on the 3-minute 78s. Popular singers ... were originally disregarded in terms of the LP.
>
> The first popular inroads into the new medium came with the LPs of original cast recordings of such major musicals as *South Pacific* and *Guys and Dolls*.
>
> In 1950, however, Ella Fitzgerald was among the first to strike a blow for the popular singer when ... she recorded eight songs by George and Ira Gershwin, released as *Ella Sings Gershwin* (six years before the first of her celebrated Songbook series). And while it sold in healthy quantities, it would be four years before Ella would make another complete album.

Peggy Lee was ahead of her time with the release of *Black Coffee*. Why she succeeded where others had achieved only marginal success is difficult to say. It probably had to do with the fact that the album was so methodically planned and executed.

Lee now brought to the recording studio what she had been bringing to her nightclub audiences for a number of years: a highly polished performance with a personal theme, all supported by the finest caliber of musicians.

For *Black Coffee* Peggy employed three of the musicians she worked with at La Vie en Rose: Jimmy Rowles (piano), Ed Shaughnessy (drums), and Pete Candoli (trumpet).

Candoli is billed as "Cootie Chesterfield" on the LP. This was due to the fact that Pete was under contract with one of Decca's rivals. Max Wayne rounded out the group on bass. With her rhythm section, Peggy recorded eight songs in three recording sessions between April 30 and May 4. The finished product showcased her versatility.

***May 6, 1953—DownBeat* magazine.** Leonard Feather wrote the following review, the closing sentence of which would become an oft-quoted description of Peggy Lee's talent:

> Being very cautious about overstatement, we will only say conservatively that Peggy gave the greatest performance we have seen delivered by any other singer in a Manhattan club in the last five years—and that includes everybody, male or female, from Lena Horne and Sinatra on down. If you only know Peggy Lee from records, or radio and TV and theatres, catch her some time in an intimate nightclub like this. If you don't get a genuine thrill—Jack, you must be dead.

May 10, 1953—New York Daily News. An article entitled "The Fargo Express," written by Eckert Goodman, appeared in the *New York Daily News*. Subtitled "Peggy Lee, many-talented daughter of a North Dakota railroader, has been high-balling down the tracks of success ever since her radio debut 15 years ago," the article saw Goodman marveling at Lee's seemingly never-ending energy and artistic interests:

> Directors know that a session in front of the cameras can be as intensive an effort as a GI's hike in the hot sun. A lot of them make sure their stars are tenderly tucked into bed almost as soon as the cameras have stopped grinding.
>
> But to Peggy, such work is like an hors d'oeuvre before dinner. All it does is whet her appetite for activities yet to come. Here, for instance, is a typical Lee schedule—after a day's shooting of her new film, *Everybody Comes to Rick's*, when the cameras have been tucked in for the night.
>
> An hour or two at the typewriter, working on a novel.
>
> A breather in her art studio, where she may work on either a piece of sculpture or an oil painting.
>
> A session at the piano in the "moody music room" of her Norman French home in Westwood Hills, to polish the lyrics she's doing for a Disney cartoon.

May 23, 1953—"Who's Gonna Pay the Check?" The single of "Who's Gonna Pay the Check?" made the charts on this date. It remained there for two weeks and peaked at number 22.

November 11, 1953—Colgate Comedy Hour. Peggy appeared on the NBC show singing "Baubles, Bangles and Beads."

Peggy Lee, of course, is one of the top pop singers of this day. She purveys a tuneful variety of sex which was evident even when she sang the Halo shampoo commercial, which is still a cavalier way of treating an artist. Her top number done in a cloud of artificial smoke was "Baubles," which made an interesting sequence.—*Variety*, 11/11/53

***November 15, 1953**—Bing Crosby General Electric Show.* Peggy joined Bing and the Collegiates for a medley of "Ain't We Got Fun?," "Netty Co-ed" and "The Varsity Drag." She soloed on "I've Got a Crush on You." The show was heard on CBS radio.

***November 29, 1953**—Bing Crosby General Electric Show.* Bing's CBS radio show featured Peggy singing "You and the Night and the Music" and "What Is This Thing Called Love?" She also sang three duets with Crosby: "Exactly Like You," "I Got Rhythm" and "They Can't Take That Away from Me."

***December 5, 1953**—*"Baubles, Bangles and Beads."* The single of "Baubles, Bangles and Beads" hit the charts on this date, remaining there for one week and peaking at number 30.

***January 1954**—* Peggy Lee and Brad Dexter divorced.

***March 1, 1954**—*"Johnny Guitar."* Peggy recorded one of her signature songs, "Johnny Guitar," with Victor Young and His Singing Strings. Lee and Young wrote the exquisite ballad for the Republic picture of the same name.

Peggy's love for David Barbour was the inspiration for "Johnny Guitar." The song became a worldwide hit. Peggy included it in her act until the end of her performing career. A small blurb in *DownBeat* said, "Only good moment in *Johnny Guitar*, Joan Crawford's first bad picture in years, is unseen Peggy Lee singing the title song."

***March 13, 1954**—*"Where Can I Go Without You?"* The single of "Where Can I Go Without You?" made the charts on this date, remaining there for two weeks and peaking at number 28.

***March 14, 1954**—Bing Crosby General Electric Show.* Peggy and Bing vocalized on "That's Amore." Peggy's solo was "Rock-a-bye Your Baby with a Dixie Melody." This was Peggy's last appearance on Bing's CBS radio show.

***April 1954**—Everyone Comes to Peggy's.* *DownBeat* reported that Peggy was being pursued for a TV series. The show, titled *Everyone Comes to Peggy's* (formerly titled *Everybody Comes to Rick's*), would incorporate jazz, a first for the medium. *DownBeat* reported that Peggy was "determined to adapt the use of good jazzmen to TV as she has to her night club act." The show never came to be.

The *DownBeat* item appeared while Peggy was enjoying a three-week stint at the Venetian Room, located in San Francisco's Fairmont Hotel. This engagement was her debut at the Venetian Room. She would perform yearly at the venue from 1954 until it closed in 1990. During this first engagement, *Variety* reported:

> You don't have to have your hip card punched to get a belt out of Peggy Lee's singing, and that's one thing that makes this gal an exception to most jazz vocalists. She has crossed completely over the bridge between jazz.... Miss Lee, like Nat King Cole — makes the squares love it ... the wallop of a barrelhouse blues shouter ... soft-voiced warmth of a café thrush ... practiced showmanship of a born trouper.

***June 13, 1954**—San Francisco Chronicle.* Jazz critic Ralph J. Gleason wrote about Peggy's early career and her dedication to music. In the article, titled "Peggy Lee Sees Mountains When She Sings Nowadays," Lee talked about a fascinating topic — what she visualized while she sang.

> Peggy is very serious about music, loves all the swinging bands and almost any good vocalist you can name. Her favorite Peggy Lee record is the sexy, moody "Baubles, Bangles and Beads," which was a Rhythm Section "Record of the Week" some time back, and she thinks about music in two distinct ways. When she is listening, she thinks of lines and figures that move with the structure and the mood of the music. When she is singing, she thinks of all kinds of things. "Lately, I've been seeing mountains and scenes from life with me in them," she says. When she recorded "Baubles, Bangles and Beads" she thought of a great crystal chandelier with lights shining on it and the whole spectrum of color refracted through a prism.

***June 14, 1954**—DownBeat magazine.* Another Ralph Gleason article appeared in *DownBeat*. This time the title was "'Retire? No!' Declares Peggy Lee; Eyes Video." This was an edited version of the article that appeared the day before in the *San Francisco Chronicle*.

***October 13, 1954**— The Perry Como Show.* Peggy sang "I Feel a Song Coming On" on Como's CBS show.

***November 9, 1954**—"It Must Be So" and "Straight Ahead."* On this date Peggy recorded two of her compositions with the Mills Brothers. Lee wrote the words and music for "It Must Be So" and "Straight Ahead."

***Winter 1954**—Colgate Comedy Hour.* Peggy appeared with Eddie Fisher. Songs included "Love, You Didn't Do Right by Me," "From This Moment On" and "Lover."

***December 18, 1954**—"Let Me Go, Lover."* The single of "Let Me Go, Lover" hit the charts, remaining there for two weeks and peaking at number 26.

***January 1, 1955**—Selections from White Christmas.* Peggy appeared with Danny Kaye and Bing Crosby on this album of songs from the popular film. The album

Peggy records with the Mills Brothers. They recorded Peggy's compositions "It Must Be So" and "Straight Ahead" on November 9, 1954. This photograph appears courtesy of Daniel Clemson of The Mills Brothers Society.

made the charts on this date, staying there for four weeks and peaking at number two.

Rosemary Clooney wasn't able to sing on this "soundtrack" as she was with the Columbia recording label. Peggy scored with Rosie's solo "Love, You Didn't Do Right by Me." (Peggy's songs were recorded on April 10, 1954, and May 24, 1954.)

February 1955—*Cosmopolitan* magazine. "John Whitcomb Visits Peggy Lee" was the title of a *Cosmopolitan* article, which featured Whitcomb's paintings of Lee. The piece focused on Peggy's involvement in the forthcoming *Lady and the Tramp*:

> Take two powder-blue eyes, a seductive shape, a short platinum-white haircut, and a husky voice designed for candlelight and late hours, and you have Miss Peggy Lee, the lady who helped whip up the songs for Walt Disney's forthcoming *Lady and the Tramp*. Miss Lee not only co-authored the score and lyrics, she also sings several of the songs and acts four parts on the soundtrack. By now, you've heard "Bella Notte" and "He's a Tramp" on local jukeboxes and over the air, so you know a Lee number can be a very foot-tapping proposition.

February 16, 1955 — ***Walt Disney's Cavalcade of Song.*** A *DownBeat* article titled "Disneyland Will Show How Peggy Lee Sings for the Cats" promoted the TV program:

> In Walt Disney's forthcoming CinemaScope cartoon feature, *Lady and the Tramp*, versatile Peggy Lee does the voices for four characters. In addition, she and Sonny Burke wrote all but one of the numbers in the score.... Two of the characters Peggy "voices" for are Si and Am, a pair of mischievous Siamese cats, and she'll reveal on the TV show how she sings a duet with herself.

"We Are Siamese" (also known as "The Siamese Cat Song") is one of the film's best-loved songs. Peggy supplied the voices of both Si and Am. To do this she first recorded the voice of one cat. Next, while the first recording was played back, she sang in harmony with herself. Peggy found that if she sang the second cat's part a fifth away from the first, it gave the recording a tonal quality that sounds like Asian music.

Other voices Peggy provided were Darling, Lady's human owner, and Peg. As Darling, she sang the touching lullaby "La La Lu" to her newborn child.

The character of Peg, a chanteuse who once performed in "the dog and pony follies," was originally named Mamie. Walt Disney felt that first lady Mamie Eisenhower might be offended, so he asked Peggy if they could name the character Peg after her. Lee draped herself in feather boas to inspire the animators. When one hears her sexy and silly rendition of "He's a Tramp," her joy is apparent. The song has endeared her to several generations. Other songs for the film include the romantic "Bella Notte" and the spiritual "Peace on Earth."

"Peace on Earth," which opens *Lady and the Tramp*, is probably the least known of the Lee-Burke songs from the film. While the choir sings "Silent Night," you hear "Peace on Earth" in counterpoint. That two twentieth century songwriters like Peggy Lee and Sonny Burke would dare write a song to be played along with the time-honored "Silent Night" took great courage. The fact that they succeeded is nothing short of brilliant.

A publicity photograph taken to promote the 1955 Disney film *Lady and the Tramp*. Lee wrote the score of the film with Sonny Burke. She also supplied the singing voices of Darling (the human mother), Si and Am (the mischievous Siamese cats) and Peg (the dog pound chanteuse).

April 1955 — ***Redbook*** magazine. Kirtley Baskette's in-depth article "Peggy Lee: She Can't Stop Giving" appeared, covering Peggy's childhood and her rise in the world of show business. The article also addressed Lee's workaholic nature:

Left: Recording the soundtrack for Disney's *Lady and the Tramp*. *Right:* A pensive moment during the filming of Disney's *Cavalcade of Song*. The Disney television show, featuring Peggy's talents as a singer and songwriter, was broadcast on February 6, 1955.

> Not long ago vivacious, husky-voiced Peggy Lee stood on the stage of a Baltimore theater singing her final number, a lively favorite called "Why Don't You Do Right?" Halfway through, the spotlight failed. In the sudden black-out she had a wild thought: "Now I've killed myself."
>
> Peggy was almost right. She had pneumonia. Stricken the first day of her engagement, she had carried on for a week with a high fever. That night she fainted in the wings and later, fortified with antibiotics, was helped aboard a train bound for her home in Hollywood. But not before she voluntarily returned part of her fee to the management. "Because," she explained, "I wasn't up to standard."

May 31, 1955—*Look* **magazine.** For Peggy Lee, the lyricist, *Lady and the Tramp* would be her biggest artistic challenge to date as she, along with Victor Young, not only wrote the entire film score, but voiced four characters as well.

Look magazine quoted Peggy as saying, "I changed voices for each character and sang the comedy broad to give the artists a chance to make the drawings amusing."

Before the excitement generated by the premiere of *Lady and the Tramp* had died down, journalists were talking about Peggy's much anticipated dramatic turn in *Pete Kelly's Blues*. One Hollywood movie magazine had this to say about director Jack Webb's faith in Lee's acting ability:

> "I want to predict right now," Webb said, "that Peggy Lee will surprise everyone with her wonderful dramatic performance. I think she'll be right up there among the select few when the Academy voting starts."

During the 1950s and '60s Peggy was frequently seen with Texas oilman Bob Calhoun.

The role that had Webb talking Oscar so early in production was that of Rose Hopkins. Rose is an abused, alcoholic singer, and Lee captures both the character's strength and fragility. Fran McCarg, acted with menace by Edmond O'Brien, is Rose's racketeering boyfriend.

At McCarg's insistence, Rose auditions as the singer for Pete Kelly's band. Kelly is hesitant to hire Rose, telling McCarg "People come to listen to the noise, it's not that kind of band." McCarg won't listen and informs Kelly that Rose "…comes for free."

At this, Rose replies, "He's known me for ten years, and all he can say is 'she comes free' … but I guess that covers it."

In Rose's audition scene Peggy sings two songs that were popular in the 1920s. The hopeful "He Needs Me" illustrates the relationship Rose wishes she had with McCarg. Next she performs "Sugar," swinging it lightly.

These songs convey Rose's hope that this job will lead to better times, but her future seems doomed. As the days go by she begins to drink heavily. When she drinks before a performance, Kelly expresses his concern. Rose says, "I always starts around noon, in case it gets dark early."

In 1955 Peggy appeared in the Jack Webb film *Pete Kelly's Blues*. She received an Academy Award nomination for her moving portrayal of alcoholic singer Rose Hopkins.

While singing the prophetic "Somebody Loves Me," Rose is unable to finish the performance. McCarg is enraged. Rose leaves the stage, with Pete following, intending to protect her. McCarg's thugs stop Kelly, and McCarg beats Rose savagely in her dressing room. Darkness has indeed come early for Rose.

These scenes alone would have been enough to secure Peggy the nomination for Best Supporting Actress. In just a few minutes of screen time she established the most sympathetic character in the film.

When Peggy, as Rose, leaves the screen, audiences long to see her again. Her presence is felt even when she isn't on-screen. Still, there was one more scene; it would prove to be Peggy Lee's most memorable moment on film.

Pete Kelly, with the help of hardened detective George Tennel (played by the comedic actor Andy Devine), intends to stop McCarg. But McCarg has gone into hiding, and in order to find him, Pete goes to see his friend Rose Hopkins.

The effects of McCarg's treatment, coupled with her drinking, have landed Rose in an insane asylum. Kelly finds Rose seated at a toy piano, wearing a shabby robe and carrying a baby doll. She is singing a heart-wrenching rendition of "Sing a Rainbow."

Although Rose really has no memory of Kelly, she warns him not to go near McCarg. She transfers her feelings for McCarg to her doll, telling Kelly, "He was mean to my baby."

Rose fears for Kelly's safety, telling him to stay away from McCarg because, "He's a bad man." When she asks Pete, "Were we good friends?" Pete responds with a somber "I hope so." Of all the scenes in *Pete Kelly's Blues*, this is the most haunting. Peggy's understated acting is devastating, a tour de force.

Jack Webb's prediction that Peggy would be nominated for an Oscar came true. The *Los Angeles Times* called her performance "sensational" and there was no shortage of further accolades.

> The surprise of the film is the performance of popular vocalist and songwriter, Peggy Lee, who plays the role of an aging, alcoholic nightclub singer. Whether she is taking one unsteady drink too many, or babbling pathetically in a mental ward, Miss Lee demonstrates that she can have a movie career without the aid of music.—*Newsweek*

A highlight from *Pete Kelly's Blues* takes place when Pete Kelly (Jack Webb) visits Rose Hopkins (Peggy Lee) in the mental ward. Rose, having been brutally beaten by her gangster boyfriend, has reverted to the age of five. Lee sings the haunting "Sing a Rainbow" and gives the scene a painful sadness.

> Most pleasant surprise comes from Peggy Lee, who turns in a standout dramatic job, proving she has the makings of a fine dramatic actress.—*Variety*

***February 20, 1955**—The Colgate Comedy Hour.* Louis Armstrong and Gordon MacRae appeared with Peggy on this NBC program. She soloed on "I've Got a Right to Sing the Blues" and "Come Rain or Come Shine." MacRae joined her for duets of "Long Ago and Far Away" and "The Birth of the Blues."

> Typical of the production elements that went into the show was the finale, in which MacRae and Miss Lee sang from a balcony, with harlequins standing there throwing down streamers.—*Variety*, 2/23/55

***June 19, 1955**—New York Times.* Helen Gould's article "Words, Songs and Performances by Peggy Lee" described the creative process that went into the making of *Lady and the Tramp*. Gould quoted Lee:

> You come to work and there is a ten-foot story board, which serves as a sort of synopsis. The directors talk to you lovingly about the characters. There were three directors assigned to the picture, but it was always the same. A couple of seconds

Jack Webb celebrates his birthday with Jayne Mansfield, Peggy Lee, and cast and crewmembers on the set of *Pete Kelly's Blues*.

> after you started you forgot the characters were dogs. You prerecorded the material for the artists, who worked from that. Vocal interpretation influences artists a great deal; they seem to be able to get a lot of things from one little inflection.

Peggy also revealed the secret behind her ability to sing in so many different dialects:

> When I was a little girl, ... I wasn't around children very much. I had an interesting childhood, but kind of rough; my mother died when I was four. I was interested in older people, some of whom had accents. The people I knew were very kind to me.
> Someone you like, you remember how they sound, and many of them are still fresh in my mind."

***July 24, 1955**—Colgate Variety Hour.* Peggy, Ella Fitzgerald and Jack Webb appeared together, promoting *Pete Kelly's Blues*. The *Colgate Variety Hour* was broadcast on NBC.

> The Misses Lee and Fitzgerald, who are in the film along with Webb, are expert singers, for sure, and they turned in quite a number of tunes for the major share of the entertainment." — *Variety*, 7/27/55

***Summer 1955**—Music '55.* Stan Kenton hosted this CBS series, which ran from 7/12/55 through 9/13/55. Peggy's songs for this production are unknown.

Peggy accepts the Audie Award (audience award) for her work in *Pete Kelly's Blues*. From left to right: Jack Warner, Peggy Lee, Tab Hunter, and Natalie Wood.

September 17, 1955—*Songs from Pete Kelly's Blues.* This album of songs from the film featured Peggy and Ella Fitzgerald. The album charted for 10 weeks, peaking at number seven.

October 1955—*Record Whirl.* Mary English wrote this piece for *Record Whirl.* This article and Peggy's book of poetry shared the same title, "Softly, with Feeling."

In the article, Peggy described her first job in Palm Springs, where the Peggy Lee style was born. English wrote:

> She had landed a job in a small cocktail lounge in Palm Springs. Things went well the first week — until Saturday night — when she found herself trying to sing to that typical roomful of noisy drinkers that has broken the hearts of so many singers. Later, she told me how it went:
> "I knew I couldn't sing over them, so I decided to sing under them. The more noise they made the more softly I sang. When they discovered they couldn't hear me, they began to look at me. Then they began to listen. As I sang, I kept thinking, 'softly with feeling.' The noise dropped to a hum; the hum gave way to silence. I had learned how to reach and hold my audience — softly, with feeling."

October 8, 1955—*Melody Maker* **magazine** (UK). The UK jazz magazine published Laurie Henshaw's article "Peggy Lee — The Old, Old Tale." Henshaw looked at the "eternal paradox" of Peggy's being a good singer who didn't necessarily sell to the mass public. The question of whether she was a popular singer or a jazz singer would remain throughout her career.

Lee's stage fright during the early days with Benny Goodman was also covered.

> Peggy opened with Goodman in New York—and froze up. As one onlooker put it, she "sang lyrics like a mechanical doll."
> The critics licked their lips with relish and turned out enough vitriol to scorch Peggy for keeps. Even the band chipped in. They urged Goodman to send her packing.
> Goodman's confidence was rewarded. Especially when she made "Why Don't You Do Right?" Collectors still cite this as one of her best efforts, and with it they bracket "On the Sunny Side of the Street," made with the Goodman Sextet.

November 5, 1955—*New York World Telegram.* "Peggy Lee Wants to Quit the Road" by Dick Kleiner appeared in the *New York World Telegram* on this date. In the article, Peggy related to Kleiner how her daughter, Nicki, wanted her to stay home:

> "She's such a sweet girl," says Mother, her eyes lighting up. "She hates me to go on the road, but she'll always do something sweet anyhow. Once she bought a book and put it in my suitcase, together with her favorite doll. When I unpacked and found them, I almost cried."
> "Another time, my canary, Jo-Jo, which I loved very much, died. I was heartbroken. Well, Nicki secretly saved up from her allowance and bought me a canary that was an exact duplicate of Jo-Jo. She bought a cage and bird food and a book on the care of canaries, too. Now, wasn't that something?"

November 13, 1955—*New York Times.* The *New York Times* featured "Peggy Lee's One-Way Ticket from Dakota" by J.P. Shanely. Peggy was in New York to give a benefit performance.

> Peggy Lee visited Manhattan the other day and, during a conversation over lunch, talked about future plans, but mostly about memories.
> Miss Lee will be singing tomorrow night on the Producers' Showcase presentation, *Dateline 2*, to be televised over the National Broadcasting Network in cooperation with the Overseas Press Club. Proceeds from the show will be used for the Memorial Center that the club has established at 35 East 39th Street.

Lee related to Shanely her memories of performing with Benny Goodman at New York's Paramount Theatre:

> "We played the Paramount and did six or eight shows a day," she said. "Some people used to get in line at about 6:00 in the morning to get into the theater. I remember seeing a line of people waiting outside in the rain.
> "I had never experienced anything like it before," she continued. "The theater was so enormous. The stage had been extended temporarily out over the old orchestra pit. I remember the first time I walked out to the apron of the stage to sing. I was in a giant spotlight and I thought 'I just hope I don't fall into the audience.'"

January 1956— Sands Hotel, Las Vegas.

> Peggy Lee is not only being accorded kudos for her role in *Pete Kelly's Blues* ... given solid tribute here.... The Lee approach to a nitery act encompasses the entire songa-

log as an overall presentation rather than as a string of tunes in the pop category. A fine balance and pace is offered.—*Variety*

March 3, 1956 —"Mr. Wonderful." The single of "Mr. Wonderful" hit the charts on this date, remaining there for 20 weeks and peaking at number 14.

March 15, 1956 — Dramatic Television Debut. Peggy's first dramatic role on television was the part of Mary Rigley in George Kelly's one-act play, *The Flattering World*. The play was part of a CBS production called *Shower of Stars*. The color special also featured skits and songs with Jack Benny, Fredric March and Elsa Lanchester.

> Miss Lee came off okay warbling "Riding High" and "Mr. Wonderful," and the foursome, Benny, March, Lee and Lanchester, romped through "Heart" from ... *Damn Yankees."—Variety*, 3/28/56

March 14, 1956 — Cocoanut Grove in Los Angeles.

> Few saloon entertainers today get billing as "Miss," as Miss Peggy Lee does for this three-week stint at the Cocoanut Grove. She earns it.... There are few singers extant who can handle a song as she does, or generate the driving rhythm that marks many of her numbers.—*Variety*

March 21, 1956 — *The Academy Awards.* Peggy and Jack Lemmon appeared together at the Oscars, presenting the awards for "Art Decoration" and "Set Decoration." Peggy did not win the Oscar for Best Supporting Actress; the honor went to Jo Van Fleet for her work in *East of Eden*.

Lee's portrayal of Rose won her the Laurel Award and the New York Film Critics Award. She also won the Audie Award presented by the Council of Motion Pictures Organization (COMPO). Since there was no "Best Supporting Actress" category for the Audie, moviegoers named her "Newcomer of the Year."

March 31, 1956 —*Sea Shells.* Peggy recorded *Sea Shells* at Decca's Los Angeles studios. Some of the songs had been recorded on February 7, 1956. Producer Ken Barnes referred to this album as "...the most intensely personal album of her career ... a wondrous listening experience for those who appreciate Peggy's sensitivity. It may ask a little more of the average listener, but in the end it repays the attention and leaves a special glow of pleasure that bears repeating."

As a lyricist, Peggy contributed three songs to the album: the playful "Little Old Car," the love-wise "The White Birch and the Sycamore," and the hauntingly beautiful "The Golden Wedding Ring." An original issue of *Sea Shells* is a treasured possession for any fan of Peggy Lee.

April 21, 1956 — Peggy Lee marries Dewey Martin. Dewey Martin appeared in several movies, including *The Thing, The Big Sky,* and *The Land of the Pharaohs*.

Peggy attends the 1956 premiere of *Giant* with her third husband, Dewey Martin. Martin appeared in such films as *The Thing*, *The Big Sky* and *The Desperate Hours*.

May 5, 1956—*"Joey, Joey, Joey."* The single of "Joey, Joey, Joey" made the charts. It remained on the charts for six weeks and peaked at number 76.

Spring 1956—*Black Coffee* (reissued). Decca released an extended 12-inch version of Peggy's classic *Black Coffee*. Four new songs were added: "It Ain't Necessarily So," "Gee Baby Ain't I Good to You," "You're My Thrill" and "There's a Small Hotel."

A combo, including pianist Lou Levy, backed Peggy. It would mark the start of a long musical association with Levy, whom Lee nicknamed "the Good Gray Fox" due to his premature gray hair.

***June 6 and 7, 1956**—Dream Street.* Lou Levy accompanied Lee as she recorded songs for the upcoming *Dream Street* album, an album designed for lovers listening late at night.

Dream Street included another Peggy Lee innovation. The first bars of Victor Young's "Street of Dreams," which opened side one of the album, were used to introduce several other selections. Hence, "Something I Dreamed Last Night," "My Old Flame," "Last Night When We Were Young," and others were all linked by the same opening theme. Peggy had taken the concept album another step further.

***June 8, 1956**—Miss Wonderful.* Lee and company recorded five more songs on June 8, 1956. These were coupled with another seven recorded on January 6, 1956, to make up Peggy's *Miss Wonderful* album. Critics and listeners alike received both albums with enthusiasm.

***December 1956**—The Walter Winchell Show.* Peggy and Tony Martin appeared on Winchell's show. Peggy's songs included "I Don't Know Enough About You," "Mañana," "Last Night When We Were Young" and "Them There Eyes."

> Fortunately, Winchell had two top-notchers for the song department in Peggy Lee and Tony Martin. They carried the bulk of the show in duet and solo and made it all an ear-appealing affair.—*Variety*, December 12, 1956

February 1957— Sands Hotel, Las Vegas

> Peggy Lee returns to the Copa Room in a program which proves her distinctive style is getting more versatile with each Vegas stint…. Her lack of animation perfectly fits the cozy numbers presented with a velvety huskiness…. When she purrs "That Old Feeling" and "Smoke Gets in Your Eyes," she gets the point across to each male in the audience that it is he alone to whom she is singing.—*Variety*

Peggy's contract with Decca expired in 1957. She chose to return to her home at Capitol Records. There she would team up with Frank Sinatra, and together they would create an exquisite collection of love songs.

She would also record what would become her best-known signature song, one that would set the music world ablaze.

• FOUR •

Return to Capitol: 1957 to 1967

***March 1957—DownBeat* magazine.** Peggy appeared on the cover of *DownBeat* magazine. In the article, entitled "The Trifles Count," she discussed her quest for perfection. *DownBeat*'s John Tynan wrote the piece, which began:

> There's a quotation from Michelangelo emblazoned on the wall of Peggy Lee's picturesque studio dressing room. It read, "Perfection is made up of trifles; but perfection itself is no trifle."
>
> Realizing the innate truth ... in this observation, Peggy Lee, in everything she undertakes, watches out for the trifles. Whether she always achieves perfection in the finished article, be it a ... painting, song lyric, music score, animated cartoon, or night club act, is not our purpose to say. What is certain, however, is that few contemporary figures in show business possess her many applied talents and fewer still can match her consistent record of distinguished artistic achievement. In paying attention to the trifles, she believes, the major problem at hand becomes that much simpler.

March 31, 1957—The Steve Allen Show. As Steve Allen's guest, Peggy sang the wistful "That Old Feeling," before moving onto a torchy rendition of "St. Louis Woman." Allen's other guests were Tennessee Ernie Ford, Dinah Shore and the Collins Kids. The show was seen on NBC.

April 1957—The Man I Love. If Peggy Lee had any one counterpart among male singers, most would agree it was Frank Sinatra. Sinatra, like Lee, paid attention to the trifles. He was a perfectionist with few peers. In the first week of April 1957, the two perfectionists headed to the Capitol studios to record the LP *The Man I Love*. From the beginning, *The Man I Love* had been Sinatra's special project, his way of honoring Lee's talent.

Frank hired one of the finest arrangers in the business, Nelson Riddle, who gave Peggy lush, warm orchestrations. Sinatra conducted the entire album.

Frank's sure knowledge of what a singer needed gave Peggy a solid foundation. With the possible exception of her 1961 release "If You Go," she has never sounded better in a romantic ballad setting.

A charming publicity photograph from 1957.

Gershwin's "The Man I Love" opens side one of the LP, setting the mood for the entire record. Side one closes with a truly beautiful reading of Rodgers and Hammerstein's "Something Wonderful."

In his book *The Great American Popular Singers*, music historian Henry Pleasants relates how Peggy "opens on a low E and stays there as she enunciates a monotone introductory recitative." She proceeds to build a deeply moving, eloquent rendition of the song. "Something Wonderful" has never enjoyed a truer reading.

The song that closes the album has special significance. Devoted fans know that "The Folks Who Live on the Hill" is Peggy Lee's favorite song. From start to finish, Peggy and Frank's *The Man I Love* album remains a timeless classic.

Peggy and Frank Sinatra would work together again in the later months of 1957. The blue-eyed Peggy Lee fan had this to say about his musical peer:

> Peggy and I met early in our careers when we both started out in New York and have been great friends ever since. All vocalists should study her wonderful talent; her regal presence is pure elegance and charm.

April 13, 1957—"Baby, Baby Wait for Me"/"Every Night." It was the early days of rock and roll, and Peggy Lee always enjoyed exploring new avenues in music. With Nelson Riddle continuing as arranger, Lee romped through "Baby, Baby Wait for Me" and "Every Night," a definite departure from the lushness of her efforts on *The Man I Love* album.

Peggy and Nelson continued to record together. Their next single was the swinging "Listen to the Rockin' Bird," while the flip side offered "Uninvited Dream," one of Burt Bacharach's early compositions.

June 8, 1957—*The Jackie Gleason Show.* Johnnie Ray took over for Gleason. Ray and Lee performed a duet on "Anything You Say Is True," and Peggy went solo on "Baby, Baby Wait for Me" and "They Can't Take That Away from Me." Of the show, *Variety* said, "Miss Lee did her usual socko job." The program was broadcast on CBS.

June 16, 1957—*What's My Line?* Peggy appeared on the popular NBC show.

June 22, 1957—*The Jackie Gleason Show.* Peggy returned to host *The Jackie Gleason Show*. Her guest was Tony Bennett. Songs included "The Man I Love."

Steve Allen, Peggy, and Tennessee Ernie Ford. Lee and Ford were guests on Allen's variety show. Peggy sang "That Old Feeling" and "St. Louis Woman." The program was broadcast on March 31, 1957.

> Miss Lee ... the hostess with the mostest.... Her work on the finale, relaxed and charming and typically low-key Lee.... Another highlight in a variety outing overloaded with songs was Miss Lee's capers with guest Tony Bennett, in which they traded off each other's trademarked numbers for a winning session. — *Variety*

Frank Sinatra and Peggy appear on the cover of *TV Life* for the week of March 12–18, 1957. Peggy was Sinatra's guest on *The Frank Sinatra Show*. Sinatra also chose all of the songs and conducted the album that marked Peggy's return to the Capitol label, *The Man I Love*.

September 23, 1957—*The Man I Love.* Lee and Sinatra's collaborative album made the charts on this date and stayed for one week. It peaked at number 20.

September, 27 1957—*Crescendo.* The premise of *Crescendo* had Louis Armstrong giving Mr. Sir, a visiting Englishman played by Rex Harrison, a tour of American music. Peggy's numbers were "Lullaby of Broadway" and "Blues in the Night."

Other performers on *Crescendo* included Julie Andrews, Eddy Arnold, Diahann Carroll, Carol Channing, Benny Goodman, Mahalia Jackson, Stubby Kaye and Dinah Washington. *Crescendo* was broadcast on CBS.

October 18 and November 8, 1957—*The Frank Sinatra Show.* Peggy opened with "Listen to the Rocking Bird." Then, with Sinatra conducting, she sang a beautiful rendition of "He's My Guy." Lee returned to the Sinatra show just a few weeks later. For her November 8 guest appearance, she sang "Old Devil Moon" and then joined Sinatra for a duet of "Our Love Is Here to Stay."

She also sang with Nat "King" Cole on his television show at this time. Songs included "My Heart Stood Still" and "Don't Get Around Much Anymore." Nat and Peggy were joined by Julius LaRosa for a novelty tune called "Makin' Records," sung to the melody of "Makin' Whoopee." The exact airdate of this NBC program is unknown.

December 1957 and January 1958—*Jump for Joy.* Between December 1957 and January 1958 Peggy entered the Capitol studios to record another album with Nelson Riddle. On *Jump for Joy* Nelson employed his trademark driving brass section. The album includes "Cheek to Cheek," "I Hear Music," and "Just in Time." Peggy swings with great freedom on the title song and the infectious "Back in Your Own Backyard."

February 1958— Copacabana, New York

> ...Nothing quite like an in-person version of Miss Lee.... The phrasing, the articulation, the authentic charm and the sincerity show all the way through, finally to encase the audience in an indefinable aura.... There's hardly anyone in the business more artful, that way and in others, than Miss Lee.
>
> Her rendition of "My Heart Stood Still" is an andante cut about in half, or slower than Rodgers & Hart intended it to be, perhaps, but as done by this thrush, a thorough winner. She has a carload of other stuff in other tempos, with "You Give Me Fever" a particular smash, complete with spotlight and tom-tom effects.—*Variety*

This marks the first time that "Fever" is mentioned in a review. It is incorrectly identified as "You Give Me Fever."

February 7, 1958—*New York World-Telegram.*

> You could hear the proverbial pins dropping all over the Copacabana last night as the well-behaved customers paid tribute to Peggy Lee at one of her greatest tri-

umphs. As I recall the richness, the warmth, the exciting rhythm and the naturalness of her performance, I try to pinpoint the high spots. Since there were no low ones, this is a task.— Robert W. Dana

At this time, one New York paper ran the headline, "Lee Captures New York!"

February 1958—Tom Thumb. Peggy continued to work as a songwriter. Three of her songs were heard in the 1958 film *Tom Thumb*: "One for You and One for Me," "Tom Thumb's Tune," and "Are You a Dream?"

***February 1958—McCall's* magazine.** Here Peggy discussed the writing process. At the time, she had written the verses for several greeting cards for the Buzza-Cardozo Company. In *"McCall's* Visits Peggy Lee," she told readers:

> It's kind of an outlet for me. These things have always been for my own pleasure.... It depends on what kind of mood I'm in and how close the Muse is. I'm apt to write a more poignant lyric when I'm happy. I write a happy one when I'm sad. It's kind of ... satisfying ... to write something.... I'd like to write a musical. That would be the epitome. One of my biggest thrills is to hear something I wrote performed — not by me.

April 1958—The Eddie Fisher Show. Peggy sang "Fever" for the first time on television.

May 1958—Things Are Swingin'. During this time Peggy wrote several songs with Jack Marshall. Marshall would act as Peggy's conductor on her next two Capitol LPs. Together they wrote the title songs for both *Things Are Swingin'* and *I Like Men!* Recorded in four sessions (May 19, 25, 27 and 30), *Things Are Swingin'* is one of Peggy's most pleasing albums.

In addition to writing "Things Are Swingin'" for the album, she also penned "It's a Good, Good Night."

"It's Been a Long, Long Time" swings gently, to charming effect. "Lullaby in Rhythm" is delight from the first note (a rare example of Peggy "scat" singing) to the last. "Alright, Okay You Win" really jumps and is one of Peggy's finest efforts. "You're Mine You" employs that unique Peggy Lee use of carefully placed pauses.

***June 11, 1958—* Venetian Room, San Francisco.** *Variety*'s critic seemed more interested in her figure than her music, writing, "Blonde Peggy Lee, nicely curvy in a white, sequined gown, gets a good hand in her 40-minute show at the Fairmont's cavernous Venetian Room.... Her accompaniment is good and she doesn't clutter up act with a lot of unnecessary chatter."

***July 14, 1958—Jump for Joy* and "Fever."** The swinging album *Jump for Joy* hit the charts on this date. Peggy and Nelson Riddle's record remained there for 5 weeks, peaking at number 15.

"Fever" charted on this date as well, staying there for 15 weeks and peaking at number eight.

Sometime in 1957 Peggy's musical associate, Max Bennett, brought a new single to her attention. Little Willie John was the singer of this John Davenport and Eddie Cooley–penned song. The title was "Fever."

Peggy loved the song. However, she didn't feel that the lyrics (about the fever a man gets for a woman) were appropriate for her to sing. She set out to tailor it to her own style.

Peggy wrote several new verses to the Davenport-Cooley tune. She included references to great love affairs, like Romeo and Juliet, and Captain Smith and Pocahontas.

Lee then created a daring new arrangement for the song. Her accompaniment was sparse: drums, bass and her own snapping fingers. When she turned the number loose on her listeners she smoldered, simmered and sizzled.

"Fever" is hers alone. Others have attempted to cover it over the years, but it will forever be associated with Peggy Lee. Peggy had another hit, another signature song.

August 20, 1958—*New York Mirror.* Don Bailer contributed "Peggy Sets a Feverish Pace" to this issue of the *New York Mirror*:

> "It's a blues type of song," she points out. "it has a moderate tempo, but a very intense tempo, a good, simple, basic rhythm.
>
> "The young people, and anyone else for that matter, will respond to good songs if they have a basic good rhythm."
>
> "Fever" illustrates her point in more ways that one, because it was taken away from the rock 'n' rollers.
>
> About November of last year, bass player Max Bennett came to Peggy and said he wanted her to hear a song, a real bang-away rock 'n' roll version of "Fever"—but which he said had a great bass line, that basic roadbed upon which a song is built.
>
> They then sat down and stripped the song to the bass line—and rebuilt it à la Lee.

October 1958—*I Like Men!* Peggy was back in the recording studio with Jack Marshall, completing her next album in three sessions (October 17, 19 and 22). On the Lee-Marshall release *I Like Men!* Peggy sang about all the types of men she loved. She mentioned "Jim," "Charley, My Boy," and "Bill."

Her rhythmic timing on "I'm Just Wild About Harry" and "Oh Johnny, Oh Johnny, Oh!" offers a lesson on how to really swing. The Peggy Lee style was very much in evidence in a hard-driving "My Man."

October 1958—*The George Gobel Show.* Peggy appeared with George Gobel. She sang her latest hit, "Fever." The exact airdate of this show is unknown.

October 25, 1958—*Melody Maker* **magazine (UK).** The UK jazz magazine printed the Steve Race article "'Fever' by Peggy Lee: Sanity in the Top Twenty." Race was pleasantly surprised to find jazz singer Peggy in the top twenty:

> Quite the most cheering sign in recent months has been the rise of Peggy Lee's "Fever" (Capitol 45 CL-14902), a record which combines strong jazz qualities with a number of proved Hit Parade ingredients, and by satisfying both sides qualifies for a place in my series.
>
> Unlike any other member of the current Top Twenty aristocracy, 38-year-old Peggy Lee has a sound jazz background. Originally discovered by Benny Goodman's wife, she has long been prominent in the top jazzmen's own list of favourites.

Race went on to praise the song's unique arrangement and Peggy's phrasing:

> Here, Peggy Lee works to the absolute minimum of accompaniment: one bass, one percussionist, and two or three finger-snappers. The result is novel and extraordinarily compulsive.

Race cited her "subtle inflections" and "conversational, almost mocking way in which she tells her story" as the "planned artistry" that earned her a Top Twenty spot.

November 3, 1958—**"Light of Love."** Peggy's single "Light of Love" hit the Top 100 chart on this date, remaining there for a total of six weeks and peaking at number 63.

November 24, 1958—**"Sweetheart."** "Sweetheart" made the charts for two weeks. It peaked at number 98.

December 1958—**Moulin Rouge, Hollywood.**

> Peggy Lee, looking great and sounding better ... there's one of the most moving moments on the nitery circuit when, in a single spotlight Miss Lee sings ... the haunting "When the World Was Young."

December 8, 1958—*Things Are Swingin'.* This album reached the charts on this date, staying there for one week and peaking at number 16.

January 19, 1959—**"My Man."** "My Man" charted on this date, remaining there for six weeks and peaking at number 81.

January 26, 1959—**"Alright, Okay, You Win."** Peggy's swinging rendition of "Alright, Okay, You Win" made the charts, remaining there for six weeks and peaking at number 68.

March 15, 1959—*The Dinah Shore Chevy Show.* The songs and network for this program are unknown.

April 10, 1959—*Swing Into Spring.* Benny Goodman and Peggy Lee were reunited on his *Swing Into Spring* television show. Other guests included Ella Fitzgerald and Andre Previn. Lionel Hampton played his vibes with unequaled style. Peggy turned loose a very sexy, insinuating rendition of "Why Don't You Do Right?"

In a medley about relationships between men and women she sang "I'm Just Wild About Harry." Next she devastated all concerned with "When a Woman Loves a Man." During this number Ella could be heard off-camera giving Peggy "ohs" and "uh-huhs" of support and awe. Peg and Ella then sang "The Glory of Love" together; it was glorious.

April 15, 1959—"**The Peggy Lee Story.**" The exact (New York) newspaper that ran this article is unknown, as is the author. This was a standard piece covering Peggy's rise to fame.

In it, Peggy spoke of her love for the craft of songwriting:

> "I just drifted into composing," Peggy says. "It sort of comes naturally to me. And I find a certain pleasure out of the creative end of music that I can never get as a singer. Sure singing is fun, and making record sides gives a performer the satisfaction of knowing that the song can achieve the permanence of a standard—if it's a hit, but still I get the greatest satisfaction of all in the field of composition."

May 17, 1959—*The Dinah Shore Chevy Show.* As with the earlier Dinah Shore program, the airdate and songs for this show are unknown.

May 28, 1959—*DownBeat* **magazine.** Once again Peggy was on the cover of the latest issue of the venerable jazz magazine. The article, "Peggy Lee, Girl in the Middle," was written by George Hoefer.

Hoefer discussed how Peggy was caught between the worlds of jazz and pop music. His opening paragraph summed up the tone of the four-page article:

> Peggy Lee's combination of talents tends to keep her identification dilemmatic. She has been too successful in several areas to win acceptance in the jazz world, and not quite commercial enough to attain the pinnacle of fame awarded to lesser stars by an indiscriminating mass public. Musically, she's too good for her own good, and fads have not shaken her taste.

Hoefer went on to report that, in a true jazz setting, Peggy Lee could and did turn in unparalleled jazz performances:

> Peggy Lee has given jazz performances on records that mark her the greatest white female jazz singer since Mildred Bailey. Her "Ain't Goin' No Place" and her interpretation of Willard Robison's "A Woman Alone with the Blues," both on Capitol, are outstanding jazz renditions. The record with Benny Goodman that originally gave her nation-wide recognition, "Why Don't You Do Right," is a jazz classic.

May 29, 1959— **Disc Jockey Convention.** Peggy performed in Miami, Florida, at the Disc Jockey Convention. Her performance that night was recorded live. It was a once-in-a-lifetime meeting of two musical greats: George Shearing on piano and Peggy Lee on vocals. Shearing's famous quintet was aided and abetted by conga drummer Armando Peraza.

Peggy sang three Cole Porter songs: "Do I Love You?" was her swinging opener;

"Always True to You in My Fashion" was given a Latin flavor; and she closed with "Get Out of Town."

Peggy's renditions of "There'll Be Another Spring" and "All Too Soon" proved to be two of the most moving moments in the show. Carl Sigman and Duke Ellington's "All Too Soon" was sung as a tribute to one of Peggy's musical heroes, Mildred Bailey. "There'll Be Another Spring" spoke of eternal love and faith.

This show, recorded live by Capitol, was released as the Lee-Shearing album *Beauty and the Beat*.

August 12, 1959—Latin ala Lee. August 1959 found Peggy in the Capitol studio recording what promised to be a groundbreaking collection of songs. Again, she went to work with a specific musical theme guiding her. *Latin ala Lee* was recorded in three sessions (August 12, 13 and 14). The new album was released in January 1960. For this venture Peggy surrounded herself with authentic Afro-Cuban sounds.

Latin ala Lee was received with great acclaim. One critic wrote, "She has an unerring ability in spotting strengths and weaknesses in songs and lyrics, with corresponding ability to take advantage of both, either with humor or heart."

The *Latin ala Lee* album was so popular it launched a whole series of similar recordings, including Rosemary Clooney's *A Touch of Tabasco*, Nat "King" Cole's *Cole en Espanol* and Peggy's own follow-up albums *Ole ala Lee* and *Guitars ala Lee*.

August 18, 1959—"Hallelujah, I Love Him So." "Hallelujah, I Love Him So" entered the charts for a two-week run, peaking at number 77.

September 12, 1959—Beauty and the Beat. Peggy and George Shearing made the charts with this album and stayed there for a solid 18 weeks. The album reached a peak of number 19.

September 29, 1959—The Bing Crosby Show. For this television outing four of the greatest singer-musicians in show business joined forces: Louis Armstrong, Bing Crosby, Peggy Lee and Frank Sinatra. For her solo spot Peggy was seen in a skin-tight, bugle-beaded gown singing a pulsing "Baubles, Bangles and Beads." She was surrounded by crystal chandeliers for this number (a very appropriate setting, as she always visualized chandeliers when she sang the song).

When she finished the song, Crosby said, "She certainly casts a spell, doesn't she!" to which a grinning Sinatra replied, "She do! She do!"

Crosby, Lee and Sinatra also participated in a medley of songs. A superb pianist accompanied each vocalist. Bing joined forces with Joe Bushkin, Peggy was reunited with George Shearing, and Frank sang with Paul Smith.

> Sophisticated, smart, breezy, snazzy and solid entertainment. Whether it was Satchmo's blowing up a storm or vocalizing, or Crosby, Sinatra and Miss Lee singing, dueting or as a threesome, or yet again as a Bushkin-Shearing-Smith grand-slam in their 88 virtuosing, it came out like TV being restored to the showbiz

Peggy is Steve Allen's guest for his November 9, 1959, special on NBC. Here she is seen singing a hypnotic medley of sad love songs, including "How Do You Erase a Memory?," "Baby, All the Time," "I've Grown Accustomed to His Face," "I Get Along Without You Very Well," and "Here's That Rainy Day." (Lee wrote "How Do You Erase a Memory?")

pedestal. These Crosby outings have a habit of upgrading the medium.—*Variety*, September 1, 1959

November 9, 1959—*The Steve Allen Show.* Peggy opened the show with special lyrics to the tune of "It's Alright with Me." Next she segued into a sizzling "Smack Dab in the Middle."

The highlight of the evening came when Steve called her back to do a medley of forlorn love songs. With Allen at the piano, the beautiful Miss Lee proceeded to tug at viewers' heart-strings with "How Do You Erase a Memory?," "Baby, All the Time," "I've Grown Accustomed to His Face," "I Get Along Without You Very Well," and "Here's That Rainy Day." *Variety* simply said, "Peggy Lee was a standout in her song assignments."

December 17, 1959*—The Big Party by Revlon.* In her last television appearance of the year, Peggy continued in top form. Guests included Benny Goodman, Carol Channing and John Gielgud. Once again *Variety*'s review was to the point: "Miss Lee overcame the handicap of the opening spot with a tasteful in-time medley and a rendition of her disc ... 'Fever.'"

At the close of 1959 Peggy was voted *Billboard*'s number two "Favorite Female Vocalist." Her friend Ella Fitzgerald took the top spot. *Billboard* acknowledged Peggy's recording of "Alright, Okay You Win" as the "Best Female Vocal Performance." Frank Sinatra was *Billboard*'s "Best Male Vocalist" that year.

As she entered 1960, the release of *Latin ala Lee* wasn't the only big Peggy Lee project. Lee was about to make showbiz history. Once again she would take New York by storm. She was preparing to open at a small jazz club. Until her arrival, the club had only done marginal business; but within hours of her opening night, Basin Street East became the only place to be for jazz fans.

January 18, 1960*—The Steve Allen Show.* Peggy sang her own composition "El Toro (My Matador)."

February 1960*—Pretty Eyes.* A new Peggy Lee record hit the stores. *Pretty Eyes* was recorded in February 1960 (February 15, 18 and 19). As the album cover says, "Peggy Lee sings softly of romance — in twelve wonderful songs with the lush but rhythmic string and woodwind backgrounds by Billy May."

She created magic with her reading of Bart Howard's time-honored classic "In Other Words" (also known as "Fly Me to the Moon"). "Moments Like This" was sly and insinuating. The Cy Coleman and Carolyn Leigh tune "You Fascinate Me So" gave Peggy a chance to swing with great humor. Her own "Because I Love Him So" ended the album with a pulsing blues feeling.

February 24, 1960*—United Press International.* The UPI article, written by Joe Finnigan, was entitled "Peggy Lee Back to Acting: Set for G.E. Theatre Stint."

> "I don't intend to let acting drop this time," she said. "I should have continued it more closely after making the Kelly picture."
>
> Miss Lee left to enter the recording booth for a rendition of "As You Desire Me," only to take a "break" a short time later when she decided her vocal cords weren't in the mood for singing.
>
> Sitting in the control room with a hot lamp placed against her throat to relax the

cords, Peggy said, "I've got more of a challenge coming from acting than from singing."

"You know, I never wanted to sing just to make a living. I sing because I love it. It's most important to me that I have a good time singing."

March 10, 1960 — *The Revlon Review.*

> Miss Lee, svelte and glamorous in a white gown, warbled her trademarks.... That blues are Miss Lee's forte was aptly shown in a medley which had her throatily chirping such standards as "Basin St. Blues" and "When the Saints Go Marching In." — *Variety*

March 1960 — Basin Street East.

Club owner Ralph Watkins hired Peggy on the recommendation of her "old boss," Benny Goodman. True to form, Miss Lee the perfectionist had the club remodeled for her opening. A new stage was built, as was a new lighting and sound booth. Duke Ellington's "Queen" was in attendance, and nothing was left to chance.

This would be one of her greatest successes. The following reviews attest to the fact that Peggy Lee was in peak form.

> In all her yesteryears, Peggy was never better than last night. Only a superlative artist could sell out a club the size of Basin Street East on such a raw, snowy night.... Peggy's phrasing is crisp, her diction faultless, every song a delight. She uses her hands constantly; their action becomes part of and enhances her routine. She's magnetic and exciting, exhibits rare stage presence. Everyone loved her last night, and their affection was not misplaced. — Nick Lapole, *New York American-Journal*
>
> The svelte blond thrush is more in her element here than she was at the Copacabana in her last New York date three years ago. This is strictly a music room and what comes out of Miss Lee's pipes is strictly music.... Her work here is bound to get talked up around town which will keep the captain at his post directing the heavy load of traffic. — *Variety*, March 16, 1960
>
> Peggy Lee turned the presentation of a song program into a fine art during her recent Manhattan stint. Rarely has there been a more carefully prepared and tastefully executed nightclub act.... Over the years, Peggy has acquired a great deal of stage presence for in-person appearances of this type. She seems to be calmer and more in control of the situation on a nightclub floor than in front of a television camera. — *DownBeat*, March 26, 1960

The compliments did not stop there. New York columnist Dorothy Kilgallen dubbed her "the Marilyn Monroe of the chanteuses." Famed Broadway director Abe Burrows, who had worked with Peggy on her Revlon TV specials, told reporters that, "Peggy is one of those rare performers who can handle silence." Her musical hero, Count Basie, said it all with just two words: "She's solid."

March 13, 1960 — *General Electric Theatre.*

Peggy returned to the field of dramatic acting, appearing in a teleplay called "So Deadly, So Evil" (in which a masked murderer pursues her character, Natalia Cory). Peggy's co-stars were Ronald Reagan, Gavin MacLeod and Terry Loomis.

Peggy plays a dramatic role on the *General Electric Theatre* production "So Deadly, So Evil." The program was broadcast on March 13, 1960. Lee's co-stars were Ronald Reagan and Gavin McLeod. (CBS)

March 21, 1960 — ***Newsweek.*** *Newsweek* discovered that Peggy Lee was "As Hot as a Torch":

> For any female who can look so sexy and sing so lowdown, Peggy offstage is surprisingly reminiscent of a small-town librarian. She's pretty, she's friendly, she's intelligent, and she's genuinely unaffected.
>
> How does she account for the appeal that has kept her on top for so long? "The basic thing is choosing my material," she answered — "material which is commercial yet is good musically." Director Abe Burrows, who had been rehearsing her for her Revlon show on television last week (she has five in six weeks), had another explanation: "Peggy is one of those rare performers who can handle silence. She has amazing control. Also, she's somebody who likes herself — in other words, she likes what she does, and the audience gives her respect."

March 24, 1960 — ***Paul Whiteman — A Tribute.*** Peggy's next television appearance was to celebrate the 70th birthday of bandleader Paul Whiteman. On the show she sang a heartfelt tribute to Mildred Bailey, who had been one of Lee's early vocal influences. In Mildred's honor, Peggy sang a medley of songs associated with Bailey, including "Ol' Rockin Chair," "Gypsy in My Soul," "Georgia on My Mind," "It's So Peaceful in the Country," and "Hold On."

Lee also teamed up with the legendary trumpet-playing vocalist Jack Teagarden, harmonizing with Jack on "Jeepers Creepers," "Lazy River," "Them There Eyes," and "Christmas Night in Harlem."

This program was released on the album *Paul Whiteman — A Tribute* in 1986 (Sounds Great Records — SG 80150).

April 7, 1960 — ***Revlon Presents: Night Clubs, New York.*** April 1960 found Peggy appearing on two Revlon television specials. The first, *Revlon Presents: Night Clubs, New York*, aired on April 7, 1960. *Variety* said of her segment: "Peggy Lee, who recently wound up a smash engagement at Basin Street, got the biggest layout of time and made the most of it."

Peggy sang "It's All Right with Me" and "(He Called Me) Baby, Baby All the Time." Other guests included Mike Wallace, Felicia Sanders, Earl Grant and the comedy team of Bob and Ray.

April 11, 1960 — ***Latin ala Lee.*** Peggy's Latin-tinged album charted on this date, remaining on the charts for a very respectable 59 weeks. It peaked at number 11.

April 14, 1960 — ***Revlon Presents: 76 Men and Peggy Lee.*** Peggy was the star of this spectacular. The 76 men were Mel Tormé, the Chad Mitchell Trio, the Yale Glee Club, and the Vagabonds. Atra Baer, writing for the *New York Journal-American*, had this to say about Peggy's latest Revlon show:

> A highly individual variety: a silky voice softening that pulsing swing, her eyes fixed not at the audience or camera, but riveted on some faraway star, a performer whose offbeat sultriness lies in the fact that physically and vocally she sizzles while simultaneously projecting a mental aloofness.... She never looked or sang better...

When Peggy made her triumphant return to New York's Basin Street East, the nightclub came up with this famous "Peggy's back!" ad. (1960)

Peggy sang many of her hits, including "I Like Men" and "Mañana." Mel Tormé joined her for "Alright, Okay, You Win."

May 1, 1960, and May 8, 1960—*New York Daily News.* Journalist Ben Gross conducted a two-part interview with Peggy. On May 1, 1960, the *New York Daily News* ran "Peggy Lee Pines for Big Bands on TV," in which Lee spoke of the bygone Big Band era:

> "In those days," Peggy explained, "it was radio that made the bands. They played hotels and clubs for months at a time, occasionally even at a financial loss. But that didn't matter, because practically every night their music was broadcast from those spots by network radio from coast to coast.
>
> "So at the end of such an engagement, they'd hit the road, playing one-night stands. The ballrooms were packed as a result of the radio buildup, and these bands made fortunes. Such people as Benny Goodman, Glenn Miller, Tommy and Jimmy Dorsey were idols."

On May 8, 1960, Gross' second installment appeared. This was titled "Peggy Lee Says Rock-n-Roll Will Influence Music for Years." Lee was quoted as follows:

> "Dancing should be romancing, not just physical culture," singing star Peggy Lee told me as we were discussing the frantic gyrations inspired by rock 'n' roll. And, as a matter of fact, she believes that eventually rock 'n' roll may evolve into a form of music acceptable even to moon-bedizened lovers.
>
> "As we all know, the old type of rock 'n' roll is disappearing," she told me. "I mean the numbers with poor, nonsensical lyrics and the monotonous tunes. But the original foundation of rock 'n' roll, the work songs and the blues, will remain. They are true American music and for years to come they will influence pop songs and dance numbers, especially the beat."

June 1960—*Christmas Carousel.* During the summer month of June, Peggy recorded her first Christmas album. She recorded five songs, including "White Christmas," on June 15, 1960. Another five were completed on June 19, 1960. The final two tunes needed to round out the album were recorded on October 10, 1960. Peggy wrote five charming songs for this album.

June 4, 1960—*Melody Maker* **magazine** (UK). Laurie Henshaw spoke the truth when she titled her article "Artistry Is the Secret of Peggy Lee's Greatness," published in the UK's top jazz journal:

> Some singers stay the pace. And the reason can be found in one word—artistry. Talent helps, but talent and artistry are not always synonymous.
>
> Who better to illustrate the point than Peggy Lee? No one—or, at any rate, none of the "pundits"—would bracket Peggy Lee with Ella Fitzgerald or Sarah Vaughan as a singer.
>
> But Peggy Lee is an artist. Moreover—and this is not to detract from the quality of her contemporaries—she possesses a poignancy of delivery that wrings the heartstrings....
>
> [I]n the gilded world of pop, she contrives to bring a touch of greatness to all her performances.

She did it in "Lover" and "Would You Dance with a Stranger?"—two tracks issued on the defunct 78s that are still fresh in the mind—and she has since done it on successive LPs.

Summer 1960—Ole ala Lee! A fourth Peggy Lee album was released in 1960. *Ole ala Lee!* was recorded on July 16, 23, 24 and 30. This was the first follow-up to her wildly successful *Latin ala Lee!* album. Highlights from this LP include the Duke Ellington–Galnes tune "Just Squeeze Me" and the beautiful Brown-Kahn classic "You Stepped Out of a Dream." As a songwriter, Peggy contributed "Ole" to the collection.

July 3, 1960—American Weekly magazine. Neil Hickey's piece for *American Weekly* was simply titled "Peggy." Hickey wrote of the many different colors and characteristics that Peggy's voice could take:

> Singer Peggy Lee was at work earning the $12,500 a week Basin Street felt she was worth. In the crowded supper club's smoky silence, her voice grew successively sensual, blatant, desolate, flinty, intimate, and languorous, as she caressed the lyrics of a whole spectrum of blues and jazz songs.

He quoted Peggy on how she found strength in the words on Emerson:

> "Ralph Waldo Emerson has a great deal to say to our generation," she says. "I wouldn't still be working today if it weren't for the strength I've derived from some of his essays. He said: 'God will not have his work done by cowards.' To me, that means: 'Don't let your personal problems get in the way of your life's work.' I've had to remember that rule several times during my career."

August 1960— **Ciro's, Hollywood.** She was back at Ciro's in Hollywood.

> Peggy Lee's ripe quality and her exceptional good taste in arrangements, staging, lighting, etc. give fans what they crave during this 40-minute show.—*Variety*

October 16, 1960—See America with Ed Sullivan. In this pilot episode for a travelogue program, the sights and sounds of San Francisco were featured.

Peggy performed her own "I Love Being Here with You." She also sang "Yes Indeed" and "Fly Me to the Moon."

Later, *Variety* caught her next Las Vegas stint in November. As 1960 came to a close, Peggy was preparing for her much-anticipated return to Basin Street East.

Winter 1960—Person to Person. Host Charles Collingwood joined Peggy at home for this intimate look at her life. The exact airdate of the program is unknown.

January 1, 1961—The Chevy Show. Peggy joined Frankie Avalon, George Gobel and Percy Faith on this NBC program. There is no record of the songs she sang.

January 1961— **Basin Street East.** New gowns and songs were carefully selected, and the musicians meticulously rehearsed. Peggy was ready for opening night; she wasn't prepared for one of the worst snowstorms of the season.

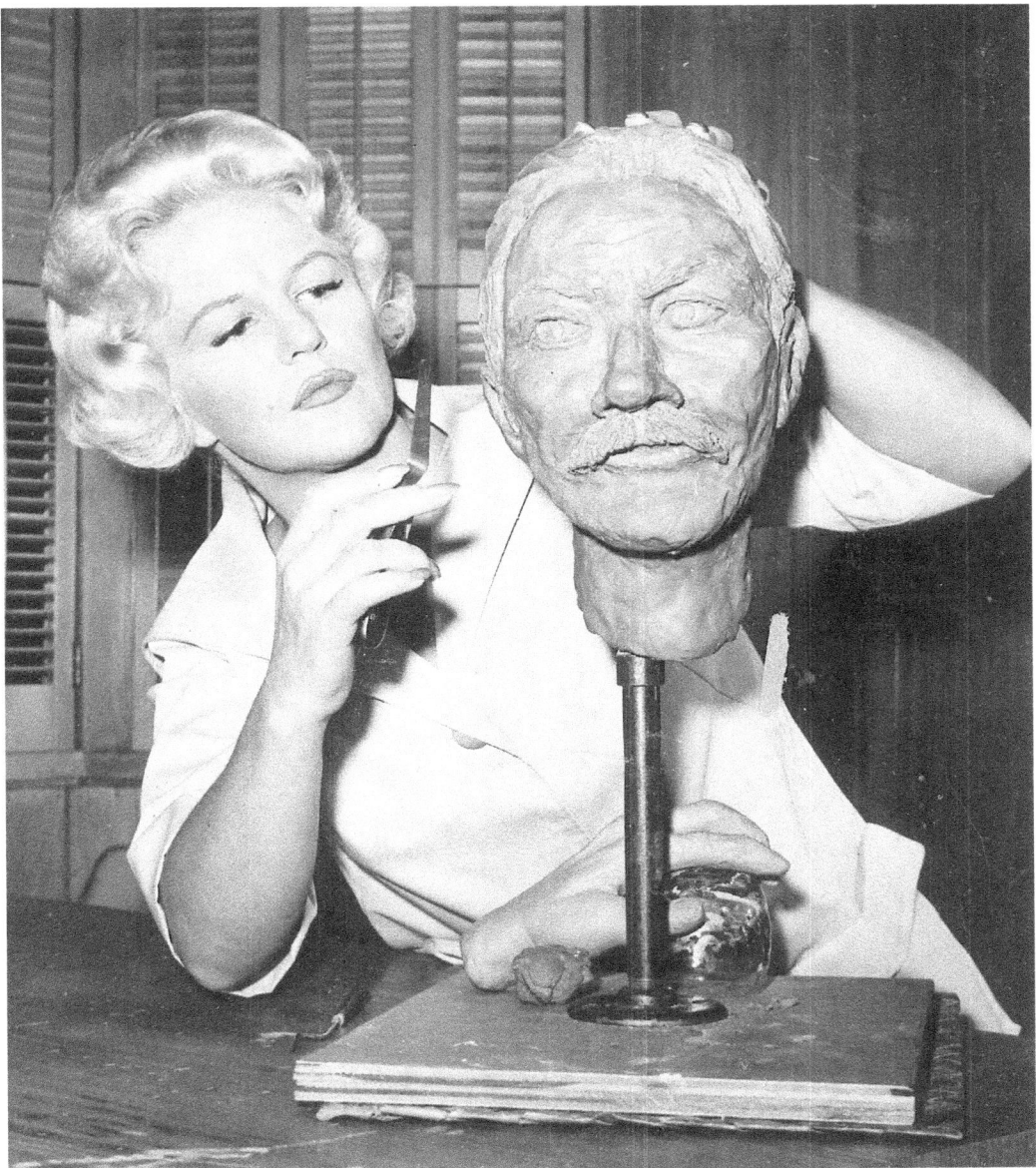

Peggy with her sculpture of Albert Schweitzer. Lee was also an accomplished painter. This photograph appears to have been taken during Peggy's 1960 appearance on the CBS program *Person to Person*.

New York shut down. The management at Basin Street East was certain that no one would brave the weather to see Peggy.

They were wrong—the club was packed. People came on foot and by horse-drawn sleigh. Hundreds had to be turned away. Then another storm hit—the blizzard of Peggy's rave reviews.

Peggy is seen in her bedroom for the 1960 broadcast of *Person to Person*. Charles Collingwood interviewed Lee for this segment. (CBS)

Her efforts proved that while the business is replete with both singers and performers, Peggy Lee is one of a handful who legitimately are superlatives as both ... beautiful and vital ... it is pretty tough to match her in any department.... Another side of the Lee talent is perhaps even more unique; her way with a very deliberate tempo, so slow that few other singers would even essay them lest they show up vocal deficiencies...

If ever a performer "owned" a club and it's audience, it's Peggy Lee at Basin Street East. Since such atmosphere brings out the best in a performer, Capitol could well consider cutting an album on location here... — Sam Chase, *Billboard*, January 16, 1961

Capitol had, in fact, planned to record Peggy's latest stint at Basin Street East. The resulting album captured the energy and feeling that Peggy generated at the club.

> The former band vocalist is one of the hotter pop singers around — also one of the most savvy. She knows how to excite moods, infuse humor and insert sly and wicked connotations into what the customers had previously imagined to be devoid of ulterior meaning. Miss Lee sells jazz and sex in copious quantities ... mixing her moods and tempo of her numbers for an extremely colorful and satisfying session.— *Variety*
>
> Breathy but truly on pitch in her pensive periods, she is firm in her declarative sentences, and as she approaches her climaxes of exultation her orchestra rises with her, but never is it so intense and closely woven that there are no loopholes through which her words shine clear....— *The New Yorker*, January 28, 1961

These reviews demonstrate that that Peggy was at the top of her craft — as did the fact that she was earning upwards of $12,500 a week. Her services were now very much in demand.

One of the songs for this engagement was her own "I Love Being Here with You." It would be her opening number for many years to come. The lyric mentions her desire to kiss Jimmy Durante on the nose. Soon photos of her kissing Durante's famous "schnozzola" made the front page of the New York papers.

The Capitol LP, recorded "live" at the club, was an instant best seller. The album finds a husky-voiced (she was suffering from a cold) Peggy Lee in captivating form. "Day In, Day Out" opens side one with a charge. Next she changes mood for a sultry "Moments Like This." Then comes an outstanding live version of "Fever."

Side two begins with "I Love Being Here with You." Again she shifts moods from hot and swinging to quietly romantic. She sings of all the many facets of love in "But Beautiful." In a "part of a tribute" to Ray Charles she tears at your heart with her shattering "Just for a Thrill." Those who were there describe this number as "hair raising!" She closes with an exultant "Yes Indeed!"

Unfortunately, Capitol left out the entire centerpiece of her act. This problem was solved with the 2003 release of *Peggy Lee — Peggy at Basin Street East* on the Collector's Choice Music label. The recording was captured on Peggy's closing night (February 8, 1961).

The previously unreleased material includes "Call Me Darling, Call Me Sweetheart, Call Me Dear," "The Most Beautiful Man in the World," "I Never Left Your Arms," "By Myself," "Heart," and the Lee-Ellington tune "I'm Gonna Go Fishin'."

Fans were also treated to a medley of the following Peggy Lee hits "I Don't Know Enough About You," "Mañana," "Why Don't You Do Right," "Lover" and "It's a Good Day." Sadly, Peggy's tribute to Billie Holiday is still missing.

February 3, 1961—New York Times. The *Times*' Arthur Gelb reported on "An Unrehearsed Performance at Basin Street East," during which Peggy's old friend Jimmy Durante joined her on-stage:

> The temperature was one degree above zero at 2 A.M. yesterday, but inside Basin Street East it was sizzling. The scheduled entertainment, provided by Peggy Lee, the singer, can heat up the room more than adequately, but early yesterday morning she had the impromptu assistance of Jimmy Durante and a couple of his friends.
>
> Mr. Durante ... walked to a ringside table shortly before Miss Lee appeared on stage for the 1 A.M. supper show.
>
> Mr. Durante, growling cheerfully that Miss Lee's pianist played "too maudlin" for him, dispossessed him, sprawled at the keyboard himself and gave an informal preview of his show that opened at 9 o'clock last night at the Copa. He tore into "Inka-Dinka-Do"....

February 12, 1961—Ed Sullivan. Ed Sullivan invited Peggy to perform a portion of her nightclub act on his TV show. For the broadcast Peggy and her combo presented "Non Dimenticar," "One Kiss," "My Romance," and "The Vagabond King Waltz." Sullivan rarely let a singer do more than one song, so this additional airtime was a real honor. This also gave the nationwide viewers a chance to see what Basin Street East audiences were raving about.

February 18, 1961—Melody Maker magazine (UK). In an article entitled "Peggy Lee: Most Teenage Music Makes Me Sick!" by Ren Grevatt, Peggy related her newfound love for Ray Charles:

> I'm terribly sick of so much of the kind of music the kids are getting today. It's so unmusical and unfeeling when you compare it with the music of Billie or Ray Charles.
>
> My 17-year-old daughter Nicki introduced me to the music of Ray Charles. He's so far above the run-of-the-mill rock-n-roll.
>
> He's the blues. He's real and down-to-earth rhythm and blues. I give him so much credit for teaching our kids something real and authentic about music.
>
> I've put together a sort of medley of Ray Charles in my act, too, and when I don't do my Lady Day group, I do the Ray Charles numbers. There's so much feeling and soul in them.

April 1961—Blues Cross Country. Peggy returned to the Capitol studios with Quincy at her side. Together they recorded two very diverse song collections. The first was an album of blues-themed material called *Blues Cross Country* (recorded during four sessions on April 14, 15, 17 and 19).

Quincy Jones and the orchestra provided the appropriate blues-flavored backing. Peggy invites us along as she visits "Kansas City," "Goin to Chicago Blues," and "St. Louis Blues."

Lee added several of her own blues compositions to these standards. She wrote six songs for the album; three of them penned with Quincy Jones. Their finest song is the rocking "New York City Blues."

April 1961— Basin Street East. For this April stint Peggy performed several of the songs from the *Blues Cross Country* record. Her "Blues Cross Country Suite" was

A stunning portrait by John Engstead. Engstead's photographs graced many of Peggy's album covers. (Circa 1961)

received enthusiastically, especially among New York residents who loved her "New York City Blues." Jazz legend Benny Carter headed up the orchestra.

> If any one person can be credited with the buildup of Basin Street East as one of the 'must' jazz rooms in town, it's Peggy Lee.... Current stand is Miss Lee's first since a siege of pneumonia forced her to cancel a four-week booking here last November …

Longtime fan Ron Towe took these candid photographs of Peggy outside Basin Street East. Towe was extremely devoted to Lee. Over the years he compiled a 2,400-page scrapbook containing hundreds of items, including rare photographs, concert and record reviews, interviews, sheet music, and candid and publicity shots.

> there are no ill effects from the sickness in either her vocal style or stage deportment.... She's one of the few song stylists who puts humor into her work and it gives the performance the necessary lifts and colorings.—*Variety*

April 23, 1961— **Associated Press.** Gene Handsaker penned "Peggy Lee's Voice Promotes Meals for Millions," in which Peggy spoke of her desire to promote humanitarian efforts:

> "I've had a long-time desire to contribute in some manner to peace in the world," she explained.
> An afternoon interview at her home produced these reflections:
> "The arts are very closely related to some spiritual sense. They must be. Where does inspiration come from?
> "I get my ideas from odd little things. Birds in the garden. Trees. Trees always make me think of patience...
> "If I write a song, I suppose it's a kind of prayer..."

June 22, 1961—***If You Go.*** The next Lee and Jones collaboration was a collection of melancholy love songs entitled *If You Go*. Recorded in four sessions (June 22, 23, 24 and 27) *If You Go* is, along with the Sinatra-conducted *The Man I Love*, Peggy's most pleasing album of wistful ballads.

Jones' orchestrations are superb; they support the singer without overwhelming her. She sings "As Time Goes By," the beloved theme from "Casablanca," with tender ease. Other classics include "I Get Along Without You Very Well," "Here's That Rainy Day," and "Smile." Peggy and Harry Sukman wrote "(I Love Your) Gypsy Heart" for the album.

At this time the work of Peggy Lee the painter was featured at a showing in Los

Angeles. She also showed great talent as a sculptor. Her bust of Albert Schweitzer was among her best work. Ten of Peggy's paintings were displayed at the Hollywood Museum of Art. Four of these were for sale; they sold immediately.

Summer 1961—Summer on Ice. Peggy debuted her next Capitol single, "Hey, Look Me Over," on this program. She also performed a duet of "I Love Being Here with You" with guest Peter Lawford.

July 1961— **Club Pigalle, London (UK).** In July Peggy traveled to London for the first time, where she was scheduled to appear at the club Pigalle. Several of her albums were best sellers in England. One of the best-loved songs in the UK was her version of "The Folks Who Live on the Hill." Her reviews for her first London show indicate that she appealed to audiences everywhere.

> Miss Peggy Lee, the woman who brought artistry to pop singing, displayed her art last Monday evening at London's Pigalle restaurant.... Masterly arrangements interpreted with such supreme skill and delicacy of timing that the audience was snapped up in the spell cast by this shimmering singer ... the whispered fragments of a slow, slow ballad, Peggy created an atmospheric silence....— Jack Hutton, *Melody Maker*, July 22, 1961
>
> She has risen above her competitors ... in kind as well as degree.... She operates on a higher plane: as she performs she shows unmistakable signs of thinking. The sexual promises and laments that express, in simple rhymes, the essential feelings of jazz are rendered by her miraculously fresh. Tin Pan Alley banalities pass through her head and emerge as poetry.— Patrick Skene Catling, *Punch*, August 2 of 1961

Peggy traveled to Monaco to perform at a gala benefit hosted by Princess Grace for the International Red Cross. She also promoted her own humanitarian efforts for "Meals for Millions." Few people knew that she was not just a spokesperson for ending world hunger, she was the president of "Meals for Millions." Lee helped co-found the organization with actor Eddie Albert.

July 8, 1961—Melody Maker **magazine (UK).** Peggy's longtime friend, jazz critic Leonard Feather, wrote "Peggy Lee, Perfectionist" for the UK magazine.

In the article, Feather talked of Peggy's "insatiable thirst for knowledge," and how she taught herself to play piano, before addressing the focal point of the piece:

> Peggy is the complete perfectionist. She has no patience with impatience. When she went to New York last year for her first date at Basin Street East, she had the whole bandstand rebuilt to provide her with a more effective entranceway; had the orchestra enlarged from five to 13 men (Neal Hefti led it); brought Sid Kuller from Hollywood to provide extra lyrics. The electrician had to follow more than 130 lighting cues in a 35-minute show. All this effort paid off; she did the biggest business in the history of the club, every musician and singer in town raved about her, and she now has a deal to return there regularly.

August 1961—Big Night Out **(UK).** Peggy appeared on this BBC show with Bing Crosby and David Kossoff. She and Kossoff performed a duet of "Mary Ellen." Peggy's other songs included "I Love Being Here with You," "Moments Like This," "Till There Was You," "Fly Me to the Moon" and "All the Way."

> The show was built around Peggy Lee.... It was Peggy's first outing on British TV, and she scored with a relaxed and polished selection of standards, sprinkled with the odd novelty....—*Variety*

September 1961—Happy with the Blues. Peggy appeared with Vic Damone, Bing Crosby and songwriter Harold Arlen on the TV special *Happy with the Blues*. The program was a salute to Arlen's work.

Lee and Arlen wrote the title song for the show. Peggy also sang Arlen's "Come Rain or Come Shine" and "The Man That Got Away."

September 1961—Jazz Journal magazine (UK). Sinclair Traill wrote an editorial for the UK publication:

> Now Miss Peggy Lee, ever since I listened some while back to her LP *Black Coffee*, has always struck me as being something very special in jazz singers. Maybe she hasn't had as much publicity as some of the coloured girls, but I have always considered her up amongst the top ones for genuine aptitude. Like the greatest of all jazz singers—I refer of course to Billie Holiday—Peggy has the ability to improvise in such a distinctly musical manner that she becomes as much a part of jazz as any of the instrumentalists accompanying her.

Peggy makes her first trip to London (July 13, 1961), where she'll appear for four weeks at the Pigalle.

September 11, 1961—Basin Street East. Peggy's live album from Basin Street East debuted on the charts. It was on the charts for 22 weeks and peaked at number 77.

November 1961— Basin Street East. Peggy had an exciting new conductor—a talented young musician named Quincy Jones. Quincy had conducted her Capitol single of "Hey, Look Me Over." He continued in that capacity for her current single, "Boston Beans," with lyrics by Peggy. Miss Lee and the handsome Jones enjoyed an intimate musical relationship. It has been suggested that had the social climate been different in 1961 the two might have married.

Peggy performing in London, July 1961. Lee's UK fans are among her most loyal.

Variety summed up this visit to Basin Street in the following review:

> Peggy Lee, who virtually put this jazz room on the map when it was just getting started in 1959 ... carries a brand of excitement that few singers can match, and her hour-long set is paced with such savvy.... Her musicianship is always at the forefront no matter what style she's tackling.

Two atypical portraits of Peggy by John Engstead. (Circa 1961)

Near the end of this engagement Peggy collapsed. She was having difficulty breathing. She asked a doctor to tape her abdomen, thus blocking her pain so she could continue to perform. This only worked for a short time, and she was hospitalized with double pneumonia.

Lee faced a long recovery period. Her lungs were damaged. For the next ten years she would require daily treatments from an IPPB lung machine. With her usual sense of humor she nicknamed the lung machine "Charlie." Despite orders from her doctors, she continued to travel and perform.

During her recuperation period Capitol issued a "best of" Peggy Lee album. This collection bore the title *Bewitching-Lee*. The album included "Fever," "My Man," "Hallelujah, I Love Him So," and the Lee classic "Don't Smoke in Bed."

November 26, 1961—New York Herald Times. Jazz critic George T. Simon wrote about "Peggy Lee: Sentimental Realist":

> Peggy's a sentimentalist all right. It has shown through ever since in so many of her records, including her new Capitol album *If You Go*. But she's also a realist, and it's this unusual combination that has contributed so much to her phenomenal success.
>
> Unlike most jazz singers, who leave so much to chance and just hope (they like to use the ad lib aspect of jazz as an excuse for not being better prepared), Peggy labors over each of her routines, examining each nuance carefully, planning every move, and never settling for anything less than the best she thinks she can do.

Peggy, Harold Arlen (at the piano) and Vic Damone. This trio appeared on *Happy with the Blues*. The television show, saluting Arlen's music, was broadcast in September 1961. Lee wrote the lyrics for the title song, and performed "Come Rain or Come Shine," "Two Ladies in the Shade of the Banana Tree" and "The Man That Got Away." She also joined Harold and Vic for a medley of Arlen songs.

> "I've been given a talent," she says, "and I feel a responsibility to try to improve the presentation of it."

During the months between November 1961 and April 1962, Peggy recuperated from her bout with pneumonia. She attended two recording sessions on March 29 and 30. The songs recorded on those dates would be included on her 1963 release *Mink Jazz*.

***April 4, 1962*—*Sugar 'n' Spice*.** Peggy went to a recording session at Capitol on April 4, 1962, the last of four sessions (the first three were on March 28, March 31 and April 2). The resulting album, which featured Benny Carter charts, was called *Sugar 'n' Spice*. Lee was in excellent form.

Selections on this LP were extremely varied, displaying Peggy's versatility. She was heard scolding one lover on "See See Rider," and asking to be taught by another on "Teach Me Tonight." Lee turned the steam up on an intense rendition of "When the Sun Comes Out." If there's any single track that educates first-time listeners on what Peggy Lee does best, it is "The Best Is Yet to Come."

Lee wrote two songs for this record. The first is her hopeful plea to be kissed again, "Embrasse Moi." Then she shouts "I Don't Wanna Leave You Now" with great blues-laden emotion.

***April 22, 1962*—*New York Mirror*.** Sidney Fields wrote that Peggy had "Silk, Fire and Ice in Her Voice":

> Peggy Lee has earned enduring and increasing acceptance as a music maker with a unique style that combines silk, fire, and ice. These are the gifts of her durability. What is the key to them?
>
> She has sung and sorrowed and loved much, and knows she must sing and sorrow and love more.
>
> Ask her what success is and she answers, "A fulfillment of what you were born to do. I know I was born to sing, but there's more. I want to write more music, to paint more...."
>
> The key to her durability? The music inside Peggy Lee.

***May 19, 1962*— President Kennedy's Birthday.** Norma Delores Egstrom and Norma Jean Baker, better known as Peggy Lee and Marilyn Monroe, were among the entertainers who paid tribute to President Kennedy at Madison Square Garden.

This event featured Monroe's now legendary "Happy Birthday, Mr. President."

***May 26, 1962*—*The Ed Sullivan Show*.** Peggy performed the Lee-Jones swinger "New York City Blues." Three other songs on this Sullivan visit were "The Sweetest Sounds," "I'll Get By," and "I Believe in You."

The forty-two-year-old singer had come a long way from her early days on North Dakota radio broadcasts.

***June 1962*— World's Fair, Seattle.** Peggy was the headliner at the Seattle Opera House.

***June 16, 1962*—*Melody Maker* magazine (UK).** Peggy's longtime pianist Lou Levy wrote an article entitled "Behind the Scenes with Ella and Peggy" for the UK's premiere jazz magazine:

> I don't know of two more generous and understanding singers to work for than Ella Fitzgerald and Peggy Lee. Peggy presents more of a thoroughly planned act, usually

These photographs were taken at President Kennedy's birthday party, Madison Square Garden, May 19, 1962. This is the same event at which Marilyn Monroe sang her now legendary version of "Happy Birthday." Monroe used Lee's lighting scheme for her song.

doing the same show during an entire engagement. Ella's concert or nightclub performance is carefully planned, but she makes certain changes while on stage.
   Working with Ella is more of a jazz job. There's more room for variations.... Peggy creates a very strong feeling, but it's not strictly because of the jazz phrasing she brings to her singing, but because of the way she projects the lyrics and creates a mood as she sings. Ella sings with less dramatic qualities overall. Despite the fact that Peggy works strictly non-jazz nightclubs, she still maintains a jazz feeling in her singing.

Summer 1962—The Lively Ones. Peggy's next television appearance was on a summer replacement show entitled *The Lively Ones*. In her first segment on the program she was seen at Basin Street East performing several songs from *Sugar 'n' Spice*. A subsequent visit to *The Lively Ones* found her standing alone in Dodger Stadium, wrapped in fur, belting out "When the Sun Comes Out."

August 25, 1962—Bewitching-Lee! This greatest hits album was on the charts for six weeks. It peaked at number 85.

September 27, 1962—The Andy Williams Show. This was Peggy's first appearance on *The Andy Williams Show*. Williams clearly admired his guest star. The honey-voiced singer, best known for his singular renditions of "Moon River" and "The Days of Wine and Roses," never sounded better than when he joined Peggy in duet. For this show she sang "Them There Eyes" and "But Beautiful." She joined Andy and guest George Gobel on "You Are My Sunshine."

November 17, 1962—Sugar 'n' Spice. Peggy had another album hit the charts in November 1962. *Sugar 'n' Spice* spent 21 weeks on the charts, peaking at number 40.

November 17, 1962—New York Daily News. Alfred T. Hendricks reported that Peggy's gowns, totaling $21,000, had been stolen from Basin Street East. One popular story has Peggy telling the police officers, "Look for a drag queen. No self-respecting woman would wear those gowns on the street."

November 1962— **Basin Street East.** The critics wrote of her wide scope of material and her ability to handle any style, mentioning "talking blues numbers to wailing up-tempo tunes to soft and sentimental ballads." Bob Rolontz, from *Billboard*, was there. His comments appeared in the November 17 edition:

> The lovely and winning Peggy Lee returned to her favorite night spot, Basin Street East ... with a whole new act ... a new band, led by her new arranger-conductor, Benny Carter.... She can turn a phrase on a rhythm tune or a ballad that is distinctly her own.... She can move from a mood of sorrow to a mood of swinging happiness within one song.... She knows how to use her hands, her body and her eyes, as well as her voice ... there are few singers around today who can compare with her.

Columnist Earl Wilson wrote a "Love Letter to Peggy Lee" during this engagement. He told her: "You overwhelmed all of us—you were so wonderful doing an hour and a half of songs on your return to Basin St. Get your flu shots, doll, and don't go getting sick; we need you around reminding us there's you and there's Judy Garland and that's it."

***November 4, 1962**—The Ed Sullivan Show.* The winter of 1962 saw Peggy making two visits to *The Ed Sullivan Show*. On the November 4 episode she provided a tribute to songwriter Richard Rodgers, singing with Steve Lawrence a delightful version of "(I'll Take) Manhattan." She soloed on an easy swinging "Mountain Greenery" and a quiet "It Might as Well Be Spring."

***November 14, 1962**—"I'm a Woman."* Peggy recorded her latest single on this date. Like "Why Don't You Do Right?," "Mañana," "Lover," and "Fever," this tune would be forever associated with her. The songwriting team of Jerry Lieber and Mike Stoller wrote it for her. Lieber and Stoller had also penned Elvis' hit "Hound Dog." Later the songwriting team would play a very important role in Peggy's career.

"I'm a Woman" was a smash hit. It was nominated for Best Solo Vocal Performance, Female Grammy in 1962. Capitol knew how to promote a hot-selling single. They soon released an album, titled *I'm a Woman*, containing the hit single and other new material. The selections for the album were recorded at various sessions between March 1962 and January 1963. Since the album was released in 1963, it received a Grammy nomination—for Best Album—in that year.

I'm a Woman showcased Peggy's unparalleled versatility. She gave listeners a very salty "There Ain't No Sweet Man That's Worth the Salt of My Tears," and a sweet, dripping "A Taste of Honey."

Peggy's humorous reading of "Mack the Knife" made the song her own. She breathed new life into the Tony Bennett classic "I Left My Heart in San Francisco." When she sang "I'm Walkin'," listeners saw her turn and leave her lover in the rain. Then she clears away the clouds with a brilliant rendition of "Come Rain or Come Shine."

***December 9, 1962**—The Ed Sullivan Show.* Lee returned to the Sullivan show to sing a great set, including "The Best Is Yet to Come," "Nice and Easy," "Close Your Eyes," "Like Someone in Love" and "I'm a Woman."

***January 5, 1963**—"I'm a Woman."* Peggy's one-of-a-kind rendition of "I'm a Woman" reached the charts at the beginning of 1963. It stayed there for nine weeks and peaked at number 54.

***January 19, 1963**—The Peggy E. Lee.* Peggy received the honor of christening a special boat. The *San Francisco Chronicle* covered the event:

> A 20-foot river boat was christened in Union Square at noon yesterday on behalf of a "swinging" organization—the Thomas A. Dooley Foundation.
> Singer Peggy Lee, chairman of the foundation's board of directors, announced she was "honored to be associated with such a wonderful group," then smashed a bottle of champagne against the bow of the craft.
> The $4500 vessel, named the *Peggy E. Lee* ... will be based at Ban Houei Sai in Laos and will ply the Mekong river, between Laos and Thailand, as a floating medical clinic.
> In addition to the boat, a trailer and a jeep, plus a ton-shipment of food from the "Meals for Millions" campaign are due to be shipped soon to Laos.

Peggy continued to work for "Meals for Millions." Her philanthropic efforts did not go unnoticed. In gratitude, the Dalai Llama of Tibet give her a gift of a rare Lhasa Apso. She named the beloved dog Genghis. Lee also donated several of her paintings to help fund SHARE and National Educational Television.

***February 2, 1963*—Mink Jazz.** Capitol released another superb Peggy Lee album, showcasing the subtle arrangements of Benny Carter. *Mink Jazz* stands as a treasured classic among Lee's vinyl catalogue. Not since *Black Coffee* had she been placed in such a pure jazz setting. Carter's charts, aided by legendary trumpeter Jack Sheldon, possess a feeling of spontaneity.

Every song is a highlight. The best of the best is the swinging "Whisper Not." Peggy excelled in gentle readings of "My Silent Love," "Days of Wine and Roses," and "Cloudy Morning." "Close Your Eyes" makes listeners do just that, as she lightly swings her audience toward peaceful sleep. She even tops herself with a supreme rendition of her previously recorded composition "Where Can I Go Without You."

Mink Jazz was recorded in five sessions. The first two were on March 29 and 30, 1962. The remaining three sessions took place on February 2, 5 and 7, 1963.

***February 1963*— Diplomat Hotel, Florida.** Peggy performed for the first time at the Diplomat Hotel, located in Hollywood Beach, Florida. The critic for *Variety* called it "a tour-de-force for the warm, easy-working, attractive, blonde vet of song." Her next stop was the Latin Casino in Cherry Hill, New Jersey. Here *Variety* noted that "Miss Lee believes in making each word intelligible and using arrangements geared to her knowing style."

***March 1963*— Basin Street East.**

> It's a common sight during Miss Lee's run to see a line outside of the café waiting to get in…. There's little wonder about Miss Lee's constant lure. She seems to work hard on a repertoire between engagements here. She comes in with a batch of new numbers, new treatments for previously used items and, not incidentally, a come-hither viewpoint that seems to make all of her offerings bedroom ballads.—*Variety*

***March 9, 1963*—I'm a Woman.** Peggy's *I'm a Woman* album entered the charts for a 26-week stay. It reached a peak of number 18.

Wowing the crowd at Basin Street East. Lee put the jazz club on the map in the early '60s. The live album she recorded at the nightclub received a Grammy nomination. (Circa 1963)

July 27, 1963—Mink Jazz. The great Benny Carter–Peggy Lee album *Mink Jazz* debuted on the charts. It remained there for nine weeks and peaks at number 42.

Summer 1963—The Jo Stafford Show and Las Vegas. The summer months of June and August found Peggy appearing in Las Vegas and warbling on songbird Jo Stafford's television show. *Variety* wrote, "Miss Lee's 'Day In' and a darling ballad taken at a slow-walking pace showed her versatility at its peak."

In addition to "Day In, Day Out," Peggy sang "Dearie, Do You Remember?" with Jo Stafford. She also reprised her first hit, "Why Don't You Do Right?"

Her act at the Riviera Hotel in Las Vegas included songs like "Mack the Knife," "It Amazes Me," "The Alley Cat Song," "The Doodlin' Song," and her new sultry favorite, "I'm a Woman."

November 12, 1963—The Andy Williams Show. Lee and Williams joined forces for a blues cross-country medley that included: "Kansas City," "Goin' to Chicago" and "St. Louis Blues." Peggy's solo spot featured her satirical "Mack the Knife."

November 22, 1963—*New York Post.* Joseph Wershba reported on Peggy's blues:

> "I keep getting deeper into the songs," she says. "I learn from musicians. I like variety—folk songs, jazz.

Citing Ray Charles, who "sees nothing wrong in singing country-western," as an inspiration, Peggy notes in the article that "variety ... [has] always been my conception of singing."

Wershba writes of Lee's "insinuating, lowdown growly, hushed, provocative, lullabyish" style, noting: "When sex is deliberate, she humors it; when she means business, the audience has to sense it. Audiences never seem to have any trouble."

He continues:

> "Of course," she says, "if I tried to vamp and manufacture the sexiness, then I'd really be funny. Anything that is forced comes over fake." Onstage, she comes over as the apotheosis of one of her songs: "I'm a W-O-M-A-N." Offstage, she has been quite properly compared to a friendly, small-town librarian. "But I don't know why people have written that I'm moody or depressed. I'm not that at all. I've had a lot of sadness in my life, but sadness is not my nature," she says.

A candid photograph of the beautiful Miss Peggy Lee. Photograph by Ron Towe circa 1963.

November 2, 1963—*In Love Again.* November and December recording dates culminated in Peggy's 1964 release *In Love Again.* For this album she decided on an interesting format. Every song on side one is a swinging number propelled by big band horns. Side two found Peggy singing lush love songs with a string section.

The album opened with "A Lot of Livin' to Do" from the Broadway hit *Bye, Bye Birdie.* This was followed by "I've Got Your Number," penned by Cy Coleman and Carolyn Leigh for the show *Little Me.*

Peggy told us that her man's "Got That Magic" in a tune she wrote with Bill Schluger. Side one closed with one of the best swingers Peggy wrote: Her give-up-and-give-in-to-love lyrics for "That's My Style" were set to Cy Coleman's music.

"I'm in Love Again" was a warm, romantic side two track, as were "I Got Lost in His Arms" and "How

Insensitive." Peggy also performed a memorable rendition of Nat "King" Cole's "Unforgettable."

Recording dates for the *In Love Again* album included May 29, October 30, November 2 and December 7, 1963.

December 1, 1963*— *The Judy Garland Show. On this date two of America's best-loved singers worked together for the first — and, regrettably, last — time. Judy Garland had always placed Peggy at the top of her list of favorite singers, and honored Peggy's songwriting talent in her opening number, "It's a Good Day." Garland introduced Peggy's solo moment by calling her "the Magnificent Peg."

Peggy gave a dramatic, theater-of-the-mind reading of the haunting "When the World Was Young." The Johnny Mercer–M. Philippe-Gerard song had been in her repertoire since Decca's *Black Coffee*. Her connection to the lyric was stronger than ever. At forty-three she had lived the song, and it showed.

In his well-written book *Rainbow's End: The Judy Garland Show*, author Coyne Steven Sanders tells of the admiration the two showbiz pros had for each other:

> "We had a lovely time and really enjoyed singing together," remembers Peggy. "Mel [Tormé] suggested some of the songs for the 'I Like Men' medley, but they're all songs that are known or identified with me."
>
> She adds, "I wish Judy and I could have done more shows together. We had a wonderful time, and just told each other a lot of jokes. What I enjoyed most about Judy, I think, was her sense of humor.... People always think there was sadness all the time with Judy. But she was really very, very funny, and anyone that knew her would say the same thing."

Journalist Adela Rogers St. Johns was close to Peggy. Her book *Some Are Born Great*, contains a chapter devoted to Judy Garland. Adela recalls being at Peggy's home to watch the Garland show, where Peggy summed up Judy's greatness for St. Johns:

> One thing she has that no one else ever has had — remember how they begin to applaud and shout before they can see her? The mere announcement of her name, the news of her approach, fires them with enthusiasm, and she gets a welcome as no one else in our profession ever has. They'll do the same on television.

***February 1964*— The Riviera Hotel, Las Vegas.**

"Peggy Lee's still the chirp to beat as a top jazz singer..."—*Variety*, February 5, 1964.

***February 22, 1964*— Peggy marries Jack Del Rio.** It was during her February Las Vegas engagement that Peggy met the man who would be her fourth, and final, husband. She was forty-three when she married the thirty-nine-year-old Argentine-born musician Jack Del Rio.

Her marriage to Del Rio was very short in duration; they were divorced four months later. Lee told reporters, "We were a little hasty. It simply didn't work. There seemed no point in dragging things out and making ourselves suffer."

***April 1964*—Americana Hotel, New York.** During her appearance at the Americana's Royal Box, journalist Charles McHarry had happy news to report in his "On the Town" column:

> Miss Peggy Lee is about to become a grandma, and while she is thrilled at the prospect she does not intend to allow the event to become a milestone in her career.

***May 7, 1964*—*New York Times*.** Robert Alden wrote "Peggy Lee, 'Fever' and All, at Royal Box":

> As anyone who has seen Miss Lee work in a nightclub can testify, the experience can be overwhelming. If the listener supplies a basic appreciation of popular music, Miss Lee does the rest. Using her voice, the music, the lights, the costumes, one is carried back and forth across and through a variety of emotions—happy, sad and in-between.
>
> When Miss Lee sings "Sometimes I Feel Like a Motherless Child," she looks like a motherless child. When she turns to a percussion accompaniment, her conga drums, her bongos, her bass, her tom-toms are as fresh and exciting as if they had never been used before in a nightclub act.

***July 2, 1964*—*In the Name of Love*.** Peggy and pianist Lou Levy joined together again for her next project. Her 1965 release was recorded in July 1964.

The Kenny Rankin–Estelle Levitt tune "In the Name of Love" provided the album's title and swinging opener. Peggy's fun treatment of "The Boy from Ipanema" left no doubt that she could breathe new life into songs associated with other vocalists. She took listeners to an ethereal "Shangri-La."

One of the highlights on side two was her bitter "After You've Gone." With Lalo Schifrin she wrote "Just Call Me Love Bird," the theme for the Jane Fonda film *Joy House*. She found great tenderness in Gene Paoli and Alec Wilder's "Senza Fine." Peggy breezed through Leigh and Coleman's "When in Rome (I Do as the Romans Do)."

February 22, 1964 — Peggy married Jack Del Rio. This was her fourth and final marriage.

***September 26, 1964*—*In the Name of Love*.** The *In the Name of Love* album made the charts. It was there for nine weeks and peaked at number 97.

October 10, 1964—***Saturday Evening Post* magazine.** Thomas C. Wheeler discussed the "Timeless Charm of Peggy Lee":

> Significantly, the only comparable American singer is Ella Fitzgerald, who is a peer, though perhaps less electrifying on a nightclub floor. Miss Lee sings old and new show music with an unmistakable white voice, and blues as if she were black. Duke Ellington, who has been in the business almost 50 years, calls her "The Queen." "I consider her as great a musician as Frank Sinatra, who in that world is king," he says.

November 24, 1964—***New York Post.*** The venerable Earl Wilson wrote "Peggy Lee Stages a Comeback":

> The get-well telegrams and phone calls to Peggy Lee had come from such friends as Frank Sinatra and Doris Duke.
> There was a note of alarm in them—for Peggy was under an oxygen tent, fighting pneumonia, at Polyclinic Hospital.

Lee soon recovered.

December 9, 1964—***Pass Me By.*** The "Pass Me By"/"That's What It Takes" single was a hit. Capitol called Peggy into the studio to record nine more songs. Peggy's *Pass Me By* album included her first foray into the world of the Beatles. She recorded their "A Hard Day's Night" to great effect.

The album also included the theme to the popular *Bewitched* TV series. One particularly beautiful track in this collection was Antonio Carlos Jobim's "Quiet Nights," with lyrics by Gene Lees.

January 4, 1965—***The Andy Williams Show.*** Peggy and Art Carney were Williams' guests. Peggy sang "Fever" and "You've Got to See Mama Every Night." She also joined Andy for a medley of "Language of Love," "Let Me Love You," "Maybe It's Because I Love You Too Much," "Fly Me to the Moon," "My Blue Heaven," "Alone Together," "Lover," and "I Love You."

February 1965—**Basin Street East.** This would be Peggy Lee's final appearance at the club she "put on the map." She would continue to perform for another thirty years, but the magic she created at Basin Street now belonged to show business lore. In the final review of her appearances at the club, *Variety*'s critic wrote:

> Miss Lee presents new facets every time she makes an appearance here. This time, Miss Lee is out to make the most of every phrase in her rhythm tunes. Her mood is one of let's enjoy everything about it, but we've got all night to make it.
> She cools down the ardor in the numbers and controls the moods of her auditors. This is not easy for an audience ready to gallop at any command she purrs out.... In her finale, Miss Lee does some of her stalwarts and it's a strong send-off.

February 27, 1965—**"Pass Me By."** Peggy's single "Pass Me By" from the Cary Grant film *Father Goose* reached the charts. It peaked at number 93 and stayed on the charts for three weeks.

Four • Return to Capitol

Performing "Fever" on *The Andy Williams Show*, January 4, 1965. (NBC)

Performing "The Boy from Ipanema" on the *Jack Paar Show*, March 12, 1965. Paar was so taken by Lee's performance he asked her to sing the song again. She did, creating a television first. (NBC)

March 12, 1965—*Jack Paar Show.* This Paar appearance was a great success. The jovial host was thrilled by her rendition of "The Boy from Ipanema." He asked her to encore it then and there, a television first. Lee obliged. Paar was in awe of her figure as well, saying, "Man, you're stacked!" and then he sang the Jell-O jingle. When Peggy asked him if he was following a story she was relating, Paar said, "Honey, I'd rather follow you than lead you."

March 13, 1965—"Pass Me By." "Pass Me By" enjoyed another success on the Adult Contemporary charts. From this point forward all of Peggy's chart hits would be in the Adult Contemporary category. "Pass Me By" was on the charts this time for one week. It peaked at number 20.

March 15, 1965—*Newsweek* magazine. *Newsweek* discovers that "Peggy Is a Red Hot Blama":

Her serious illness in 1961 changed Peggy Lee. While at Basin Street East in New York she collapsed suddenly with double pneumonia. She was left with permanent lung damage, which has restricted her engagements, made long rests a necessity, and "Charlie" her inseparable traveling companion.

Charlie is a large oxygen tank which Peggy must use four times a day to keep her lungs from filling up with fluid. "Charlie has helped me understand people, too," she said. "And so has David," she added, meaning her five-month-old grandson. "He calls me 'Blama' ... You know, grandma."

April 28, 1965 — Los Angeles Times. Charles Champlin reported on the reunion of Peggy and Benny Goodman in his article "Peggy, Benny in the Swing of It":

> When I first heard that she and the Benny Goodman band were going to be reunited — for a week at Melodyland starting May 3 and later at San Carlos — it was like being offered a stroll into the better parts of your past. Not entirely, of course, because Peggy has never been a "remember when" institution, but has kept on top of the swinging present every day of her musical life. Still, it's a reunion that triggers a memory, or three or four or more, and I jumped at the chance to say hello at her penthouse above the Sunset Strip.
>
> "'Where or When,'" she was saying. "We recorded that at Liederkranz Hall in New York, I remember. Must've been 1942. The place was so live that we all had to take off our shoes while we worked. The mikes were picking up the foot-tapping."

May 22, 1965 — Pass Me By. The *Pass Me By* album charted for four weeks and peaked at number 145.

July 9, 1965 — Happy Holidays. "Happy Holidays," "The Little Drummer Boy" and "Winter Wonderland" were used, along with nine songs from her *Christmas Carousel* album, to create a new Christmas album titled *Happy Holidays*.

September 21, 1965 — Then Was Then and Now Is Now. Another album was released shortly before her Copa stint. "Then Was Then and Now Is Now," a love song written by Peggy and Cy Coleman, provided the title for the album. This collection was arranged and conducted by Sid Feller. Several of the new songs had a decided "rock" feeling, proving that Peggy Lee was still a contemporary artist.

Then Was Then and Now Is Now was hailed by critics as a triumph. *Stereo Review* gave it their "Recording of Special Merit." Writing for *FM Guide*, critic Ron Towe said that Peggy sang with "astonishing skill and oceans of cool."

She displayed those "oceans of cool" on songs like "The Shadow of Your Smile" and "(I'm Afraid) The Masquerade Is Over." Her "astonishing skill" is evident on "I Go to Sleep" and "Seventh Son." The title song was recorded on December 9, 1964. The sessions that completed the album were held on June 18, 1965, July 7, 1965, and September 21, 1965.

September 23, 1965 — The Dean Martin Show. Peggy joined Dean and guest stars Jack Jones, John Wayne, Shari Lewis. She sang a medley of "Alright, Okay, You Win" and "I Can't Give You Anything but Love" with Martin and Jones.

October 23, 1965—"Free Spirits." Peggy's single "Free Spirits" made the charts. It would stay for seven weeks and peaked at number 29.

November 11, 1965—*The Ed Sullivan Show.* Peggy sang three solos, including "It's a Grand Night for Singing" and "Come Back to Me." Her ballad selection was a mesmerizing "How Long Has This Been Going On?" Peggy was joined by the Righteous Brothers for a rocking, electric "Yes Indeed."

November 1965—Copacabana. After the Sullivan show, Peggy opened at her new performing home in New York. The famous Copacabana had lured her away from Basin Street East. Her reviews were glowing.

> As Miss Lee pitches the lower decibels they respectfully hang on every lyrical nuance and, considering that she was uncorking a flock of newies, it was a personal tribute to her audience identification and control. She played it to the hilt... —*Variety*, November 17, 1965

December 11, 1965—David Barbour Dies. The man Peggy described as "the love of my life" passed away on this date. Peggy and David remained friends throughout the years. Barbour even played "Here Comes the Bride" on his guitar at the rehearsal for one of her other marriages. His obituary in *Variety* mentioned that the two discussed the possibility of marrying again before he died.

January 29, 1966—"Big Spender." The brassy hit from Broadway's *Sweet Charity* charted and reached a peak of number nine. "Big Spender" stayed on the charts for 12 weeks.

January 6, 1966—*The Dean Martin Show.* Her solo moments included "It's a Wonderful World" and a stunning reading of "When the World Was Young." Dean paid tribute to Peggy Lee the songwriter when he joined her for a medley of "I Love Being Here with You," "Mañana," and "It's a Good Day." Martin and Lee obviously enjoyed working together; they recorded one duet, "You Was," on the Capitol label.

February 1, 1966—*Big Spender.* On this date Peggy went into the Capitol studios to wrap up her *Big Spender* album. Material for this album had also been recorded on October 27 and 29, 1965.

The singles, recorded in October 1965, of "You've Got Possibilities," "Come Back to Me," and "Big Spender" sold well. Capitol gathered the three singles, added eight other songs, and released Peggy's *Big Spender* album in the summer of 1966.

Peggy's swinging rendition of the blues tune "You Don't Know" added the trademark Peggy Lee sizzle to the album. Ballad highlights on this LP were "I'll Only Miss Him When I Think of Him" (from the Broadway musical *Skyscraper*) and her warm reading of Michel Legrand's "Watch What Happens" (from the film *The Umbrellas of Cherbourg*).

"THERE'S FEVER IN THE AIR"—Peggy appeared at the famous Copacabana in New York City in 1965.

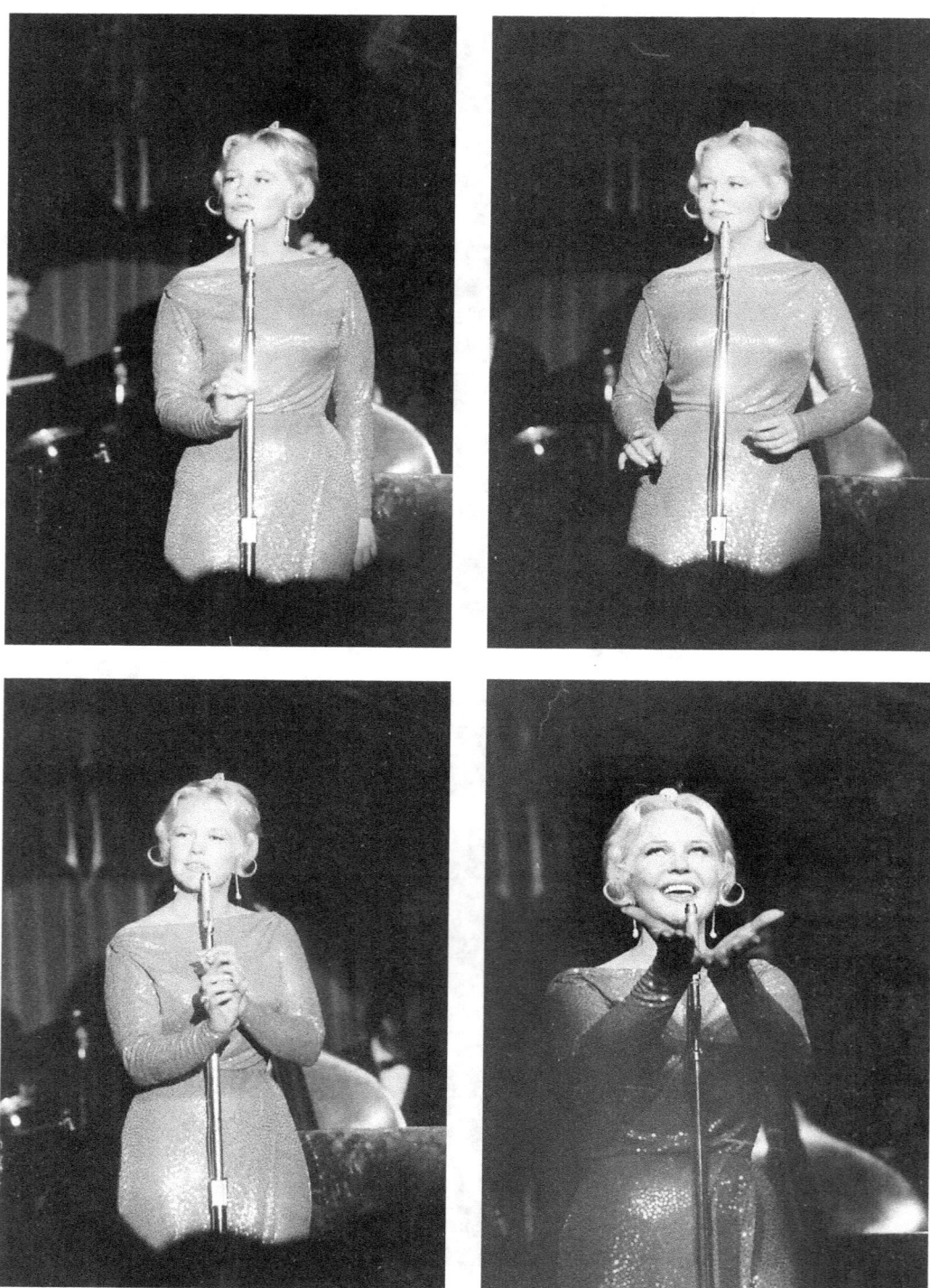

Peggy takes center stage at New York's famous Copa.

February 1966 — The Nugget, Reno, Nevada.

> Catalog, lighting and staging have been given careful attention, and result is as anticipated: singer is the consummate diseuse. Her black off-shoulder gown contrasting her light complexion and blond good looks, she soothsays what to come via "Grand Night for Singing." It is. — *Variety*, February 23, 1966

March 7, 1966 — *The Andy Williams Show.*

This program found Williams in the company of two of America's finest singers — Tony Bennett and Miss Peggy Lee. The three gifted vocalists joined forces for a medley of "Day" songs that included "It's a Lovely Day Today," "It's a Good Day" and "On a Wonderful Day Like Today." Peggy turned in a wicked "Bird in a Gilded Cage." She joined Andy again for Cole Porter's "I've Got You Under My Skin."

Dean Martin and Peggy. Peggy was a frequent guest on Martin's NBC show. This photograph is from the January 6, 1966, program.

March 16, 1966 — Diplomat Hotel, Florida.

> Miss Lee, looking lush in a red sequined gown which drew applause before she started chirping, was in a great mood for her opening and seemed to be enjoying herself completely. — *Variety*

April 9, 1966 — "That Man."

Peggy's spoof of the *Batman* theme song charted on this day to stay for five weeks. It peaked at number 31.

May 1966 — *Something Special with Peggy Lee*

In May, New York's WOR-TV broadcast a musical special Peggy had taped earlier in the year. *Something Special with Peggy Lee* would mark her first solo effort in the medium of television.

Something Special with Peggy Lee was gimmick-free entertainment. Peggy opened with "As You Desire Me." Viewers' desires were satisfied with "Moments Like This" and "The Best Is Yet to Come." Peggy's blues cross-country suite was a showstopper. However, the highlight of the evening was her dramatic theater-of-the-mind rendition of "Funny Man" and "What Kind of Fool Am I?"

Three of America's great singers — Andy Williams, Peggy Lee and Tony Bennett — perform on *The Andy Williams Show*, March 7, 1966. (NBC)

> In her fine jazz-pop style, Miss Lee paced out a solid hour, swinging a set of her own compositions, a travel medley, her well-known standards and the clown turn, which included a touchingly effective "What Kind of Fool Am I?" She is that gifted that she can take an hour out on a low, low key with proper dramatic projection. — *Variety*, May 25, 1966

May 21, 1966 — "The Shining Sea"

In 1966 Lee contributed to two motion pictures. Composer Johnny Mandel ("The Shadow of Your Smile") brought his theme for "The Russians Are Coming, the Russians Are Coming" to her, asking her to write the lyric.

When he returned to pick up the finished work he was stunned to discover that

Peggy had written a lyric that perfectly matched a major scene in the film. Peggy had not seen any footage from the film, nor did she have a script of the movie, yet her lyric for "The Shining Sea" told the story of the film's lovers.

For the Cary Grant film *Walk, Don't Run* Peggy collaborated with her beloved Quincy Jones. Together they wrote two songs for the film. This movie would mark the last time that Peggy's lifelong friend Cary Grant appeared in a film. The Lee-Jones team wrote "Happy Feet" and "Stay with Me" for the picture.

"The Shining Sea," "Happy Feet" and "Stay with Me" were all recorded on May 21, 1966.

June 1966— **Shoreham Hotel, Washington, D.C.** Peggy's new act included a song from the Broadway stage entitled "You've Got Possibilities." Over the years Peggy had interpreted numerous Broadway tunes, breathing new life into them and saving them from obscurity. Now she was working her magic with three new show tunes: "You've Got Possibilities" (from *It's a Bird, It's a Plane, It's Superman*) "Come Back to Me" (from *On a Clear Day You Can See Forever*) and "Big Spender" (from *Sweet Charity*).

June 18, 1966— **"You've Got Possibilities."** Peggy's rendition of the Broadway tune "You've Got Possibilities" charted on this date for a four-week stay. It would peak at number 36.

July 30, 1966— ***Big Spender.*** The sultry *Big Spender* album debuted on the charts. It peaked at number 130 during its three-week stay.

July 18, 1966— ***Guitars ala Lee.*** *Guitars ala Lee* continued in the Latin-tinged realm of her previous "ala Lee" recordings. The album opened with two songs associated with Frank Sinatra. Peggy's "Nice 'n' Easy" was just that, and she gave "Strangers in the Night" a tender reading.

> Aside from Miss Lee's wonderful singing, the most striking thing about this album for me is the fact that at last someone has made something decent out of ... "Strangers in the Night" ... a few guitars and a rhythm section moving in a smooth bosa nova. Because of Grusin and Miss Lee's artistry, the song's lyric is less odious than usual.
> There's a stunning song on this album by Dick Manning and Luis Bonfa entitled "An Empty Glass" ... Miss Lee is superb with it. Also notable is a funky, rock-style song by Dallas Frazier called "Mohair Sam." Miss Lee is the only quality singer ... who can get down into this sort of material.—*High Fidelity* Magazine

The recording sessions for *Guitars ala Lee* were held on July 18, 22 and 26.

Fall and winter 1966 found Peggy making a flurry of television appearances.

September 15, 1966— ***The Dean Martin Show.*** Dean's guests were Peggy, Buddy Hackett, Dorothy Provine, Dan Rowan and Dick Martin. Lee soloed on "You've Got Possibilities" and "The Shining Sea." Dean and Peggy sang a medley of "All Alone,"

Another appearance on *The Andy Williams Show*. This time Al Hirt (left), Peggy and Jack Jones join Williams (in sweater). Here the quartet is seen singing "Smack Dab in the Middle." October 2, 1966. (NBC)

"Call Me," "I Couldn't Sleep a Wink Last Night" and "Good Mornin'." The entire cast performed a finale of songs from the Broadway musical *Guys and Dolls*.

October 2, 1966 — *The Andy Williams Show.* Peggy and Andy Williams performed a breathtaking duet of the Peggy Lee– Quincy Jones composition "Stay with Me." Peggy soloed on "Put the Blame on Mame." Lee joined Andy Williams, Jack Jones and Al Hirt for "Smack Dab in the Middle."

October 15, 1966 — "So What's New?" The Peggy Lee and John Pisano composition made the charts. It stayed for seven weeks, peaking at number 20.

October 22, 1966 — "Walking Happy." Peggy's second song to chart in October stayed on the charts for 11 weeks and peaked at number 14.

October 23, 1966 — *The Ed Sullivan Show.* Peggy sang "Nice 'n' Easy" and "Walking Happy" on this Sullivan appearance.

October 30, 1966 — *World Journal Tribune.* Journalist Robert Salmaggi reported "This Gal Goes by the Book":

> When this gold-topped gal is being caressed with a baby-blue spot, and lofting the inimitable Lee sound, you find yourself admiring the letter perfect precision of her act. The lead-in cues, the accord between vocalist and band, the split-second timing of the sound man, and the click lighting liaison, are the constant envy of Peggy's songbird contemporaries.
>
> It's because Peggy goes strictly by the book. Literally. It's a large, black-leather-bound looseleaf affair, jammed with neatly typed-and-mimeo'd notes and data, all lovingly compiled and looked after by Peggy's gal Friday, Phoebe Jacobs. If Peggy were to lose her "show-book" (and she did, for a few harrowing hours, just before a Copacabana stint last year), things wouldn't be half so sweet on stage. Peggy knows it: "That book is half of me — the better half."

November 27, 1966 — *What's My Line?* Peggy appeared on the popular celebrity panel game show.

November 1966 — The Copacabana. Her guest shot on *The Ed Sullivan Show* was to promote her annual appearance at the Copa. She sang her latest hit single, "Walking Happy." The phrase "Walk in Happy!" was used in the Copa's ads for the show.

Her opening at the Copa saw many celebrities in the audience, including football great Joe Namath. Following the show, Namath visited Peggy in her dressing room, telling her, "Wish I could play football like you sing."

December 21, 1966 — *The Danny Kaye Show.* Danny and Peggy performed a Christmas medley. "Here's That Rainy Day" and "So What's New?" were solos for Lee. "So What's New?" was written by Lee and John Pisano.

1967 — *Peggy Lee Songs for Singers.* This folio, published in 1967, contained thirteen of her compositions. The exact date of publication is unknown.

January 1967 — Diplomat Hotel, Florida. Peggy began the new year with her annual appearance at Florida's Diplomat Hotel. The critic for *Variety* found her to be "...working very easily on some fine charts, well read by the musicians, and is in full control as she styles her way through the show..." Next she would style her way through a very unique television appearance.

January 1967 — *Hi-Fi/Stereo Review.* Peter Rielly wrote "Peggy Lee: The Voice of Experience." This was largely a review of Peggy's *Guitars ala Lee* album:

> Miss Lee is too good and natural to bother with such nonsense as the vanishing American myth that a woman's attractiveness ends at the age of thirty. How could any young woman evoke the chilling finality of the opening phrase "Close the door" in the song "An Empty Glass?" ... And who else but someone who had lived and observed could inject the right note of ribald good humor into the delightful "Nice 'n' Easy"? There is a very healthy sort of earthiness here that has been a Lee strong

point since the long-ago "Why Don't You Do Right?" and it is a talent that, to my knowledge, has never been shared by any other young white female singer.

February 21, 1967 — The Girl from U.N.C.L.E. NBC's *The Girl from U.N.C.L.E.* was a hit show in 1967. The program, starring a young Stefanie Powers, was a spin-off of the highly successful *The Man from U.N.C.L.E.* The script for "The Furnace Flats Affair" called for a sultry Texas-born rancher named Packer Jo. Peggy was hired for the part.

She played Miss Jo with a touch of Mae West, her comedic talents coming to the fore as she flirted outrageously with co-star Noel Harrison. Public response to Peggy's character was so great it was rumored that MGM executives negotiated with Peggy for her own series based on Packer Jo, but the series never came to be.

March 9, 1967 — The Dean Martin Show. Peggy joined Dean for a medley of "You" songs, including "Just You, Just Me," "Exactly Like You," "For You," "The Very Thought of You," "You're Driving Me Crazy" and "Then I'll Be Happy." She sang "Three Little Fishes" with Martin and Joey Heatherton. Her solo moments came with "Walking Happy," "I Feel It" and "The More I See You."

May 1967 — Something Special. As with her 1965 *Something Special*, this 1967 update saw Peggy singing for an entire hour, backed by top musicians. A highlight of this program was her playful duet with Toots Thielemans.

Thielemans, the composer of the jazz waltz "Bluesette," played harmonica while Peggy sang "Makin' Whoopee." Lee's solos included "Things Are Swingin'," "Fever," "You Fascinate Me So," "Greensleeves," "Then Was Then and Now Is Now," "Come Back to Me," "So What's New?," "Big Spender," "Alright, Okay, You Win," "Mañana," "Unforgettable," "I Can't Stop Loving You," "Lonesome Road" and "Stay Well."

The show closed with Peggy's daring new rock rendition of "Lover." She was still an innovator.

June 6, 1967 — "***I Feel It.***" Peggy remained current by singing contemporary music by young composers like Randy Newman, Kris Kristofferson, John Lennon and Paul McCartney.

On June 6 she recorded a gentle pop-rock song entitled "I Feel It." The song was recorded during the sessions for her 1967 album *Somethin' Groovy*. It did not appear on that album; however, the single did make the charts.

June 1967 — Somethin' Groovy. The *Somethin' Groovy* LP was just that. Lee sang a wide variety of material in her singular fashion. In a review of that album that appeared in *Stereo Review* magazine, critic Rex Reed said that this record confirmed his belief that Peggy "...is one of the greatest magicians a good song could ever wish for.... [She] fashions an entirely new tone poem out of 'You Must Have Been a Beautiful Baby.'" Reed concluded that *Something Groovy* was a record of "largely expressive and perceptive songs sung with warmth and taste and an almost supernatural class."

July 19, 1967 — Roostertail, Detroit.

> She alternately shook 'em up with rhythm numbers and soothed 'em with the blues, withal maintaining a romantic mood. — *Variety*

September 30, 1967 — "I Feel It." "I Feel It" made the charts on this date. In a 10-week stay, it peaked at number eight.

October 1, 1967 — *The Ed Sullivan Show.* Peggy sang "I Feel It" and a spellbinding version of "The More I See You." This Sullivan appearance also included a medley of songs performed with Sergio Franchi and Nancy Sinatra. Peggy was currently performing at the Copa, where she sang "Somethin' Stupid," which had been a hit for Nancy and her famous dad.

October 1967 — The Copa

> The range of professionalism between a master of song like Capitol Records' Peggy Lee and a novice — everybody else — was never demonstrated better than Thursday night at the Copacabana nightclub.... One can't help getting the impression that she's a blues belter — or could be, or can be when she wants to be — but she has every note locked up tight and is in control. — Claude Hill, *Billboard*, October 14, 1967

October 22, 1967 — *Newark Evening News.* "Singer Peggy Lee 'Proves' Old Is New," author Daphne Kraft quotes Peggy:

> "One thing remains constant for me, whether I am giving a concert, living and experiencing a song in a nightclub, or singing for a recording. That is concentration about what the song means. That remains the same. Love must have an object, and it is the more gratifying and pleasing things that make me want to sing."

November 2, 1967 — *The Dean Martin Show.* Peggy performed her hard-driving rendition of "Lonesome Road." Then she became teary-eyed and romantic for an ethereal reading of the current hit "Alfie."

Prior recordings of this Burt Bacharach–Hal David song offered the listener very little. It was merely sound without substance. Peggy Lee was the first artist to really examine the lyric and bring forward its spiritual message; in her expert hands the song made sense. Unfortunately, she did not record her unparalleled interpretation.

November 3, 1967 — *Time* magazine. Parsimonious Peggy" was the title of this article (the author is unknown):

> A lavish spender in private life, Peggy Lee hoards her musical resources, parceling them out with a parsimony that makes every jot count. Her sound, never big or brassy, is growing thin at the top and breathy at the bottom. So she spends her notes ... with frugal selectivity but stylish aplomb.

Peggy clowns with Dean Martin (left) and Van Johnson, *The Dean Martin Show*, November 2, 1967. (NBC)

The anonymous author wrote that the 47-year-old singer has toned down her act "to a quieter hush" and "makes the lifting of an eyebrow do what other singers strike poses to accomplish."

Noting Peggy's ability to overcome her physical difficulties (including a crushed disk in her back and the pneumonia-damaged lungs that required periodic sessions with the compressed oxygen tank Peggy playfully christened "Charlie"), the writer concludes: "When her warm, smoky voice curls languidly around a lyric or teases it along with up-tempo jazz phrasing, familiar material reveals unsuspected meanings and yields new freshets of feeling. "There are always deeper layers to discover in a song," she says. "That's why I'm never bored." Neither are her listeners.

• FIVE •

Grammy Winner: 1968 to 1972

January 1968 — **Stereo Review magazine.** In *Stereo Review*, critic Rex Reed wrote:

> Honey-drippin', honey-sippin' Peggy Lee seems to turn out almost as many discs as Nancy Wilson.... But for my taste, they're all a welcome relief from the slush that piles up at my door every month.
>
> Have you ever seen her perform? The lights have to be just right, the gowns designed just right, the hair coiffed just right, the orchestra tuned just right, the mikes adjusted just right, the air-conditioning turned up just right (she generates a lot of heat) or she just doesn't go on. This does not mean she is temperamental; it simply means she is a perfectionist, one of the few performers who care. That perfection is the key to why she is just about the best singer in the business today, and why, like brandy in the cask, she gets better every year.

February 1968 — **Diplomat Hotel, Florida.**

> Miss Lee has her usually skillful control, style, poise, showmanship and total believability, and she combines the elements into as good a show as any femme singer puts on. — *Variety*

February 1968 — ***The Hollywood Palace.*** Peggy appeared on *The Hollywood Palace* with her friend Bing Crosby. She performed contemporary songs, including "What Is a Woman?," "Do I Hear a Waltz," and "Something Stupid." She and Bing sang a duet of one of her newer compositions "So What's New?"

March 7, 1968 — ***The Dean Martin Show.*** In addition to a medley with Dean, she soloed on "Come Back to Me" from the Broadway show *On a Clear Day You Can See Forever*. She also sang her own touching ballad "Here's to You." Written with Dick Hazard, "Here's to You" is a gentle waltz that salutes Peggy's audiences. It would be her closing number for years to come.

April 1968 — **Copacabana, New York.**

> Peggy Lee's sultry, jazz-oriented song style has been a national sound for more than a score of years.... Blues, jazz, folk, rock, standard — any and all are this girl's forte

... audience applaud wildly with ... a beg-off rendition of the liberal folk rouser, "Hand on the Plow."—*Variety*, April 17, 1968

April 1968 — **"Who's Got Soul?"** The April 1968 edition of *Esquire* magazine offered a photo essay that asked the question "Who's Got Soul?" The magazine defined "soul" in the following terms:

> As a life-style, soul has no color. The only rule is that a soulful person must be at harmony with himself and that everything he does must be an honest form of self-expression. Sound simple? Try it.

Photos showing celebrities were captioned with an explanation as to why *Esquire* felt the person did or did not have soul. Politicians Hubert Humphrey, Barry Goldwater and Richard Nixon did not have soul. Muhammad Ali got the rating of "He's all soul." Ray Charles received a similar rating, which stated that, "His inner eyes have 20–20 vision, and he sings the way he sees it. He *is* soul."

Singers who had soul included Sammy Davis, Jr. ("...he's still cool"), Lena Horne ("Sophisticated soul") and Lou Rawls ("Plenty of it"). Peggy was the only white female among the entertainers. *Esquire* wrote, "She's got more soul than Ella Fitzgerald. Peggy puts real savvy into a song."

April 1968 — ***Two Shows Nightly.*** Based on the past success of Peggy's annual Copa engagements, Capitol Records decided to record her April 1968 stint. The album was given the title *Two Shows Nightly*. Unfortunately, something went awry during the live recording. As a result, the sound quality was not up to Peggy's standards.

Lee attempted to salvage *Two Shows Nightly*, going into the Capitol studios to re-record her vocals. An applause track was added (for reasons unknown). The "looped" applause featured a discernible break, clearly evident to a vigilant listener. Capitol distributed several "free" copies of the album to disc jockeys and record promoters.

Peggy was still dissatisfied with the uneven and muddy sound. She pulled the album from release. Today a copy of *Two Shows Nightly* on vinyl is a treasured collector's item.

Two Shows Nightly was recorded on April 22, 23 and 24, 1968.

May 1968 — **Frontier Hotel, Las Vegas.**

> Her taste in repertoire is stunning and her involvement in music is total.... Being a musician and composer, Miss Lee can most effectively bring audiences into her personal sphere quickly and hold them fast until her final notes.—*Variety*, June 5, 1968

Spring 1968 — **Aretha Franklin.** The equally soulful Aretha Franklin spoke with Leonard Feather about Peggy Lee, awarding Peggy's hard-swinging version of "Hallelujah, I Love Him So" high marks:

Peggy and Bing Crosby on *The Hollywood Palace*, February 1968. Lee and Crosby sang a medley that featured "Do I Hear a Waltz?," "Sing a Rainbow," "Something Stupid" and Peggy's own composition "So What's New?" Peggy and Bing had been friends since the early 1940s. The famous singers performed duets on film, radio and television. (ABC)

Peggy Lee is always very tasty in her arrangements, and they're always very complimentary to her. It's a good song.... You're going to hear it completely different to the way you've previously heard it. She always picks something that's good for her.... Everything I've heard her do is very good.

June 1, 1968—*Melody Maker* **magazine (UK).** Longtime friend Leonard Feather wrote an article entitled "Peggy Lee Tries Some New Wine in Old Bottles" in which Lee spoke of her desire to remain contemporary. Feather ended his piece with these words:

> "Musician's musician" is a cliché-compliment too loosely thrown around among jazzmen. Peggy Lee, as a musician's musician and singer, has shown that perfectionism becomes her. In bringing it to the new sounds she displays the same matchless taste with which she has always graced the old.

July 1968— **The Consummate Artistry of Peggy Lee.** In an article for *High Fidelity* magazine jazz historian and songwriter Gene Lees discussed "The Consummate Artistry of Peggy Lee." Lees compared her to Sinatra, saying, "Sinatra and Miss Lee began to deliver songs as if they were spontaneous creations."

Calling her "...the most mature, the most authoritative, the most sensitive, and the most consistently intelligent female singer of popular music in America," Lees observed:

> As her act unfolds, you realize that Peggy Lee is a great actress. In one song, she'll be the fragile rejected girl of the Dick Manning–Luis Bonfa ballad "An Empty Glass." Then, with a wink and a bawdy wave of the arm, she becomes instantly the frowzy London hooker of "Big Spender." Then, perhaps, she'll become the mature woman finding love on a new level in "The Second Time Around...."
>
> To see a fine actress build a convincing characterization in the ninety minutes of a movie is impressive enough. But to see Peggy Lee build fifteen characterizations in the course of an hour is one of the most impressive things I've seen in show business.

September 1968— **New York, Copacabana.** A press clipping (dated October 5, 1968) noted that Peggy was still exploring new areas in music: "Newcomer-wise, she's unearthed some interesting material, including two Randy Newman numbers—both of which expand the pop-singing idiom—and a great supper-club ballad by Jimmy Webb, 'Didn't We.'"

During this run at the Copa, Peggy had a surprise for her audiences.

> Peggy Lee did something unusual at her big opening at the Copacabana ... after singing about 20 minutes, she introduced her drummer Grady Tate, who came out and sang "The Windmills of Your Mind," title song of *The Thomas Crown Affair* which he successfully recorded. Then Peggy resumed.—Earl Wilson, *It Happened Last Night*
>
> Peggy Lee, like all artists worth their salt, has never been static... she conquered the Big Band, Brazilian beat and rock eras because of tremendous natural talent and perseverance.... [S]he showed the stuff she's made of by dazzling the audience with a new wave performance that was effortless and full of surprises.— Robert Sobel, *Billboard*

***October 30, 1968**—Passaic Herald News*. Peggy spoke philosophically to Hal Boyle for his article "She's No Perfectionist":

> "To me life is awareness," said the silky-voiced singer, "awareness of everything possible—from music trends to world problems and the flowers in your garden.
>
> "People who don't stay aware eventually become vegetables. It would be awful—a waste of life not to be aware.
>
> "Live with as much love, humor and courage as you can—and try to learn from your experience.
>
> "I have the feeling sometimes that the public thinks I am sad because I sometimes sing sad songs," she said. "I have had sad times"—her three marriages ended in divorce—"but I have a sense of humor and love to laugh."

***Autumn 1968**—The Hits of Peggy Lee and Broadway ala Lee.* The year 1968 came to a close without the release of any new Peggy Lee albums. Two compilations are released, however—*The Hits of Peggy Lee* and *Broadway ala Lee* (a collection of the best songs from her *Latin ala Lee* and *Ole ala Lee* albums).

***January 26, 1969**—New York Daily News.* This first part of Ruth Kling's two-part article on Peggy was titled "The Singer's Singer":

> Peggy Lee is often referred to as the singer's singer. She is greatly admired and imitated by those starting out in show business as well as by those who have been around a long time....
>
> Her talents are many, although most people know her best for her beautiful voice. She makes frequent appearances in supper clubs, television and motion pictures and makes recordings, but she has also won acclaim as composer, artist, actress, writer and philanthropist.

***January 29, 1969**—"Is That All There Is?"* A new Peggy Lee single hits the airwaves. Leiber and Stoller, the team that gave Peggy her smash hit "I'm a Woman," wrote this new masterpiece, described by Eugene Boe as "a haunting Kurt Weill-ish minor key refrain." Of the song, Peggy said, "I've lived that whole thing. The fire, the circus, marriage—all of it." The fact that she had experienced the lyric first hand showed in her thoughtful and thought-provoking handling of the material.

"Is That All There Is?" almost didn't get recorded. Jerry Leiber and Mike Stoller had difficulty finding the correct artist to record it. The talented Leslie Uggams recorded the tune, but it didn't catch on with the public. Next the team offered it to Merv Griffin; he turned it down. Finally, it was brought to Peggy's attention.

She struggled with the song for a full year before deciding to perform it. The message of the lyric, if not handled properly, ran the risk of sounding depressing. Peggy went to the executives at Capitol to ask them if she could record the song. Capitol's powers-that-be told her, "No. The song is too long and too weird."*

Undaunted, Peggy recorded a demo of the tune and took it to Capitol founder Glenn Wallichs. He was appalled that she had gone to the trouble of making a demo,

---

*The Reporters, broadcast 1990.

telling her, "You helped build this company. You don't ever have to record a demo to convince anyone. You record whatever you like."

January 31, 1969—A Natural Woman. This album was a bold departure from her previous work on vinyl. She embraced the rock sound completely on this album. Her arrangers and conductors, Mike Melvoin and Bobby Bryant, surrounded her with all aspects of the "rock" experience.

There is the Rhythm and Blues sounds of Otis Redding's "(Sittin' on) The Dock of the Bay," the psychedelic-flavored rock of "Spinning Wheel," and the folk-rock of Randy Newman's "I Think It's Gonna Rain Today."

Other areas Peggy explored on the album were the gospel-tinged "A Natural Woman" and the pure, hard rock of Sly & the Family Stone's "Everyday People."

She also performed a painful, wailing rendition of the old Billie Holiday composition "Don't Explain." Her finest moment comes in Percy Mayfield's R & B classic "Please Send Me Someone to Love." When she sang, "Heaven please send to all mankind understanding and peace of mind," the lyric became an earnest prayer. "Please Send Me Someone to Love" is Peggy Lee at her dramatic best.

In addition to the January 1, 1969, recording date, there were also sessions on February 12, 15 and 28, 1969.

A Natural Woman received outstanding reviews, including the following:

> Peggy Lee can work with any vocal fashion and flatter it without betraying herself. What other white singer, for instance, can get into Ray Charles material on his terms as well as her own? I was wondering if she would care to interpret the latest fashion, and if so, how would she define it.
>
> Now we know. As usual, Miss Lee takes over once she decides to, singing market hits with more natural instinct than any other of our classic pop singers, including Frank Sinatra.—Morgan Ames, *High Fidelity*

> The amazing Peggy Lee of the impeccable taste, unfailing phrasing and versatile style continues to reveal an uncanny ability to adopt to every shifting mood of the music business with complete success.... Aretha Franklin's "A Natural Woman" is ... effective ... her cover of the Blood, Sweat & Tears "Spinning Wheel" has some funky sound all its own.... Incredibly enough she has managed to produce another album which is even better than her last one. Long may she continue to reign.—*FM Guide*

February 28, 1969—Is That All There Is? The single of "Is That All There Is?" spawned a Capitol album of the same name. Lee included the compositions of several new artists among the album's material. She sang Randy Newman's "Love Story" and "Johnny" (titled "Linda" when sung by a male). She rocked hard on Neil Diamond's "Brother Love's Travelling Salvation Show." In Peggy's hands, "Something," written by the Beatles' George Harrison, was treated warmly.

Lieber and Stoller were definitely indebted to Peggy Lee. In addition to "Is That All There Is," the album also included their earlier smash, "I'm a Woman," and another new Lieber-Stoller tune entitled "Whistle for Happiness."

Peggy's "Me and My Shadow" featured a superb arrangement by her guitarist Mundell Lowe. She also revisited her past hit "Don't Smoke in Bed," with a new, heart-breaking intensity. The material on the *Is That All There Is?* album completely lives up to the excellence of the title song.

Subsequent recording sessions for the *Is That All There Is?* album took place on April 5 and October 15, 1969.

February 23, 1969*—New York Daily News.* Part two of Kling's profile of Peggy was titled "Peggy's Career an Open Book":

> Peggy is a perfectionist about many things in her life, especially her performances. "I literally go by the book. It's a black loose-leaf book, filled with typed and mimeographed notes and data, all kept in order. I simply don't think I could function without it," she says.
>
> The book is a record of every show that Peggy has done for the past two decades, each song she sang, where the performance took place and what she wore.
>
> "I often want to revive a number or medley that really went over big with the audience, and having all the information at my fingertips saves so much time," Peggy explained.

March 1969*—* **Sherman House, Chicago.** One startling new addition to Peggy's repertoire was a song written by singer David Clayton-Thomas called "Spinning Wheel." She introduced the song during her appearance at the Sherman House. *Variety* said of this engagement "Everything she fashions seems easy and natural."

April 5, 1969*—* **Cue** **magazine.** Peggy's reign continued in regal fashion as she premiered the material from "A Natural Woman" at New York's Waldorf-Astoria Hotel.

Cue magazine journalist Eugene Boe revealed just how important this show was to Peggy. Boe's article, "Peggy Lee — An Artist Tunes Up for the Waldorf," described an afternoon rehearsal at Peggy's Beverly Hills home. The rehearsal was her fifth for the upcoming engagement at the Waldorf's Empire Room. The article explained how she remained up-to-date with musical trends:

> It can be argued that musically Peggy Lee is as hip a singer as they come ... she's also proof that the blacks by no means have a corner on soul, if soul signifies the capacity to feel — and project feeling — down to the fingertips and nerve endings.

For years Peggy had recorded the details of her act in a large notebook. Everything was accounted for there, including her hand gestures. Boe commented on the notebook:

> There it all is, the magnificent organization, like a military manual of Standard Operating Procedure. The programs for Chicago and New York, with alternate selections. The lyrics ... all the wardrobe and accessories that will fill a score ... of luggage. Memos. ("Important, Please Note: Need organ, timpani.") Lists of musicians in the cities where she performs....

When the afternoon rehearsal ended, a "party ambience" took over the Lee household. The musicians, journalist and friends—like neighbor and fellow jazz singer Carmen McRae—stayed for a buffet dinner.

April 6, 1969—*The Ed Sullivan Show.* On this Easter telecast Peggy introduced the nation to "Spinning Wheel." Seeing the elegant Miss Lee backed by dancers dressed in "hippie" garb and psychedelic lighting may have surprised some of her fans. It was apparent, however, that Peggy was in command of the material. There was no question now that Benny Goodman's former girl singer could indeed rock.

Lee also sang Aretha Franklin's hit "A Natural Woman," making it her own. Soon Capitol would release a single of "Spinning Wheel."

The flip side of the "Spinning Wheel" single contained a pure rock song written by Peggy, Mike Melvoin and guitarist Mundell Lowe. Lee, Melvoin and Lowe's "Lean on Me" was as gritty, driving and up-to-the-moment as "Spinning Wheel."

April 12, 1969—*New York Post.* The *Post*'s Bill Burrus wrote about Miss Lee's artistic abilities and philanthropic efforts in "Peggy Lee: At Fever Pitch":

> On the side, she is finishing a portrait of Moshe Dayan she is painting from photographs, because "he has a marvelous face." And she is a honorary national chairman of a fund campaign for the Salk Institute for Biological Research in San Diego.
>
> "It's the 15th anniversary of the Salk vaccine," Miss Lee said. "They are doing marvelous work at the institute. I went out there and I was thrilled," she said. "I felt if I could be of any help this summer I'd like to be."

April 1969—**Empire Room, Waldorf-Astoria, New York.** Peggy hadn't officially released "Is That All There Is?" when she opened at the Waldorf. She included the song in her act, and it was a hit with her audiences.

Eugene Boe continued to write about Peggy, this time in his "Nightlife" column for *Cue*:

> Peggy Lee packed such an emotional wallop strong men were reduced to tears. The standing ovation that greeted her finale was a genuinely spontaneous uprising.... What's predictable ... is the exciting musicianship. What's new — and she's always evolving — is the big leap into the contemporary idiom.... The sensation of the show is that new haunter, not yet recorded: "Is That All There Is?" Leiber and Stoller wrote it; Randy Newman gave it the super arrangement; and nobody but Peggy Lee could put it across half so well. It's *her* song.

Variety ran a full-page ad with quotes from various critics and stars. The critic for the *New Yorker* wrote, "There is only one singer who belongs in the Peggy League and that is Miss Peggy Lee herself." Petula Clark was quoted as saying, "It's Peggy Lee I patterned myself after. She's my favorite singer.... Peggy Lee is my musical bible."

June 1, 1969—*Family Weekly* **magazine.** As reported in *Family Weekly* magazine, Peggy was friendly with a cousin of Dr. Salk and asked to meet the doctor, saying, "Some of my favorite people are scientists; their sense of humor is really wild, and they have a great, quiet strength about them." Dr. Salk was impressed by the intelligent, spiritual singer and her humanitarian nature. Peggy was soon appointed chairman for Dr. Salk's "Tree of Life" foundation.

As she did with "Meals for Millions" and "The Thomas Dooley Foundation," Peggy would quietly support Dr. Salk's efforts for years. Shortly after she was named chairman she hosted a dinner dance for the foundation. As a result, the Salk Institute was benefited with $60,000.

July 13, 1969 — Los Angeles Times

"N.E.T. Plans Peggy Lee Special for Fall" was the headline of an article by Cecil Smith. David Prowitt produced this television special, filmed for educational TV. He had planned to do a documentary on Peggy for five years.

Peggy was shown at work, rehearsing her new nightclub act. Smith commented on Peggy's youthfulness, saying, "Maybe her music keeps her young. Between concerts and nightclubs, she is ever working at it, rehearsing, composing, writing lyrics. She's a painter and a poet, but more than anything else she is the singing voice of American life…"

Peggy is filmed at home, in rehearsal and in performance for a NET program. The special was broadcast on October 16, 1969.

Prowitt's cameras followed her as she previewed the new act at the Mark Taper Forum, located in the Los Angeles Music Center. The television crew would also follow her to Las Vegas and her premiere at the new International Hotel.

The warmth and love that she gave to, and received from, her audiences was attested to in every review.

> Peggy Lee, in 500-seat Casino Theatre, fared better preem-wise than did Miss Streisand, possibly because she's at home with live audiences, and because the room is pleasantly intimate. — Forrest Duke, *Variety*
>
> Reviews were surprisingly negative to La Streisand. Her patter was deary, her repertoire inappropriate, her delivery cold. Her numbers earned her only a smattering of applause, while Peggy Lee, in the smaller room a few hours later, received a standing ovation. — Joyce Haber, Hollywood
>
> Within hours after the opening of the International Hotel here, word went racing through New York show-biz circles that Barbra Streisand — the inaugural performer in the main showroom — had bombed. The acclaim a glossy first-night audience withheld from her it lavished extravagantly on Peggy Lee in the smaller Casino Theatre, giving her a moist-eyed, table-pounding, triple-standing-ovation send-off she could never forget.
>
> …One is warm and the other's chilly. One comes on humble and the other has

The 90-minute NET special shows Peggy receiving visitors in her dressing room backstage after a performance.

> that image of boastful, arrogant egocentricity. One receives love by giving it and the other apparently assumes love is a one-way street.— Eugene Boe, *Cue*

July 17, 1969*—Christian Science Monitor.* "Peggy Lee — Lyricist, Composer, and Singer" by Amy Lee graced this issue of the *Christian Science Monitor.*

> For refreshment she paints. For good purpose, also. "Paintings are so good for charity. They can be auctioned." In May she contributed several paintings for a benefit for retarded children in Los Angeles. For the dedication of the Hollywood Museum in 1962 she contributed 10 works of art....
> "My things are impressionistic, I guess you'd say. New York is my favorite subject. Now I'm painting small things, flowers in bowls, happy things."

October 11, 1969*—The Andy Williams Show.* This program also included guest stars Danny Thomas and Victor Borge. Peggy sang her current hit "Spinning Wheel." She joined Andy for a medley of California-themed songs, including "California Soul" and "California Dreamin'."

October 16, 1969*—The World of Peggy Lee.* Five days after the Andy Williams appearance, N.E.T.'s *The World of Peggy Lee* made its debut.

> The vocalist is seen in the labors of preparing a show and the giving of a performance.... She is in the best of form and the viewer also learns something, though far

from enough, about the individual herself.... [The program shows] Miss Lee, a composer herself, searching for the right interpretation of lyrics, working on her phrasing and seeking to preserve the overall mood of her choosing. The comparison with the early trials and the final results are a reminder that, be it jazz or classical music, the sheer physical toll of achieving a desired end is central to the act of creativity....— Jack Gould, *New York Times*

***October 1969*— Peggy Lee and Johnny Cash.** *The Kraft Music Hall* was a popular program in the 1960s and early '70s. At the end of October 1969, country music legend Johnny Cash hosted the show. Ben Gross, television critic for the *New York Daily News*, called Johnny and guest star Peggy "Two members of the royalty of song."

Gross went on to say that the two stars "brought distinction to the Music Hall last night." His review singled Peggy out with the following praise: "...[Miss Lee,] as always, put over her numbers in her familiar impeccable style, which is a merger of deep emotion and the restraint of good taste."

Peggy and Johnny Cash had tremendous admiration for each other. The Lady in White and the Man in Black appeared together on two television specials. This photograph is from the October 1969 broadcast of *The Kraft Music Hall*. Peggy sang her hypnotic new song "Is That All There Is?" She and Cash joined forces for a medley that included "Down in the Valley" and "Kisses Sweeter Than Wine."

Peggy sang "Is That All There Is?" on *The Kraft Music Hall*. She also performed it on her last television appearance of 1969.

***November 13, 1969*—*The Dean Martin Show*.** In addition to her new theme song, Peggy joined Dean for a medley that included "Zip-a-dee-doo-dah," "I Got Rhythm," and "Beer Barrel Polka."

By the time Martin's show aired, people were predicting that Peggy would win the Grammy for "Is That All There Is?"

December 13, 1969*—*Is That All There Is? Peggy's hallmark album arrived on the charts to stay for 18 weeks, peaking at number 55.

January 1970. This is how the critic for *Variety* summed up Peggy's first concert engagement of the 1970 season:

> Peggy Lee is not just a singer of songs. She's a complete musical artist. Each tune delivered shows meticulous detail. The complete picture is Peggy Lee with spot and stage lights illuminating the occasion of song.... She is not the same lady of song who frequents every TV show. From those video appearances it would never be suspected that she has a keen sense of humor. Apparently much of the chatter unleashed here was unrehearsed, because her mini-symphony orchestra reacted with laughter, much as did the audience.... Young singers should look to Miss Lee for professionalism in her approach to, and quality of, a vocal act.

***January 22, 1970*— *DownBeat* magazine.** Leonard Feather's "TV Soundings" discussed the N.E.T. television show:

> Her voice-overs were used here and there to point up certain aspects of the designing of her show. Lighting cues, electronics, the public address system, orchestration, transportation, and the rest were dealt with, never too technically, but in sufficient detail to assure an air of authenticity.
>
> Having watched Miss Lee at close quarters before several of these nervous opening nights, I can attest to the genuineness of the manner in which this insight was presented, even to the mandatory good-luck kissing of each musician, the last-minute ditching of an arrangement that didn't seem to work out, the great concern for pacing, the rest.

***February 17, 1970*— *Bridge Over Troubled Water*.** The album *Bridge Over Troubled Water* was released during her 50th year. Peggy's ever-contemporary material included Paul Simon's title song and nine others. She performed two popular songs by the team of Burt Bacharach and Hal David—"(There's) Always Something There to Remind Me" and "Raindrops Keep Falling on My Head." Her romantic "What Are You Doing the Rest of Your Life?" is the finest version ever recorded of the Legrand, Bergman and Bergman composition.

There was also a recording session for this album on February 20, 1970.

***March 1, 1970*— *The Ed Sullivan Show*.** For this broadcast, a tribute entitled "The Beatles Songbook," Peggy sang "Something" and a silly rendition of "Maxwell's Silver Hammer." She joined Dionne Warwick and Paul McCartney (via film) for a trio of "Yesterday."

In his "Second Look" column, critic Scott MacDonough wrote, "Faring best was Peggy Lee, whose renditions of the haunting 'Something' and the witty 'Maxwell's Silver Hammer' were flawless. But then, Miss Lee and the Beatles are musicians as well as singers, and exquisite ones at that."

***March 11, 1970*— *The 12th Annual Grammy Awards*.** "Is That All There Is?" won for "Best Contemporary Vocal Performance — Female." A grateful Peggy Lee accepted her award from presenters Glen Campbell and Della Reese. The single was nominated for "Record of the Year"; unfortunately, it did not win. However, it did win *Stereo Review*'s "Record of the Year" award.

Peggy accepts her Grammy Award from Glenn Campbell and Della Reese. Lee won for her singular rendition of "Is That All There Is?" The song won the Best Female Vocalist award for 1969.

March 26, 1970 — *The Dean Martin Show.* On Dean's show Peggy soloed on "Almost Like Being in Love" and "Watch What Happens."

March 30, 1970 — *The Carol Burnett Show.* Both the Martin and Burnett shows featured medleys saluting Peggy's compositions, including "I Love Being Here with You," "Mañana," and "It's a Good Day."

April 1970 — **The Waldorf-Astoria's Empire Room.** The Grammy winner wowed her audiences with "Is That All There Is?" Also included were "Raindrops Keep Falling on My Head," "Bridge Over Troubled Water" and "You'll Remember Me." These songs would all appear on her next album.

> She provides comfort with a demonstration of how to cater to audiences in intimate moments and still enjoy yourself as well. The lesson is amply appreciated. — *Variety*, April 15, 1970

April 18, 1970—New York Daily News.

> Some people have got upset over the fact that Peggy Lee's latest hit, "Is That All There Is?," is an uncredited musical version of a Thomas Mann story, "Disillusionment...."
>
> The criticism upsets her and puts an expression in her face that might be a glower if it were stepped up a few notches in intensity, but it doesn't interfere with her delivery of the song in her act at the Waldorf-Astoria's Empire Room.
>
> Look at it this way: How many people did Mann reach with his story and how many does Peggy reach? If the aim is communication, there's no contest.

April 26, 1970—The New York Times. In the article "Peggy Lee Is Still on Top—Is That All There Is?" Peggy discussed adjusting to the rock scene with journalist Judy Klemesrud:

> "When rock first came in, I was very upset," she says, emphasizing her words with left-hand jab into the air. "I felt very insecure, and I turned it off whenever it came on the radio. When you feel left out of something, you don't like it at all."

Klemesrud pointed out: "Critics say that one of Peggy's strengths through the years is that she is such a good actress *while* she is singing; she *thinks* about every lyric." Peggy commented on her thought process during a song:

> "I guess you could compare it to the way an actor or actress works," she says. "I draw on memories or my subconscious while I am singing. To me, each song is like a little story. Sometimes, when I get into the mood of a song, I almost start to cry. I did cry once during a show, on 'Don't Explain.' I had heard that a friend was ill, and I was feeling very bad."

April 29, 1970— **Duke Ellington's 70th birthday.** While in New York Peggy performed at a star-studded show honoring her beloved friend Duke Ellington. The NAACP sponsored the event. Peggy opened the show, which took place at Madison Square Garden. Also performing that night were Sammy Davis, Jr., Ray Charles, Roberta Flack, Leslie Uggams, Louis Armstrong, Stevie Wonder and B.B. King.

May 26, 1970— **Peggy Lee's 50th birthday.** Peggy decided to disguise her birthday with a lavish circus theme. Her home on Tower Grove Drive was transformed with a huge tent and authentic circus items. Guests were instructed to come as clowns. Fred Astaire's longtime choreographer, Hermes Pan, and Rita Hayworth won Peggy's "Best Costume" award. Peggy would laugh about this party years later, asking, "Have you ever seen 150 clowns in one room?"

June 6, 1970—Bridge Over Troubled Water. The album debuted on the charts on this date and stayed there for nine weeks, peaking at number 142.

June 1970— **Royal Albert Hall, London** (UK). In June 1970 Peggy made a triumphant return to England. Her engagement at London's Royal Albert Hall was sold-out. This was the first time her fans in the UK heard Peggy's new sound in person.

June 1, 1970—*Variety* (UK).

It would have been understandable if Peggy Lee ... had chosen to play it safe by giving her fans a nostalgic selection of her past hits. However, it was a measure of the smoky-voiced songstress' integrity and courage that she concentrated on contemporary material.... As an interpreter of modern love songs, she is close to perfection. Her affinity to the roots of jazz, often underplaying but always present, enabled her to rejuvenate jaded and trite lyrics.—*Variety*, June 1, 1970

June 20, 1970—*Guardian* (UK).

"The first thing is that you don't just walk on to the stage and sing. I produce maybe three new shows a year and each one takes months of work. First we have to edit the new songs, rejecting some of them but with the promising ones, trying to see how to interpret them best."

"Then we work on the song with the rhythm group, to get interpretation in more detail, to get the style right for me. Once that is done we probably do a cassette for the arrangers so that they can see what we are aiming at. We might work for two hours on four bars or we might work all day and still reject the song at the end. Then there are some that don't fit when you get on the actual stage you are using, that somehow are not suited to the room — so you have to put another in."

June 21, 1970—*Daily Telegraph* (UK). Journalist and jazz critic Peter Clayton shared his experience of seeing Lee in rehearsal in his article "Unsquare Peg":

Watching a singer rehearse has the same collusive intimacy about it as staying for breakfast. It was good to be able to stand close and hear how that disturbingly erotic sound is made, how she glides languidly into a note the way the late Johnny Hodges used to. Not that there was much actual singing on Friday, which was mostly devoted to getting the measure of the hall.

June 21, 1970—*London Times* (UK). Philip Oakes took a trip to Peggy Lee country in "On the Lee Side":

Peggy Lee country lies on the edge of night-town, jumpy with sexual encounter and parting, sometimes jubilant, always electric. She celebrates good times and bad with an extraordinary awareness. She summons mood and meaning, incident and occasion with total assurance. She offers a sentimental education: passes guaranteed.

June 23, 1970—*London Times* (UK).

She has this enchanting manner of whispering, half-teasing the words of a song, and employs her jazz training in the superb manner of handling a lyric. How much the shrill-voiced young pop singers of today could learn from her.—Michael Wale, *London Times*, June 23, 1970

July 21, 1970—*Make It with You.* Arranger Benny Golson and Peggy teamed for her next Capitol release. Songwriter David Gates' current hit provided the albums title song. Other contemporary offerings included C.C. Courtney and Peter Link's "Let's Get Lost in Now," Lennon and McCartney's "The Long and Winding Road," and Paul Anka's "That's What Living's About." As a songwriter, Peggy contributed

"Passenger of the Rain," a sad rainy-day love song she had written with Francis Lai for the film *Rider on the Rain*.

Peggy paid tribute to her former boss Benny Goodman on this album. The final song is an ethereal rendering of Goodman's theme "Good-Bye."

Variety reviewed her *Make It with You* album, saying in part, "Miss Lee delivers with her easy beat on the rhythm numbers and projects the atmospheric ballads with her usual savvy."

The critic for *Playboy* magazine stated that, "Peggy Lee, who has been making all the right sounds for many a moon, has a new LP, 'Make It with You,' that is super-right.... If you're looking for a beautiful album, head Leeward."

Other recording dates for *Make It with You* included February 20, August 5 and August 27, 1970.

July 27, 1970 — Wollman Rink, Central Park, New York City.

On July 25, 1970, *Cue* magazine awarded Peggy its Salute of the Week:

> The incomparable Miss Peggy Lee, the lady with the after-midnight voice, is back in town to sing it at the people, in a one-night appearance at the Schaefer Festival in Central Park on July 27th. In recent interviews, Miss Lee has often expressed concern that her fans and friends can't afford to see her... frustrating the beautiful love affair between her and her fans. So she's decided to go a lot heavier on the outdoor concert thing.... We like it just fine... our admiration for the Lady Lee knows no bounds.

Peggy's two shows at the Schaefer Festival on the evening of July 27, 1970, were a huge success. The concert venue could hold up to 10,000. So many showed up to see Peggy that hundreds had to be turned away; they sat out on a grassy area where they could still hear her over the sound system.

> ...Miss Peggy Lee put on one hell of a show in Central Park. The lady has never been in better form, and the overflow crowd loved every minute of her show ... She is that rare kind of artist who makes every song sound as though it were written for her — not just her own steamy "Fever," but Burt Bacharach's lilting "Raindrops," the hard, sad "Remember Me," the wistful, quiet "What Are You Doing the Rest of Your Life," and the brash, sexy "Hey, Big Spender." The audience, a delirious mix of young and old, simply wouldn't let her leave the stage. — Nancy Hughes, *Cue*, August 8, 1970

August 10–20, 1970 — The Racquet Club, Sheraton Hotel, Hyannis, Massachusetts.

September 23, 1970 — *The Kraft Music Hall.*

> Anthony Quinn, the compelling actor ... [and] Peggy Lee, the sultry singer, were paired last night.... A performer such as Mr. Quinn can hold his own with Miss Lee, no slouch herself in understanding that lyrics are no less important than a beat. In their climactic rendition, the duet managed to capture the elusive durability of love, no matter what the reasons. It was a strangely effective and poignant oddity... Miss

> Lee is a winning and experienced hand in retrieving awkward moments by drifting into a song that eases the strain.—Jack Gould, *New York Times*

The songs Peggy drifted into included "What Is a Woman?," "Love Story," "Don't Explain," "Me and My Shadow," "He's Got the Whole World in His Hands," "Lost in the Stars," "But Beautiful," "I'm Glad There Is You," and "Until It's Time for You to Go." The most riveting of these was her stark, tension-filled reading of "Don't Explain." This was musical theater-of-the-mind at its highest level.

***Autumn 1970*—*The Glen Campbell Show*.** Peggy performed George Harrison's "Something." She joined Campbell for a duet of "Leaving on a Jet Plane." The original airdate for this show is unknown.

Lee also appeared on *The Tonight Show* and *The David Frost Show* at this time. Again, the date of the broadcasts are unknown. David Frost devoted an entire 90-minute show to Peggy. She performed songs with co-composer Cy Coleman.

September 23, 1970 — Peggy and Anthony Quinn join forces on *The Kraft Music Hall*. Lee wrote the script for the program, entitled "A Man and a Woman."

***Autumn 1970*— Peggy and Johnny Cash.** Lee and Cash were re-united when she visited his television show in Nashville. This time their natural chemistry illuminated Kris Kristofferson's song "For the Good Times." Peggy's solos included the sultry "I'm a Woman" and her new single "One More Ride on the Merry-Go-Round."

***October 5, 1970*—*Senior Scholastic*.** "Roy Hemming Interviews Peggy Lee" was the title of this article. Hemming wrote about Lee's continued success and popularity:

> You can count on one hand the number of singers who were popular 20 or 25 years ago and who still are — especially with "the kids" who determine the Top 40. Peggy Lee is one of them.
> What's kept her on top? A uniquely warm and communicative style, to begin with. Also an ability to do more than keep up with changing trends, but to recognize the best of the newcomers and new things. That's why Peggy was singing the songs of the Beatles, Jim Webb, Randy Newman and others long before everyone else got on their bandwagons. As composer-arranger Johnny Mandel has said: "Peggy is one of the few singers who can bridge the generation gap without making it sound like a tree graft."

December 9, 1970—***Petula.*** While in London, Peggy taped a television special with Petula Clark. Petula, a devoted Peggy Lee fan, was thrilled to work with her musical hero:

> "She is definitely my favorite singer. We had a relationship before we ever met. She's unbelievable! I can hardly believe that it's happened — that I'm actually singing with her. I've admired her for so many years and it's almost like a dream come true to find myself singing with her. We make a funny sound together. I think Peggy got it right when she turned to me and said, 'We sound like four girls instead of two.'"

The December 10, 1970, issue of *Variety* contained the following:

> ..."Petula" featured another rare talent, Peggy Lee. The two teamed for "I'm a Woman," "Wedding Bell Blues," and an extremely moving "When Johnny Comes Marching Home" ... Watching Peggy Lee lying propped up in a brass bed, rain dripping from the windows and a man sleeping silently beside her as she sings "What Are You Doing the Rest of Your Life?" is nothing short of beautiful. One doesn't even dare breathe loudly or even sigh. When professionalism like hers is put to use like this it is a joy.

Winter 1971— **Peggy Lee, professional painter.** The following is an excerpt from Dave Dexter's autobiography *Playback*:

> I received a query a while back from the Sylvania firm in Chicago asking if I could recommend a "big name star" capable of painting a series of oils which they would reproduce in full color and offer as a premium to persons purchasing their new television sets.
>
> Sylvania received her four lovely still-lifes three weeks later. It took only a little longer for Peg to get a check for $5,000 in the mail. Everyone was pleased.

In addition to giving prints of Peggy's paintings to their customers Sylvania also created a new Peggy Lee album. The special collection, entitled *The Sounds of the Seventies* included a full color artist's portfolio.

February 1971— **Palmer House, Chicago.**

> As always, Miss Lee's turn is virtually a dissertation on introspection ... accomplishing much with apparent little effort, depending upon consummate skill at shading and phrasing to achieve strong ends.... [She offers] thoughtful commentaries on the various emotional levels of interpersonal relationships, with some numbers imbued with an undeniably restrained but nevertheless spirit-lifting enthusiasm, while others are cloaked with moving poignancy.—*Variety*, February 24, 1971

March 1971— **The Empire Room, Waldorf-Astoria, New York.** In addition to "Is That All There Is?" Peggy sang several songs from the *Make It with You* album, including: "You'll Remember Me," "Let's Get Lost in Now" and "Good-Bye." Another new song was Joe Raposo's "Sing," which she would record several months before the hit version by the Carpenters.

> Miss Lee's performance seems the epitome of simplicity and directness. There are no gimmicks, no big productions. She just sings ... in an understated, low-keyed fash-

ion. Yet within this seemingly constricting range, she finds an astonishing variety of colors and emotions.... It is a model of what one hopes a popular singer's presentation will be but very rarely is.—John S. Wilson, *The New York Times*, March 31, 1971

One of Miss Lee's major attributes is her attention to musical detail. With her pianist-conductor Lou Levy, she brings in one of the most polished music crews in the industry.... This outfit, when necessary, cradles her, spurs her on, and helps burnish her turn to its top brightness....—*Variety*, March 24, 1971

When Peggy left the Empire Room she traveled on to the Shoreham Hotel in Washington, D.C. This was followed by an engagement at the Frontier Hotel in Las Vegas. She returned to Los Angeles for an appearance on *The Pearl Bailey Show*.

Lee's solos on the Bailey program included "My Sweet Lord" and the déjà vu love song "I Was Born in Love with You."

April 1, 1971—*The Dean Martin Show.* Peggy sang her current hit "One More Ride on the Merry-Go-Round." Dean joined her for a medley of "Together Again," "For the Good Times," and "Raindrops Keep Fallin' on My Head."

April 5, 1971—*Where Did They Go?* **Album.** *Where Did They Go?* offered several top-notch Lee performances. "My Rock and Foundation" was not "imitation Bacharach-David," it is the real thing, with a buoyant Peggy Lee vocal. She becomes a vulnerable young woman on Kris Kristofferson's "Help Me Make It Through the Night." She shines on "I Don't Know How to Love Him" from the Broadway musical *Jesus Christ, Superstar*.

Side two contains three highlights. Peggy made Stephen Sondheim's "Losing My Mind," from the Broadway show *Follies*, sound better than it actually was. Her rocking rendition of George Harrison's "My Sweet Lord" lifted the record off the turntable, ending with a triumphant "Hallelujah!" The aforementioned "I Was Born in Love with You" is another example of how beautifully Peggy sang the works of Michel Legrand (with lyrics by Marilyn and Alan Bergman).

Additional recording sessions took place on April 6 and May 11, 1971.

May 13, 1971—*DownBeat*: "Grady Tate: He'd Rather Sing."

> Mention of Peggy Lee led to a question about Tate's association with the singer. It was Miss Lee who really let him be heard as a singer by very graciously giving him a spot in her show.
>
> "You know, that was not only a great thing Peggy did for me, it was also unprecedented," was his response. "Singers are a funny lot. The stage is all theirs... quite often they don't want anything that has the remotest chance of upstaging them.... But Peggy Lee is a beautiful lady... She is first and foremost a musician and because of that she wants everything to enhance the whole of her show. She wants the band to be the best, the charts as hip as possible. I have a great deal of love for Peggy. She is a beautiful, beautiful person.
>
> "The way the singing thing came about was that after each night's show we would congregate in Peggy's suite. One night she decided she wanted all of us to sing with her. By us, I mean the guys in the band, the guys she calls her 'jewels.' She seemed to

like my voice and said that there should be a place for me on the stage and that she would present me. And that's exactly what she did. It's funny, my first singing engagement was at the Copa, so where do you go from there? It's like starting at the top."

May 25, 1971—*New York Daily Mirror.* Peggy wrote an article for the *New York Daily Mirror* in which she speaks of her love for her audiences:

> Audiences are really the most important things in performing, and I feel a great sense of responsibility to them. If you can't capture your audience, the best musical material in the world won't be of any help to you.
>
> You can't just stand up there like a star saying, "Here I am." You have to give to an audience. Some of our younger performers haven't learned this yet. I guess I'm kind of old-fashioned. I'm very hard-working and low-keyed. I love to talk and sing to an audience as if they were my friends.

July 1971—"Where Did They Go?" Single. "Is That All There Is?" was released in 1969. Almost a full two years later, Capitol decided to do a "follow-up" single. A press clipping from July 1971 stated: "Peggy Lee's latest Capitol single has for its plug side a tune, 'Where Did They Go?,' that is a blatant and awful attempt by an unknown to repeat the success of the Lieber-Stoller 'Is That All There Is?' that worked so well for her last year. The flip side, 'All I Want,' is imitation Bacharach-David but serves her much better."

July 6, 1971—Louis Armstrong Dies. On July 6, 1971, the world received the sad news that international jazz legend Louis Armstrong had died. The funereal was held on July 9 at the Corona Congregational Church in Queens, New York.

Peggy was invited to sing "The Lord's Prayer." Louis' lifelong friend Ella Fitzgerald was also asked to sing. Ella declined, stating that she would be too emotional to get through a song.

Peggy almost demurred as well, feeling that the song was not within her range. When a Science of Mind friend told her that she had to do it, and that she would help her with positive prayer, Peggy felt that she was "lifted" up to the high notes.

That evening *CBS News* hosted a tribute to Louis Armstrong. Footage of Peggy singing "The Lord's Prayer" was part of the program. Then Peggy joined a "Who's Who" of jazz in the CBS studio. The group reminisced about the man they called "Pops" with Charles Kuralt. Then, backed by Earl Hines, Buddy Rich, Bobby Hackett, Tyree Glenn, Dizzy Gillespie, Milt Hinton and Budd Johnson, Peggy sang "I Can't Give You Anything but Love."

July 1971—*The Merv Griffin Show.* Peggy and Tony Bennett are Merv's only guests for the 90-minute program. The two jazz greats performed Joe Raposo's "Sing" together. Peggy also sang three solos: "Things," "If" and "All I Want."

July 19, 1971—Schaefer Music Festival. Peggy performed for capacity crowds in Central Park on July 19, 1971. The concert was followed by engagements at the Latin Casino in New Jersey and the Racquet Club at the Sheraton-Hyannis Inn.

"A tribute to Louis Armstrong" was broadcast on the night of Louis Armstrong's funeral, July 9, 1971. Peggy is seen here with an all-star line-up of jazz musicians: Tyree Glenn (trombone), Milt Hinton (bass), Buddy Rich (drums), Budd Johnson (saxophone), Bobby Hackett (cornet), Dizzy Gillespie (trumpet) and Earl "Fatha" Hines (piano). The fact that these legendary jazz musicians invited Peggy to sing with them speaks volumes about the esteem in which she was held. Host Charles Kuralt is seen on the far left.

***August 1971—Companion* magazine.** The *Companion* piece, written by Robert Amsel, was titled "Peggy Lee: If That's All There Is, It's More Than Enough." Peggy discussed numerous topics with Amsel, including what she tried to bring to each show:

> "I can't be upset by anything before I do a show. It may sound corny, but I try to bring to each show a feeling of love that I hope is conveyed to the audience. Just within the last few years, I've felt more the value of trying to make each appearance as special as possible. I think I have been able to do this because I've been singing so long."

She expressed her amazement at, and appreciation of, the rapt attention her audiences gave her, noting:

> "But sometimes when I sing, it's so silent that it almost—frightens would be the wrong word. I sort of stop and say to myself, 'What are they listening for? I'd better have it—whatever it is.'"

Amsel concluded his insightful profile by recalling the praise Peggy received from another showbiz legend:

> ...Perhaps one of her greatest tributes came from actress-singer Marlene Dietrich. After one of Peggy's performances several years back, Miss Dietrich left the audience, came on stage, knelt down and kissed Peggy's hand. It was homage paid by one great lady to another.
> In a book Marlene wrote, she described Peggy Lee thusly: "Honey-dripping, singing, timing, phrasing; awakening no memories of other voices but awakening all the senses to a unique feast."

***September 1971—Cosmopolitan* magazine.** Larry King, writing for *Cosmopolitan* magazine, explored the downside of show business. His article on Peggy, titled "Rapping with Peggy Lee," offered insight into the demanding world of touring and performing.

This revealing look at Peggy, and the stress under which she frequently performed, may have shocked some fans. However, King's piece is illuminating, giving the reader some idea of what Peggy endured in order to remain on top:

> "She works. Lord, how that woman works," King marvels, citing hours spent each day with public relations experts, lawyers, managers, and musicians. "Life is a dim rehearsal hall ... chain-smoking and sometimes looking a bit wan, taking her numbers from the top again and again—compulsively seeking perfection."

Ultimately, this profile reveals just how lonely life can be for a star who "drew thirty thousand to a concert at Expo in Montreal and ten thousand to an outdoor concert in New York's Central Park":

> One has the notion she feels a compulsion to communicate, as she does with an audience, but prefers to keep her relationships at a distance. There are other clues that, having achieved fame, she sometimes thirsts for a long-lost anonymity. Leaving Washington for her Cherry Hill engagement in a charter bus, she enthused over a lovely green park and its displays of flowers: "Oh, I'd love to sit in that park for an hour. Just goofin'...." Then why don't you? She looked startled: "Oh, no, it wouldn't work...."

***October 19, 1971—Look* magazine.** In "Peggy Lee — The Name Is Woman," Charles Mangel wrote of the Montreal concert, where she drew thirty thousand fans:

The afternoon before the concert in Montreal, heat was building up under the band shell, and a humid wind played with the sheet music. Peggy Lee and 20 musicians worked on arrangements of songs each already knew well. Would an emphasis here be handled better by a reed? What about a tuba there? A violin? The work in the sun went on, polishing musical nuances. Peggy Lee could have been back at the hotel. But instead she chose to lead the band.

***October 1971—* Kennedy Arts Center, Washington, D.C.** Peggy was invited to be the first performer at the Center's presentation of "The Art of the American Jazz and Pop Singer." Albert Goldman covered the event for *Life* magazine. His title referred to Peggy as "A Queen on a Lonely Peak":

A rare outdoor portrait by John Engstead.

A remarkable performer who has sustained herself for an astonishing total of 30 years in a business that takes its toll swiftly and often fatally, Miss Lee and her music now represent one of the peaks to which popular art has climbed in America.

October 1971— the Fairmont Hotel, Dallas, Texas.

There are legends and there are legends. Miss Peggy Lee is a legend among legends. Time has a way of standing still when listening to Miss Lee. The huge, overflowing audience in the hotel's showroom instantly was silenced when she appeared and remained thus until they could control their admiration no longer.— Mike Alexander, *Dallas Times Herald*

She takes full measure of all the sensuality inherent in the lyrics of "Help Me Make It Through the Night" and handles the exquisite "If" in such a fragile, tender style that one false note would have shattered the effect. Miss Lee, though, seems incapable of false notes, either emotional or musical.— Phillip Wuntch, *Dallas Morning News*

November 1971— Mill Run Playhouse, Chicago.

For years I have pondered the mystique of this extraordinary person, certainly no great singer in purely vocal terms. But she grows steadily more captivating with her straightforward, but always prismatic, vocalism and a technique that allows her to whisper a song that others shout in order to hold an audience. In Miss Lee's case, her sotto voce is spell-binding.— Sam Lesner, *Chicago Daily News*

December 12, 1971— *New York Times.* John Lissner's insightful record review for the *New York Times*, entitled "Lady Day and Peggy Lee," reads:

Miss Peggy Lee ... has successfully survived in show business without abandoning the musical ground rules she learned as a vocalist with Benny Goodman.... In an interview with author-musicologist Henry Pleasants, Miss Lee once stated: "Band singing taught us the importance of interplay with musicians. We had to work close to the arrangement.... I learned more from the men I worked with in the bands than I've learned anywhere else. They taught me discipline and the value of rehearsing and how to train."

Some of the best moments of that early Goodman-Lee collaboration are now available on a recent re-issue, *Miss Peggy Lee* (Harmony H 30024).

Lissner notes that the "sexy, cashmere-like quality Miss Lee has developed over the years" is already evident in such songs as "All I Need Is You," "My Old Flame," and "The Way You Look Tonight." He observes the influence of other singers ("a bit of Holiday phrasing, some smoky strains a la Lee Wiley on 'I Got It Bad and That Ain't Good'") and concludes that "it is the bright up-tempo numbers that are the big kick as Peggy sings and swings with a natural, easy gait on 'We'll Meet Again,' 'Elmer's Tune,' 'Not a Care in the World,' and her big moment with Goodman, 'Why Don't You Do Right?'"

Peggy arrives in Dallas for her first appearance in that city, October 21, 1971.

January 5, 1972 — *The Carol Burnett Show.* Peggy sang one of her favorites, "Sing a Rainbow," from the film *Pete Kelly's Blues.* She also joined Carol for a medley, including "Happy New Year," "Great Day," and "Something's Coming."

February 17, 1972 — *Owen Marshall, Counselor at Law.* Peggy played the part of singer Jenny Rush. The *New York Daily News*' Kay Gardella wrote an article promoting the show, whose episode is titled "Smiles from Yesterday."

> Miss Lee, over 50 now, but still soft, sweet and womanly, will portray a former singer-songwriter who becomes involved in a music plagiarism suit…. Co-starring with her … are Hoagy Carmichael and Joe Campanello. The title song, written by the show's producer, Jon Epstein, and Jerry McNelly, will receive a voice-over rendition by Miss Lee, who otherwise will confine herself to acting in the hour drama.

January 15, 1972 — Playboy Club, McAfee, New Jersey.

March 6–25, 1972 — Empire Room, Waldorf-Astoria, New York. Earl Wilson reported: "She gets standing ovations at the Waldorf Empire Room."

March 18, 1972 — *The New Yorker* magazine. *The New Yorker* magazine ran a "The Talk of the Town" piece titled "Miss Peggy Lee." Snooky Young, Count Basie's lead trumpet player for many years, was with Peggy for this engagement and he talked about her professionalism:

> "Some singers don't go to rehearsals — they leave it to the conductor, and then come in after everything is ready," Mr. Young said. "But Peggy is always there. She knows just what she wants. We're supposed to be here for three or four hours today, but you watch. We won't be out of here before six."

According to the article, Peggy arrived at one on the dot. She opened her notebook and began the rehearsal. The working relationship between Peggy and her musicians was described as follows:

> Throughout the rehearsal, Miss Lee spoke to the musicians in a gentle, friendly way, but she spoke to them often. She stopped "Fire and Rain" several times because a guitar figure didn't sound right, and she hummed what she wanted until she got it.

When asked about her reputation as a perfectionist, Peggy answered:

> "Well, it's true that I'm interested in the whole process of the show … the gowns, the lighting, and especially the music. Now, you don't have an audience of musicians, but the music still has to be just right…. I think the audience enjoys it more if it comes off well, simply because I enjoy it more…. I think preparation is the key to the whole thing."

This article concluded with Peggy's entrance into the Empire Room that night. A few minutes before the show, "her expression was grim." This in spite of a phone call from her "good-luck token — Cary Grant." Then the magic of a live performance took over and all her hard work paid off:

She was transformed. Her eyes flashing ... she looked happy ... full of herself. Halfway up the ramp, she caught the eye of a moonstruck male fan, paused for a second, and made a mischievous, catlike gesture at him with her long fingernails. Then she was before the mike and into her first tune. We knew instantly that everything that had looked ragged a few hours before would be made smooth, and it was.

Other critiques of this performance include the following:

The voice seems able to do anything she wants, with no apparent effort; the phrasing is always provocative and low-key. The trappings, the ambience may be a bit rococo, but the lady herself is a magnificent understatement. You couldn't imagine Peggy Lee reaching for a note, could you? Or straining for an emotion? Never. She heats you up without once losing her cool.—Jerry Parker, March 8, 1972, *Newsday*

Her catalog seems to be one of the longest she has brought around. Miss Lee makes it evident that her accomplishments in many varieties of tunes are considerable. She brings to the Waldorf floor a transcription of a Carl Sandburg poem and an adaptation of the Spanish "Romanza." There are the oldies that she wrote including "Mañana" and others that make her an ASCAPer of considerable impact.—*Variety*, March 15, 1972

March 20, 22 and 24, 1972—*New York Post.* Journalist Alfred G. Aronowitz penned a three-part article on Peggy for the *New York Post*. The series was titled "Miss Peggy Lee." Gossipy in nature, the article reveals nothing.

From Part One: At the Empire Room, she sang James Taylor's "Fire and Rain," George Harrison's "My Sweet Lord," Carole King's "I Feel the Earth Move" and a medley of her own hits, including "Why Don't You Do Right?" "Is That All There Is?" and "Fever." She recited poetry of Carl Sandburg and Lois Wyse and she asked for requests. "You're beautiful, you're beautiful," she told the crowd. She sang "Sing a Rainbow" and she sang "I Love Being Here with You."

April 12, 1972—Elmwood Casino, Windsor, Ontario.

The Mother Superior of Jazz with quick, breathy introductory patter between numbers, moves through James Taylor's "Fire and Rain," vaults an uptempo "Just in Time," offers a strong "My Sweet Lord," but doesn't forget to give the folks a shot of her own "Fever," along with "Mañana," "Hey, Big Spender" and others.—*Variety*

April 24, 1972—*Norma Deloris Egstrom from Jamestown, North Dakota.* Peggy's final Capitol album was released in the summer of 1972. She had recorded it in April. Rumor has it that she wanted to call the album *Super Bitch*. Was this her wicked sense of humor, or her anger at being dropped by the Capitol label? A few album copies carried a pink *Super Bitch* sticker on the cover.

It is evident from the first track that Peggy Lee had reached another artistic peak, as she gave every song in this superb collection an incandescent light. This album, the author's all-time favorite, truly shines.

Jazz critic Peter Reilly wrote a full-page review for the October 1972 issue of *Stereo Review*. The insightful piece discussed the album, Peggy's craft and the changing climate of the recording industry:

Class, in every aspect, has always been a Lee hallmark. She is at her classiest — and sexiest — here in "Someone Who Cares." She treats the mountingly emotional lyric lines with the leisurely expertise of a Colette heroine, all the while underlining them with that insistent vocal eroticism she is famous for, finally exploding into a rock coda. "Just for a Thrill" is a different kind of sexiness, reminiscent of her earliest recording days, the long, lazy jazz line projected with great humor and immaculate musicianship. "Razor (Love Me as I Am)" is more vintage Lee — only she, I think, could so nonchalantly drop the line "You can love me as I am/or goodbye" and still leave so many inviting options open.

Reilly went on to discuss the youth-oriented entertainment industry. Whether or not he knew that Capitol had dropped Peggy when he wrote the article is irrelevant.

He was speaking with searing honesty when he addressed the fact that recording industry executives felt that the "...future lies with acceptance by the younger generation." He felt, and rightly so, that in Peggy's case this concept was not valid, based on the following reasons:

> First, I don't think it matters whether you are young or old; if you know quality, you will like Lee. Second, Lee is a performer who radiates honesty; no age limit on that. Thirdly, she knows and loves music and communicates that love. Last, she is a superior actress (ever catch her in the film "Pete Kelly's Blues"?) who gives a hell of a performance every time out.
> If I thought the people, young or old, would ever stop responding to such an arsenal of talent, I would be tempted to throw in my lot with the morons at either pole; those who claim that everyone under thirty is a drug-crazed degenerate, or their opposite numbers who want everyone over thirty put out to pasture. One thing these groups have in common is that they don't listen — to anything. But in every generation there are those who do listen — and one listen is all Peggy Lee needs.

Unfortunately for Peggy and her fans, the executives at Capitol had stopped listening. In their pursuit of a "younger audience" they let one of their finest artists go. Considering all the years of work and dedication that Peggy had given to the company, plus the fact that she was succeeding in her bid to remain contemporary, that she had just won the Grammy, and that tickets sold out wherever she performed, then letting her contract lapse appears not only ungrateful, but bad business.

In spite of the flawless performances on *Norma Deloris Egstrom from Jamestown, North Dakota*, arguably her finest album since *Black Coffee*, Peggy Lee was, for the first time in her career, without a record label. True to form, she would continue to excel. Having Capitol's executives turn their backs on her must have been devastating, but Peggy's motto had always been "Straight ahead and straight up." Her last song on her final Capitol record was "I'll Be Seeing You." Her fans would be seeing and hearing her for many years to come. Peggy Lee, the legend, was not about to quit.

Spring 1972 — **Black & White Scotch.** "What makes her the singer's singer makes us the Scotch drinker's Scotch." So reads the advertising copy on an ad for Black & White Scotch. The ad featured a stunning, un-retouched photo of the glamorous fifty-two-year-old singer.

June 7, 1972—Westbury Music Fair.

Her presence is one of icy elegance while her songs and conversation communicate a personal, intimate warmth.... More than anything else, Peggy Lee is an interpreter of songs. Each piece of music is colored and shaped by her vision and feeling. With each tune, she attempts to say something, to communicate a personal statement.—Len Cohen, *The Evening Star*

• SIX •

Becoming a Legend: 1972 to 1982

If the powers-that-be at Capitol thought of Peggy as "over-the-hill," the critics certainly did not agree. "Two Sides of a Love Affair — Peggy Gives and Peggy Gets," "Perfection by Peggy Lee," and "Peggy at Peak as a Pop Singer" were but a few of the headlines garnered by her show at the Lake Geneva Playboy Club and Hotel in August 1972.

Peggy's all-new show featured music from the *Norma Deloris Egstrom from Jamestown, North Dakota* album. With her matchless artistry she continued to gain new musical ground.

> Next to Pat Nixon, the last person on earth you'd expect to become a rock and roll star is Peggy Lee. But that's what she threatens to become. Her new act ... is 80 percent rock — hard, soft, gentle and strong — and nearly 90 percent spanking new....—Bruce Vilanch

Sam Lesner, who wrote the article titled "Peggy at Peak as a Pop Singer," reported that, "New songs pour out of her with all the assurance and vocal poise of the old songs that have become her hallmark."

April 6, 1972 — ***Chicago Tribune.*** Harriet Choice interviewed Peggy for "Two Sides of a Love Affair — Peggy Gives and Peggy Gets":

> [Peggy Lee's] mercurial Gemini personality allows her to "take care of the business" so that her shows are near-perfect. And then, afterwards, when she's given the audience everything they've wanted and more, she can hang out with the musicians. She is one of their kind. With them, she exudes the rare combination of cooing mother hen and "let's play" little girl.
>
> "We just liked each other. It's just different with this group of musicians. It's a genuine affection, and I respect them more than any group I know."

August 9, 1972 — **Schaefer Music Festival, Central Park, New York.**

> Miss Lee, 30 summers after she came to prominence with Benny Goodman's orchestra, has become the most popular singer to be heard anywhere. The songs from her

new album provided an interesting insight to the balance of elements that keep her performances on such a high level.—John S. Wilson, *New York Times*, August 11, 1972

November 1972—**The Carol Burnett Show and Las Vegas.** Peggy was scheduled to appear at Caesar's Palace with the great comedian Alan King. Prior to the Las Vegas opening, Peggy made another appearance on *The Carol Burnett Show* (broadcast on November 1, 1972). She performed "The Rhythm of Life" with the entire cast. Carol and Peggy joined forces for a duet of "Girl Talk." Her solo moment came with Leon Russell's "A Song for You."

Peggy also hosted a party in Alan King's honor before leaving for Las Vegas. Journalist Janie Greenspun, who wrote a column called "Hollywood-Vegas Line," attended the party. Greenspun was amazed at the "Who's Who" of show business that she encountered that night. In addition to Peggy's "Good Luck Charm," Cary Grant, the guests included Carol Burnett, Jack Benny, Dick Martin, Carl Reiner, Lee Grant, Walter Matthau, Joan Rivers, Harvey Korman, Sheila MacRae, Richard Chamberlain and Vincent Price.

November 19, 1972—*New York Times.* "Sing a Song of Peggy Lee, Producer" was the title of A. H. Weiler's article. Peggy revealed that she intended to produce a film version of *Clair de Lune*:

> What's a nice girl like Peggy doing in the producing game? "It's one big, beautiful accident," she says. "I had *Clair de Lune* on my bookshelf for a long time, but I didn't read it until a house guest recommended it to me. The story fascinated me: it was so romantic—so sensual, without being pornographic. Then I found out that La Mure lived only a few blocks from me in Los Angeles, so we got together and made the deal."
>
> Does the deal include the services of actress Peggy Lee? ... "Well, I think I'd be right for the role of an older woman whom the hero falls in love," she says modestly.
>
> We think she'd be right for the younger woman.

The project never came to be.

December 9, 1972—*Melody Maker* (UK).

> As an incomparable singer, as a nightclub artist, as a weaver of moods, Peggy Lee is about as close to perfection as any singer who ever lovingly fashioned a performance for an audience.... It was a long show, but not a moment too long. It never is when Peggy Lee is onstage."—Leonard Feather (reviewing her Caesar's Palace engagement)

December 10, 1972—*Los Angeles Times.* Leonard Feather also wrote "The Pleasures and Pains of Peggy Lee," in which Peggy again mentioned her desire to produce the film version of *Clair de Lune*.

> A few years ago I had to spend a great deal of time in bed and I asked somebody to get me some biographies. One of them was *Claire de Lune*, the story of Claude

Debussy by Pierre LaMure, who also wrote *Moulin Rouge*. Well, I was just fascinated, and I bought the rights to the book. I've been living, breathing and sleeping with it ever since.

This is a first, because there never has been a woman producer. Woman director, yes, Ida Lupino, but no producer.

January 1973—*This Is Your Life*. Peggy became the subject of the popular *This Is Your Life* television show. She was clearly surprised, as when host Ralph Edwards appeared and announced "This Is Your Life—Miss Peggy Lee," the shocked singer tried to hide behind Alan King!

Among the special guests who paid tribute to Peggy were Ken Kennedy (from WDAY in Fargo), Peggy's brother Claire, her daughter Nicki and longtime friend Duke Ellington. The latter gave Peggy his customary five kisses on the cheek. Peggy was deeply moved during a medley of her hit songs; when she heard "I Don't Know Enough About You" and "Mañana," she became tearful, saying, "It's all David." Her beloved David Barbour was never far from her thoughts.

The final guest was Lucille Armstrong. Louis' widow brought a special orchid with her, explaining to viewers that whenever Peggy had an opening night Louis always sent an orchid to Peggy. As she handed the flower to Peggy the voice of Louis was heard singing "It's a Wonderful World." During the show the teary-eyed Miss Lee commented that she thought she was "dreaming."

January 1973—*The Julie Andrews Hour*. Peggy soloed on "Someone Who Cares" and "Make It with You." Julie and Peggy sang a lengthy medley that included "Sing," "Up, Up and Away," "I Believe in Music," and "Love Is Just Around the Corner." Peggy joined Julie and Robert Goulet in a tribute to Broadway producer David Merrick. With Goulet she sang "Make Someone Happy." She also turned in a low-down, sultry "Who Will Buy" from the Broadway show *Oliver*.

January 13, 1973—*Duke Ellington—We Love You Madly*. Those paying tribute to the Duke on this CBS special included Count Basie, Ray Charles, Sammy Davis, Jr., Billy Eckstine, Roberta Flack, Aretha Franklin, Quincy Jones, Sarah Vaughan and Joe Williams. Ellington's "Queen" performed their composition "I'm Gonna Go Fishing." Peggy joined Sammy Davis, Billy Eckstine, Roberta Flack, Sarah Vaughan and Joe Williams for a medley of Ellington tunes.

February 1, 1973— Café Cristal, Diplomat Hotel, Florida.

> She is one of those performers who can lean 100% on her past hits for effect, as so many do when playing the Miami area, but she eschews the easy way to combine what the crowd knows her for with more than a touch of the contemporary.... Emerging in a long white gown, Miss Lee makes contact with her audience from the top and holds them for almost an hour before she gently releases them.—*Variety*, February 7, 1973

March 17, 1973 — *The Carol Burnett Show.* Carol Burnett loved singing and joking with Peggy Lee. Here Peggy made her fifth appearance on the show. Carol and company paid tribute to Peggy Lee the songwriter when they joined Peggy for a medley that included "It's a Good Day," "I Don't Know Enough About You," "So, What's New?," "Where Can I Go Without You?," "I'm Gonna Go Fishin'" and "Mañana." In her solo spot Peggy sang the uplifting "When I Found You" from her *Norma Deloris Egstrom from Jamestown, North Dakota* album.

March 19, 1973 — *The Tonight Show with Johnny Carson.* Peggy joined Johnny and his guests Carroll O'Connor, Tommy Leonetti and Ralph Pearl. The songs she performed are unknown.

March 25, 1973 — *New York Daily News.* Christina Kirk visited Peggy during an afternoon rehearsal, then wrote "Peggy Lee Productions Presents Miss Peggy Lee in an Evening with Norma Egstrom":

> The voice — cool and clear — comes in like another instrument as the band runs through her elaborate, driving arrangements. The blonde head bobs and the foot taps until her ear hears a discordant sound. She stops singing and the band slides to a halt. "Look," she says, pleasantly, "can we possibly do it this way on that chorus?" She sings her suggestion, the band tries it and she approves. "Okay, just give a little more bite to it."

Among Peggy's mix of new and old songs is James Taylor's "Fire and Rain." Kirk relates that, "[Peggy] was proud that he [Taylor] was at her opening with his bride, singer-songwriter Carly Simon, to join in the standing ovation. She likes a young audience as well as her old faithfuls."

March 28, 1973 — Empire Room, Waldorf-Astoria, New York.

> Peggy Lee shows new facets of her art at virtually every engagement at the Waldorf-Astoria's Empire Room.... Miss Lee apparently spends a great deal of time in preparation. Her arrangements are imaginative and she has impeccable musical backing.... Miss Lee remains a singer of top quality, mixing humor, sensitivity and rhythmic feeling with a keen sense of musicianship and meaningful lyricism. — *Variety*

April 27, 1973 — *The Bobby Darin Show.* The great Bobby Darin had long been a friend and fan of Peggy Lee. Bobby invited his friend to appear on the final installment of his television show, airing on April 27.

> "In the final show (of the series) the atmosphere was virtually all nightclub — Bobby and the band pouring it on. Brash Bobby and Peggy with the richly sensuous, smoky tunes — it was a good way to go." Peggy soloed on "Someone Who Cares" and "When I Found You." She joined her host for a medley of "Just Friends," "Something to Remember You By," "Skylark," "Spring Is Here" and "Long Ago and Far Away." — Don Freeman

May 1973 — St. Louis. Peggy made an appearance in St. Louis. Dick Richmond, writing for the *St. Louis Post-Dispatch*, said: "She was onstage for an hour that melted away. When she finished, the hundreds of persons in the audience rose en masse to applaud."

June 18, 1973—*Newsweek.* The Franklin Mint had commissioned several celebrity artists to contribute paintings to a special portfolio that would sell for $1,500.

Peggy painted a portrait of Claude Debussy's mistress Gabrielle DuPont. Peggy's "Gaby" was seen alongside paintings by Tony Bennett, Candice Bergen, Duke Ellington, Kim Novak, Dinah Shore, Red Skelton and Henry Fonda.

Newsweek ran a photo of "Peggy Lee with her 'Gaby,'" and commented that, "Sunday painter Peggy Lee listed her favorite artists as 'Renoir, Monet and Henry Fonda.'" The Franklin Mint also produced an 11-minute film, entitled *Celebrity Art*, to promote this collection.

On April 27, 1973, Bobby Darrin hosted the last episode of *The Bobby Darrin Show*. Peggy, his beloved friend, was his only guest that night. (NBC)

June 1973— Playboy Hotel at Lake Geneva, Wisconsin.

> She was superb. In fact, by the time the applause from her standing ovation died away, everyone in the room realized they had heard one of the finest performances in show business today.... At risk of all superlatives for her performance, there was absolutely nothing at all that could detract from any number she did.—Alex Thien, *Milwaukee Sentinel*, June 30, 1973
>
> Lee's stint is a study in preparation. Nothing—not a note, gesture or comment—seems left to chance, and this dedication to detail resulted in a superb 55-minute layout that nabbed a standing ovation at final bows. The top-liner has a knack for imbuing each song with equal parts soulfulness and sophistication, a technique that gives every item a very personal feeling.—*Variety*, July 4, 1973

September 13, 1973— Venetian Room, Fairmont Hotel, San Francisco. San Francisco audiences became the first to see the new Peggy Lee. She had lost 30 pounds. "The New Peggy Lee Is Glowing," reported Michel Lomax of the *San Francisco Examiner*. Lomax commented: "Behind that gilded Buddha façade, Peggy Lee is as beautiful a woman as you've ever seen..."

During this engagement veteran photographer Fran Ortiz took an exquisite, candle-lit photo of Peggy.

Many years later, in December of 1980, the photo was reprinted in the *San Francisco Examiner & Chronicle*'s "Sunday" magazine. In "A Photographic Essay" Ortiz related the story behind the photo:

> I spent the entire day with Peggy Lee and must have shot a dozen rolls of her in many, many situations, but after the last show at the Venetian Room she said she wanted to buy me a drink. We went to a small bar in the Fairmont. She still had her stage makeup on. The only light was from the candles on the tables, but I decided to experiment. The exposure was about ⅛ of a second at F/2. This image said more about her than anything I had shot all day.

The Ortiz photo caught both the glamorous star and the shy little girl. Like Philip Elwood's review, it was glowing. Elwood, writing for the *Examiner*, exclaimed, "The New Peggy Lee — Great!" His review opened with "Hail and glad tidings, Miss Peggy Lee — a good weekend, and next week to you; and how nice it was last night to have you singing the way we all have always wanted, looking bright, mellow, confident and frisky." He closed the review by noting that her act was "an expensive show rich in rewards."

October 1973— Palmer House, Chicago.

> She was in top form both vocally and physically.... During her 60-minute program, Lee goes in several musical directions for material. Broadway musicomedy items are contemporary and fare standard, with all tailored to her distinctive style. Per usual she treats her carefully constructed show in a casual manner, dishing up the kind of thrushing, charm and grace that had premier night auditors making with cheers.—
> *Variety*, October 10, 1973

During her stay in Chicago, journalist Todd Mason interviewed Peggy for the *Chicago Daily News*. Mason's article, entitled "The Legendary Lee, So Supremely Herself," appeared in the October 13, 1973, edition of the newspaper. In it, Peggy shared her views of success with Mason:

> "Success isn't all money, or living on a mountaintop in Beverly Hills next door to Frank Sinatra. My father worked for a small railroad and he was a success.
>
> "I think it's really the character of a person, how they relate to others, and their attitude in general. Someone with a straight-ahead attitude who reached success without cutting throats. It's the ability to laugh at oneself. It is an inner strength that if someone needed to, they could lean on for a few minutes.
>
> "It's funny, but people often think that successful people never need to lean on anyone, but they do. They're very much alone. The higher they go the more alone they really are. You know what I mean? People think of them as being invincible, but tomorrow they could fall into the gutter. And there's no satisfaction in accomplishing something if you have no one to tell it to, or to share it with."

She also told Mason about what kept her going:

> "Music itself is my driving force. It's closely examining the lyric so that I can believe every word. It's trying very hard not to let the next performance be less than the last, but, I hope, better."

October 1973*—Stereo Review.* Peter Reilly titled his review of Peggy's *Norma Deloris Egstrom from Jamestown, North Dakota* album "Peggy Lee and That Old Vocal Eroticism":

> For some years now her best material has been that which allows her to project the ripe autumnal womanliness of someone who has been glad, been sad, and often been had, but who has extracted a wry wisdom from it all....
>
> By the standards Peggy Lee herself has set (no others can take her measure), the new album isn't particularly outstanding. But, as always, there are three or four stunning bands—"I'll Be Seeing You," "I'll Get By" and "Someone Who Cares" here—that reach the highest level of her accomplishments, and that is high indeed.

November 1973*—Julie Andrews' Christmas Show*, **London.** On November 25, 1973, the *Sunday Express* reported that Peggy was visiting England to appear with Peter Ustinov on the upcoming *Julie Andrews' Christmas Show*.

In the show, Peggy played the Sugar Plum Fairy in a dream sequence and sang a sultry, pulsing version of the "Dance of the Sugar Plum Fairy," luring Julie into her unique universe.

Julie and "Sugar" performed a lengthy duet, having great fun with "Row, Row, Row," "I Can't Give You Anything but Love," "I Talk to the Trees," "Is It True What They Say About Dixie?," "Swingin' on a Star," "Siamese Cat Song," "Where Has My Little Dog Gone," "Just in Time," and others. Peggy turned on her delightful sense of humor when she implored Julie to stay by singing "Baby, It's Cold Outside."

Peggy's solo was one of her finest pieces of work in the medium of television. She sang a medley of David Gates' "Clouds" and the time-honored classic "Have Yourself a Merry Little Christmas." The setting was an airplane, with Peggy flying home to her lover (as the lyrics of "Clouds" suggested).

Julie's Christmas special was broadcast on December 14, 1973.

November 17, 1973*—Daily Express* (UK). Victor Davis' article, titled "How I Walked Into Chapter Three of the Legend of the Perils of Peggy," covered some of Peggy's mishaps and health problems:

> She's been in this country only three times—and on her first visit we almost killed her.
>
> So Miss Peggy Lee arrived in London this week treading very warily.
>
> Here to record a Christmas show with Julie Andrews, Peggy recalled the first time she dropped in twelve years ago.
>
> "I'm not blaming London, you understand. But things do seem to happen to me here," said Peggy, who has the title of her biography all worked out. It will be called *The Perils of Peggy*.
>
> "I was doing three shows a night in cabaret and performing for the BBC. I had no time to get back to my hotel to rest. I ran myself into the ground, contracted pneumonia and pleurisy and spent seven months in bed."

December 5, 1973*—Punch* (UK). David Taylor interviewed Peggy for his article "Passing Through: Peggy Lee Talks to David Taylor." In it, Peggy discussed her feeling for her audiences:

> "I do not pretend that in the beginning I could gauge an audience. It comes, with practice, with work. I suppose that I do try and think about them for some time before I step out, to achieve some quiet about me at that time. Perhaps I shouldn't tell you this, but what I then do is stomp my foot in a girlish, hystrionic way and right on cue — Ladies and gentlemen, Miss Peggy Lee — I come flying out. Without wires. Or wings. Well, then, once out, the music takes charge.... But I don't like to have the thought that there may be celebrities, or family, or anyone I know out there in the audience. Perhaps because I'm really two people — I'm not even me when I'm out there. Now I've really confused you, yes? Peggy Lee is a schizophrenic? It's not an easy thing to describe; it is, as you suggest, just about the most self-conscious way there is to make a living...."

December 1973 — **Empire Room, Waldorf-Astoria, New York.** High praise came from critic Rex Reed, who told his readers that "For a Musical Education Listen to Peggy Lee":

> I caught Peggy Lee's opening, and was once more amazed at her grace, beauty and musical craftsmanship....
>
> Mike Nichols says she is his favorite actress, and I understand why. She does more than sing. She works over a song until it is a three-act play. Peggy Lee's singing surpasses ordinary artistry. It has the usual requisites of art — emotion, imagination, intellect — but it has verisimilitude, too, and communication uncommon even among the biggest stars.

March 1974 — **Ohio Theatre, Columbus, Ohio.** Gene Garrard, writing for the *Citizen-Journal* on March 5, 1974, remarked that, "Peggy Lee is an illustrious American institution, and one of the joys of the world." Garrard also felt that she was "an enchantress" who should be "charged with vocal witchcraft."

March 20, 1974 — **Toronto, Canada.**

> Some singers woo an audience; some caress a crowd by crooning to it. Peggy Lee paralyzes people. She did it opening night at O'Keefe Centre, making that hollow hall virtually cough-less — has anyone ever done that before? — as her enraptured audience, hushed and reverent, hung on her every whispered note. — George Anthony, *The Toronto Sun*

Spring 1974 — ***The Great American Popular Singers.*** Henry Pleasants was a music historian who had written several well-known books on the worlds of opera and classical music. In his book *The Great American Popular Singers*, published in 1974, Pleasants turned his fine-tuned ear toward popular vocal music and wrote insightful essays on a wide variety of artists, including Bessie Smith, Louis Armstrong, Mildred Bailey, Billie Holiday, Frank Sinatra, Mahalia Jackson, Hank Williams, Elvis Presley, Johnny Cash, B.B. King, Aretha Franklin, Judy Garland and Ethel Merman.

Pleasants' essay on the artistry of Peggy Lee proved extremely informative. He opened his essay with quotes from journalists seeking to illuminate how she constructed her shows. In one quote Peggy comments that, "I think preparation is the key to the whole thing." Pleasants notes that while such professionalism characterizes Peggy Lee, it does not define her, and concludes, "Other singers have been as painstaking as Peggy without ever evoking the magic of her singing."

Pleasants goes on to discuss the physical strength Peggy gains from this careful preparation, explaining, "from it she derives the security she needs to do with a song the things that she does," including employing interpretive devices that are distinguished from those of other excellent singers by "their delicacy, their small scale, their subtlety, their ultimate refinement."

Speaking of her vocal longevity, Pleasants opined, "No other singer ... has asked less of a voice while using it so much. No other has done more with what the voice has given her." Noting that Peggy had never pushed her voice beyond its natural range, Pleasants observes that "she has mined a wealth and variety of color, inflection, eloquent lyricism and even grandeur hardly matched by any other singer, male or female...."

Pleasants pointed out that while Peggy's range was similar to Judy Garland's and Ethel Merman's, her approach to singing was entirely different. Lee rarely "belted," as both Garland and Merman did. There was a shrewd, wise reason behind Peggy's gentler technique.

"With Judy Garland and Ethel Merman, unless they are belting, one is always aware of an approaching register break around D flat and D. The sound suddenly trails off, as if the singer were running out of vocal steam" causing the voice to become "girlish and tenuous." With Peggy, however, "If she couldn't do more at the top, she saved the weakness, or inadequacy, from exposure by doing less in the middle and at the bottom."

Pleasants posited that Peggy's self-imposed vocal softness allowed her greater interpretive scope, since "there is greater interpretive return from a slight variation on next to nothing, or pianissimo, than there is from a considerable variation between mezzo forte and forte, or between forte and fortissimo."

Pleasants noted that Peggy's subtlety extended to her physical performance as well (illuminating the lyric via acting), concluding, "She works from very little, does very little — just what is right, and no more — and makes everything count."

Mr. Pleasants pointed out that her dramatic gifts helped Peggy survive the ever-changing musical climate and become "more consistently successful than any other singer of her generation in adapting her art to the new song styles that came in with rock in the mid–1950s." In short, "where most singers shape a song to suit their style, Peggy shapes her style to suit the song."

In his closing comments, Pleasants indicated that Peggy Lee was truly in a league of her own: " Her knack of characterization, her adaptability and her dedication to her art and craft over a span of thirty years have sufficed to place Peggy Lee in a class by herself among the scores of girl band singers, many of them delightful singers and accomplished musicians...."

April 10, 1973—*The Academy Awards.* Peggy sang "The Way We Were," the Oscar-nominated song from the film of the same name during this award-show broadcast.

Barbra Streisand was asked to sing the song by producer Jack Haley, Jr. When Streisand refused, Haley asked Peggy to perform. Upon learning that Peggy was replacing her, Streisand suddenly changed her mind. Haley stuck to his guns, and Miss Lee performed the song.

May 2, 1973—Venetian Room, Fairmont Hotel, Dallas.

> It has been said before, but it is worth repeating. Peggy Lee is one of the great song stylists of our time....
>
> Being the expert performer that she is, she saved the best until the last. After doing one of her biggest hits "Is That All There Is?" she picked up a book of verse from the nearby piano and read a love poem by Edna St. Vincent Millay and then quietly slipped into "Touch Me in the Morning." The effect was nothing short of dazzling, poignant and sensuous. A magnificent, captivating number.—Mike Alexander, *Dallas Times Herald*, May 2, 1974

June 1974—*After Dark* magazine.

The cover story, entitled "Miss Peggy Lee: ... quite simply the finest singer in the history of popular music," was five pages in length. In it, Peggy discussed a wide variety of topics, and spoke a bit more openly about her past (hinting at her stepmother's cruelty and her desire to escape North Dakota):

> As a child growing up in Jamestown, North Dakota, I was always daydreaming.... I had six brothers and sisters, and a stepmother who hired us out as day laborers. I wanted to get out, but I didn't know how. I was always impressed with show business. I loved the glamour of it.
>
> When I was sixteen I borrowed my Dad's railroad pass and eighteen dollars, and I took off for Hollywood. I wanted to sing, but no one would listen to me. So I got a job as a short-order cook and later as a shill in a carnival.... And I fell in love with the Strong Man. He let me touch his tattoo. Oh, I was so young and trusting of everyone. I made a lot of mistakes, but I learned. That's why someday I'd like to write a book for young singers. And after I tell them to lie about their age, I'll tell them what to look out for.

June 3, 1974—*People* magazine.

People featured a piece on Peggy's dramatic weight loss, reporting that, "Peggy's loss of 50 pounds in three months was Her Admirers' Gain." Lee told the magazine:

> "I spent 10 days in the hospital once on a diet of 250 calories per day and only lost a pound and a half. Nothing worked."

What worked this time was a "regimen of 700 calories a day (heavy on raw vegetables), a restriction on salt and horizontal rest for 45 minutes three times a day."

People also reported on the effect that the weight gain had had on her self-esteem:

> For a woman who is such a perfectionist that she bristles when one note or one hair is misplaced, her own lack of self-control rankled to the point where she often seemed to be trying to coax extra applause out of even receptive audiences, as if seeking reassurance.

Her belief in herself and her talents returned with the weight loss:

Perhaps most important, she has regained that celebrated self-confidence. When a band hit a clinker behind her recently, she turned to the conductor and said, "I don't think we are in the same key. I'm in tune with the infinite, so you figure out where that leaves you."

July 1974—Boston Pops Orchestra, Boston. The infinitely in-tune Miss Lee wowed Arthur Fiedler, who, in his own words, had "wanted her to appear with [him] for a long time." Peggy sang the following eight songs during her *Evening at Pops* visit: "Love Song," "Clouds," "Always," "Wait Till You See Him," "I've Got a Crush on You," "When I Found You," "The More I See You" and "I'll Be Seeing You."

> "What she has is a good voice, a good ear, good taste, a wonderful way with ballads, and an actress's ability with lyrics." That's how a *New Yorker* article summed up the talent of Peggy Lee, who is making her first appearance with the [Boston] Pops. In a half-hour set, she sings numbers old and new and mostly on the torch side.—*TV Guide*, July 28, 1974

July 17, 1974—*Let's Love* album. *Let's Love* was the name of a song written for Peggy by Paul McCartney. The former Beatle reported that when he was invited to Peggy's hotel for dinner he decided to bring a song instead of a bottle of wine.

The *Let's Love* album would be her first—and only—record for the Atlantic label. Peggy produced the record along, with Dave Grusin—another first for her.

With *Let's Love*, Peggy continued to explore contemporary music. She sang the McCartney song with great tenderness. Melissa Manchester's "He Is the One" enjoyed the finest reading it had ever received. Listeners felt Peggy's real longing when she pleaded "Don't Let Me Be Lonely Tonight." She gently enveloped us with her soul on the gospel-flavored "Sweet Lov'liness."

As a songwriter she contributed "The Heart Is the Lonely Hunter" from the film of the same name. She and co-producer David Grusin wrote and published the film theme in 1968. "Sometimes" by Henry and Felice Mancini was a love letter to Peggy's friends and fans.

Stereo Review gave *Let's Love* its Recording of Special Merit honor. The magazine labeled the recording "Excellent" and the performance "Pure gold." The critic for *Stereo Review* had this to say:

> [Peggy Lee] is ... still the most mesmerizing popular recording performer of our time, and still brings to bear on every piece of material she records her musical elegance, her dramatic sensibility, and her uniquely stylized voice. Let Streisand stomp around chewing the scenery, Aretha construct what by now have become Byzantine three-act plays out of a simple blues, Helen Reddy tell us off in song after song; Peggy Lee continues on her self-sufficient way, apparently content in the knowledge that when you get lonesome for the real thing you'll come home to Mama.

July 18, 1974—*Zoo World*. "The Generation Bridge," by Len Epand, appeared in *Zoo World* magazine. The article discussed the friendship and musical collaboration between Peggy and Paul McCartney, who produced his song "Let's Love" for Peggy's album:

Arthur Fiedler welcomes Peggy to *The Boston Pops*, July 1974. Peggy sings "Love Song," "Clouds," "Always," "Wait Till You See Her," "I've Got a Crush on You," "When I Found You," "The More I See You" and "I'll Be Seeing You." (PBS)

After a hard day's work, Paul ... and Peg ... held a mini press conference/photo session around Studio C's grand piano. In high spirits, they casually sang a couple of songs together, elaborated on their surprising collaboration and then took the small mob into the control room to hear the finished track.

"Well, of course," said Peggy to Paul, "I was a fan of yours before you knew about me."

"No, that's not right," answered McCartney. "No. I was a fan of yours before you knew about me, Peggy."

"Yeah, I used to have records of Peggy. I did 'Til There Was You' because I had Peggy's record of it [see *Latin ala Lee*].... So I've been a fan of hers for a long time, you know. And she came to London and she invited us for dinner over at her hotel. So I thought 'I'm going along to dinner. Well, I'm either gonna take a bottle of champagne or a song...'"

Later, in the same article, Peggy talked about some of her early musical influences, citing Maxine Sullivan (a black singer in the 1930s who "had a soft tone and marvelous sense of time"), Billie Holiday, Mildred Bailey, Bessie Smith and "of course" Ella Fitzgerald, before adding: "But I always feel that the biggest influence on my work has been listening to musicians."

Photographs of Peggy's profile are rare. This portrait was taken in 1974.

***September 24, 1974**—New York Post.* In this edition, Jan Hodenfield discovered how "Miss Lee Endures":

> She brings to mind, Miss Peggy Lee, Liz Taylor's 40-carat diamond.... [S]he is perfection overblown to the grandiose.
> Her songs are new and of the moment, by James Taylor and Thom Bell and Linda Creed and Paul McCartney and Melissa Manchester, and each one interpreted with immaculate grace and a total precision incorporating gesture of infinite degree, is a movie of her mind projected with spellbinding efficiency.

***September 26, 1974**—Village Voice.* Jazz critic Gary Giddins discussed the ongoing careers of three of our great jazz singers in his article "Jazz-in-the-Boite: O'Day, Lee, Tormé." Of Peggy Lee, he opined:

> Peggy Lee ... enters a phrase like a balsam glider riding a breeze. Only sometimes the breeze is a misjudged gust which sends her sailing flat or sharp or somewhere in the great uncharted middle. Peggy is a performer pickled in aspic; violinists churning to the left of her, an orchestra riffling to the right, two pianists and a drummer who socks his cymbal every time the third beat of a measure rolls around.

***October 10, 1974**—Soho Weekly News.*

> Like a Zen master who carefully transforms a simple activity such as archery into a religious ritual, Peggy Lee focuses her power of concentration and controlled energy to lift pop music into a realm it rarely occupies....

With three black female back-up singers, her act (as seen at the Waldorf) is largely a re-working of the material from the album into an effective evening that builds and rests gently with a hushed air of excitement....

Just as a Zen master formalizes and spiritualizes all aspects of her art, Peggy Lee's astonishing subtlety allows her to communicate more with the wave of a hand, the lift of a brow, or the twist of a note more than most pop musicians get across in an entire evening.—Henry Post

***October 1974*—Blue Room, Fairmont Hotel, New Orleans.** "Peggy Lee Spins Her Web at the Fairmont" was the title of Mark Hemester's concert review. Hemester wrote, "Miss Lee, an original stylist still equipped with a voice of limited range if unerring musical instinct, somehow achieved the effect of turning back the pages 20 years.... Miss Lee of youthful maturity and blissful ardor, had spun her web."

***October 1974*—*The Best of the Music Makers* by George T. Simon.** George T. Simon had been covering the music scene for several decades. He was there when the young Peggy Lee performed with Benny Goodman at the New Yorker Hotel's Terrace Room. His new book, published in 1974, contained a profile of Peggy entitled "She seems to be most concerned with love." Simon wrote about Peggy's great sensitivity:

> The feelings Peggy projects in her numbers run the gamut from good, strong, healthy sex to cute, pixieish humor, to sweet, little-girl sentimentality. But she seems to be most concerned with love (love of all kinds: light, heavy, happy, dismal), with presenting those various feelings through her songs and with receiving love in return from those close to her, including her audiences. She loves people easily, making her quite vulnerable.

Simon also focused on her unrelenting quest for perfection and acceptance from her public. He reported that she often worked "to the point of utter exhaustion" polishing her craft for her audiences.

When she was feeling wiped out or blue, what lifted her spirits? What kept her going? In answer to these questions, Simon quoted Peggy as saying, "Appreciation is the best vitamin I've found."

In closing, Simon quoted Peggy again, this time talking about the importance of nurturing her talent:

> In turn, she appreciates good musicianship and insists on it from her co-workers, who she feels should share one of her strongest beliefs: "I've been given a talent, and I feel a responsibility to try to improve the presentation of it."

***May 24, 1974*—Duke Ellington Dies.** Peggy wrote a personal tribute to Ellington for *Stereo Review*. This is how she expressed her feelings for her friend:

> We all know and will not forget Duke Ellington's musical genius, but any woman who was ever privileged to meet the great man almost always carried away with her a very special feeling because the Duke had an extraordinary way of making a woman feel beautiful and very special.

He seemed to give his exclusive attention and soon you were pleasurably showered with a poetic phrase which he felt would suit and please you ... you just walked away smiling. I shall always remember him that way ... and smile.

Summer 1974 — **Blackglama advertisement.** The Blackgama mink "What Becomes a Legend Most?" campaign was the brainchild of ad man Peter Rogers. Rogers hired photographers Richard Avedon and Bill King to take beautiful portraits that captured the essence of some legendary ladies.

Prior to Peggy's posing for the ad campaign on this date, Rogers and his photographers had enshrined such legends as Lauren Bacall, Bette Davis, Judy Garland, Marlene Dietrich, Rita Hayworth, and Claudette Colbert.

Autumn 1974 — *Dinah!* On *Dinah!*, the talk show hosted by Peggy's friend from the early days at Capitol Records, Dinah Shore, the two singers had a great time reminiscing, and Peggy sang her funky version of Irving Berlin's "Always." Peggy appeared several times on Dinah's show; unfortunately, the exact airdates of the programs are unknown.

November 20, 1974 — **Studio One.** This party at LA's famous Studio One would mark the first time Peggy had sung in Los Angeles in eleven years. It was her understanding that this was to be a small party to celebrate the release of *Let's Love*. She was genuinely surprised when 2,500 people showed up to honor her.

Studio One was a gay-owned and operated club. With this concert Peggy graciously acknowledged the support and love she had received from the gay community throughout her career.

Glen Spencer covered the event for *In Touch* magazine, with photographs by Hy Chase. Spencer reported that when Peggy sang "she was that little girl again at the Roseland Ballroom, caressing those lyrics and taking those pregnant pauses as though the nine months necessary were compressed in a single breath."

November 21, 1974 — *The Tonight Show with Johnny Carson.* Peggy appeared with Carson the night after the Studio One bash. She talked about the party and plugged *Let's Love*. The album was selling well, but her stay with the Atlantic recording label was destined to be a short one.

On the show, Peggy sang "I'm a Woman," "Just for a Thrill" and "Fever" for Carson.

January 1975 — **Palmer House, Chicago.** During this engagement Peggy was interviewed by Dick Saunders of the *Chicago Sun-Times*. She spoke with him about meditation:

> Beneath that enigmatic exterior, in the quietest and gentlest way, Peggy is the personification of Positive Mental Attitude — a disciple of transcendental meditation who hardly seems capable of expressing a negative thought.

Peggy in full flight. A concert appearance circa 1975.

"It has helped me enormously. I think more clearly and there is a great flow of creative ideas. I am more in tune with life, with the environment, with people. I have this feeling of oneness with nature."

January 19, 1975—Chicago Tribune. Rick Soll titled his article "Celebrations Laced with Loss Are Songs of a Languid Lady," and discussed the artistry that Peggy displayed at the Palmer House:

The constantly shifting tones, the ever-changing mood, the sadness the flickers in the middle of the joy, the depth and sincerity of her voice — it all should have led the way, at least a little, to the woman whose sight and sound seems a spiritual pantomime of the richness she broadcasts on stage....

Sometimes the songs were celebrations, but always they were laced with a tearing quality that inevitably led to some private place in the night where you had to deal with loss and loneliness.

"If that's all there is, my friend, then let's keep dancing" are words in her famous song — there is music even in the bad places, it is easier to dance and cry than drown in tears.

February 1975 — **Café Cristal, Diplomat Hotel, Florida.**

Café Cristal audiences oohed and aahed on seeing a strikingly streamlined blonde who looks enchanting after a ruthless weight reduction. The message is gracefully upbeat, almost all the way. There are outstanding new compositions by young composers the caliber of Steve Wonder, Leon Russell, Melissa Manchester and James Taylor. — *Variety*, February 26, 1975

May 1975 — **Peggy Lee, Doctor of Music.** Peggy received a special invitation from North Dakota State University, who honored her as "the state's most widely known woman" by bestowing upon her the honorary degree of "Doctor of Music."

May 19, 1975 — *The Tonight Show with Johnny Carson.* Della Reese acted as Carson's guest host. Reese welcomed Peggy, Carroll O'Connor and Sandy Duncan. The songs that Peggy sang are unknown.

Spring 1975 — *Dinah!* Peggy made two visits to the *Dinah!* show. On the first she and Dinah performed a duet of "Sing." Then Peggy charmed the viewers with her classic "I'm a Woman."

David Niven was a guest the next time Peggy appeared with Dinah Shore. Peggy sang two Cole Porter songs this time: "I've Got You Under My Skin" and "Too Darn Hot."

Peggy appeared on two other episodes of *Dinah!* For episode 42 she sang "Let's Love" and a medley with Dinah Shore. On episode 1030 she sang "Love Me or Leave Me" and "Saved" (a duet with Shore).

Dinah's show was syndicated. The exact airdates of Peggy's appearances are unknown.

July 1975 — *Mirrors.* During the spring and summer Peggy prepared a new act based on some special material written for her by the team of Leiber and Stoller. The songwriters, responsible for Peggy's "I'm a Woman" and "Is That All There Is?," were given carte blanche by A&M Records to produce Peggy's next album. Given that great financial and artistic freedom, Leiber and Stoller came up with a daring concept album titled *Mirrors*.

Mirrors has always been a treasured album for Peggy Lee fans. No other album uses theater of the mind so brilliantly from beginning to end. For insightful reviews of this album, see the December 1975 *Mandate Magazine* and March 1976 *Stereo Review* entries.

July 24, 1975*— *The Tonight Show with Johnny Carson. Johnny greeted Peggy, Joan Rivers, David Brenner and Buck Henry. Peggy's songs on this episode are unknown.

***August 1975*— Flamingo Hotel, Las Vegas.** Peggy premiered the new material at the Flamingo Hotel.

> Peggy Lee is back with top drawer sound and appearance blending with classy charm.... Most songs in the program are Leiber-Stoller cleffed, and tailored for Lee's delivery and personality. One of her own compositions [with Dave Barbour], "Mañana" gets warmest reception. Memorable is her familiar sound underlined by a gracious, almost regal attitude. —*Variety*, August 27, 1975

***September 1, 1975*— 10th Annual Jerry Lewis Labor Day Telethon.**

Fall 1975*— *The Merv Griffin Show. This guest spot found Peggy surrounded by several top-notch stars. In addition to Peggy, the host greeted Rosemary Clooney, Tony Bennett, Pearl Bailey, Johnny Mercer and the legendary Fred Astaire.

***September 28, 1975*— Dallas Symphony Orchestra.** This concert took place in Dallas' Music Hall.

October 10, 1975*— *The Tonight Show with Johnny Carson. Comedian Joey Bishop was Carson's guest host. Bishop's guests were Ricardo Montalban and Susan Sarandon. The songs Lee performed are unknown.

***October 16, 1975*— Empire Room, Waldorf-Astoria, New York.** The songs from "Mirrors" were extremely innovative. In the hands of a lesser talent the subtlety and irony of the Leiber and Stoller songs would have been lost. Peggy, in her best Stanislavsky singing method, illuminated the songs from within.

> Lee shows why she is still among the top echelon of posh club attractions.... A little Lee philosophy interspersed with the 20 tunes helped the 70-minute set fly by, including her comments on *Mirrors*—'It reflects people, their experience, memories, happiness, sadness, and takes you on a cruise — a voyage of the mind.' —Stephen Traiman, *Billboard*, November 1, 1975

Peggy's comment about the "voyage of the mind" is the key to the mysteries of *Mirrors*. This album, and her show, was pure theater-of-the-mind. This was the type of material that Peggy Lee did best.

> Lee's present turn has a theme threaded through it. Act is labeled "Mirrors" and is based on her current A&M album of that name. Much of it is a series of reflective songs which are contemplative and retrospective to give her dimension.... Lee deliv-

ers meaningfully. Ballads frequently have a haunting and penetrating quality and there are times when her rhythmic tunes have a bounce to lift the audience several notches.—*Variety*, October 22, 1975

October 19, 1975—*Los Angeles Times*. "Is That All There Is? A Lady of Many Moods Finds There's Much More" is the title of Marshall Berges' article. In a lengthy question and answer session Berges uncovered some interesting insights:

> Q: What's your gift to music?
>
> Peggy: I see it less as a gift than an expression of love between music and me. With that love I can interpret lyrics and bring out a feeling from way down inside myself. A singer builds an emotional bridge to an audience, and understanding travels across that bridge.
>
> Q: Just how well do you understand yourself?
>
> Peggy: Not nearly well enough. Sometimes I lose sight of the humor in a situation and I'm abrupt or lose my temper with people who are very dear to me…. Afterward I'm sorry.
>
> Actually, when my voice is raised, no one need worry. It's only when I become quiet and terribly elegant that I'm really angry. Fortunately, most of the time I'm a happy person.
>
> Q: What makes you happy?
>
> Peggy: Simple things…. [M]y idea of a lovely experience is to have a quiet evening at home, curled up with a good book. Books open new worlds to me, and I'm sort of an eager explorer, always trying to make discoveries, always looking for ways to improve myself.

December 2, 1975—*Christian Science Monitor*. In "Peggy Lee: A Vocal Style That Weathered the Rock Era," David Sterritt wrote of Peggy's staying power.

> "There are certain things that I really object to singing about, and I won't sing them. I prefer to sing about—oh, love. And life supporting things."
>
> One of the sturdiest personalities on the pop music scene, smoky-voiced Peggy Lee has built a fabulous career out of those life-affirming songs and sentiments.
>
> When faced with a huge potential hit on a skeptical subject—"Is That All There Is?"—she thought for months about her interpretation. "Being a very positive person, I didn't want to sing anything that was negative…. My approach was positive, and now I'd say that 85 percent of my listeners regard the song as being on the positive side. I do believe that there is more to life…. I like humor, and torch songs, too, but they have to show deeper emotion."

December 27, 1975—*Record World* magazine. Peggy discussed the process of recording *Mirrors* with David McGee:

> RW: Did the new album, *Mirrors*, start out as a concept album?
>
> Lee: Leiber and Stoller had originally hoped for that, but they weren't prepared for the whole album when they came to California. In the meantime I had to go to Japan, so we set the keys on the things they did have and when I returned they had written new things. By then it had become a concept album.
>
> RW: How long did you spend recording the album?

Lee: Well we started in 1942. Seriously, we did set keys in April and then I went away and when I returned we recorded for awhile and I went away again and came back and finished it.

RW: Do you like to take awhile to record an album or do you prefer to go in and get it done?

Lee: I really like to go straight ahead and get it done. 'Cause then it's a whole consuming thing. I can devote my full attention and not break that.

December 1975—***Mandate* magazine.** *Mandate* printed Freeman Gunter's review of *Mirrors*:

> The melodies range from lush and romantic to a dry, storytelling form which is highly reminiscent of the German theater music of the thirties. Johnny Mandel has arranged the songs to achieve a wide range of instrumental color and texture, with a transparency that is remarkable considering the fact that an 82-piece orchestra was used.

Gunter singled out several songs for praise, including "Some Cats Know" ("a sly song, in the traditional Peggy Lee manner") "Professor Haupman's Performing Dogs" ("the closet Peggy Lee has yet come to making a political statement in a song"), and the enigmatic "The Case of M.J." ("Just what Mary Jane's problem is remains a mystery, even to Peggy; I asked her what the composers had to suggest and Peggy replied, 'I don't think they know either'").

One of the album's highlights is the song that closes side one. The brilliantly written and performed "Tango" is the classic example of theater-of-the-mind. Peggy, the actress, projects vivid images. It is as if she has set up a movie screen in her listener's mind. When she sings of the phonograph playing an old broken record you can actually see the Victrola.

Freeman Gunter describes "Tango" as follows:

> The most startling song in the album, "Tango," is a still and poetic description of a murder scene, that of Ramon Novarro, the silent film star who was killed in his apartment by a sailor he had brought home. This bold and provocative, even ugly subject is rendered delicate, beautiful and intimate by the unique sensibilities Peggy Lee brings to the song.

"Tango" is the masterpiece among many exquisite vignettes found in *Mirrors*. Peggy's singing is rich and warm, hinting at secret worlds.

January 30, 1976—***The Tonight Show with Johnny Carson.*** M*A*S*H star McLean Stevenson was the guest host. Peggy joined Rich Little, Jack Warden and Jose Molina. She sang "Send a Little Love My Way" and "Touch Me in the Morning."

February 1, 1976—***San Francisco Examiner and Chronicle.*** Calvin Ahlgren in "Miss Peggy Lee: The Legend Leaves the Mountaintop to Sing":

> An intelligent, industrious professional, [Peggy Lee] was reported as cool, distant, even phony at times by those who could have been rebuffed in their attempts to penetrate her personal seclusion.

> Years ago, she moved to a mountaintop overlooking the Los Angeles area, where she could work ... garden, entertain her friends, and recuperate from a series of respiratory illnesses and unsuccessful marriages. From there, she emerges periodically to take on singing engagements, such as her upcoming, annual return to the Fairmont's Venetian Room, Thursday though February 18.

February 6, 1976— Venetian Room, Fairmont Hotel, San Francisco.

> When Miss Lee is good, she's very, very good. And last night's house rewarded her highly-polished performance with a standing ovation.
> You didn't just watch Peggy Lee — she watched you. She sang with utmost control and confidence, playing to the audience's intelligence — never doubting that the entire room wasn't just as attuned to the lyrics of her ironically funny, esoteric ballads as she was.— John Stark, *San Francisco Examiner*, February 6, 1976

February 1976— *Inner View.* During her February run at the Venetian Room Peggy was interviewed by critic and author Gene Arceri. He wrote:

> She moved like an ethereal, elusive dream, her moon-toned voice taking you on a voyage of the soul. A&M Records have aptly titled her new album *Mirrors*. Certainly, the lady reflects many-sided emotions vocally.
> Peg speaks of the arts as part of some spiritual sense, "They must be where inspiration comes from..."
> "...A writer, that's perhaps what I should have been most of all. I never wanted show business. I wanted to sing, nothing else but sing..."
> Peggy Lee has been coming to the Fairmont for over twenty years. Anya G. Ushakova, in public relations, used to the demands, problems and headaches of the stars booked there, said of Miss Lee, "I really love her, she has an incredible amount of compassion for humanity, for other people." I mentioned to Anya Miss Lee's aloofness, toughness one hears about. "Perhaps when you first meet her, but when you talk to her, know her, she is totally unlike the image presented."
> Peggy Lee's accounting of her success: "...a fulfillment of what you were born to be."

March 1976— *Stereo Review.* The final word on *Mirrors* belongs to critic Peter Reilly. His critique, "Peggy Lee: Ready to Begin Again," appeared in the March 1976 issue of *Stereo Review*:

> The consistent level of quality this finest of all our popular singers has maintained over two and a half decades in the entertainment firmaments is unique, I think, in the

Promoting a San Francisco Venetian Room appearance in 1976.

annals of American music, for Peggy Lee does not merely survive—she triumphs. *Mirrors* ... it must be confessed, is not—for me, at least—the ideal Peggy Lee album. It is at times pretentious, gimmicky, and rather overdecorated even for her, but she nonetheless finds room in between the furbelows to demonstrate, incredibly, that she continues to grow as an interpretive artist—one would have thought that she had already scaled all the peaks, that there was nothing left to conquer.

May 1976—Caesar's Palace, Las Vegas.

August 1976—Japan. Japan was also celebrating America's Bicentennial in 1976. Peggy's visit was part of this celebration. Her tour was sponsored by the Mitsukoshi department stores. She had been invited to Japan by Mitsukoshi's president, Shieru Okada. Okada told the press that Peggy was their choice for musical entertainer "because her great warmth and lovely personality are representative of the American people."

Peggy told Associated Press writer Bob Thomas that the Japanese fans amazed her:

> The Japanese have sent 30 requests for songs they would like to hear," said the singer as she prepared for the trip at her Beverly Hills home. "I'm amazed at how much of my work they know. They asked for songs that go back to when I was writing with Victor Young. They want not only 'Fever' but 'Johnny Guitar' and 'Autumn in Rome.' I've also written a special song for Japan, 'Dreams of Summer.'"—August 8, 1976

During this time Peggy wrote "Dreams of Summer" with a Japanese music student named Utakaka Kokakura. Peggy also learned two songs in Japanese, which she would bring back to the United States for future concerts. The tour of Japan included performances in Tokyo, Sapporo and Osaka.

September 8, 1976—*The Tonight Show with Johnny Carson.* David Brenner acted as guest host. His guests were Steve Allen, the Mills Brothers and Ricardo Montalban. Peggy sang "Have a Good Time" and "Everything Must Change."

September 1976—Drury Lane Theater, Chicago. On September 22, 1976, the critic for *Variety* wrote "Lee's impeccable taste and professionalism" suited the 1,700-seat theater.

September 18, 1976—*Chicago Tribune.* During this visit Peggy was made an honorary citizen by Chicago's Mayor Daley. Fred Orehek covered the event for the *Chicago Tribune*:

> "It's great to be in Chicago," said Miss Lee, "because this is where I was discovered by Mrs. Benny Goodman when I was singing at the Buttery in the Ambassador West Hotel in 1941."
>
> The blonde star, wearing a dramatic white cape and a black silk pantsuit with a long string of white pearls, kissed the mayor on the cheek and whispered something in his ear as he awarded her a medallion, making her an honorary citizen.

She agreed to sing "Chicago" for the mayor and his wife, Eleanor, when they attended her show in the Water Tower Drury Lane Theater Friday night.

October 1976— **Empire Room, Waldorf-Astoria, New York.**

> Peggy Lee's annual appearances ... are always somewhat of an adventure. There have been times when her performances there have been brilliant and others, such as the last two, when, because of material, orchestrations, or battles with the sound system, she has been surprisingly ineffective. This year is one of her good years—one of her very best, in fact.
>
> Everything—sound, orchestrations, programming, her voice—are under control and in balance. Looking slimmer and more relaxed than she has in several years, she is singing songs that, for the most part, do not pretend to be anything but good songs, songs that ride easily and smoothly on the low, throaty, shimmering tones of her voice.... Overall, this is a polished performance that avoids some of the heavy mannerisms she has tripped over in the past.—John S. Wilson, *New York Times*, October 16, 1976

Rex Reed sang her praises during this visit:

> Praise the Lord for Peggy Lee. She saved the week... I suggest you pay her a visit if you want to learn something about the craft of turning popular music into art.
>
> ...Peggy does a sublime Rodgers-Hart medley of "Glad to Be Unhappy," "It Never Entered My Mind," "Bewitched" and "Who Are You?," switches to a disco beat on "Love for Sale," and warms the coldest reaches of the heart with her own lyrics to a song by a young Japanese student named Yutaka, called "Dreams of Summer."
>
> This wunderkind can stand there and not sing one note during the last eight bars of "I'll Be Seeing You" and the audience is destroyed. That takes guts and greatness. This is class. This is art.

Winter 1976— **Television appearances.** During the final months of 1976 Peggy appeared on the following television shows: *Andy* (hosted by Andy Williams, exact airdate unknown), *Good Morning America*, broadcast by ABC on October 15, 1976, and *America Salutes Richard Rodgers: The Sound of His Music.*

The original airdate of the Richard Rodgers salute is unknown (the special was so popular that CBS re-broadcast it on June 3, 1978). Peggy looked glamorous as she and Vic Damone sang a medley of Richard Rodgers' tunes with the stunning Lena Horne.

February 1977— **Venetian Room, Fairmont Hotel, San Francisco.** Peggy shared some of her philosophy with Marian Zailian of the *S.F. Sunday Examiner & Chronicle* just prior to her opening on February 4, 1977:

> "Learn to be considerate of others. If you make an appointment, keep it. Don't be late. The further you go, the more difficulties you encounter. Set a standard for yourself to keep or rise above. Improve your performance. Hone. Probe."

Addressing her reputation as a perfectionist, Peggy explained:

> "I have been accused of having an obsession with perfection. I get the impression that what that means to the general public is that everything I do has to be perfect.

That's not so. It's striving to be better, striving for perfection—but there is no perfection."

March 7, 1977—Peggy. During this visit to England Peggy recorded a studio album for Polydor. The recording sessions took place sometime between March 7 and March 12. Like the *Live in London* LP, this record was produced by Ken Barnes. Peter Moore conducted the studio orchestra. The album was simply titled *Peggy*. Stunning portraits of Peggy taken by photographer Hans Albers grace the cover.

She brings a heart-wrenching sadness to Neil Sedaka's "The Hungry Years." On Peter Allen's "I Go to Rio" she displays good humor. Her rendition of Johnny Mercer's rarely heard "Star Sounds" takes the listener to that unique Peggy Lee universe. "What I Did for Love," the hit from the Broadway musical *A Chorus Line*, is bittersweet and poignant. The emotional subtext rings true here.

The album's finest performance is Peggy's extremely tender reading of "Just for Tonight." With one magic phrase, "…let's dance a slow dance," Peggy brings you into her arms for one more night of love. *Peggy* closes with a new rendition of Peggy's classic "Lover." This time she set the song to a '70s disco tempo.

March 8, 1977—Daily Express (UK). Peggy, in London for a series of concerts at the London Palladium, is interviewed by journalist Herbert Kretzmer for a piece titled "Peggy's Dancing Trees":

> Peggy Lee's suite on the eighth floor of the Dorchester is knee-deep in house plants. She bought them for company and keeps up a friendly communication every day with the surrounding vegetation.
>
> "I don't actually go up to them and say, 'Hi Fern!' but they know I'm there, and that I like them. I have felt this thing about plants since I was a child. The trees in my Beverly Hills garden actually dance to music. I've seen them move when there's no wind. I don't often speak about this because people will tend to think that I'm bonkers.…"
>
> Besides being a painter and sculptress, she is a splendid songwriter in her own right, with an eagle eye for a clean, uncluttered line in lyrics.
>
> "I believe I simplicity. A great man once said that the eternal struggle of art is to leave out all but the essentials."

March, 13 1977—London Palladium. The Polydor label was there to record her London Palladium concert on March 13, 1977. Her musical director was Peter Moore. Ken Barnes produced the album. The impact of the live album is summed up in the following concert reviews:

> There is nothing very spectacular about Peggy Lee except that she happens to have about the finest voice of any female in popular music.… It is natural, unforced and direct, but then the advantage that popular singers enjoy over their concert counterparts is that they are all natural and direct. Where most of them let themselves down, though, is in pushing that naturalness to the utmost, whether becoming melodramatic like Shirley Bassey or too perfect like Cleo Laine. Peggy Lee is a genius at just being herself, in the same way that a very good actress persuades you that she is always like that.—Miles Kington, *The London Times*, March 14, 1977

> The impersonal Palladium was transformed into a hall of nightclub intimacy as the singer caressed her songs of lost love and forlorn hopes, unique and brilliantly sung.... Peggy Lee is an essentially elegant singer to whom words are all-important, and it was particularly interesting to observe that not once throughout the show did she let rip. In her handling of warm ballads, she was the epitome of cool and her physical mannerisms were finely Economical.... It was a peerless performance from a singer with a load of charisma.—Ray Coleman, *Melody Maker*, March 19, 1977

The Polydor album *Peggy Lee—Live in London* captured the excitement of the Palladium concert. The record has a tangible energy that makes it difficult to single out individual songs. Two of the songs in the concert were special requests from the British fans, and these are definite highlights: "The Folks Who Live on the Hill" and "I Don't Want to Play in Your Yard."

"The Folks Who Live on the Hill" had been one of Peggy's biggest hits in the UK. It was also her favorite song. Her rendition, warm and touching, possesses a rougher, sadder edge than the studio version recorded for *The Man I Love* album. She sings like a woman shattered; somehow you know these dreams won't come true. Then in the next song, "I Don't Want to Play in Your Yard," she becomes an innocent little child taunting a playmate who hurt her feelings. It is an amazing transformation.

This album finally made her much-talked-about rendition of "Touch Me in the Morning" available to record buyers. She takes the song at a slower, more thoughtful pace than Diana Ross did on her hit version. Peggy makes the song her own. It is a portrait of a woman who will survive in "the cold morning light." Another highlight was her delightful reading of "Mack the Knife" as she brought new life to the over-recorded song.

Critic Miles Kington singled out "Mack the Knife" in his review, writing:

> Her version of "Mack the Knife" last night, for instance, was the only one I have ever heard that did not develop into a heavyweight brass band parade; she controlled it the whole way through, acting it, timing it beautifully, and making you think you had never heard the song before.

This concert album also includes a soaring "Mr. Wonderful" and the haunting "Sing a Rainbow" from *Pete Kelly's Blues*. The record closes with two Peggy Lee compositions, "Dreams of Summer" and "Here's to You."

March 19, 1977—*Yorkshire Times* (UK). Reginald Brace wrote of "Peggy Lee's Serene Tempo of Life." In the article, producer Ken Barnes spoke of Peggy's ability to sing behind the beat.

> Miss Lee beamed, and confirmed that she had enjoyed having her first British album produced by Barnes for Polydor. "We got on famously," she said.
> Around us, in a suite on the top floor of the Dorchester Hotel, boomed the Barnes remake of "Lover," one of Miss Lee's classic hits: a small, subtle voice fighting a winning battle against a thunderous arrangement by Pete Moore. "The original was an enormously influential record in the business in terms of percussion," said Barnes. "We've revived it without destroying the essential magic. Peggy likes to keep up to date.

"I don't know of any other singer who can play with the tempo like Peggy. She can let a bar go by and catch up. She telescopes her phrases with a finesse and authority which nobody has shown since Nat Cole and Mel Tormé."

***March 19, 1977**—Melody Maker* **(UK).** The venerable Max Jones wrote "Purrfect Peggy" for the UK's top jazz magazine:

> The singer keenly looked forward to her Palladium debut, having always nourished an ambition to appear in what was widely known to be England's number one variety spot. Her delight was doubled by the fact that Polydor was recording the concert live for Peggy's second LP for the label, which may be released first.
> "I think the studio album worked out very nicely and I'm hoping the concert one will, too. I have planned a programme to make everyone as happy as possible; it will include a selection of Rodgers and Hart songs, also certain requests."

***December 1977**—Peggy,* **Thames Television Special.** Peggy taped a concert for Thames Television in the UK. Peter Moore and Ken Barnes continued in their respective roles as conductor and producer. Peggy's special guest was the French cabaret star Charles Aznavour.

This program, like the Polydor album, was entitled *Peggy*. Miss Lee recaptured her old magic in her renditions of "The Folks Who Live on the Hill" and "Sing a Rainbow." With Aznavour she performed "I Love You" and a perfect "La Vie en Rose."

***December 30, 1977**—The Tonight Show with Johnny Carson.* Johnny welcomed Peggy, Suzanne Pleshette, Beau Bridges and Merie Earle. Peggy sang "When I Need You."

***January 13, 1978**—Second Annual People's Choice Command Performance.* After a rest of nearly nine months Peggy returned to perform on this CBS program. By request Peggy sang her two best-loved songs "Fever" and "Is That All There Is?" (Some sources list the airdate as January 8, 1978.)

***February 1978**—* **Venetian Room, Fairmont Hotel, San Francisco.** Writing for the *S.F. Sunday Chronicle Examiner*, James Kelton commented:

> The spotlight focuses on her snapping fingers when she begins "Fever".... [S]he evokes a realistic poetry when she whispers the words to Billy Joel's "Just the Way You Are." She sings "What I Did for Love," with a constrained, experienced beauty. Her versions of a pair of Charles Aznavour songs are lovely, lilting exercises in the practice of saloon singing—a form of jazz-nostalgia expertise to which she has staked apparently irrevocable charm.

***February 9, 1978**—San Francisco Chronicle.* In an article by Blake Green entitled "Singing About Romance and Disappointment," Peggy discussed a wide variety of topics with Green, including her interpretation of "Is That All There Is?" She told Green, "My attitude is that there is more. In the final sense the things that never let you down are what you are within yourself."

During her February Venetian Room engagement, Peggy gave a special birthday party for her musical hero, Mabel Mercer. The amazing Mercer was still performing at the age of 78. Like Sinatra, Peggy gave credit to Mabel, a master storyteller, for influencing her approach to the content of the lyric.

Ezekiel Green covered the birthday party for the *San Francisco Sunday Examiner & Chronicle*. Green's article, which appeared on February 26, 1978, observed:

> Two immensely popular singers. Not just singers. Two women who have taken words and songs we've heard in too many elevators and on too many meaningless afternoons and given them meaning. They make you listen to the words of standards you never realized had words.

February 19, 1978 — "Peggy Lee Casts a Vote for Class." Prior to her February 22, 1978, concert, the *Los Angeles Times* printed an interview between Peggy and jazz critic Leonard Feather. The piece featured the usually cautious Miss Lee speaking without restraint about the direction music was taking:

> "I still have a strong conviction that beauty is important in life, whether it's in singing, writing, literature, paintings. We'll never lose those values. I do feel that people in the arts have a duty to maintain certain standards of excellence, to counteract..." She paused for a moment, as if uncertain whether to point the dagger, then plunged in:
>
> "Take this rock group Kiss ... they're never seen without make-up, and the young kids have this illusion that they are romantic idols or something, when in fact it's just a total put-on. Grotesque."
>
> "The Sex Pistols—when I first was in London I was so embarrassed, because at first I was under the impression they were an American group, and they did this dreadfully offensive song about the queen.... Remember the days of the carnival, when they had men called geeks? They made them eat live chickens and lizards.... I just hate to think of show business slipping back to a stage that isn't too far removed from that."

The interview ended on a lighter note, with Peggy listing several contemporary musicians she liked, including Billy Joel ("love his writing"), Carol Bayer Sager, Carly Simon, Miles Davis with Gil Evans, Satie. "Depending on my mood, I can go from Hurricane Smith to Carmen McCrae.... Of course, there are all the forgone-conclusion people whom I shouldn't even have to mention—Ella, Sarah, Frank, Tony."

Peggy's wonderful, sly sense of humor surfaced in her closing comment:

> "I guess you could sum it up by saying I can appreciate almost anybody who doesn't eat live chickens."

February 22, 1978 — **Dorothy Chandler Pavilion, Los Angeles.** Harvey Siders wrote a review for the *Los Angeles Times* entitled "Time Stands Still to Peggy Lee Beat." Siders observed:

> Few jazz-oriented singers today can boast her uncanny rhythmic sense, whether she lags almost imperceptibly behind the beat or floats her bittersweet soprano in legato fashion over a busy pulse.
>
> After running the rhythmic gamut, she opted for the slow tempos, and the rest of

her long program was dominated by the type of ballad that allows her to disappear into the lyrics: "Folks Who Live on the Hill," with opulent string voicings, a thoughtful Charles Aznavour medley and an excellent Rodgers and Hart medley.

April 1978—Easter Seals Telethon. Jack Klugman hosted the annual telethon. The original broadcast date (although one can assume April 1978) and the songs Peggy performed are unknown.

In April she also performed in Detroit with her musical hero, Count Basie. She later told Lee Melville of *Drama-Logue* magazine that her appearance with Basie was "a dream come true—a total pleasure. We hope we can do it again."

April 19, 1978—The Tonight Show with Johnny Carson. Comedian Don Rickles acted as guest host. Rickles' guests were Shecky Greene, Peter Isackson, Rinette Reno and Carlos Palomino. Peggy sang "The More I See You" and Billy Joel's "Just the Way You Are."

June 3, 1978—America Salutes Richard Rodgers: The Sound of His Music. Peggy sang a medley of Richard Rodgers songs with Vic Damone and Lena Horne. Other guests included Gene Kelly, Diahann Carroll, Sammy Davis, Jr., Sandy Duncan and John Wayne. This program was first broadcast in the winter of 1976.

August 3, 1978—The Tonight Show with Johnny Carson. In top form, Peggy stepped on stage and sang a hard driving, swinging "Kansas City." She told Carson the chart was written by Quincy Jones and that she had performed it on the road with the Basie band.

Her delightful sense of humor was fully on display during this visit with Carson. Talking about the remodeling of her home, Peggy told how the work was disrupted when several snakes suddenly appeared in her yard. Peggy requested that Animal Control remove the snakes, but nothing could be done due to an EPA (Environmental Protection Agency) ruling.

One of the snakes was six feet in length. Peggy had Carson and his audience in stitches when she said, "I don't think it would do much good to spray Raid on a six-foot snake." She told Carson she liked the deer and the raccoons (who washed their faces in her swimming pool), but she was "not too fond of snakes."

At Carson's request, Peggy sang "Los Angeles Forevermore," a song she and Dick Hazard wrote honoring the city.

After a commercial break Peggy moved to the grand piano and performed a riveting rendition of "Send in the Clowns," a difficult song to sing. Peggy, accompanied only by piano, demonstrated her superb musicianship.

August 4–10, 1978—Drama-Logue magazine. This Lee Melville–penned article made the first mention of Peggy's upcoming engagement at the new Scandals nightclub, located in Hollywood.

June 3, 1978 — Peggy, Vic Damone and Lena Horne join forces for a medley of Richard Rodgers songs during the CBS special *America Salutes Richard Rodgers: The Sound of His Music.*

On being a perfectionist: "I'm trying to kill that word perfectionist; I'll sell it cheap," she laughs. "I hear every once in a while that I'm difficult and I can't quite understand where that comes from. If there's a wrong chord and I'd like the right chord — if that's being difficult, then, of course, I am. It's really more toward trying to do the best you can."

I tell her I had read that she has perfect pitch. "No, I'd say I have relative pitch, which is next to perfect. I'm grateful that I have a very good ear and I do hear things in a relative way — pick things out of the air and not be able to understand that myself... it came with the package."

August 8, 1978 — San Francisco Symphony.

Peggy traveled to San Francisco to replace singer Pearl Bailey at the opening of the San Francisco Symphony's Concord Pavilion series. Bailey was hospitalized for the removal of a kidney stone. Upon her return to Los Angeles, Peggy would also be hospitalized.

An Associated Press blurb reported that Peggy entered St. John's hospital with "a bout with viral flu." A piece in *Variety* made her illness sound a bit more serious, stating that Peggy was "suffering from an acute viral infection which has apparently invaded her blood stream and liver." Della Reese replaced Peggy at the Scandals opening. Peggy did not work for the remainder of 1978.

There was some good news during Peggy's recovery. It was announced that she had signed a contract with DRG Records. Hugh Fordin, DRG's president, would be producing her first album in two years.

September 6, 1978—**The Advocate.** Peggy spoke with *The Advocate*'s David Galligan about her spirituality and her singing style. Galligan's article was simply titled "Miss Peggy Lee."

> On Science of Mind: "I don't go to church, but I'm still in touch. One of the things you learn is that you really go to church within yourself. I once asked Ernest Holmes [the late founder of Science of Mind], 'Now that you've made me a free thinker, how do I differentiate between what's good and bad?' He said, 'Well, I think that if it's beautiful, it must be good.' He was a great influence in my life."
>
> On her voice: "Sometimes people say my voice is thin. I use the thin part for a certain reason. I can belt a song, but I can't express the proper feeling by doing that unless the song calls for it. I can make it very small because it's an intimate experience."

March 1979—**Opera House, Sydney, Australia.**

> After several months of illness, Peggy Lee's comeback at the Sydney Opera House was a wow.... Despite the house and its notoriously bad acoustics, Lee succeeded in giving one of the best shows the concert hall has seen.... The self-assured warm and lazy attitude of Lee affected fans as she rolled with ease through George Benson's "Everything Must Change," Erroll Garner's "Misty," and Billy Joel's "Just the Way You Are." At other times, in "Touch Me in the Morning" and Boz Scaggs' "Let It All Begin," her virtuosity was equally apparent with a strength and range undiminished... She encored with "Our Love Is Here to Stay" after roaring and stamping from the 2,000-strong SRO audience.—*Variety*, March 28, 1979

April 7, 1979—**Claremont, California.** Peggy gave a one-night concert at the Bridge Auditorium in Claremont, California.

May 30, 1979—**Los Angeles.** Peggy entered the Filmways Heider Studios in Los Angeles, recording ten songs in just two days. The new album, *Close Enough for Love*, would be released in a few months.

June 30, 1979—**Radio City Music Hall, New York.**

> The singer, who has been ill, said she had thought of retiring during the last year. But she told her audience on Thursday that she was feeling well again, and her appearance and voice seemed to confirm that.... Miss Lee seemed like her old confident, assured self in her opening numbers. Her voice had its familiar dark, throaty quality as she swung through "Love for Sale".... Her closing number, "I'll Be Seeing You," was a reminder that Miss Lee is essentially a mood-weaver, a spellbinder, who can use a catchy rhythm as well as a throaty whisper to gain her effects.—John S. Wilson, *New York Times*

July of 1979—***People* magazine.** During her visit to New York, Peggy's DRG album *Close Enough for Love* was released. *People* magazine gave the album a favorable review, saying of Peggy, "she is still one of the most durable jazz-pop singers." *People*'s critic also noted that she "retains her adventuresome ability to choose material," and concluded that the album was "vintage Lee, refreshing proof she hasn't run out of mañanas."

***December of 1979—Stereo Review* magazine.** Reviewing the album *Close Enough for Love*, critic Peter Reilly wrote:

> The very great Peggy Lee is recording on a new label, but she hasn't changed much else; she still sounds superb.... Peggy Lee's style is instantly recognizable and still one of the seven wonders of the world of entertainment.

Reilly illustrated how Peggy's talent transcended the so-called generation gap when he played the record "for someone young enough not to know the difference between Pinky and Peggy Lee." The reaction? "Outasight! Really outasight! Was she with a group before?"

Reilly felt this was "an album of pure gold." He singled out her rendition of Cole Porter's "Just One of Those Things" as the "Mont Blanc" in this outing. Other highlights include the title song and two ballads by Carole Bayer Sager. "Close Enough for Love" is delivered in Peggy's best tender, near-whispered fashion. She also shines on the Bayer Sager tunes "Come in from the Rain" (written with Melissa Manchester) and "Through the Eyes of Love" (penned by Bayer Sager and Marvin Hamlisch). All three ballads display a thoughtful and thought-provoking artist at her interpretive peak.

As a songwriter Peggy contributed two lovely tunes to this album. With Richard Hazard she wrote the Sunday-lazy "Easy Does It." She delivered the song in her most suggestive style. Peggy and jazz pianist Marian McPartland collaborated on "In the Days of Our Love." The album closes with a warm rendition of Arthur Hamilton's "Rain Sometimes."

December 29, 1979—Kennedy Center Awards. Peggy was there to honor America's "First Lady of Song," the venerable Ella Fitzgerald. Lee hosted the segment honoring Fitzgerald and Count Basie, Joe Williams and Peggy joined forces on "Alright, Okay, You Win." Other honorees that year included Martha Graham, Tennessee Williams, Henry Fonda and Aaron Copland.

Peggy salutes her friend Ella Fitzgerald. The *Kennedy Center Awards* were broadcast on December 7, 1979.

February 13, 1980— Blue Room, Fairmont Hotel, New Orleans.

> She creates mini-dramas with her superb voice and with good orchestrations from the Dick Stabile group. Especially effective is her ability to hit a note, flatten it for dramatic effect and return it to its proper place on the scale.... While Lee respects her audience by trying new, unusual material, she also respects backup musicians by turning toward them during bridges, riveting audience attention on their fine music.—*Variety*

February 23, 1980— Venetian Room, Fairmont Hotel, San Francisco.

> Peggy Lee still has an aura, a mystique, an ineffable essence that she uses to hold sway over her audiences.... She presides over her show like a good, white witch (so to speak) and yet, it seemed she wasn't always there. I mean, in the here and now.... Her most effective moments Thursday were those where she sang as if from a cocoon, oblivious to the band, the audience, to everything but the words.—Conrad Silvert, *San Francisco Examiner*

May 26, 1980— Peggy Lee's 60th Birthday.

June of 1980—"Side by Side by Sondheim." This engagement marked Lee's first in a "legitimate theater" production. She performed in the show for five weeks at the Birmingham Theater in Michigan. The pianist for this production was Paul Horner. Soon Peggy and Paul would begin writing songs for her autobiographical musical *Peg*.

September 12, 1980— Chicago Mill Run Theater, Chicago.

October 1980— Hollywood Palladium. Peggy returned to Los Angeles to perform at a Big Band Bash at the Hollywood Palladium. The show was hosted by Mel Tormé and featured Buddy Rich, Harry James and Lena Horne.

October 19, 1980— San Diego Union. "Peggy Lee at 60: Old Flame Still Shines Brightly" was the title of an article by Vernon Scott. Peggy spoke of songwriters and her plans to perform in a Broadway musical based on her life.

> Of contemporary songwriters, she likes Paul Williams, Barry Manilow, Melissa Manchester and Carol Bayer Sager. She suggested that most of the big hits are being written for groups, adding that she does not lament the demise of disco.
>
> Peggy is forced to pass up many new songs because of sexually explicit lyrics or veiled reference to drugs.
>
> "I'm still writing songs," Peggy said. "Right now I'm involved in writing a Broadway musical based on highlights of my own life. I'm writing the lyrics and Paul Horner is writing the music. I hope to star in it myself.
>
> "I'm very careful with lyrics. There are a lot of romantic words and phrases that have gone out of style. You don't use 'darling' or 'honey' in contemporary music because they have a dated quality.
>
> "I guess I'm still going strong because I've kept up with the times and styles in music. And I plan to keep it up as long as people want to hear me."

November 1980— **London Palladium.** Peggy was invited to perform at a London Palladium Gala honoring the Queen Mother.

In London she was greeted with the same enthusiasm she received during previous visits. *Music Week* magazine published this review by Rodney Burbeck in the November 1980 edition:

> Staying on at the Palladium for two nights after the Royal Variety Performance, Peggy Lee sadly attracted a less than capacity audience, but those that were discerning enough to attend were treated to a spellbinding performance of stunning virtuosity. Barely moving from the same spot by the piano, she simply sang, but commanded attention, respect and admiration through the deceptively laid-back power and control of a voice that has not dimmed over the years.

November 20, 1980—*Daily Mirror* (UK). Alan Markfield wrote that Peggy still had a "Fever for Living":

> She won't name the illness or its symptoms in case anyone thinks Peggy Lee, at an age when most women look forward to retirement, can't stand the pace of a major tour. The only reminder she has of it comes late at night when she is tired. The left side of her face still goes numb.

About the illness, Peggy said, "My fans didn't know what was happening to me... I kept it all secret.

"There was quite a bit of doubt about whether or not I would survive. But as you can see, I'm fine. I'd like to think of it as having had a little rest. I am so grateful to be feeling well and able to enjoy my work again.

"It certainly makes for a new beginning—but don't you dare call this a comeback."

November 27, 1980—The Stage (UK).

> Blonde bombshell Peggy Lee took the Palladium by storm last week with her overplayed ice queen glamour and her ultra-cool—even underplayed—set. The extravagance of the whipped honey halo of hair and the diaphanous feathered gown was in marked contrast to the taut, controlled performance in which not one bar of phrase was wasted...
>
> Perhaps the most remarkable facet of the American's performance was her ability to communicate the intimacy of a nightclub setting as she draped herself across the piano in slinky fashion, and yet be received with the revered hush of a concert hall audience.—Moira Petty, *The Stage*

January of 1981— **A Tribute to Leonard Feather.** Peggy's first performance of 1981 came at a tribute for her lifelong friend, Leonard Feather. *Variety* reported that the special concert, which took place at the Cocoanut Grove, was a "celebration of Duke Ellington's music to raise funds for a Leonard Feather scholarship at the Duke Ellington School of the Arts in Washington, D.C."

Variety also noted that critic Feather played the piano "while Ella Fitzgerald, Peggy Lee, Sarah Vaughan and Joe Williams scatted on Duke Ellington's "It Don't

Mean a Thing." Peggy's solo moment was described as follows: "Peggy Lee, looking and sounding gorgeous, essayed a poignant 'Solitude,' supported by the fluid and creative background of Nat Pierce on piano and John Pisano on guitar."

February 17, 1981 — **Dorothy Chandler Pavilion, Los Angeles.** Peggy returned for another "Special Evening" at the Dorothy Chandler Pavilion. This evening was hosted by her friend, Steve Allen. The *Los Angeles Times* printed Paul Grein's review on February 19, 1981:

> Peggy Lee is a singer of great subtlety and understatement. In fact, she's at her best when she's cool, blasé and detached.... Lee was in wonderful voice, easily belying her [*sic*] 58 years (40 of them in show business). Her effortless, unforced style combines great taste with purity and precision, though she spices it up occasionally with saucy numbers like Leiber and Stoller's "I'm a Woman."

February of 1981 — **Diplomat Hotel, Florida.** Tony Bennett and Peggy Lee performed together for the first time. The two legendary jazz singers received kudos:

> For their first co-billed engagement, Peggy Lee and Tony Bennett have put together an evening of musical nuggets comprising 36 songs tied into three long medleys.... Both singers are in good voice, the songs are standards and the arrangements are top-notch. The main thrust of the evening is the quality of the music and the singers, and there are no problems there. The show's only problem can be solved by working out the kinks in the presentation and pacing it to provide a bit more pizzazz if they want to continue pairing, as they say they do. — *Variety*, March 4, 1981

Peggy flew to England after her stint with Tony Bennett and filmed a new special for the BBC. This television concert would be aired during the summer. Her next stop would be San Francisco.

March 7, 1981 — *Billboard.* Dave Dexter, Jr., wrote "A Whole New Ball Game Coming Up for Peggy Lee."

April 1, 1981 — **Venetian Room, Fairmont Hotel, San Francisco.**

> Standing statuesquely in the curve of the piano, her eyes near-glazed much of the time, her hands and arms waving around in what might be called her inimitable Lee whirl, she can, indeed, distract one visually — but not, in fairness, to the point of not realizing that here, still, is one of the very best singers of popular songs in our time. — Philip Elwood, *San Francisco Examiner*

July 1981 — *The Tomorrow Show.* At age sixty-one the singer still looked stunning, and here turned in an equally stunning vocal performance. Tom Snyder and his studio audience were clearly enthralled when Peggy sang her own "I Love Being Here with You" and Ellington's "I Got It Bad."

Snyder welcomed her by saying that after a year of being "rocked and rolled and punked and steamed" by other musical guests he was delighted to spend "a quiet moment with Peggy Lee."

She closed *The Tomorrow Show* with a charming rendition of "I Could Write a Book."

July 31, 1981*— *New York Times. Peggy discussed her early influences with John S. Wilson in an article titled "Peggy Lee Sings Tonight and Mañana":

> "I was a big fan of Lil Green," she recalled. "When I joined Benny Goodman, I traveled with a wind-up phonograph and some records by Lil Green and some Debussy records. What a mixture! My dressing room was next to Benny's. He heard me play Lil Green's 'Why Don't You Do Right?' over and over. 'Do you like that?' he asked me. I told him I did. 'Would you like to sing it with the band?' he asked. I told him I'd love to."

According to the article, Peggy's other influences inclluded Laura Rucker ("I got my style for the piece ['Let's Do It'] from her"), Maxine Sullivan (who "had a happy talent for knowing where to draw the line, having the good taste to cut some things"), Billie Holiday ("for her soul"), and Ella Fitzgerald ("for her technical ability").

***July 31, 1981*— Garden State Arts Center, Holmdel, New Jersey.** Peggy and Tony Bennett performed together again this time in New Jersey. From there the two jazz-influenced singers traveled to Indianapolis.

At this time a television show called *A Gift of Music* aired. This program celebrated the 200th anniversary of Los Angeles. Peggy performed "Together (Wherever We Go)" from the musical *Gypsy*. The exact airdate of *A Gift of Music* is unknown.

August 3, 1981*— *Peggy Lee Entertains. The hour-long concert broadcast over the BBC. Ever the glamorous star, Lee made several costume changes during the show. She included nearly all of her best-loved songs—"I Love Being Here with You," "Mr. Wonderful," "Why Don't You Do Right?," "I'm a Woman" and "Fever."

Highlights from this special included her ethereal reading of "Everything Must Change" and her tender, warm and open rendition of "But Beautiful." The latter proved that Peggy still knew more about the use of silence than any other singer. Judy Collins' "My Father" became a masterpiece in Peggy's hands; the listener could see the lyrics as Peggy painted her memories and hopes in glowing pastels.

November 8, 1981*— Sunday Datebook, *SF Chronicle & Examiner. "Peggy Lee at 61— She Still Gives Them Fever" was the headline of an article written by Colin Dangaard.

Dangaard found the star in her garage. She was dressed in judo clothes and refinishing a chair in a color she called "embarrassed shrimp." When questioned about romance, Peggy said, "I tell men I need a little time, like 300 years."

December 31, 1981*— *Los Angeles Times. In jazz critic Leonard Feather's article "The Many Faces of Peggy Lee," Peggy told Feather that she had written a book called "The Men I've Loved." The book was never published.

She also revealed that she was writing her autobiography at that time, as well as a play based on her life. This was the first mention of the project that would eventually become the Broadway musical *Peg*. About the proposed play, Lee says:

> "We have 18 songs, I wrote the lyrics, and the music is by a fellow from England, Paul Horner. Although the songs are tied in with my life story, they can all be sung independently.
>
> "Tony Bennett is very anxious to get at the score. People who have heard it seem to be enthusiastic. When someone like Mel Powell thinks it's a great score, there must be something worthwhile about it."

At the end of the interview Feather asked Peggy if she had any regrets. Peggy responded:

> "I don't know that I honestly regret anything. I know I've made a lot of mistakes, but I think, given the same set of circumstances, I'd make the very same mistakes again."

In the article, Feather reported that Peggy's latest single could be heard on the soundtrack of the Burt Reynolds film *Sharky's Machine*. Critic Rex Reed felt that the soundtrack was "the best thing about *Sharky's Machine*," and advised his readers to "buy the soundtrack and skip the movie."

Burt Reynolds hired an amazing group of jazz all-stars to record the songs for the film. Julie London came out of retirement to record a singular "My Funny Valentine" for Reynolds. Chet Baker, the Manhattan Transfer, Sarah Vaughan and Joe Williams were also heard on the film score. Williams' solo "8 to 5 I Lose" was nominated for a Grammy. Writing for *Stereo Review*, Peter Reilly singled out Peggy:

> As with most such galas, one star outshines all the rest; in this case it is the unsinkable Peggy Lee. Wrapping her sloe-gin voice and lambent lyric style around a really lousy song—"Let's Keep Dancing," probably best described as a sort of idiot son of "Is That All There Is?"—she is still able to produce the kind of effects that send the listener back to the recording to play her track again and again.

• SEVEN •

There'll Be Another Spring: 1982 to 1988

August 17, 1982*—*The New York Times. *The New York Times'* "Briefs on the Arts" section ran the headline "Peggy Lee to Make Debut on Broadway in Her Story." Like other articles on the upcoming show, this one claimed that *Peg* would boast a "22-member cast, [and] the musical has a score of 21 original songs." During the creative process of staging the show, the cast and musical numbers would be trimmed down.

***August 19, 1982*—"Stage Watch."** Lawrence Christon's "Stage Watch" column reported "Peggy Lee Set for 'Personal' Musical." Writing songs in a biographical vein was new to Peggy, who commented:

> "In the old days you kept your life out of your songs, even when you wrote them. But times have changed. Singers write about themselves and their experiences now much more freely. I've kept my life as a writer fairly secret, but there are many astonishing things that have happened to me and have never been publicized. A lot of it will deal with my life with Dave Barbour. It'll be my Broadway debut, and I'm training for it like an athlete."

September 1, 1982*—*The Youngstown Daily Vindicator. Syndicated columnist Bob Thomas wrote an article that was picked up by the Associated Press. Thomas' piece, "Broadway Musical to Be Staged as Autobiography of Peggy Lee," revealed that Zev Bufman and Irv Cowan would produce the show. Bufman and Cowan had a Broadway hit with *The Little Foxes*, starring Elizabeth Taylor. In fact, it was rumored that Taylor was a financial backer of *Peg*.

***September 6, 1982*— Associated Press.** Bob Thomas reported on the luncheon where the producers officially announced that *Peg* was headed for Broadway:

> Miss Lee took the microphone and remarked, "This is one of the happiest days of my life." She admitted that in the past she wouldn't have been able to speak more than a few words to such as gathering, "but now my shyness has sort of left me. I want to get out and live life to the fullest." Reviewing her life to create "Peg" may have been therapy, she conceded.

Then she performed three of the songs, with Horner playing piano. The room was silent as she sang about a player piano she had known as a child, about how she learned to sing the blues, about her love for Dave Barbour. The voice was sultry and insinuating as ever, but the songs seemed to emerge from deep within her.

Asked if there would be a road company of "Peg," Bufman replied: "I can't conceive of anyone filling those shoes."

September 13, 1982—**Capitol Reunion Concert.** Peggy traveled to Hackensack, New Jersey to perform at a reunion of Capitol artists. At the special concert, six hours in length, Peggy shared the stage with Gordon MacRae, Keely Smith, Nelson Riddle, Margaret Whiting, Betty Hutton, Andy Russell, Ella Mae Morse, the Four Freshmen and the Pied Pipers.

September 14, 1982—*The Star-Ledger.* George Kanzler's review of the Capitol Reunion concert, "Capitol Singers Prove They Still Got That Swing," appeared in New Jersey's *The Star-Ledger*. From the all-star line-up, Kanzler singled out two performers: Keely Smith and Peggy Lee. Of Miss Lee, Kanzler made these comments:

> Except for Peggy Lee, none of the other singers on hand were as notable, or likely to be immortalized, as such other Capitol Records artists of the early decades as Frank Sinatra, Nat King Cole or Judy Garland, all of whom were seen during the opening film hour.... Lee's rich, insinuating voice was in top form, and she was an appropriate tiara to the Capitol Records salute.

November 1982—**Silk Cut Festival of Jazz, England.** Peggy and a troupe of jazz greats traveled to England. Lee, happy to be in the company of her beloved Carmen McRae, was also joined on this tour by Sarah Vaughan, Billy Eckstine, Joe Williams and Blossom Dearie. The BBC televised Peggy's Silk Cut concert.

November 7, 1982—*The Observer.* Dave Gelly reviewed the Silk Cut concert for *The Observer*:

> There was a moment, a few minutes into Peggy Lee's performance... when it became obvious that something quite extraordinary was happening. It came as she embarked on a version of the old Gershwin ballad 'S Wonderful,' and the word for it, I suppose, is inspiration. For the best part of an hour thereafter, every phrase she sang had a poise and spaciousness that not even her best recordings have captured.... Even at the slowest of tempos she could leave a long pause without fear that the momentum would be lost.... There were no histrionics or showbiz tricks, just the merest of hesitations, a droop of the voice, a couple of altered notes which transformed the melody and made it infinitely more moving than its composer could ever have imagined.

December 1982—**5th Annual Kennedy Center Honors.** Peggy was there to salute her "old boss," Benny Goodman, who was being honored alongside George Abbott, Lillian Gish, Gene Kelly and Eugene Ormandy.

Peggy thanked her former boss for "all those bus rides" and then sang a haunting rendition of the déjà vu classic "Where or When." Forty years after she had

Benny Goodman was honored with the Kennedy Center Award. Goodman became teary-eyed when Peggy sang "Where or When" and thanked him "for all those bus rides." The show was broadcast in December 1982. (CBS)

recorded the song with the Goodman sextet, it was apparent that her magic and skill had grown. The usually taciturn Goodman sat teary-eyed, amazed at his once fledgling "girl singer."

February 13, 1983 — *Chicago Tribune News.* The year 1983 began with more press about Peggy's upcoming Broadway debut. Larry Kart of the *Chicago Tribune News* service interviewed the singer. His article quoted Peggy at length, as she spoke of the emotional danger of becoming too involved with a song:

> "Of course it's necessary for me to keep some distance between myself and the songs. In performance I've lost control of that only twice, maybe — to the point where I wound up weeping and had to leave the stage. Why? Well, a relation suddenly developed between the song and something that occurred to me, something that gave the song a dimension I just couldn't handle."

Lee knew that playing herself in "Peg" would be difficult. Every lyric touched on her personal life. She would have to separate herself from the painful memories, while remaining honest:

> "Writing the show I really had to confront my past. The truth is one of the things I promised myself it would be because I knew it wouldn't be fair to write a fairy tale. At one time I started to put in all down in a book, but I stopped because it became so dark and violent. But somehow, maybe because it's a musical, the show seems to be doing itself."

Peggy ended this interview with a bit of philosophy about great artists and their apparent need to suffer:

> "I used to think that Sophie Tucker was wrong when she said that you had to have your heart broken at least once in order to sing a love song.... I've found out that she was right."
>
> ..."I've often wondered why so many great singers have had a lot of grief and pain in their lives.... Maybe it's because the soul needs to be pressed down or heated up in a flame, tested in some way in order to promote future growth."

March 1983 — **The Peggy Lee Rose.** The American Rose Society honored Peggy by naming the 1983 American Beauty Rose of the Year after the singer. The Peggy Lee Rose was described as a "beautiful pink Hybrid Tea Rose with blooms so enchanting they're like a song that haunts your memory."

May 1983 — *Crescendo International* (UK). Record producer Benny Golson spoke of working with Peggy.

> "[W]hat a delight to work with Peggy Lee. I mean, she's a real professional. I had an experience with her that I've never had with any other artist as the arranger/conductor of the music for a complete recording session [*Make It with You* on Capitol[. Incidentally, at a time when people were all overdubbing the strings, the horns and everything, she insisted on doing the whole date live. The strings, the whole orchestra was there, and she was singing in the room.... She wasn't there for the mix, and when she heard it, it had been mixed so that the singing was very loud and you

could hardly hear the arrangements—the vocal was just wiping the brass and everything. She said: "The voice is too loud." They went back in and remixed it, and she went with 'em this time—that's the way it should be.

July 1983—Los Angeles. Journalist Maurice Zolotow penned an in-depth article for *Los Angeles* magazine, focusing on *Peg* and the personal history behind the songs. The article, titled "Is That All There Is, Peggy?" delineates her early childhood ("Mama had died giving birth, and her paradise had been lost," [and] she was under the stern, cruel domination of a stepmother who hated her"), her early exposure to 1930s bands on the radio ("she memorized lyrics ... she was born a singer ... and because her mother had died and her stepmother beat her, she had the blues"), and how she ran away from home and "got a job singing and playing piano for 15 minutes on Fargo station WDAY ... changed her name to Peggy Lee.... She killed a lot of time, but she always kept good time. She already had the style and the looks. She looked fresh and believed in the music. She could get the meaning of the words. She was a writer herself and had begun writing poetry."

August 29, 1983— **Associated Press.** In the AP article "The Life and Music of Peggy Lee," Jay Sharbutt wrote:

> The singer: Peggy Lee. The musical: *Peg*, about both the bad times and the good times in her life and career. It is propelled by 29 songs, some her hits of yesteryear, others new tunes written for the show.
> It is scheduled to premiere in November, and it will be her Broadway debut in three respects—as a lyricist, co-author and star....
> "I didn't intend to be in it at all, originally," says Lee, a shy, soft-spoken woman. "I was writing it for someone else to do."
> That changed when she invited Irv and Margie Cowan, friends who own a hotel, to a party at her Beverly Hills home. Someone urged her to sing a bit of the score from the work-in-progress.
> "They loved it," she reports. "They said, 'We'd like to produce it.'" Then they summoned Broadway producer Zev Bufman to hear it. He also flipped, and asked to co-produce it. All insisted she be the star.

November 1983— "Fight for Sight—Lights on '83." Peggy shared the bill at this fundraiser with Bob Hope, Eddie Fisher, Tony Randall, Eartha Kitt and the cast of *Dreamgirls*.

November 7, 1983— **Lincoln Center, New York.** "The Stars Shine for Liberty" was the first major benefit for the preservation of the Statue of Liberty. In addition to Peggy and Bob Hope, this show starred tap legend Charles "Honi" Coles and Luciano Pavarotti.

December 1, 1983—Peg. *Peg* has its first preview at the Lunt-Fontane theater.

December 14, 1983—Peg. Opening night of *Peg*.

***December 15, 1983*—Reviews for *Peg*.** For the first time in a career that spanned almost fifty years the critics proved universally harsh towards Miss Peggy Lee. Most of the critics praised her singing and the new songs she had written; however, they dismissed the show as nothing less than an ego-trip.

> Dressed in a flowing gown of white and silver, her head crowned by a halo of glitter, Peggy Lee takes to the stage of the Lunt-Fontanne like a high priestess ascending an altar. And *Peg*, the "musical autobiography" that Miss Lee has brought to Broadway, is nothing if not a religious rite. In this evening of songs and chat, one of our premier pop singers presents herself as a spiritual icon. There is some entertainment in *Peg*, not to mention some striking musicianship, but the show is most likely to excite those who are evangelistically devoted to Peggy Lee and God — ideally in that order.... Though Miss Lee's voice is a small instrument, it is usually sure in pitch. Her rhythmic attack can't be beat.— Frank Rich December 15, 1983, *New York Times*
>
> Along the way, we hear some harrowing stories about the future star's childhood including the fact that her step-mother started her doing housework at the age of five, beat her and poured boiling water on her hands as she did the dishes.... And while she tells of her punishments, a cheerful, almost funny Miss Lee curiously enough sings a calypso-style song called "One Beating a Day," which has a choral arrangement by Ray Charles.
>
> When Miss Lee sings she still sings memorably.... She sings warmly of the joys of her life, her husband, guitarist Dave Barbour, and her daughter.... Here deft and often witty in her upbeat numbers, and glisteningly soulful in her more sentimental ballads, Miss Lee sings with a compelling intensity.— William A. Raidy, December 15, 1983

***December 18, 1983*—*Peg* closes.** After thirteen previews and five performances, the show was shut down. It was a devastating blow to Peggy Lee. There were reports of a 45-minute standing ovation on closing night. Reviews continued to be printed long after the closing.

***December 21, 1983*—*Variety*.**

> When Peggy Lee is singing, "Peg" is an entertaining show. But the concert revue which arrived Wednesday at the Lunt-Fontanne Theater has been clouded by awkwardly written, mawkish autobiographical material that veers close to self-glorification....
>
> Musically the show is virtually flawless.... It's not that the singer is an unattractive or cold personality. But the myopic and maudlin writing, which omits introspective insights, ironically distances her from the audience.

***December 1983*—*Mandate*.** The gay men's magazine featured Freeman Gunter's article "Peggy Lee: Blonde Soul." Freeman revealed that "blonde soul" was the nickname bestowed upon her by Louis Armstrong.

***January 9, 1984*—*People*.** The magazine featured J.D. Reed's article "Peggy Lee's Broadway Show Was a Bust, but the Lady Has Seen Hard Times Before," in which Reed found Lee turning the negative feelings about *Peg* into something positive:

Lee is already viewing the setback with practiced calm. More fond of quoting literature than lyrics, she cites Emerson: "God will not have his work made manifest by cowards...."

Since *Peg* folded, Lee's spiritual view of life has supported her. "I've been trying to figure out," she says, her eternal lassitude intact, "what I'm supposed to learn from it." The answer seems to lie in activity. She and Cy Coleman are planning to re-stage *Peg* and record an album of the show. "Retiring doesn't interest me," she says. "I've got ideas for other shows and film scripts stacked up and waiting. After all, intelligence conquers age. My slogan is straight ahead. And straight up."

January 15, 1984— Palace Theatre, New York. Before leaving New York, Lee performed at two special events. The first, "We Write the Songs: A Celebration of the American Songwriter," was hosted by the Songwriters Guild. Other songwriters who shared the stage with Peggy included Sammy Cahn, Cy Colemen, John Kander and Fred Ebb, Burton Lane and Jule Styne.

February 13, 1984— Madison Square Garden's Felt Forum. Peggy's radio home in New York, WNEW, was celebrating its 50th anniversary by sponsoring a benefit concert for the National Kidney Foundation of New York/New Jersey. Peggy performed alongside Tony Bennett, Rosemary Clooney, Vic Damone, Joe Williams and Mel Tormé.

June/July of 1984—*Crescendo International* (UK). *Crescendo*'s Les Tomkins enjoyed a question-and-answer session with Peggy during her 1984 tour of the UK. The resulting article was titled "On a New Plateau of Vocal Artistry: Peggy Lee."

> LT: On the subject of your early listening—back in Jamestown, North Dakota, what music around you was inspiring you?
>
> PL: I used to listen to Kansas City on a five-dial Atwater Kent radio. I'd hear Bill Basie... I think they called him Bill Basie and His Kansas City Coon Shouters—so funny, it sounds so ridiculous now! Yes, and the Blue Devils. And then—oh, the Kid from Red Bank. Oh, what a giant to go! Gordon, and now Count Basie—oh, my goodness.
>
> LT: Yes, we're losing some great people. From the beginning, did you feel that your self-expression was going to be your voice?
>
> PL: Mmmm—absolutely. I always knew that. No, I wasn't listening to singers at that time—I did as soon as I could. But I knew it before I heard anyone else sing. Strange, knowing that. The great desire was there in me to do that, and a kind of a will for it to happen.

June 1984— Festival Hall, London.

> Star quality, as the still running masterpiece *Evita* observes, is what it's all about.... You either have it or you don't. Peggy Lee has it, with sexuality to match, and her outrageously successful concert at the Festival Hall on Thursday was a memorable demonstration of its effect.... Evita-like, too was the feeling that flooded back from the audience. You could sense it, almost touch it—a kind of loving for the good

years which plainly moved the sexagenarian who received it to a degree rare in the emotive-tinsel world of stage performance. I have seen standing ovations, but never one so meant.—Derek Jewell, June 3, 1984, *London Times*

***June 1984**—The Westwood Playhouse.* To promote her Westwood engagement, Peggy spoke to Michael Kearns of *Drama-Logue* magazine. In the magazine's June 21–27, 1984, issue, Peggy discussed her feelings about *Peg*. Her carefully chosen words to describe the Broadway fiasco were "It was *wonderfully interesting.*" Her sadness became a bit more evident when she related the following:

> "I worked on the story for six years—the story of my life. Paul Horner and I worked on the score—that was a wonderful experience, too. We are going to record it eventually—probably when I get back to New York. It was a shock because we all loved it. The audience certainly showed they loved it—18 performances, 18 standing ovations, at least one per show. The last show—which, unfortunately, the producers didn't even see—a 45-minute standing ovation with tears and pleading, 'Don't go.' None of us know why."

***June 1984**—The Merv Griffin Show.* Peggy visited with Merv and sang her swinging version of "Heart" with the marvelous Jack Sheldon on trumpet. Sitting next to Griffin, she sang her Grammy-winner "Is That All There Is?" The exact airdate of this show is unknown.

***June 19, 1984**—Los Angeles Times.* Reporter Terry Atkinson covered Peggy's appearance on *The Merv Griffin Show* for the *Los Angeles Times* in his article "Lee's Quest for Meaning in Life":

> This version of "Heart" was... Peggy Lee at her best. The phrasing was as delicious as ever, the pitch right on.... The interview with Griffin was mildly interesting but meandering, and greenroom attention was lagging....
>
> Suddenly, though, the room became completely quiet, except for the sound from the monitor. Lee, sitting right there next to Griffin, was going "Is That All There Is?" And it wasn't merely a good-for-her-age performance. The half-sung, half-talked interpretation was top-drawer—beautiful, chilling. Leiber and Stoller's song of hopeful disillusionment may fit Lee better than ever at this stage of her career.

***June 21, 1984**—Los Angeles Times.*

> It was immediately clear that all the elements had fallen into place. The [Westwood Playhouse] theater is just small enough to enable her to establish a rapport, even with fans in the back row.... Peggy Lee works too seldom in the city where she has lived for so many years. Her presence in the right place, with the right repertoire and musicians, is a needed reminder that she is still one of a kind.—Leonard Feather

***June 21, 1984**—Los Angeles Herald Examiner.*

> In a way, it's good that Peggy Lee visits Los Angeles as seldom as she does. Seeing her in person makes it difficult to appreciate most other popular singers; compared to her, there's no comparison....

Although aware of every word (every syllable, really), Lee delivers each subtly. You see and hear her going through the emotions and other thought processes of a song, but subtly. For instance, the recent country hit "The Wind Beneath My Wings" is usually given an all-stops-out treatment. Lee caresses the number, which comes out all the better for her underkill.— Todd Everett

June 25, 1984 — The Tonight Show. Lee joined guest host Joan Rivers. The singer looked elegant and "svelte" all in black. She performed her own "I Love Being Here with You." Chatting with Rivers, she discussed her newfound ease on stage, telling the host she was still very shy and that she had only recently "learned to talk." After the laughter died down, Peggy added, "Pretty soon I'll get to read!" Then she wrapped the audience up in a silky yet strong "I Got It Bad (and That Ain't Good)."

July 11, 1984 — Variety. Variety noted that the "rather sudden booking of Peggy Lee for a two-week concert stand at the Westwood Playhouse had some ramifications opening night, but Lee has a way of making "untogether" an asset, and the charm and slightly spacey wit she applied to the various staging and behind-the-scenes snafus evident that evening made her two-hour plus performance all the more personal and appealing."

Though reporting that Lee complained of having a slight cold, the review talked of the "effusive fan response," and singled out "an understated version of 'The Folks Who Live on the Hill,' a quintessential Lee treatment of "S Wonderful' and a striking rendition of 'Fly Me to the Moon'" as standouts, not to mention the two "recent country hits" "The Wind Beneath My Winds" and "Help Me Make It Through the Night" (both of which "suit Lee's breathy, appealingly diffident singing style very well").

August 1984 — Resorts International Casino Hotel, Atlantic City. Next on her schedule was a concert with the New Jersey Symphony Orchestra. PBS aired the Atlantic City concert in August 1984. The concert, now titled "The Quintessential Peggy Lee," was released on video, laser-disc and DVD.

> Peggy Lee at 62 is still an intensely absorbing pop-jazz vocalist. Health problems... have given Miss Lee's dreamy passivity an occasionally disconnected air, but the singer hasn't lost her ability to invest the subtlest hesitations of phrase and bending of notes with intimations of mischief and eroticism. This blend of playfulness and glamour, along with an aura of metaphysical contemplation, helps make the musical special ... a compelling retrospective....— Stephen Holden, August 31, 1984, *New York Times*

August 25, 1984 — Associated Press. The AP's Bob Thomas was on the scene again for "Peggy Lee Credo: Go Back to Work":

> One of the entertainment world's ablest survivors, singer Peggy Lee, last winter suffered a blow that would send most stars to their psychiatrists. Her autobiographical show, *Peg*, was rejected by the Broadway critics and closed December 18 after 18 performances.

"Self-pity is a waste of time," she said recently. "I decided the best thing to do was go back to work."

In January, she made appearances in Canada. She followed with a trip to Japan, then a triumphant tour of England and Wales....

Obviously on a roll, Lee decided to make a rare appearance in her hometown. The Westwood Playhouse, an intimate theater on the fringes of the University of California at Los Angeles, was available, and she moved in for a sellout three weeks.

October 3, 1984— Venetian Room, Fairmont Hotel, San Francisco.

> I've never understood just what wheels had to be turning, what galaxies had to be in proper juxtaposition, what cosmic vibes had to be functioning for singer Peggy Lee to perform a show just the way she wanted. But, whatever, last night in her opening set of a two week run in the Fairmont's Venetian Room, Lee had her act as much together (I think) as she'll ever accomplish and the overall effect was both memorable and stunning.— Philip Elwood, *San Francisco Examiner*
>
> She sang a long program — 21 songs— but an hour and a half with her seemed like 20 minutes. She sang songs without gimmicks or the slightest affectation.... Her sometimes spacey rap was delightful. "The piano is out of tune," she said at one point, "and it could use a polish too... Like my new dress?" ... When she sang "Is That All There Is?" you knew she'd been there, too, and the feeling was painfully real.— Jesse Hamlin, *San Francisco Chronicle*, October 4, 1984

October 1984—Interview. The October 1984 edition of Andy Warhol's *Interview* magazine offered an extensive interview with Peggy Lee. A glorious photo by Matthew Rolston accompanied the interview, which was conducted by George Christy.

In his introduction, Christy brought readers into the delightful world of Peggy Lee. Christy clearly enjoyed Peggy's sense of humor, reporting that, "When asked about politics she muses, 'My favorite color is plaid,' and when queried about marriage, she winks, 'I don't discuss politics.'"

Peggy seemed to be opening up not only on stage, but in interviews as well, discussing many topics with great candor. Perhaps the experience of *Peg* gave her the desire to share more of the private Peggy Lee. Christy mentioned the play and Peggy told how she came to forgive Min for all the years of abuse:

> GC: *Peg* was much more personal in the sense that you revealed a great deal about your growing up....
>
> PL: Everything.
>
> GC: You did bring humor into a lot of the sad situations.
>
> PL: Oh, yes. In the case of my stepmother, for instance, I had long ago forgiven her. When I began writing *Peg*, I felt compassion for her because, if hers had been my lot in life, to feel that way and inflict physical and mental violence on someone, I wouldn't want to be alive. I feel sorry for her, really sorry.... I can also thank her for giving me a stronger motivation to work.

Peggy spoke with fondness about the early days in Jamestown. She remembered working at the Gladstone Hotel. When George Christy expressed his disbelief about Peggy working as a waitress, she responded, "Yes, and I was a very funny waitress. I think I'm a better cook than a waitress."

She also recalled how nervous she was at the audition with Ken Kennedy at WDAY in Fargo. Peggy's songwriting talents were discussed at length, with special attention given to the fact that she had written new lyrics for "Fever." She called the great Johnny Mercer "my mentor for writing."

Peggy paid tribute to her favorite singers. She singled out Ray Charles, Frank Sinatra, Mel Tormé, Joe Williams, Sarah Vaughan, Ella Fitzgerald and Carmen McRae. She called these six "the Tiffany of singers." When asked what she did for relaxation, Peggy responded as follows:

> Reading relaxes me tremendously. I had these books about 20 years ago and started to read them, and then lost track of them somewhere. On this trip back I found them in my library—*The Lives and Teachings of the Masters of the Far East*. Four volumes, all of them fascinating. I understand there are five volumes and I'm going to find that last one.

The singer told George Christy that her favorite book was *Letters of the Scattered Brotherhood*, a collection of anonymous spiritual letters edited by Mary Strong. Peggy still followed the teachings of Dr. Ernest Holmes. In fact, she told Christy, "Ernest Holmes also was a great influence on my life, perhaps the biggest influence."

***October 27, 1984*—Lewisham Festival of Jazz, England.** Peggy performed at the Lewisham Theatre as part of the Lewisham Festival of Jazz.

***January 1985*—Sundome Center, Phoenix, Arizona.** Following her engagement in Arizona, a late January Associated Press article reported the following:

> Singer Peggy Lee has undergone surgery to open constricted arteries and now is resting at her home. Lee's publicist, Gino Empry, said yesterday that the 63-year-old singer had the successful operation last Wednesday at St. John's Hospital in Santa Monica. In the surgery, balloon catheters were used to push aside obstructions in the heart arteries. The problem was discovered after Lee developed chest pains on January 21.

***February 1985*—Venetian Room, Fairmont Hotel, Dallas.**

> Hardly a week after undergoing heart surgery, Lee stepped onto the stage Wednesday.... At her best—with those ultracool, smoky vocals—Lee can transform any song into the most delicate work of glass.... Whatever the flaws, whatever the expectations from a performer like Lee, she is a master of timing, her phrasing is frequently exquisite, and she is, above all a consummate musician. That in itself—with a little touch of "Fever"—is a rich living legacy.—Russell Smith, *The News*

***May 23, 1985*—Drury Lane Theater, Chicago.**

> In the world of popular music, Peggy Lee is one of the permanent people—a singer of such special gifts, especially in the area where technique and emotion meet, that the term "popular music" doesn't begin to describe her artistry. If the performance Lee gave Wednesday ... had been labeled a "song recital" instead of a show, and been measured against the work of, say, Janet Baker or Elly Ameling, I'm sure that any unprejudiced listener would agree that Lee was in the same league. In fact, I'd go

further than that and claim that Lee is, at her frequent best, something close to a composer —for she reshapes her material with a subtlety and taste that go beyond mere interpretation.— Larry Kart, *Chicago Tribune*

July 5, 1985 — **Associated Press.** "Starwatch: Peggy Lee" was the title of Mary Campbell's article:

> "It was a terrible shock when *Peg* closed," Miss Lee says. "I only had one day's notice. I'd invested six years of my life in it. As soon as I got over the shock, I just continued to work.
>
> "I kept my quintet together after *Peg*. I love music and I love working with these fellows. They're jazz musicians, although they can do everything. We just finished playing the Drury Lane Theater in Chicago and I got the most magnificent review in the *Chicago Tribune* I think I've ever had."

July 7, 1985 — *New York Newsday.* Bill Kaufman wrote about Peggy's return to New York in his article entitled "Peggy Lee Is Back, in a Chelsea Cabaret":

> "I'm terribly excited. What I'm mostly excited about — a dream of mine — is being able to keep the quintet together," said Lee the other day. She was referring to her taut, ever-present group led by pianist Mike Renzi, which features Grady Tate on drums. Lee said her new show runs in two acts with an intermission. "It's not the way I used to usually perform. I treat it as a sort of a theater experience," she said, describing previous club acts in which she sang an unbroken set of numbers.

July 9, 1985 — *New York Daily News.* Phil Roura and Tom Poster's article entitled "Song in Peg's Heart" appeared in the *New York Daily News*:

> Peggy Lee looked at her pretty blond granddaughter, Holly, and smiled: "Someday you'll produce my life story on Broadway."
> Peggy wasn't kidding. Someday the Peggy Lee story will be back on Broadway.
> The indomitable Miss Peggy, the ultimate song stylist, never got over the way her autobiography was bounced off Broadway.
> "My friends tell me they were depressed by the story of my life. Hell, if they were depressed, imagine how I felt. I lived that story!" Snapping her famous fingers in her famous style, Peg says: Let's look ahead.

July 10, 1985 — **The Ballroom, New York.**

> Peggy Lee has not made a New York nitery appearance in about a decade.... Her return to niteries in what she does best at the Ballroom is an event, and must unfortunately turn out to be a test of her physical stamina. In her first show, she showed great skill as a singer-entertainer, with hardly a reference to the sad parts of her life.... Lee seemed as fresh at the finish as she did at the start of her taxing show. In addition to her considerable vocal talents, she shows a gracious sense of humor, which many seemed to have forgotten during her hiatus.— *Variety*, July 17, 1985

August 5, 1985 — *The New Yorker* **Magazine.** During Peggy's visit to New York, *The New Yorker* magazine published an article written by jazz critic and historian Whitney Balliett. Balliett also included the piece in his 1988 book *American Singers*—

27 Portraits in Song. Balliett began his portrait of Peggy, entitled "Still There," by describing the unique visual image of the legend who was "still there," wowing Ballroom audiences:

> What is visible at the Ballroom is a creation that has been slowly and carefully constructed over the years by Peggy Lee herself and her image-makers. This onstage figure has grown more intricate. When Peggy Lee appeared at the Empire Room of the Waldorf-Astoria ten years ago, she was swathed in white robes and white makeup, and she suggested snow queens and Icelandic sagas. At the Ballroom, she wears a close-fitting helmet covered with glass beads, huge, round tinted glasses, an egg-size amethyst ring, a heavy rope of pearls, and various silk robes and gowns.
>
> All that can be seen of her beautiful face is the tip of her nose, the famous mole adrift on the alabaster sea of her right cheek; her mouth; and her resplendent chin. The total effect is of antimacassars and gingerbread. The contrast between this encrusted beauty and the simon-pure voice is startling.
>
> She is a stripped-down singer. She keeps her vibrato spare and her volume low. (She has a powerful voice but chooses to hold it in reserve.) She avoids long notes and glissandos, and if she uses a Billie Holiday bent note she lets it die almost immediately. Many singers confuse shouting with emotion. Peggy Lee sends her feelings down the quiet center of her notes. She is not a melody singer. She does not carry a tune; she elegantly follows it. She is a rhythm singer, who moves all around the beat, who swings as intensely and eccentrically as Billie Holiday. She is a subtle and brilliant showman. She can slink, arch an eyebrow, push out a hip and rest a hand on it, half smile, wave wandlike arms, bump, tilt her head, and slouch — all to dazzling, precise effect.... The voice slowly subsumes her image and by the end of the show has enveloped us.

To give his readers further insight into the person behind the legend Balliett interviewed three people who had known Peggy for most of her adult life. Jazz singer Sylvia Syms had a lot in common with Peggy. Syms had known and admired Billie Holiday. Sylvia Syms was also one of Frank Sinatra's favorite female singers. Sinatra referred to Syms as "Buddha." Syms had this to say about Peggy Lee:

> "She's always had great humor and great sensuality. She's very articulate. She's very intelligent. She is mannered — but Peggy Lee–mannered. She has a way of making her relationship to a song seem so simple. Her sound is like a reed. She walks away from any other singer. The colors in her voice are pastel rather than the bright greens and blues and reds of so many other singers. I have never once felt stifled in a Peggy Lee show — there is always a wonderful feeling of air. She's very caring about her audiences. There is none of the it's-too-bad-I-have-to-be-bothered-with-all-this feeling that certain performers give off. She knows what an exalted thing it is to be alive."

Peggy's one-time roommate, Jane Feather, reminisced about the early days when Peggy was still something of a naïve young farm girl:

> "I was sent up from Minneapolis, where I lived, to replace Peggy in Grand Forks, North Dakota, where she was a great favorite — Peggy Lee and the Collegians. Then we both worked in Fargo. I was at one end of town and she was at the other, in Powers Coffee Shop, and we became friends. In 1941, she got a job with Benny Goodman at the College Inn in Chicago, and I was at the Edgewater Beach Hotel, and we roomed together. When Benny went to New York for a long gig at the New Yorker

> Hotel, we rented an apartment in the Village. It was a basement place with a garden, and we thought it was fantastic. Peggy was still pretty much a wild North Dakota farm girl. Instead of buying six potatoes, she'd buy a twenty-five pound bag. And she'd make bread and put the dough to set in a warm closet — and run down to Washington, D.C., to see a boyfriend."

Pianist Mel Powell told Balliett of Peggy's difficult times with Benny Goodman. Powell spoke of his affection and admiration for the singer:

> "I was eighteen and she was nineteen, and plain human compassion made me take her under my wing.... It took her a long time to settle down with the band, and one reason was that Benny didn't subject himself to any kind of sensitivity training. He rarely took trouble to learn the names of his sidemen, so he called most of them Pops, which was O.K., but he called Peggy Pops, too, and that didn't speed up her acculturation. So a bond formed between Peggy and me, and it's still there. We talk on the phone, we see each other, and Peggy and my wife have become very close. Whenever I hear her sing, I think of what Louis Armstrong said on the set of a movie called *A Song Is Born*. It was made in 1948, and a lot of jazz musicians were in it. Somebody asked him about swinging, and he said, 'Man, if you can't swing quarter notes, you ain't going to swing.' Peggy can swing quarter notes, and all the rest — behind the beat, on the beat, in front of the beat."

Balliett also interviewed Peggy for the piece. Perhaps the most telling comment came at the end of the article. Peggy, talking about her fellow songwriter Alec Wilder, revealed that Wilder had always considered her to be a fairytale character:

> "Alec and I used to sit and talk by the hour in the lobby of the New Yorker Hotel, where Benny was playing. Or, if we had time, we'd go out and find a curb and sit on it and talk. We were great curb-sitters. We even found a curb to sit on in Beverly Hills when the band was playing in Los Angeles. I introduced Alec's 'While We're Young,' and he wrote a song for me — 'Is It Always Like This?' He also wrote the lyrics, which begin, 'Are the trees always so green? Has the sea this silvery sheen?' Alec always thought I was Alice in Wonderland. Maybe he was right."

Peggy's highly successful run at the Ballroom ended on August 3, 1985.

October 9, 1985 — Associated Press.

> Peggy Lee, the Grammy-award-winning singer-songwriter, was in satisfactory condition after undergoing four hours of double-bypass heart surgery on Tuesday, hospital officials said.... Miss Lee, 65, who checked into the Touro Infirmary on Sunday with chest pains, had been scheduled to perform Tuesday night at the White House at a state dinner for the prime minister of Singapore, Lee Kuan Yew.... Dr. Tom Oelsner, an internist who has been treating Miss Lee in New Orleans since Sunday, said surgery went well.... Miss Lee was treated in New Orleans because doctors believed it would have been too risky to send her back to her home in California, said Oelsner.... Assuming all goes well, Miss Lee should spend a week to 10 days in the hospital, then head back to California, Oelsner said.

October 29, 1985 — *Variety*.

Twenty-one days after the surgery, it was reported that Peggy "had to undergo an operation last week for an infection that had developed within the incision." Suzanne Stewart, spokeswoman for the Touro Infirmary, told reporters that Peggy would have to be hospitalized for two more weeks.

***December 17, 1985*—Variety.** Peggy had been moved to St. John's Hospital in Santa Monica. She had been there since the 9th of December. She was flown from New Orleans to Los Angeles on the private jet of her lifelong friend Frank Sinatra. Sinatra spoke with Peggy as often as he could during her stay at the Touro Infirmary. He was determined to bring her home.

***December 31, 1985*— Associated Press.** "Singer Peggy Lee leaves hospital." Not quite one month later, on January 23, 1986, newspapers would announce: "Lee to return to performing."

***March 31, 1986*—13th annual Aggie Awards.** This marked Peggy's first public appearance following her open-heart surgery. The Aggie Award was presented by the Songwriters Guild of America for outstanding work in the field of songwriting. Previous recipients included Henry Mancini, Johnny Mercer and Sammy Cahn. This year the honoree was Miss Peggy Lee.

Score, the newsletter for the Society of Composers and Lyricists, reported on the 13th Annual Aggie Awards: "The evening was filled with a wonderful musical tribute to Miss Lee, presented by many of the songwriters, musicians and performers who have worked so closely with her over the years." Among those paying tribute to Peggy were Bobby Troup, Sammy Cahn, Jerry Leiber and Mike Stoller, Lou Levy, Benny Carter, Stella Castellucci (the harpist from the *Sea Shells* album), Neal Hefti, Billy May, Lainie Kazan, Patty Andrews, Jack Jones and Danny Thomas. George David Weiss, the composer of "Mr. Wonderful," presented the Aggie to Miss Wonderful, Peggy Lee.

***April 9 through April 20, 1986*— Westwood Playhouse.** Interviews began to appear promoting Lee's Westwood Playhouse concerts. Peggy was a bit more philosophical in these interviews than she had been in the past, a bit more revealing of her tremendous spiritual strength. Peggy told journalist Don Heckman:

> "I came very close to checking out. I think when you survive what I went through, you realize that you're not finished yet for a reason. I'm not quite sure what God had in mind when he kept me around, but I know I'm still here for a purpose."

In an article printed in the *Los Angeles Times*, Peggy talked about the role that love played in her life, her music and her recovery:

> "I want to make people happy and I want to entertain them. Since love has always been one of the important themes in my music, I'll sing a lot about love. But this time it'll be about healing love as well as romantic love. When I was in the hospital I was getting love and prayers from everywhere — I've got boxes of letters — and it really helped. Now I want to give some of that love and affection back to all those people in my audience who cared so much."
>
> "I get a lot of letters from people who tell me how healing some of my music has been for them. That always makes me feel wonderful, because it makes me feel as though I do have a purpose. Who knows, maybe that's what God had in mind for me, after all."

March 31, 1986 — Peggy receives her Aggie Award. The prestigious award is presented to distinguished individuals by the Songwriter's Guild of America. Lee's songwriting talents were also recognized by ASCAP, who awarded her with their highest honor, the Pied Piper. Lee was also inducted into the Songwriter's Hall of Fame. The Society of Singers honored her with the Ella Award.

April 11, 1986 — *Los Angeles Times.*

"I want to thank you from the bottom of my new heart," Peggy Lee told a clearly sympathetic and receptive audience.... Slimmed down, radiant in a white gown and coat with white fur trimmings, wearing shades to relieve eye strain, she simultaneously reassured anyone who may have been expecting visual or vocal signs of wear and tear.... The warmth and passion still radiated their personal glow....

To quote from one of her most durable hits, Peggy Lee clearly is convinced that the time has not arrived for "that final disappointment." In short, that's not all there is, and it may even be that the best is yet to come. — Leonard Feather

April 17–23, 1986 — *Drama-Logue* magazine.

Lee Melville heralded "A Glorious Return to the Westwood." In the interview with Melville, Peggy offered this advice to young singers:

"The only thing I can think of is just sing every opportunity you can, whether it is in church or at a club, because the experience is so important. There are little places now I hear about, clubs, where you can sing. All of that helps because later on the big stage you can use all that experience. It's good, it's like boot camp."

April 23, 1986 — *Variety.*

The night was given an added dose of poignancy, as this is Lee's first engagement since undergoing heart bypass surgery. She quickly shows the curious and the hopeful that she still has a way with a song and can turn a lyric into a personal statement.... In Lee's case, it has never been a matter of great range or dynamics, but of subtlety in feeling. Her greatest asset is still a diction and phrasing that makes a tune all her own.... When she exited to "I'll Be Seeing You," it was clear that it was no casual remark, and meant as much to her as her fans. It was something more than just her music.

June 1986 — Toronto and New York.

Peggy traveled to Toronto, where she performed at the Royal York theater. Then she returned to the Ballroom in New York. As with most of her previous New York engagements, this one was greeted by a flurry of press. Peggy gave several interviews to promote her appearances.

June 10, 1986 — *The New York Post.*

Last night Peggy Lee, songwriter, received the President's Award of the Songwriter's Guild of America. Tonight Peggy Lee, singer, opens a six-week engagement at the Ballroom....

These were the opening words of "Peggy Lee: One Note After Another," an article written by Jerry Tallmer. Tallmer asked Peggy if she thought about singing again as she lay in the Touro Infirmary:

"No." Then, with a quarter-smile: "I was asked to sing a note one day. By one of the doctors. I sang one note. That's all I had strength for. Now I think my voice is perhaps stronger than ever."

Speaking of her musical influences, Peggy said:

> "I always loved black music. There were practically no blacks in North Dakota then. I would listen to Lil Green and Wee Bea Booze, a marvelous singer. Used to listen to Count Basie on the radio before he was called Count Basie. He was 'Bill Basie and the Kansas City Coon Shouters.' Shows you how far we've come."

June 12, 1986 — The New York Times.

> Peggy Lee returned on Tuesday to the Ballroom ... and gave a demanding two-hour performance that revealed a new sense of security in both her singing and her stage presence.... Miss Lee is easy, casual, confident. She has a superb group of musicians backing her, led by drummer Grady Tate, who has been associated with her for 25 years.... With this foundation, Miss Lee has refined her singing to its essence. Her voice simmers through her songs. There is nothing extraneous. Simplicity is keynote, but it is simplicity that underlines the colors and warmth in her voice. — John S. Wilson

Among Peggy's repertoire during this engagement was "Just Keep Holding On," a song that expressed the singer's philosophy about life perfectly. Alan Barcus wrote the song for an upcoming London musical entitled *Keagle Street*. Audience response to Peggy's rendition was extremely strong, and it appeared that she had found her next hit. Unfortunately, the song was never recorded.

June 18, 1986 — Variety.

> With the years, many things become increasingly evident about La Lee. She can repeat much of her material and it all seems fresh. She constantly gives these numbers new vistas. She regards many of her songs as vehicles for enjoyment and has little difficulty in conveying these thoughts to the audience.... Lee's easy, sexy and understated stylings apparently provide little wear-and-tear on her vocal equipment, which enables her to provide added color and new interpretation. She seems like a new girl in town with every date.

August 1, 1986 — The Philadelphia Inquirer.

The *Philadelphia Inquirer* informed its readers that Lee would be performing at the Golden Nugget Hotel/Casino.

September 24 and 25, 1986 — Westbury Music Fair.

Peggy shared the Westbury stage with the Count Basie Orchestra.

Fall 1986 — Los Angeles.

When Peggy returned home to perform at a special event, newspapers ran a photo of the glamorous singer, captioned, "Peggy Lee donned oodles of fur to entertain at the 15th anniversary party for the L.A. Gay and Lesbian Community Service Center." With this performance Peggy Lee became the first major star to raise money for the AIDS epidemic.

December 17, 1986 — The Joan Rivers Show.

Peggy wowed Rivers, the studio audience and viewers with a sizzling, sultry, lowdown "Fever."

This television appearance also featured a stunning performance of a new song. Peggy hypnotized the audience with her simple, ethereal reading of Ivan Lin's "Love

Dance." Like "Just Keep Holding On," this was a song perfectly suited to the singer. "Love Dance" would also go unrecorded.

Winter 1987—*ASCAP in Action*. *ASCAP in Action* featured "Women in Music." Songwriter Cy Coleman discussed his working relationships with three top female lyricist: Carolyn Leigh, Dorothy Fields and Peggy Lee. Coleman expressed his feelings about Peggy as follows:

> "She's a consummate artist at whatever she does. She knows exactly what she's doing. When you get somebody who's as good an artist as she is, you don't question the way she sings. You don't question why she does what she does. And she does everything beautifully."

January 8 to January 17, 1987—Marine's Memorial Theater. Originally only five shows were scheduled, but these sold out so quickly that another six shows were added.

> Peggy Lee — she of the fur-lined throat and indomitable sophistication — has returned to San Francisco after a two year absence with a new show, a new venue and the same old ingratiating savvy. Long may she wave....
>
> [The years] have treated Lee's larynx with notable kindness. She doesn't sustain some notes as long as you'd like, but the smoky allure is still there as well as the improvisatory air that makes "Is That All There Is?" sound as tart as it did the last 187 times you heard it. The singer's gift for breaking down rhythmic structures into fragments and then re-assembling them sounds as unassailable as ever.—Allan Ulrich, January 9, 1987
>
> You don't walk out of Peggy Lee's new show asking "Is that all there is?" There's plenty.
>
> She could always suggest more with a subtle phrase than most singers could belting it out. It's the power of suggestion, the sensuous implication that there is more to come.... Lee sang two short hours' worth of songs that expressed a lifetime of experience and feeling.
>
> One of the great things about her is her marvelous, slightly demented and off-center sense of humor. She'll stop in the middle of a song for no reason and tell a joke that has nothing to do with anything. And it's doubly funny. In the middle of a ballad called "I Love," a list song in which she reels off the things that matter to her, she forgot the lyrics. She turned to her piano player and calmly asked, "What is it I love?"— Jesse Hamlin, *San Francisco Chronicle Datebook*

January 16, 1987—"Miss Peggy Lee — Weaving the Art of Legend."

> Miss Lee is a musician; her instrument is her voice. I now understand why she is referred to as a legend, and it has nothing to do with the story or circumstances of her life. Her legend pours out of the phrasing in every syllable of each word, in all the songs she sings. She is a song stylist who passes every lyric through the prism of her artistry and reflects it back at the audience in subtly shaded hues of light. It was as if I had never heard these songs before.—Robert Julian, *The Sentinel*

February 1987—Caesars Palace, Las Vegas. Peggy joined show business legend George Burns on the stage at Caesars Palace. Between them the two showbiz vets had 150 years of experience (Burns was 91 at the time).

Unfortunately, Peggy had some bad luck during this Vegas stint. While coming onstage she slipped on a metal plate that covered an electrical outlet on the stage floor. Not knowing how badly she was hurt, Lee asked for a chair and did her complete act sitting on what she later described as "my one good hip." As she was rushed on a stretcher to the hospital, George Burns quipped, "You're a brave girl, Peg!"

Syndicated columnist Dick Maurice reported that, "Although severely hurt, her performance, according to George Burns was, 'The finest performance she's ever given.'" Maurice went on to say: "It's doubtful Ms. Lee will be well enough to return to the Palace stage, she claims she 'will return.' Sounds like Gen. Douglas MacArthur. Who knows? She very well could finish her engagement. After all, you can't keep great talent down."

February 1987 — **Northwest Airlines.** During her recovery, the in-flight magazine for Northwest Airlines published a charming article on Peggy. The article, featured in the Laureates section, was titled "Peggy Lee — The Velvet Voice Slides into Its Fifth Decade." Laurie Werner wrote the profile. In it, Peggy spoke of her traumatic childhood and her dreams: "It may sound odd, but I always knew that I'd get away and become a singer. It didn't happen all at once; it wasn't a sudden awakening. I always knew I could sing — I'd always sung in church choirs and at school — and I always knew I would sing. When I was 12, though, it really crystallized."

March 12, 1987 — **Pasadena Playhouse.**

> Lee's stage presence blends just the right touches of preparation and informality.... The romantic warmth, the rhythmic sensitivity, the touches of humor, and, above all, the indestructible vocal instrument that is Peggy Lee must rank among the rarest treasures of contemporary music. — Leonard Feather, *Los Angeles Times*

> Time and trouble, most recently a broken hip, have not dimmed the subtle, distinctive artistry of legendary warbler Peggy Lee.... The show was Lee's first since falling down during a Las Vegas concert in February, and the singer's return was, on nearly all counts, a solid success. Unable to ambulate, Lee proffered her 22-songs set sitting down (her chair was elevated amid champagne bubble balloons). She turned the limitation to good effect, drawing regular laughs and cheers with sedentary kicks and grinds.... Lee always has been a rather exotic creation, at once bluesy, ethereal and super cool, with a faintly tragic air seeping through layer upon layer of legend and mystique. — *Variety*

April 3, 1987 — **Washington Times.** In the article "'Fever' Still Burning After Lee's Comeback," journalist Lou Fournier wrote of Lee's poignancy and shy humor:

> Her most poignant moment comes during the singing of "Here's to Life," a song recently written for her by Artie Butler. "All you give is all you get," she sings. She seems to know.
> Some things in her style today are very different. She says her whole approach to performing underwent a radical change after her sobering emergency surgery. Now she aims to make her shows more personal, more sharing.

"Around the time of all the heart surgery, I think I got over my shyness—I hesitate to call it shyness—being somewhat of an introvert."

April 6, 1987— Ritz-Carlton, Washington, D.C.

> The first number Peggy Lee sings every night in the Ritz Terrace is "I Won't Dance." The Otto Harbach song is not only a good, upbeat curtain-raiser; it is, in context, an existential statement—a kind of manifesto. At the moment Peggy Lee can't dance; she even has trouble walking.
> Two months ago, while doing her act at Caesars Palace in Las Vegas, Lee suffered an accident. "I fell down and fractured my pelvis," she says. "If anyone tells you it's a fractured hip, that's because they don't want to say 'pelvis.' I have a bruised coccyx, too, but nobody mentions that; forget about that."— Joseph McLellan, *Washington Post*

Peggy handled her slow, cautious journey from the wings to center stage with great aplomb, telling her audiences, "Your part is to applaud until I'm thoroughly seated in the chair. My part is to get there." Once she was there the music took over, the singer and her audiences were transformed. "Platinum & Whimsy" was the title of Joe Brown's review, printed in *The Washington Post* on April 2, 1987:

> In its prime, Lee's voice was like a pearl sinking slooowly in honey. And though time has added a few grains to that honey, the voice retains its opalescent qualities and its sensual way with a lyric.... Last night, the evening's bookends a light-footed "Won't Dance" and a poignant and appropriately phrased new ballad called "Here's to Life," and in between was a glide through Lee's eclectic career as a singer and composer.

May of 1987—*Science of Mind.*

Elaine St. Johns, the daughter of Peggy's lifelong friend Adela Rogers St. Johns, conducted the interview which was titled "A Presence in My Life." In it, Peggy reflected on a great many things, all of them linked by a spiritual thread. That thread was Ernest Holmes and his teachings.

> "They say," Peggy shudders slightly, "that abused children grow up abusive. I don't believe that and after I met Ernest I know why. We didn't deal with this specifically—Ernest never gave me specific advice or psychological counseling; instead he would uncover the principle that applied and encourage me to work from there. In this case he showed me the value of forgiveness—to 'give for,' love for hate, joy for sadness, beauty for ashes. He explained that we can't make any growth until we can do this. And I wanted to grow!"

June 1987— Caesars Palace, Las Vegas.

Lee was reunited with George Burns. The June 24, 1987, issue of *Variety* reported that her "seated position in no way impedes her delivery and forceful presence." The critic for *Variety* went on to say, "The dynamics are instinctual as she ranges from purrs to wails, expressed in her innate jazz sense."

July 14 through July 19, 1987— Warren Star Theater, Ohio.

July 31, 1987— Caesars Palace, Atlantic City.

> Both performers can safely be regarded as show business veterans, although Burns, 91, regards Lee, 67, as "the kid." No matter, Burns and Lee continue to earn their salaries on merit, not memories. This is no nostalgia show.
>
> The Lee voice produces instant recognition. While other female singers can throw more octaves into a song, Lee's technique, her phrasing, the smoky tones, blend into a style that is hers alone.— Jack Lloyd, *The Philadelphia Inquirer*

Summer 1987— *Pete Kelly's Blues* and *Lady and the Tramp*. Two Peggy Lee classics were released on videocassette: *Pete Kelly's Blues* and *Lady and the Tramp. Video Review* magazine gave *Pete Kelly's Blues* three stars. Critic Richard M. Sudhalter recommended the video— based on Peggy's performance.

Sudhalter dismissed Jack Webb's portrayal of Pete Kelly with "He's just a jerk," then went on to say, "Miss Lee is another matter — all flesh and blood vulnerability amid the cardboard. I can think of few actresses who could improve on the big 'Sing a Rainbow' scene in the psychiatric hospital. Her singing (especially on Arthur Hamilton's elliptical, poignant, 'He Needs Me') is also memorable."

The video release of the beloved *Lady and the Tramp* became a "blockbuster." Leonard Maltin, writing for *Video Review*, gave the film four stars. Maltin commented on Peggy's contributions, saying, "I'm also quite fond of the music score by Sonny Burke and the versatile Peggy Lee, who also does several memorable voices on the soundtrack." It would only be a matter of time before Peggy found an interesting clause in her original contract with Disney. Until then she promoted the video release wholeheartedly.

October 1987— Venetian Room, Fairmont Hotel, San Francisco.

> She still can sculpt a song with the sensuous power of suggestion. Lee's art is all subtle shaping, shading and nuance. What she leaves out matters as much as what she puts in. And she can still swing a song with the greatest of ease.
>
> She introduced "As Time Goes By" by recounting what Humphrey Bogart once said to a gentleman friend aboard the Bogart yacht Santana: "There are a lot of dames in this town, but very few good broads. This is one of them. Take care of her." She brought out the best in the song, singing it with understated elegance that suggested a lifetime of experience.— Jesse Hamlin, *San Francisco Chronicle*
>
> Peggy Lee's 90-minute song recital currently at the Fairmont Hotel is the most wonderfully satisfying such performance I can recall in my quarter century of attending Venetian Room shows.
>
> My term "recital" is not chosen casually, any more than is any aspect of Miss Lee's performance. Her every selection is a musical production — her material, her accompanying orchestrations (played by a quintet), her deceptively casual entr'acte remarks, all focus on Lee's remarkably sensitive (and, of course, hip) vocal interpretations.
>
> There isn't a poor rendition or a foolish selection in the show — it's a musical evening of classical proportions.— Philip Elwood, October 8, 1987, *San Francisco Examiner*

November 15, 1987— *The New York Times* Book Review. Peggy was featured in Gene Lees' new book, *Singers and the Song.* Lees' book received good reviews in both

The New York Times and the April 1988 edition of *Jazz Times* magazine. Both reviews quoted Lees' comments on the artistry of Peggy Lee, in which he referred to her style as "a Stanislavskian approach to singing that gives a deep sense of the life behind it and the emotion within it."

1988— Peggy Lee's Fiftieth Anniversary in Show Business. If you count 1938 as the year she really began singing professionally, Peggy Lee had been illuminating the "life behind" and the "emotion within" musically for fifty years. In 1988 the singer announced that she was celebrating her fiftieth year in show business. To mark this anniversary the singer returned to the Ballroom in New York City.

January 31, 1988 *— The New York Times.* In Stephen Holden's insightful article entitled "Peggy Lee at 67: Still in the Swingtime of Her Life," Holden revealed many facets of Peggy's life, including an early desire to reach for the heights— in an airplane:

> "[As a child] I wanted to fly so badly," she recalled ... "I knew a barnstormer who was able to pick up a handkerchief with his wing tips at county fairs. He said, 'I'll take you up if you dance the Charleston.' I was so shy that I couldn't look at anyone, but I danced the Charleston for him, and he took me up in his bi-wing plane with an open cockpit. I wasn't in the least bit frightened."

Holden noted that the two-week Ballroom nightclub engagement "is being billed as her fiftieth anniversary in show business, but it is in fact her fifty-third. 'I don't like marking time,' she said with a rueful, tough-sweet smile. 'I like to think of everything as now. Haven't the scientists more or less proven that that's true?'"

Lee discussed the misconception some hold that she had merely imitated Billie Holiday: "People say I emulated Billie Holiday," she explained. "Although that is a great compliment, it isn't true.... I wasn't drawn to any particular singer ... I heard Maxine Sullivan ... I liked the simplicity and economy of her work."

Holden addressed Peggy's, observing, "Her characteristic lyrics of late have a wistfully upbeat philosophic tone." Of her own songs, Holden noted that Lee harbored "a special affection for "Johnny Guitar," and that her favorite among her 59 albums is *The Man I Love*.

When asked if the songs she sang, many of which she had done hundreds of times before, ever felt stale, Lee responded: "In the majority of songs, I always find new meanings and impressions. Finding the impressions to fit each song is like preparing for a role. But once I enter the world of a song, it never gets old."

January 31, 1988 *— New York Newsday.* Lee discussed with Stuart Troup her definition of a jazz singer for his article "New Songs in the Classic Style":

> "I've never been able to define a jazz singer," Peggy Lee said, "but I can tell when I hear one." Then she leaned back on the couch in her hotel suite, contemplating the ceiling, and said, "I think it's a composite of good taste in music and understanding of harmonic structures. It doesn't necessarily mean that they have to scat-sing at all.

I think it's a question of phrasing and choosing good material. And it's certainly a question of time, and being able to skip two measures you need to re-establish where you started out — always knowing where 'one' is."

February 1988—Where. Peggy wrote an article about her feelings for New York for *Where* magazine. "My Manhattan" was the title of her love letter to the city.

> I have been told that one of the hardest words in the world to define is "glamour." But I don't agree. I can define glamour in a single word: Manhattan.
>
> As far as I'm concerned, if you take every positive cliché uttered about Manhattan, you will find that they are all true. I ought to know. When I first saw this town I was a walking cliché myself — a young girl right off the farm (literally) who was seeing the Big Town (we didn't call it the "Big Apple" then) for the first time....
>
> T.S. Eliot wrote of "mixing memories with desire," which sums up my feelings for Manhattan. When I arrive here, many of my greatest, happiest memories come back to me, and yet I'm also eager for the new experiences that never fail to occur during each visit.

February 2, 1988—New York Daily News. Long known for her penchant for wearing white, Peggy's style was the topic of discussion for Patricia O'Haire's article "The Woman in White":

> She comes into the room, and she's dressed all in white. Platinum hair, bangs straight cut across her forehead, white pantsuit — even white nail polish on her toes....
>
> "Do you mind if I'm not wearing shoes?" Peggy Lee asks. "My latest affliction," she says, pointing to her toes. "I don't know why they hurt, but they do. The pain jumps from the left to the right, kinda like ping-pong balls."
>
> White is her color; she wears it onstage and off. In this case, "off" is a suite overlooking Central Park....

February 2, 1988—New York Post. "She's Got the Fever" was the title of a piece by Stephen M. Silverman. In it, Lee spoke of contemporary artists and her interpretation of "Is That All There Is?"

> As for other vocalists, Lee said: "I think Sade and Linda Ronstadt are wonderful. I get a kick out of Tina Turner, too."
>
> When it comes to her own voice, Lee said it took a year to find the right approach to one of her signature songs, Leiber and Stoller's 1969 "Is That All There Is?"
>
> "I had difficulty finding a positive way to sing that. I thought, well, I can think of it as one of life's learning experiences, something like Peg, for instance. That was difficult emotionally, and when it is over, what can you do? You have to get up off the ground and start over again. But you have to learn something from it."
>
> She said she finally cracked the song by shifting the emphasis in the key line from "Is That All There *Is*?" to "Is That *All* There Is?"
>
> "And to think of it," said Peggy Lee, "of course there's more."

February 2 to February 13, 1988— The Ballroom, New York.

> At the Ballroom, she walked onstage leaning on a glittering silver cane, a vision in white — white shoulder-length wig, white fur jacket, white gown and huge, amber-

> tinted glasses. She settled into a chair and, like an exotic variation of the regal Mabel Mercer, sang her entire program sitting down.... Aside from an occasional snapping of her fingers, picked out by a spotlight as she moved into "Fever," her hit of 30 years ago, all the movement Miss Lee needs is in her voice.—John S. Wilson, *New York Times*, February 4, 1988
>
> It seems unusual and pleasing that the major asset holding up best is her voice.... Physically, she comes on aided by a sequined cane, and she uses an unsequined chair. These concessions to her latter-day infirmities do not affect her performance. She looks great in her highly blondined wig and surgical overhaul resulting from some broken bones.... Many numbers have been in her folio for years. However, she gives fresh facets to the familiars. Her natural understatement of the works tend to draw the customers to her.—*Variety*, February 10, 1988

During this time Peggy signed a recording contract with the Musicmasters label. Although the recording dates of her first Musicmasters' release, *Peggy Sings the Blues*, are unknown, it was probably during this stay in New York that she recorded the album. It would be her first album since the 1979 release of *Close Enough for Love*.

April 10, 1988 — **Radio City Music Hall, New York.** Three show business legends met and performed at New York's famous Radio City Music Hall. Frank Sinatra, Sammy Davis, Jr., and Miss Peggy Lee enthralled the sold-out audience. This performance was a benefit for the Memorial Sloan-Kettering Hospital.

> Peggy Lee joined Frank Sinatra and Sammy Davis Jr. in their Radio City Hall finale April 10 to make a joyous, affection-laden recital even more joyful. Lee added luster to the event with her well-defined and deeply grooved catalog, which included most of her epics.... Lee, who has been ailing and now walks with the aid of a sequined cane, worked from a variation of a pilot's chair which allowed her to swing in all directions for better audience contact.... There is a basic humor and warmth to her natural style of presentation. She, no less, was a hit, and it's based on ability to sing rather than sympathy for her physical condition.—*Variety*, April 13, 1988

April 19–May 1, 1988 — **Moulin Rouge, Fairmont Hotel, Chicago.** "Peggy Lee misses nothing in her Moulin Rouge sets" proclaimed Lloyd Sachs in his "Jazz Notes" column for the *Chicago Sun-Times*. Sachs' April 21, 1988, review mentioned Peggy's forthcoming album:

> Those who recognize Lee's career-spanning commitment to a wide variety of American music, black and white, will be enthralled by her late emergence as a maker of spare, unshakable, wisdom-grounded blues statements.... Upon being told that Lee soon will release an album of blues songs, one couldn't help but think of how much the acclaimed, newly committed blues-dipper, Marianne Faithful, could learn from her.

April 20, 1988—*Chicago Tribune.*

> In Peggy Lee's world, intimacy equals truth or is its only hope for survival — which is why she always sings to an audience of one.... Lee can put so much meaning into the slightest shift in volume, pitch or vocal timbre that the impact of her dramas is in no way limited by the size of her voice — which, again, must sound and be intimate if she is going to tell the truth.— Larry Kart

Spring 1988 — **Peggy's autobiography.** Peggy had been working on the book for a number of years. With her publisher, Donald I. Fine, she was now putting the finishing touches on the text, and ads began to appear promoting the publication.

June 7, 1988 — **National Ballet of Canada.** While at home in Bel Air, working on the book, Peggy hosted a party for the entire National Ballet of Canada. All one-hundred-forty-seven members of the ballet company were invited to Peggy's home for hors d'oeuvres. Accompanied by piano and guitar, Peggy sang "Them There Eyes" and "Ain't Nobody's Business" for the enraptured, young dance troupe.

July/August 1988 — *DISCoveries.* Longtime Peggy admirer Gino Falzarano wrote an essay on Lee's life entitled "Thirty Years of Fever":

> Today, at 68, Peggy still performs and is recording once again. Despite changing trends in music, illness and personal setbacks, Miss Lee endures. And the reason is simple. Peggy Lee is a natural. No gimmicks. No special effects. She sings straight from the heart. No, much deeper. From the soul. She is believable. She sings as if she's lived each song ... as a matter of fact, she probably has. That's what will continue to keep her audiences coming back for more. The curiosity that maybe each new performance or recording will give another glance into her life, or a reflection into ours. Who knows? And what does Peggy Lee have to say about it all?
> "It's nice to know that you've left some kind of mark."

August 1988 — **Adela Rogers St. Johns Dies.** When Louis Armstrong died it was St. Johns who insisted that Peggy would be able to sing "The Lord's Prayer" at Armstrong's funeral. St. Johns, working for Peggy in the Science of Mind fashion, spiritually supported the singer as she performed her farewell to Louis. Now Peggy would sing "The Lord's Prayer" again at St. Johns' funeral. No doubt Peggy still felt Adela's support.

August 1988 — **Rare Songs by Harold Arlen.** At the end of the month Peggy traveled to New York to record a new album. The project, an album of *Rare Songs by Harold Arlen*, was something that her fans had been looking forward to with great anticipation. The Arlen collection was recorded for Harbinger Records between August 29 and September 2, 1988. Peggy was not pleased with the final result, however, and the CD would not be released until 1993. Waiting five full years would have been excruciating for Peggy Lee fans if it weren't for the release of another astounding album.

• EIGHT •

Peggy Sings the Blues: 1988 to 1995

Fall 1988—*Peggy Sings the Blues.* This album, her first available in the CD format, received glowing praise from every music critic in the industry. Only *Black Coffee* could rival this album. Every element worked—the musicians, the arrangements, the material and the singer's interpretations were all flawless. Peggy Lee was back with an album of pure genius.

October 22, 1988—*London Times.* Frances Dickenson and Caz Gorham interviewed Peggy for the first major article to promote and critique the new album. The journalists reported that:

> Recently Peggy Lee has detected a change in popular music, a move away from the rock she found so alien. In response, she has recorded a new album. And she is once again taking chances. Abandoning the lush productions of her later records, she has returned to a stripped-down quintet of piano, bass, drums, percussion and vibraphone. It is an album which leaves the singer exposed, making no concessions, offering nowhere for a voice, now in its late sixties, to hide.
>
> From the first notes, her voice rings out—confident, supple and perfectly clear. She says: "I don't like to think in terms of years. When you enter the world of a song, time means nothing. Your world goes on forever."

November 1988— **Peggy sues Walt Disney Productions.** At the time that *Peggy Sings the Blues* was released, Peggy also made the front pages with a major lawsuit, suing Walt Disney Productions for $25 million. The lawsuit was reported in the *New York Post*, as well as *People* and *Time* magazines. An Associated Press article printed in November of 1988 noted the following:

> In a $25 million lawsuit filed Tuesday in Los Angeles County Superior Court, she [Lee] charged that Disney ignored a 1952 contract provision that barred the company from making "phonograph recordings and/or transcriptions for sale to the public" without her consent.

The current video release of *Lady and the Tramp* was clearly a "transcription." *People* magazine reported that the movie had earned Disney "$110 million." Peggy's original salary for her contributions to the film was a mere $3,500. Her honorarium for promoting the video was $500. With typical good humor, Peggy told reporters, "My hairdresser makes more than that."

November 26, 1988*—*The Anniston Star. Bob Protzman's review, "Still Vital at 68 and Singing the Blues, Peggy Lee Makes LP That Moves," was picked up by the Associated Press and appeared in numerous newspapers:

> At 68, Peggy Lee remains a vital vocalist who can excite and move a listener without resorting, as so many do, to histrionics and sheer volume. Understated, subtle, Lee nevertheless is as convincing on this program of old and more recent blues and blues-inflected tunes as any belter or shouter ever could be.

December 1988*—*Stereo Review. Chris Albertson wrote the following:

> You'd have to look hard to find a more mellow vocal album than this one. Peggy Lee has been caressing our ears for close to half a century now, but her smooth laid-back style shows no sign of wear, and lends itself perfectly to the kind of material collected for *Miss Peggy Lee Sings the Blues*.

Albertson gave some much needed and long overdue advice to the many singers who think simply being loud shows great emotion:

> Jennifer Holliday, Diane Schurr, Patti Labelle, and all the other screamers who mistake volume for soul ought to be locked up with this album until they get it right.

December 1988*—*Jazz Times.

> This is laid-back Lee, smoky, soft and sultry by turns in an eclectic set of blues and bluesy tunes that make the most of the singer's warm and expressive voice.... Aside from a bit of false funkiness on "Kansas City," there isn't a gimmick in the group of a dozen songs, just relaxed, superlative singing and playing by musicians who have an innate sense of what's called for.— Allen Scott

Ron Towe, the former music critic for *FM Guide*, wrote the following exclusively for *Fever!* (the quarterly newsletter of The Peggy Lee Fan Club):

> From the very beginning of her career, Peggy Lee's singing has always represented what is unique and best in American jazz and vocal music.... With her new album, *Miss Peggy Lee Sings the Blues*, her first in far too long, Peggy returns to source for a glowing program of exemplary performances without sacrificing anything of what she has achieved over the years. If you want to know what true American jazz singing is all about you owe it to yourself to buy this album; it is more today than anything you'll hear anywhere else in the field of music.

January 31, 1989*—*The New York Post.

> Reaching legendary status wasn't easy. Plagued by poor health since the early '60s, Lee has had the specter of forced retirement hanging over her head for almost 30 years. But she is nothing if not resilient and determined. "I don't know how to stop," she says softly. "I have to be on a stretcher to stop."
> "I believe in a higher power. That's the one I talk to—Big Daddy! When I had my

second heart operation, I lay there for six weeks. That's a long time to just think. I came out with a great serenity. I'd already been through the death experience in 1961. They gave me six months to live if I kept working. In 1985 they said I should retire."

"But I can't stop. I mean, sit there and wait for what? My last breath? What do I have to lose? I went back to work, and my health improved. Then it got worse, then it improved again. But each time I got stronger. And each time, I've gotten a nicer attitude about life."

"I believe that whatever we believe in strongly enough, we can accomplish. It's about the omniscience of God, the omnipresence, the omnipotence. If you tap into that, it doesn't matter if it's music or writing or whatever, it's all there for us. No matter what we say, the universe says yes. If we say it's a lousy day, the universe says yes. If we say it's a very good day, the universe says yes. It's always positive. And that positive energy is there for us to use." — Bob Harrington

February 2, 1989 — The New York Times.

Peggy Lee has always been a spellbinding singer — a weaver of moods and colors. But for her new show she has created an illustrated narrative, "The Blues Branch of the Jazz Tree," in which she traces the development of the blues with spoken settings that have the same magnetically mood-evoking qualities as her singing. Moving from chain-gang songs to street cries to spirituals and gospel songs, Miss Lee mixes brief phrases of song with a languorous, almost hypnotizingly cadenced narration before she reaches a full-scale treatment of a classic blues song, Ma Rainey's "See See Rider." She sings it softly, with a sinuously rocking beat that is pure Peggy Lee without losing the emotional strength of Ma Rainey's version. — John S. Wilson

February 7, 1989 — Staten Island Advance.

Peggy Lee, who's been singing for more years than it's perhaps fair to count, has a new serenity about her.... As she casts her spell of the blues, she seems to set out certain vocal boundaries. She never strains or tries to overstep these boundaries and the result is more warmth and a new off-beat charisma.

In her autobiography, *Miss Peggy Lee*, just published by Donald I. Fine Inc., she recalls her first Ballroom engagement several seasons ago.

She writes: "When agent Irwin Arthur spoke about the Ballroom in New York City, I couldn't quite picture what it was. Taken literally, it could have been a place to stop for a one-nighter with a band, or a huge room with a stage on one end and a whirling mirrored ball hanging from the ceiling. When Irwin said, 'They have a tapas bar,' I thought he said topless! We cleared that up right away." — William A. Raidy

February 7, 1989 — New York Daily News. Journalist Patrick Pacheco found Peggy to be "Like a Statue Rising Above the Ruins":

Her face is immobile as she speaks in that soothingly soft voice about her new autobiography, *Miss Peggy Lee*, her new album, *Peggy Lee Sings the Blues* (nominated for a Grammy) or her return engagement to the Ballroom, where she is appearing through February 18. Her lips occasionally turn up into a smile, but it is a pair of Scandinavian blue eyes that register all the emotion, flashing with wit or anger or thoughtfulness, as when she responds to the inevitable question: What gives a white singer the right to sing the blues?

"I don't think the suffering that gives life and depth to the blues is a question of color," adding that among the influences of her life was jazz great Maxine Sullivan. "Under the skin, we're all the same."

February 13, 1989 — *The New York Observer.*

The first part of the show concentrates on old favorites like "Fever" and "Is That All There Is?..." It's all a lightly swinging buildup to the heavier, more cerebral section of the act, devoted to the blues. She explores the roots of blues taught to all singers of substance by Ma Rainey, Bessie Smith, Lizzie Miles and Lil Green, to name a few of her influences. She imitates the wail of the street vendors, the pain of the chain gangs and the passionate obsession of the gospel singers. But it's the homesick blues like "Basin Street Blues," "Beale Street Blues" and "Baby Won't You Please Come Home" that showcase the indelible, honey-dripping, nectar-sipping Peggy Lee style at its zenith. I've never heard her sing more securely in tune. I've never seen her make more direct contact with her musicians or her material. — Rex Reed

February 22, 1989 — *Seven Days.*

Neal Karlen received a rare backstage glimpse of how the star prepared herself for a performance. He wrote about it in an article titled "Ladies and Gentlemen, Miss Peggy Lee":

A towel has replaced the wig on her head, her huge spectacles are off, and this afternoon's makeup has been wiped away.... Only once has she gone onstage this way. And it taught her a lesson about the value of a mask. She bared all — in *Peg*, the 1983 Broadway musical of her life that offered some unvarnished truths about some unhappy times. The critics hooted; the play closed in a week.... Soon after the play bombed, she was hospitalized, near death, in New Orleans. As they wheeled her into heart surgery, Miss Peggy Lee begged the nurse not to take off her false eyelashes or fingernail polish.

So why does this proud, aching, exhausted woman still want to put up with a life of stuffy dressing rooms, grabby fans, and the strain of playing two shows a night? ... "Music," she replies to the question of ever retiring, "is a terrible, incurable disease. That's what my late husband said, and I agree." Miss Peggy Lee has actually had four husbands, but she speaks only of one — her first, who she says was her only true love.

Spring 1989 — Grammy Nominees.

Peggy Sings the Blues was nominated for Best Jazz Vocal Performance, Female. Peggy's friends Lena Horne and Carmen McRae were also nominated. Lena took the Grammy for her album *The Men in My Life.*

April 16, 1989 — New York Times Book Review.

Despite the appalling number of devastating illnesses and personal misfortunes that have punctuated her life, the great jazz singer Peggy Lee has survived in style.... Unfortunately, she has chosen to tell it without the aid of a ghostwriter, who might have suggested replacing much of the book's mundane trivia and celebrity name-dropping with more about the development of her unique art.... The story of Miss Lee's art is — like any mention of her fourth husband — absent from this book. — Burt Hochberg

April 19, 1989— San Francisco Examiner.

Sitting comfortably on a bar stool on the Fairmont Hotel's Venetian Room stage at her Tuesday (opening night) show — she's there for two weeks — Lee in midshow gracefully, without comment, slid into Duke Ellington's "Mood Indigo." The already quieted audience seemed to stop breathing as she sang....

Lee has perfect pitch, perfect intonation; her range is limited but her harmonic imagination compensates. Her warmth saturates her song, emphasize their lyric meaning.— Philip Elwood

April 20, 1989—San Francisco Sentinel. "Miss Peggy Lee Still Dazzles" was the title of a piece written by Harold Niesen to tie in with Peggy's appearance at the Venetian Room. He wrote of her many accomplishments (including her multiple awards and the fact she recorded over 600 songs) and her views of good music as communication (quoting Lee as saying, "It's like a smile or kind word that doesn't care whether you're five or 95"). Niesen also tells of how he grew up listening to Peggy Lee records ("Mom supplied her 45s to me before I could read"), and how "I always thought we felt the same way about life. Our phone conversation Monday proved it."

HN: My favorite song you've recorded is "Alright, OK, You Win." Is there any story behind it?

PL: The only story for that one is when Cary Grant heard it, he told me, "That's the most profound song." [laughter]

HN: When you're on the road, what hobbies keep you busy?

PL: I do a lot of reading, that's my favorite pastime....

HN: Do you have a favorite TV show?

PL: I have several favorites: I like *60 Minutes,* I like *Alf* [laughter], and I love nature shows like *Nova* and *National Geographic.*

HN: Any favorite performers you've worked with?

PL: I love a lot of them. It's kind of bad to say, because I don't want to show any favorites.

HN: Do you listen to any Top 40 music today?

PL: Oh yes, anything that's good, I'll listen to. I like Sade, some of those bluegrass groups, the Judds, to name a few. As long as it's good, I like anything that's good.

HN: Do you enjoy Linda Ronstadt's work with Nelson Riddle?

PL: Yes, and I'm glad that she brought all that out again. They're practically re-dos of my albums with Nelson Riddle, and I think they're wonderful.

HN: How do you feel about the large number of gay fans you have?

PL: I appreciate all of my fans. [My gay fans] have an awful lot of my shoes and gowns and things. I'm trying to help with AIDS benefits whenever I can. I gave the first benefit in L.A. and we raised $350,000 that night and I was alone on the benefit program. It was the very first one and hardly anyone knew about it.

Whenever I see Miss Lee in concert I wonder if she can imagine the special part she plays in my life. Don't miss her Venetian Room performance. Grab a copy of the

Lady and the Tramp video or put on Miss Lee's Greatest Hits collection and remind yourself what real stars are all about.

April 25, 1989—***Village Voice.*** Michael Musto reviews Peggy's autobiography for the *Village Voice*:

> She writes like she sings, with spurts of effortless declamation camouflaging a lifetime of pathos.... No ghostwriter worked on this book — another rarity — and the writing's lack of elegance creates a jazzy, casual feel that suits her. But if we don't want her to wallow, we would at least like to know how suffering has transformed her, onstage and off, and how she's different from all the other dark ladies who turned dejection into art. Instead of an in-depth analysis of her singing technique or the psyche behind the mole, Lee offers a fairly chronological telling of events from her childhood.... The book's litany of horrors, and its conclusion that "Sometimes life is sadder than death," may be all the explanation we need; singing is both Peggy's expression of angst and her escape from it. If that's all there is to the fair, then it's enough.— Michael Musto

June 1989— **Associated Press.** This article reported that Peggy was planning to sell her home. Her plan was to build a new house "with a recording studio." Her Bel Air "French Regency–style villa, listed for $3.95 million, has a circular staircase, music salon and drawing room with a marble fireplace."

September 1989—***Guideposts*** **Magazine.** The spiritual magazine featured an article written by Peggy Lee. In "Words to Grow On," the singer related an inspirational story.

> Not surprisingly, my head is filled with lyrics, with lovely lines and rhymes from favorite songs. And from poetry too. One poetic line in particular has come often to mind: Closer is He than breathing...
> For years I didn't even know what poem those words came from. I did know, however, the "He" was God, and I didn't have to be told that He was close, for He was always near to me through prayer.

The story went on to describe moments when Peggy felt God had seen her through and rescued her from despair, including her own near-drowning as a child. She continued:

> Then one day not long ago a friend showed me the poem by Tennyson containing the line that had been so meaningful to me for so long. Though I'd never read the poem before, it seemed utterly familiar, for it said everything I've ever known about prayer:
>
> > Speak to Him thou for He hears, and
> > spirit with Spirit can meet —
> > Closer is He than breathing, and nearer
> > than hands and feet.

September 21, 1989—***Rolling Stone.*** The magazine featured a photo essay section called "Sweet Inspirations" in which young musicians and singers were pictured with the artists who inspired them. Singer k.d. lang was pictured with her hero, Miss Peggy Lee.

The following quote from lang captioned the photo:

> Back in the early Eighties, I listened to Peggy Lee all the time. Her old records have this incredible sultry, shimmering quality that no one else at the time had. She always manages to transcend the physical and go directly to the emotional — she creates an atmosphere that's like a web that you can't help but get caught up in.

November 1–3, 1989— **BMG Studios, New York.** Peggy produced an album of her finest work as a songwriter. The Musicmasters release, *The Peggy Lee Songbook — There'll Be Another Spring*, would be available in the spring of 1990. It would receive the same critical acclaim as *Peggy Sings the Blues*.

January 7, 1990— *Daily Mail* (UK). "Peggy to Sit It Out on Tour," written by Victor Davis, detailed how Lee handled a recent mishap with her usual sense of humor.

> Singing legend Peggy Lee opened the door for the cat … and almost ruined her forthcoming British tour.
> As she let the pet into her Beverly Hills bedroom she fell, injuring an arm and a leg. Now she will perform from a chair for the dates which start at the Royal Albert Hall on Thursday.
> She said in London yesterday: "Is it being accident-prone when it's not your fault?"
> Peggy was helped from a plane at Heathrow yesterday, and could not stand at a book-signing for her autobiography, *Miss Peggy Lee*.
> She is due to sing on TV's *Wogan* show tomorrow, but looked fragile.
> "This may be my last tour — but I hope not," she said. "I'm tough. I've written a song that goes 'If I wasn't so healthy, I'd be dead.'"

March 6, 1990— **The Ballroom.** Peggy's new act featured all of the songs from *The Peggy Lee Songbook — There'll Be Another Spring*.

> Lyrics spill from Peggy Lee with an unmatched combination of nonchalance and credibility. Her strength is simplicity and, as Duke Ellington declared, simplicity is the most complex form. No tricks, no filigree lines, no scat. Just words, simply phrased — saucy, tender, plaintive, joyous— with insouciant artistry. Such ease of delivery isn't easy, of course; it is sculpted and polished with uncanny understanding…. The wispiness of Lee's voice has increased as she approaches her 70th birthday, but it remains vibratoless and warm, like a rhythmic soft wind.— Stuart Troup, March 8, 1990, *Newsday*

> Peggy Lee has been writing songs for more than 40 years, and she usually includes several of them in her programs. Her new show, 'The Peggy Lee Songbook,' is a showcase for lyrics she has written over the years to the music of a variety of composers…. There was a great deal of variety in her lyrics, too, but it was not always apparent because Miss Lee maintained a subdued, sometimes trancelike manner of singing that created a sense of similarity from one song to another. But the warm, throaty quality of her singing and the twinkle that lit up her eyes and touched her voice still made her music pure Peggy Lee.— John S. Wilson, *New York Times*

March 6, 1990—*New York Daily News.* Reporter Harry Haun learned that Peggy "Springs Eternal-Lee." Sadly, the second and third volumes of *The Peggy Lee Songbook* mentioned here never came to be.

> Tonight, when she bows at the Ballroom for a three-week return engagement, she'll be leafing lightly through something called *The Peggy Lee Songbook*—which, not so incidentally, is the name of her new album Musicmasters releases a week from today. The show and the record ... are brimming with primal Peggy Lee, songs she has written the words and/or music to away from the spotlight. "You'd think after a while I wouldn't be excited about anything, but I am — I still am," she declares with a slight lilt in her smoky voice. "The musicians have talked me into doing my own songs."
>
> Many of these are standards now, but she and her guitarist–musical director, John Chiodini, mixed in a few new numbers and updated others, like adding fresh lyrics to her signature "Fever." She figures she has a couple hundred others where these came from. "We have Volume One out now, and John and I hope to do Volume Two—and Three."

March 9, 1990—*The New York Post.*

> For either style or content, it would be hard to beat Peggy Lee, currently on view at the Ballroom. A consummate musician and singer, she makes it all look so easy.... Lee's cool passion invests her songs with an utterly fetching verity. You just sort of lean forward into her interpretations and let them run down your central nervous system, savoring every note and nuance.— Bob Harrington

March 1990—*The Peggy Lee Songbook—There'll Be Another Spring.* Luckily, for those who could not attend her shows at the Ballroom, every glorious "note and nuance" was captured on the new CD. *The Peggy Lee Songbook — There'll Be Another Spring* contained thirteen songs with lyrics by Peggy. She re-recorded several of her classic songs, including "Fever," "He's a Tramp," and "Johnny Guitar." Five new songs were featured in this collection: "Circle in the Sky," "I Just Want to Dance All Night," "I'll Give It All to You," "Boomerang" and "Over the Wheel."

The album has many highlights. Among the songs she had recorded previously, "Johnny Guitar" and "Sans Souci" are standouts. "Johnny Guitar" offers more poignancy than it ever held before, and guitarist John Chiodini's shimmering solo matches Lee's vocal. A wicked cello and violin opening ignite "Sans Souci." Here the singer's voice is grittier than it was on the original Decca recording, lending a marvelous evil quality to the song.

"I Just Want to Dance All Night" and "Over the Wheel" both have an easy country feel. These two songs illustrate the singer-songwriter's ability to write totally contemporary material. Unlike most of her peers, Peggy Lee was not trapped in a bygone era. In "I'll Give It All to You" the singer displayed her delightful sense of humor. The finest among the new songs was "Circle in the Sky." Penned with her pianist, Emil Palame, this beautiful ballad paints the portrait of an eternal love. "Circle in the Sky" captures Peggy Lee's personal belief that life and love go on forever. This is Peggy at her ethereal and spiritual best.

Released during her March 1990 engagement at the Ballroom, this album was recorded on November 1, 1989.

March 13, 1990 — **Pied Piper Award.** The American Society of Composers and Publishers, ASCAP, bestowed its highest honor upon Peggy Lee. Susan Heller Anderson, writing for *The New York Times*, reported on the occasion:

> Peggy Lee will join Frank Sinatra, Lena Horne and Ella Fitzgerald when she receives the Pied Piper Award of ASCAP. The organization's highest accolade, it goes to an entertainer for lifetime achievement. The award has been given nine times in the 28 years since it was established by ASCAP....
>
> Today some of her peers will pay tribute to her as a songwriter.... Miss Lee has written more than 100 songs since she began in 1941.... "The biggest thrill," she said, "is hearing other people singing your material." She will officially become a Pied Piper on May 8 in Washington.

Among the "peers" paying tribute to her at the Ballroom were composer Burton Lane, Sylvia Syms, Margaret Whiting, Cy Coleman and Tony Bennett.

April of 1990 — **Associated Press.** An article titled "Peggy Lee Wins Disney Suit Over Video with Her Music" reported that Lee had won "a summary judgment against Walt Disney." At this time Peggy and her attorneys did not know how much of the $12.5 million she was seeking would be awarded.

June 1990 — ***Pulse.*** For the article "Great Comebacks," Peggy discussed her songwriting and singing style with Eliot Tiegel.

> Of interest in this first songbook are the new lyrics for "Fever." "It's a big surprise to people that I've been so prolific a writer," Lee says unabashedly. "I've not yet figured out why I was hiding my light under a bushel. While I like writing music and words, lyrics are my forte. They're very easy for me to do."
>
> She says she's been able to keep her voice clean and strong over this long run in show business ... by not doing anything to strain it. "I think that's the basic thing, and through the years the critics have said, and rightly so, that my voice is thin. I never let it out, but I can scare you if I want to. I can really belt it, but that's not my style. If I started to yell, I don't think people would enjoy it."

June 1990 — ***DownBeat.*** Eliot Tiegel was also the author of "Riffs— Peggy Lee." In this *DownBeat* article Lee continues to discuss her songwriting talent and some of her contemporary admirers:

> For the first time in her 54-year career, the smokey-voiced singer — who turns 70 this May 26 — has released an entire album of her own tunes. The woman, whose distinct, soft, sensual voice was featured with the Benny Goodman band from 1941 to '43, and who eventually helped build Capitol into a powerhouse, has selected 13 tunes for the new album that, as she says, "are music from the heart."
>
> "I Just Want to Dance All Night" is a good example of catching a piece of life and transferring it to sheet music. Written with her musical director/guitarist John Chiodini, it reflects "the first serious love affair I ever had," Peggy explains in the

quiet of her Bel Air, California, abode. The man was a bandleader who remains unnamed. "We were in Minneapolis in this after-hours place and the band was playing 'Body and Soul,' and I wanted to dance there with him all night. I told John this story and he said, 'That's a good title.'

"Once young people hear this music, they buy it, and that goes for some of the rock people who come to my performances, and that surprises me. Elvis Costello is a fan. Boy George said I look outrageous, and that's a compliment. k.d. lang likes my work."

July 9, 1990 — Time.

Peggy Lee is an American icon. Her singing, no longer as effortless as it once was, now combines its sultry smokiness with the quality of having lived life with a capital L. These 13 songs, most co-written by Lee, have been beautifully recorded with a knockout team of studio musicians. Her fans should pounce.

August 1990 — CD Review.

Has any singer done so much with so little voice? In addition to her impeccable jazz phrasing, Peggy Lee is also an accomplished songwriter, as this collection of re-recorded hits and newly penned songs proves.... Her four new songs from 1989 are equally accomplished, with evocative lyrics and lovely melodies. As with any Lee production, the arrangements are superb, and there's a nice intimate feeling to this digital recording.

September 1990 — Pulse Magazine.

Peggy Lee's second and latest album for the Musicmasters label is the first in a series of albums that will feature songs for which Lee has written the lyrics. Of the 13 songs on *The Peggy Lee Songbook/There'll Be Another Spring*, five are new and receive their first recordings here. Two of these, "I Just Want to Dance All Night" and "Over the Wheel," are country-style ballads and are given particularly sensitive readings by Lee...

The diversity of musical styles here combined with Lee's warm and delicate vocalizing make this a winning album. The succeeding volumes in the series should be most welcome. — Steve Gruber

Unfortunately, the proposed future volumes in *The Peggy Lee Songbook* series were never recorded.

October 1990 — DISCoveries.

The Peggy Lee Songbook is a return to romanticism for the ever-charismatic Miss Lee. Throughout the songbook are lush, crisp strings; one moment soft and shimmering, the next, menacing and foreboding. And of course, there are Peggy's trademark ballads "Where Can I Go Without You," "The Shining Sea," and "There'll Be Another Spring" sung in that sultry, smoky drawl as only Miss Peggy Lee can sing a ballad.

There is a poignant wistfulness to the newer songs, "Circle in the Sky" (written with Emil Palame), "I Just Want to Dance All Night" and "Over the Wheel" (both penned with John Chiodini).... They are more than songs. They become little dramas of life and lost love.

> But the biggest surprise here is the new version of Peggy's classic, "Fever...."
> [H]ere she adds two new verses, making the lyric completely hers, and bringing it into the '90s.

The Peggy Lee Songbook — There'll Be Another Spring garnered Peggy a Grammy nomination for Best Jazz Vocal Performance, Female. This time the award went to Peggy's friend Ella Fitzgerald for her *All That Jazz* CD.

December 1990— **Interview.** Linda Ekblad reminisced with Peggy about her favorite Christmas songs in an article entitled "Peggy Lee: Christmas Fever":

> I: But it's so clear that you're a musician as well as a singer. Does that influence your choice in Christmas music?
>
> PL: Oh yes, it does. I love Sammy Cahn's song "The Christmas Waltz." And everybody loves Bob Wells and Mel Tormé's song: "Chestnuts roasting –" I particularly like some carols by a man named Al Burt, who was a young man — he died right after he wrote them. One is called "The Star Carol." A beautiful thing.
>
> I: When you listen to music, are you just listening, or are you a singer hearing a song you might like to sing, or are you a musician aware of the musical nuances?
>
> PL: Strange you should ask that right now. I was thinking yesterday about Irving Berlin and "White Christmas." I have always thought of that song with Bing Crosby. I loved Bing so much. But yesterday I was thinking about the construction of it, and Irving Berlin's talent for simplicity, in getting right to the point of things.

December 1990— **"Everybody Needs a Santa Claus."** Peggy released what would prove to be her last recording on the Musicmasters label. Two new compositions by Peggy Lee and John Chiodini were featured on this Christmas cassette single. Dom DeLuise played the role of Santa, and the Carpenter Avenue Elementary School Chorus was featured.

The other song on this cass-single was one of the finest songs ever written about the importance of human unity and world peace. In recent concerts Peggy had brought audiences to tears of joy with "We Be Friends." The song spoke of planting the seed of love and watching it grow. It expresses the common link that we all share.

February 19, 1991— ***Los Angeles Times.*** Sharon Bernstein wrote "The Lady and the Lawsuit" for the *Los Angeles Times*.

> "I put my whole heart and soul into this 30 years ago," says Lee, who continues to perform songs from the film in her concerts, "and I deserve to have my contract honored."
>
> In *Lady and the Tramp*, Lee provided the voices for the characters of the torch-singer dog Peg, the Siamese cats Si and Am, and Lady's owner Darling — and was paid $3,500. She and her writing partner, Sonny Burke, earned another $1,000 for the use of six songs he and Lee collaborated on for the movie. The pair retained all rights for phonographic recordings and transcriptions, but their contract — like the contracts of most performers of the day — didn't foresee the advent of video and the huge audience it would provide for their work.

According to attorneys on both sides, the case hangs on the court's interpretation of the term transcription.

Disney is arguing that the term, as it was used in the 1952 contract between Lee and the studio, was not intended to cover future technology, such as video.

***April 8, 1991**—People.* People magazine featured Peggy in their "Winners" section in an article titled "No Pussycat in Court, Peggy Lee Nips Disney for $3.8 Million." The seventy-year-old singer was photographed in her Bel Air home with her beloved cat, Baby. On the grand piano behind her were the Peggy Lee Rose and her Pied Piper Award. *People* reported that the jury had awarded Peggy $3.8 million. Peggy, happy it was over, commented, "The strain of the trial was tough on me."

> "You know, they always say, 'Don't mess with the Mouse,'" says Lee, referring to Disney's big-eared symbol and standard-bearer. "I'm glad my rights were vindicated."

***April 17, 1991**—Los Angeles Daily News.* By mid–April the judge decided that Disney owed Peggy $2.3 million:

> On Tuesday, Los Angeles Superior Court Judge Stephen Lachs rejected arguments from Lee's attorneys that jurors had intended for her to receive $3.8 million, the total of five separate awards in the case. He said that his ruling was based on a pretrial agreement that she would receive only the largest of the awards, not the cumulative amount.

The article noted that Lee, who felt she deserved $9 million of the $72 million Disney made from video sales of *Lady and the Tramp*, was disappointed by the ruling:

> "It's very difficult to be poised about this," said Lee, who has been confined to a wheelchair by falls that fractured her pelvis. "I feel I did not get a fair trial, and I don't feel the jurors did either."

***May 13, 1991**—* Raymond Theater, Pasadena, California.

> "I'm glad I was never afraid of mice," laughed Peggy Lee.... No mouse appeared, which was a good thing, because as everyone in the glittering Pasadena audience knew, the 69-year-old singer couldn't very well get up from her chair and flee should one get on her.
>
> But of course they also knew about her recent victory over the Mickey Mouse folks, so they knew she wasn't scared.... As her confidence built, that easy touch of hers grew surer and sweeter, and by the time she got to "See See Rider" she could do no wrong.... And the choice of Hildegard's old theme song, "I'll Be Seeing You," for the finale... told the world that Peggy Lee, who's been killing us softly for better than fifty years, knows how to spring that mousetrap.—Tony Geiske, *Hollywood Reporter*

***August 1991**—* Paintings for the Essex Hotel. Peggy returned to one of her great loves—painting. She was commissioned by the newly remodeled Essex Hotel in New York to do an oil painting. Peggy painted a portrait of her cat, Baby, which was showcased with several other celebrity paintings.

July 1992— **Hollywood Bowl.** Peggy and Mel Tormé performed in a rare concert at the Hollywood Bowl. It was a triumphant return for the singer, as she had spent most of the past year confined to her home.

> In separate turns [Lee and Tormé had] already left the audience limp, or at least well-pleased. Now it was time for their first joint appearance in 41 years.... Lee was only a hair less vibrant, but her balladic savvy is such that she grabbed the 11,000 present on the second number... And, of course, she nailed down "Is That All There Is?" with its uniquely cornfed jaundice, a perfect fit for Lee's somehow starry-eyed disillusionment. All things considered it turned out to be plenty.— Tony Gieske, July 20, 1992, *Hollywood Reporter*

Leonard Feather was there that evening. Feather's review appeared in the July 29, 1992, edition of the *Los Angeles Times*:

> It was a memorable evening for Lee and her fans. Since a Pasadena concert in May 1991, she had been inactive, due to a variety of ailments including a form of paralysis. Greatly improved now, she was able to walk onstage and sit down to offer glowing evidence that the Lee timbre, the Lee phrasing and the Lee sensitivity are undiminished.... How many singers can end a set with a slow ballad and draw a standing ovation?

July 29–30, 1992—*New York Post.* The following excerpts came from Cindy Adams' columns for the *New York Post.*

July 29, 1992:

> Terrific, fabulous, drop-dead great Peggy Lee opened at Club 53 at the Hilton last night. Before the downbeat we talked of the old days.
> "When I first played New York," Miss Peggy, age 72, told me, "It was 1941 or '42. I worked the Paramount.... Benny Goodman was headlining. And the Extra Added Attraction was a kid named Frank Sinatra.
> "That was when those little girls were swooning by the thousands. I couldn't understand how they'd get there and line up around the block so early in the morning. First show was 9 A.M. We did five to eight a day. When we just did five we thought we were laying off!
> "I'd never worked such a huge place before. Thousands of seats. And when that big blinding spotlight hit me first time I came out on stage, I thought it was a train. It was like an engine coming straight at me."

July 30, 1992:

> I'm full of Peggy Lee–isms. Like when she was working with Benny Goodman at the Paramount 50 years ago. Benny was careful with the penny. Some say chintzy. Me, I'm not saying it. Me, I don't know. I only know what some say. So some say there was this day he sent his bandboy, Popsy Randolph, out for soft drinks, and everyone had to chip in and pay for his or her own. The sodas were 15 cents in those days. Peg only wanted a little sip. She drank half. Popsy finished the other half. Popsy then said to Benny: "She only owes you eight cents."

July 31, 1992—*New York Daily News.* Howard Kissel wrote of Peggy's return to New York in "A 'Fever'-Pitch Comeback":

Only in Hollywood movies, I had always supposed, do you see a frazzled maitre d' hoisting tiny tables over crowds and jamming them into the already tight spots between the tables to squeeze in patrons desperate to get into a nightclub. But that was exactly the scene the other night at Club 53 in the Hilton as a crowd clamored to see Peggy Lee's New York comeback.

July 31, 1992 — **"Can't Think Straight."** Peggy recorded this duet with song stylist Gilbert O'Sullivan. The CD was released as a single, and later on O'Sullivan's album *Sounds of the Loop.*

July and August of 1992 — **Club 53, New York.** Her audiences and the critics were amazed by Peggy's return to New York. Miss Lee even amazed herself; she told her opening night audience, "There's something special about tonight. Not only did I get back to New York, but I walked to this chair. I've been laying prone for a year."

> Indomitable. Write that down. Then write down: Peggy Lee.... She sang a reflective and subdued "S' Wonderful," rocking slightly from side to side, and when she came to "you've made my life so glamorous," I thought, my God, how long has she been making all our lives just a little bit, just a lot more glamorous, all the way back to the Benny Goodman days.... The voice holds, only the vessel has changed. — Jerry Tallmer, July 30, 1992, *New York Post*
>
> The whole thing was indeed special.... She still knows how to control a room and the sound is still that special sound. What Lee has done is heroic, and the most amazing part of it is that she manages to make herself seem not at all heroic, but simply the familiar, unpretentious legend. — Howard Kissel, July 31, 1992, *The New York Daily News*
>
> The most remarkable thing about Peggy Lee, who at age 72 still personifies high-style nightclub glamour, is her sheer tenacity. The singer has difficulty walking. Several strokes have given her speech a pronounced slur. Her singing voice, which was never large, is now severely diminished in size and range and has a noticeable wobble. Her eyesight also seems to be failing. Yet in performance, Miss Lee treats these difficulties as minor inconveniences. Together, her willpower, musicality and professionalism enable her to project a fair degree of the old magic.... With just the tiniest adjustments in her swiveling rhythmic mannerisms she was able to suggest deep changes of attitude. — Stephen Holden, August 3, 1992, *New York Times*

August 1992 — **"You Were Meant for Me."** "You Were Meant for Me" is the title of the superb recording Peggy made with Michael Franks. The song, part of his *Dragonfly Summer* CD, would be released in 1993.

August 7, 1992 — ***New York Daily News.*** Journalist Gene Plaskin interviewed Peggy for the *New York Daily News.* Plaskin's article was titled "Lee's Triumph of Spirit." For the first time Peggy revealed the truth as to why she had been bedridden for much of the past year (and would remain so for the rest of her life). She believed many of her ailments were brought on by workaholism:

> "I did it to myself," says Lee, who battled life-threatening viral pneumonia in the '60s, then a 1978 bout with Bell's Palsy that left the right half of her face somewhat

immobile, numerous open-heart surgeries and, most recently, a devastating year-long bout with PMR: polyomelitis rheumatica, a neurological disease that left her in bed for a year.

"PMR is a distant relative of polio," Lee explains, "and it boils down to being paralyzed due to inflammation of nerves, muscles, and joints—everything from the neck down. Horrifying pain." She was spiritually sustained, she says, by her two bibles: Ernest Holmes' *Science of Mind* and Baird T. Spalding's *The Life and Teachings of the Masters of the Far East*.

"I was Ernest's adopted spiritual daughter and he taught me how to think and concentrate. I believe in mind over matter—that all my physical problems were caused by overworking, and that I will heal myself."

"Some people," she muses, "might have killed themselves" given the PMR, or considered retirement, but not Lee. "I don't believe in death, and I love life enough to say I won't give up. I don't know how to stop."

August 18, 1992—*The Village Voice*. "Always True in Her Fashion" was the title of a fine article written by Gary Giddins for *The Village Voice*. Giddins revealed that his first exposure to Peggy Lee's music was an "accident." While in college he purchased a Benny Goodman collection. Upon hearing "Why Don't You Do Right" for the first time, Giddins assumed the singer was Billie Holiday. Only after reading the record cover carefully did he discover his error. Initially he dismissed Peggy as "yet another Billie imitator."

In time Giddins would "live and learn." In the article he discussed the similarities and differences between the two jazz legends:

> I suppose it was the two-note bubble on the word "ri-ight" that girded my ignorant assumption, that and the thin voice and the legato time and the knowledge that Billie had sung early on with Goodman. Because Lee, though likely influenced by Holiday's sense of economy, swing and ability to make the most of a small range, never sounded much like her. They did share something profound, however, a candid vulnerability that draws you into the drama of what they sing and how they sing it. They slur notes, but their slurs have different pedigrees, even if they had tough childhoods in common. Read either of their lives and you may wonder if the slurs aren't a kind of musical recoiling, wounded sighs. The former Norma Deloris Egstrom of North Dakota, who started singing on radio at 14 in part to escape the ministrations of a wicked stepmother, sings in the clipped cadences of the cold country, the vowels rarely indulged, the timbre cool and coy, icily sexy, giving way to an intimate vibrato as she attains high notes she only pretends to find daunting. A noted perfectionist, Lee gets it right or she doesn't go for it at all. Yet you feel she's at constant risk.

Giddins also pointed out that both singers had their musical soulmates ("Holiday had her Lester Young, and Lee had her husband Dave Barbour"), then offered an overview of Peggy's career, mentioning her songwriting talent and the Oscar nomination for *Pete Kelly's Blues*. He went on to praise her for her ongoing battle with Disney, saying, "Every performer in Hollywood ought to thank her for waging battle against the rodents.... When she finally wins in the higher courts—Disney keeps appealing—a barrier to equitable profit sharing will be blown off its hinges."

Gary Giddins knew that the lawsuit was honorable. Peggy Lee wouldn't be the only victor; her actions would continue to help other creative artists. Giddins continued:

> Lee is a credit to her race in other ways, and it is unseemly to blame her for capitalizing on opportunities once permitted those of Scandinavian stock yet denied those of African lineage, though one suspects that is the only reason she is perennially ignored by the jazz press (even Grove Jazz lists Barbour, but not Lee). Not the least considerable of her achievements is her enduring charm on songs from a blues background—from Lil Green's "Why Don't You Do Right," at the very beginning of her career, to Little Willie John's "Fever," at its very pinnacle. Covers they may be, steals they aren't. She found her own way in those songs, as in all the others, marrying wit and theatrics. She never embarrassed herself with them, and she doesn't embarrass her audience today, at 72, singing "Fever" from a chair at Club 53 at the New York Hilton, where she is ensconced through the end of the month.
>
>   It is startling to see her. The platinum Cleopatra wig is in place, but the dark glasses of recent gigs are gone, and her face is much broadened and less tractable.... Yet the timbre of the voice is intact, the hushed phrasing, the minimalist (and North Dakotan) trust in thrift—the right note, the commanding posture, the easy wit. We are all in this together. Watch me as I glide through this song. It isn't much and so we'll laugh about it afterward. But in fact she is often most moving when you least expect, as on the bridge to "'S Wonderful," when her laid-back phrasing takes on increased strength and seems to quell the bossa nova beat that gets the song started.
>
>   Sometimes she settles for a near-parlando style, as on Jerome Kern and Dorothy Fields' neglected "Remind Me," backed only by Renzi, or even on "Fever," accompanied only by bass and drums, conducting every note with a gesturing finger, yet for all the complicit humor in the conceit making the temperature raise all the same. Everywhere she is most expansive: She has a lock on Cole Porter's "Always True to You in My Fashion," taken with her trademark Latin bounce and spelled by a soprano sax. Yet perhaps the finest moments of her opening night set were those blues-colored ballads in which she seemed to suspend every phrase from the pull of LaSpina's bass, notably Gershwin's "Our Love Is Here to Stay" (Niewood's best solo of the night, on tenor); a thrillingly shrewd and welcome revival of Lil Hardin Armstrong's "Just for a Thrill," phrased almost entirely in frugal sighs and expressive rests that subtly suggested Ray Charles, whose influence was also suggested in her treatment of Sy Oliver's "Yes Indeed" and even in a new setting for "Why Don't You Do Right," now outfitted with a "Hit the Road, Jack" vamp.

September 6, 1992—*QW*. Nora Burns wrote "Is That All There Is to an Interview" for *QW* magazine.

Burns noted that many celebrities came to see Peggy's show at Cub 53, including Liza Minnelli; Madonna, who sent Peggy some "wonderful roses" ("she was abolutely charming," commented Lee, "and looked so pretty"); and Al Pacino ("I'm a huge fan of Al Pacino and I guess he's a fan of mine, so he said").

When asked her favorite people to work with, Peggy replied, Victor Young, Johnny Mandel and Sonny Burke when we worked on the score for *Lady and the Tramp*.

With the subject broached, Burns told Lee, "I love the update on the Disney case that you do at all of your shows," to which Peggy mischievously answered, "I hope it makes them squirm a little. Michael Eisner's yearly salary is $50 million, as is

Jeffrey Katzenberg's, and I don't think that they should miss $2 or $3 million for someone who had a contract and worked for it."

When Burns mentioned Peggy's "huge gay following," Peggy quipped, "Gay men have good taste. I think they're a lot more appreciative," and went on to say, "I've lost quite a few friends to AIDS. It's the saddest thing.... I did one of the first AIDS benefits in '82 or '83. We raised $350,000. I contribute to a lot of charities and auctions. Since I've broken so many bones and can't really walk, I've donated most of my shoes, Charles Jourdain four-inch heels, to AIDS auctions."

Asked if she'd change anything if she could live her life over, Peggy concluded, "I've made hundreds of mistakes, but I'm happy with my life, honey."

September 8 and 9, 1992*—Moments Like This.* At the end of her Club 53 engagement, Peggy went into the BMG recording studio to record what would be her last album. Peggy's final complete album would be released on the Chesky label in early 1993. *Moments Like This* included fifteen songs, all of which Peggy had recorded previously, and was very nearly a song-for-song recreation of the act she performed at the Hilton's Club 53.

The singer carefully sculpts every ballad here. Peggy still retained the amazing quality of bringing new life to time-honored songs. Her readings of classics like "Remind Me," "Our Love Is Here to Stay," "The Folks Who Live on the Hill" and "'S Wonderful" made it seem as if the listener was hearing them for the first time. She placed emphasis in unexpected places, bringing freshness to her material.

With her own favorite, "The Folks Who Live on the Hill," she continues to find new, breathtaking vistas. "Don't Ever Leave Me" is a plea both tender and anguished. On the underrated—and infrequently recorded—"Amazing" she is just that. This collection also features four of Peggy's own compositions, but the earlier versions of "Mañana" and "I Don't Know Enough About You" far outshine these renditions.

However, the Lee ballads "I'm in Love Again" and "Then Was Then (and Now Is Now)" both have an added poignancy, with the 72-year-old singer delving deeper into each song's inner life. She is not merely singing notes here; she is singing emotional truths.

September 14, 1992*—* Jamestown's *North Dakota Sun.* Mary Campbell, a journalist for the Associated Press, interviewed Miss Lee for an article titled "Peggy Lee Is Still Doing Right by Her Audiences." Campbell wrote of the incredible triumph of Peggy's return to New York, and also discussed the PMR diagnosis that curtailed Peggy's ability to work, but not her spirit.

The article mentioned several of the celebrities who came into Club 53, and noted that two well-known singers asked Peggy to record duets with them:

> Madonna came into Club 53 one night and the next day she [Madonna] recorded "Fever," her way.... While in New York, Peggy sang a duet and made a video with Gilbert O'Sullivan and also recorded a duet with Michael Franks, at their request, songs each of them wrote.

And she's writing lyrics again. "I just finished a piece I'm very proud of with a gorgeous melody by Benny Golson, 'Flying Through the Sky.' Red Norvo sent me a tune he wrote; I haven't finished it yet. A lot of composers have been sending me things to write," she says. "I have quite a few ahead."

September 21, 1992 — The Circle Star Theatre, San Carlos, California.

Lee can weave spells with her voice, but she's also a truth-teller.... Her vocal power is obviously not what it was when she belted out hit after jazz hit in the '40s. But her sense of phrasing has the kind of grace and dignity that doesn't come with youth. You can hear the self-knowledge in the way she delivers a lyric. When she softly sustains a note and the pitch slightly wavers, her depth of emotion and breadth of intelligence more than compensate.— Barry Walters, September 21, 1992, *The San Francisco Examiner*

January 2, 1993 — Beverly Hilton.

What better way to break in the New Year than with the cool, caressing sound of Peggy Lee? Thursday evening, this resilient woman offered evidence of a talent that has weathered countless storms of health problems and changes in popular taste.... [T]hroughout her performance ... she displayed the capacity for understatement that has long been the key to her art.... Unlike any other singer not of African descent, Peggy Lee can sing the blues with a genuine feeling for the idiom.

Only one adjective can sum up Lee's artistry, today perhaps more than ever: Inspiring. She could give lessons to almost every singer, male or female, who currently dominates the pop music charts.— Leonard Feather

February 4 and 14, 1993 — *Cleveland Plain Dealer.*

Rebecca Freligh wrote two articles for the *Cleveland Plain Dealer*, the first, titled "Peggy Lee Still Radiates 'Miss Standing Ovation,'" was published on February 4, 1993; the second, "A Peggy Lee Valentine," ran on February 14, 1993. In the February 4 article Lee discussed the production of *Love Held Lightly*.

Interviewed recently by telephone at her home in Bel Air, Lee spoke of her respect for the lyricists represented; she is "honored to be in the midst of them," she said. And her attraction to Arlen's tunes always has been the undercurrent of the blues.

"You hear a show tune, and they're wonderful, but his work was so unique," Lee said. "It always moved me emotionally."

The producers went to work mixing the album. Lee, an accomplished musician and composer, contributed valuable ideas. But the course of "Love Held Lightly," like true love, wasn't always an easy one: During the final mix, Lee put the brake on the project.

She now says it had nothing to do with her relationship with the producers, whom she called "very thoughtful and supportive and enthusiastic."

"I've never had more fun with anyone — and I've had great producers," she said.

February 14, 1993:

Among contemporary American singers, Lee is renowned for her ability to interpret a song — to become the character behind the lyrics...

"In singing, it's all in the mind, and that's where everything starts anyway," Lee said. "I just sort of go into my own little universe."

Madonna, who covered "Fever" on her last album, came to see Lee in New York., and the senior legend pronounced the junior one "a perfect little lady."

"She dressed impeccably," said Lee. "She was quite shy. I can't figure it out — is it just a role she's playing, or what?"

Just who is Peggy Lee singing to? "I sing to one, but universally," she said. "I usually choose songs that have double meaning."

May 26, 1993 — Peggy's 73rd Birthday.

July 25, 1993 — "Musical Majesty," *The Chicago Tribune.*

The collection of rare Harold Arlen songs that Peggy recorded in 1988 was finally released. In his review, journalist Howard Reich failed to mention that the CD had been sitting dormant for five years.

Calling *Love Held Lightly: Rare Songs by Harold Arlen* "one of the most taxing and notable works of [Lee's] long career, Reich pointed out that not only did the album offer several rarely performed Arlen songs, "others are still more exclusive, never having seen the light of day."

Reich quoted Lee as saying: "I approached this music with the same kind of process I always use — as if I were given a role to play in a movie. When you're doing a movie, you analyze the character, and it's the same thing in thinking about a song."

Detailing the album's highlights, Reich wrote of the "sense of mystery" Lee brought to the song "Can You Explain?" (lyrics by Arlen and Truman Capote), "the smoldering intensity" she lends to "Got to Get You Off My Weary Mind" (lyrics by Mercer), "Happy with the Blues," which Peggy had written with Arlen years earlier, "reveals just how much she understands about the art of songwriting."

Singling out "I Had a Love Once" (which Arlen wrote for his own wife, Anya, who died in 1970), as the album's "tour de force," Reich calls the song "a terse, anguished cry of grief."

Peggy herself concurred: "I consider all the songs to be wonderful, but I agree that 'I Had a Love Once' is especially powerful. When I sing that line, 'I had a love once' … well, I think I know what Harold means, because I had a love once, too. More than once."

July 25, 1993 — *San Francisco Chronicle.*

"At 73, Peggy Lee Still Having a Good Day" was the title of Lee Hildebrand's article for the *San Francisco Chronicle*. This article was similar to the one written by Howard Reich in that it was both an interview and a CD review. Once again Peggy discussed her unique affinity for the blues and the link to Billie Holiday:

> "I think I always felt that inside," Lee, 73, said of the blues… "I could identify with any slaves."

Unlike Reich, Hildebrand *does* mention the album's five-year waiting period, indicating the reason for its long delay was Lee's dissatisfaction with the producers' original vocal mix. "'When they use limiters and high-tech things on the human voice, it doesn't even sound like yourself when you hear the playback,' she said."

Hildebrand noted that the remixed album offered 14 "mostly obscure" Arlen songs, eight of which had never been recorded before. One of the songs, "Happy with the Blues," featured lyrics by Lee herself, commissioned by Arlen for the 1961 CBS television retrospective of his music, in which Lee starred. But Lee dropped the song before the program aired.

> "I didn't like it at all," Lee explained. "My lyrics were so trite and dosey-dosey-do. Of all people, I admired Harold so much, and I wanted them to be really good. I suppose that's what kept me from writing my best." The new album afforded Lee the opportunity to revamp the words to her liking.

The article also covered Lee's latest actual recording, a duet with singer-songwriter Michael Franks on his Warner Bros. album *Dragonfly Summer*. "'You Were Meant for Me,' a Franks-composed bossa nova that reflected both artists' long-held interest in South American sounds," wrote Hildebrand, "features the two singers trading choruses, then singing the bridge in unison, their voices almost mirror images of each other."

The phrase "almost mirror images" perfectly describes the unique sound created by Peggy and Michael Franks. Fans of both singers had often referred to Franks as "the male Peggy Lee." His light touch is very much a reflection of Peggy's style. There is no doubt she was a major influence in his musical life. Both singers told Hildebrand of their admiration for each other:

> "I think it's natural for both of us," Lee said of their quiet tones and behind-the-beat phrasing. "It's a rather subtle thing; I don't think it's too explainable."
>
> "Considering the feminine voice and the male voice there were moments I thought they were so close," Franks said by phone. "And she came up with all those really pretty harmony parts at the end. She ad-libbed that. It was amazing to be there with her and just to observe at such close range how she worked."

August 31, 1993 — *San Francisco Examiner*. Lee Hildebrand's July 25 article was written to promote Peggy's participation in the Concord Jazz Festival. Peggy and Mel Tormé were reunited for this rare concert at the Concord Pavilion in Concord, California. The concert, part of the 25th anniversary of the Fujitsu Concord Jazz Festival, was held on August 30, 1993. Philip Elwood reviewed the show for the *San Francisco Examiner*:

> I doubt anyone expected the Show of the Decade performance we got from Miss Peggy Lee.... Hers was a performance for the ages. Not merely great — magnificent.... On and on the great renditions rolled, Lee in her best voice, her Mabel Mercer sit-down style, her flippant asides, her fan blowing the feathers about, the video screen projecting herself many times larger behind her — not always flatteringly. But if Lee isn't the girlish Norma Egstrom we first saw singing with Benny Goodman in 1941, she still is the voice that vocalized into our hearts with Benny and his most exciting and adventurous band. Abruptly, Lee said, "I love Basie and Leadbelly," then she floated into "See See Rider," inventing lyrics along the way — followed by an astonishing five minutes of ad-lib blues with guitarist Paul Vipiano in magnificent support.... Lee and Tormé, seated, performed a duet briefly to end the show — a tender, heart-wrenching experience.

May 1994 — **The Society of Singers.** The Society of Singers bestowed its highest honor on Miss Peggy Lee, the "Ella" Lifetime Achievement Award. Lee was the fourth singer to receive this honor, the first being Ella Fitzgerald herself (for whom the award was named), then Frank Sinatra and Tony Martin.

The May 11, 1994, edition of the *Los Angeles Times* featured Jeannine Stein's article "'S Wonderful: Society of Singers and Friends Galore Salute Jazzy Peggy Lee." Stein's article captured the electric and sentimental mood of the evening:

> She's still got it. That was the overwhelming consensus of the 800 people who heard Peggy Lee sing at her tribute from Society of Singers on Monday night at the Beverly Hilton.
> A wheelchair-bound Lee sang two songs, "S' Wonderful" and "Here's to You" for an appreciative crowd that gave her two enthusiastic standing ovations. With a little help, she stood to acknowledge them.
> "I think I've felt more heart here in this room tonight, and I know that is the shining truth," said Lee, dressed in white satin and marabou.

On receiving the award, Stein quoted Lee as saying: "This is incredible. It's like a movie of my life. This is wonderful because it's for my career, and it's absolutely the highest and the best because it's from my peers."

The Beverly Hilton was filled with stars from every generation that evening. Among those paying tribute to Peggy were Bob and Delores Hope, Tony Martin and Cyd Charisse, Chaka Khan, Hugh and Kimberly Hefner, Polly Bergen, Bea Arthur, Frances Bergen and Helen Forrest. The performers interpreting Lee's songs over the course of the two-hour show made up a virtual Who's Who of the music industry: Joe Williams, k.d. lang, the Manhattan Transfer, Jack Jones, Ruth Brown, Rosemary Clooney, Cleo Laine and John Dankworth, and Natalie Cole. Garry Owens served as emcee.

Longtime friend and admirer Joe Williams said, "I went into a puddle," upon hearing Lee's voice for the first time. At the end of the evening Williams made his way to Peggy's side, and the two jazz legends performed an impromptu "Alright, OK, You Win."

June 1995 — **JVC Jazz Festival, Carnegie Hall.** Peggy traveled to New York to perform at the venerable Carnegie Hall. This engagement was part of the JVC Jazz Festival. For this performance — and her final concert one month later — Peggy was joined by Mel Tormé and pianist Marian McPartland.

> [A]n ailing Peggy Lee wove an eerie spell that transcended a vocal capacity so diminished that her voice was little more than a wobbly murmur. Within the limited mobility left to her, Miss Lee still swings, although quietly. Looking a lot like Mae West in her later years, the 75-year-old singer also conveyed more than a glimmer of the smoldering sexuality that made her the most glamorous nightclub singer of the 1960s.... The singer's version of ballads...had the sad and disturbing quality of someone trying to remember an elusive dream. Up-tempo songs ... were phrased with a sly, finger-snapping acuity that showed Miss Lee in solid rhythmic command.... Miss Lee's mystique and Mr. Tormé's technique made for a very full and satisfying concert. — Stephen Holden, June 26, 1995, *New York Times*

> [Peggy Lee's] physical gestures and vocal inflections were minimalist. And yet with the slightest shrug, hint of a sweet/sad smile, or upturn of a warm, smoky note, she said volumes.
> "And when the kids grow up..." she sang in "The Folks Who Live on the Hill," pausing longer than other singers would risk, before finishing the line: "and leave us..." And in that pause, enough was implied about time's inexorable passage to make you cry.... She drew strength from the audience, finishing her short set with more assurance than when she started (seeming frail, tired). The audience gave her a standing ovation (which they did not give Tormé).... For the first time in JVC history, Tormé had the show stolen from him by another singer.—Chip Deffaa, *New York Post*

> [Peggy Lee is] 75 years old and so hobbled in recent years by health problems that she did her whole set sitting down. Still, this most minimalist of jazz pop giants had enough magic and power to transform the grand old concert hall into her own intimate lounge. Tony Bennett and Frank Sinatra may be the only other singers alive capable of such alchemy. Of those two, Sinatra is Lee's sole peer as a lasting presence and influence in American music.—Gene Seymour, *Newsday*

July 1995—Pulse. Will Friedwald offered his well-informed thoughts in an article for *Pulse* magazine titled "Peggy Lee: Doin' Right—Her Way":

> An early believer in tradition- and culture-spanning, Lee has tested the boundaries of pop and expanded the vocabulary of jazz when and wherever she's performed.
> Typically, Lee commands something more than detached listening from her audiences; she draws them into an emotional involvement. Her personality is both sublimely surreal and super real in its honesty.
> She swings like nobody's business, and no one's better than she with torch songs. Yet Lee is at her best in a genre she virtually invented: the song of seduction. In such numbers as "Fever," with its undulating underpinning of bass and finger snaps, and Lieber and Stoller's "I'm a Woman," Lee sold flat-out eroticism long before the '60s sexual revolution.
> At age 73, Miss Peggy Lee is still singing to make us sizzle. What a lovely way to burn!

August 4, 1995—Los Angeles Times. Peggy and Mel Tormé returned to Los Angeles for one more performance at the Hollywood Bowl. The equally legendary pianist George Shearing joined them. Although she probably didn't plan it, this would be Peggy's farewell performance. Her dear friend Leonard Feather had covered her career from the very beginning. Feather would write the last concert review she would ever receive:

> There was more than a century and a half of show business experience on stage at the Hollywood Bowl Wednesday night. George Shearing, 75, Peggy Lee, 75, and Mel Tormé, 69, have been headliners in their profession since the dark years of World War II. Perhaps, inevitably, a concert featuring veteran performers often becomes a summing up of their greatest hits, showcased within a framework of vitality and longevity.... Lee's set was long on style and manner. Various infirmities now obligate her to perform while seated, and her voice, while occasionally hardy, rarely revealed the small subtleties of inflection and timbre that were once her stock in trade. Although she sang such trademark tunes as "Fever" and "Why Don't You Do Right?," she was at her finest on an easygoing blues, "You Don't Know."

August 26, 1995— **Peggy's Final Recording.** Peggy Lee entered a recording studio (Group IV Studios in Hollywood) for the last time. Benny Carter, Peggy's arranger on her 1963 album *Mink Jazz*, was recording an album of his work as a songwriter. He asked his longtime friend Peggy Lee to record his beautiful ballad "I See You," the album's final track. Peggy's voice was supple, pure and strong.

It had been exactly 54 years and 11 days since Peggy's first recording with Benny Goodman. Somehow it seemed fitting that she make her exit with Benny Carter. Peggy's voice blended beautifully with Benny's alto sax. If all of her fans could sing to her they would probably sing Benny's lyrics, the last she sang ...

> I see you, everywhere,
> You're a flower blooming, a rose perfuming the air.
>
> When I hear music played
> There you are in every soothing serenade.
>
> Like a star shining bright,
> Near or far you're never out of my sight.
>
> From the sea to the sky above,
> I see you through the misty eyes of love.

Epilogue

Postscript: Peggy Lee

All entertainers have, to use Noel Coward's phrase, a talent to amuse, but Peggy Lee, who died last week at the age of eighty-one, had something else as well: a talent to be amused. She swung with a sense of humor, and handled lyrics with an uncynical knowingness, letting you in on the little secret of whatever song she happened to be singing, or, at least, letting you know that she had a secret. Unlike Frank Sinatra, her peer in musical intelligence, she had a voice that didn't command you to pay attention; it suggested that you might have a lot of fun if you did. There was something about Peggy Lee that didn't invite a listener all the way in, though that quality, instead of being off-putting, made the intimacy she did allow feel special. In one of the songs she wrote for the Disney movie *Lady and the Tramp*, two cats (Lee provided their voices) lay out the facts of their existence: "We are Siamese if you please. We are Siamese if you don't please." A famous perfectionist when it came to her performances— she controlled the technical as well as the musical elements of her shows— Peggy Lee knew what she was about, and that purring self-containment and sureness of footing make even her earliest recordings, which are now sixty years old, sound distinctive and mature. Her voice wasn't big, but it was womanly — it had hips. She told Whitney Balliett in 1985, "People say my voice is thin or small, but I have a lot more voice than I ever use. I ration it, and it's lasting very nicely." By that time, she had become the rather grand Miss Peggy Lee, and had sheathed herself in a weird casing of extraterrestrial glamour — the platinum wig, the beaded headdress, the heavy makeup, the sunglasses— but she was still fundamentally earthy, and that rootedness enabled her to range playfully around virtually every popular-music style during her career without seeming ridiculous and without getting lost artistically.

Peggy Lee's own favorite among her recordings was one she made for Capitol in 1957 — an album of ballads called *The Man I Love*. Her label mate Frank Sinatra conducted Nelson Riddle's arrangements, and part of what makes the album moving is the idea of these two not so old pros working together. She and Sinatra brought out tremendous tenderness in each other; he is at her service, plumping the pillows for her, making her comfortable, helping to create something of relaxed intimacy and shimmering beauty. Her voice is quiet and warm and sometimes quavery, with an occasional crack in it that fleetingly calls up Billie Holiday. In Jerome Kern and Oscar Hammerstein's "The Folks Who Live on the Hill," the last song on the album, she imbues each part of the opening phrase, "Someday, we'll build a home on a hilltop high, you and I," with its fullest possible measure of hope and wistfulness. (She created a similar feeling of vulnerability in another recording of a Kern-Hammerstein number, "Don't Ever Leave Me," a couple of years later, over George Shearing's piano accompaniment; the record is essentially a three-minute, sung kiss.) Peggy Lee had a torchy, nighttime side, but she also had an aura of natural, daytime light about her. Her bent was optimistic — she wrote songs with titles like "It's a Good Day" and "I Love Being Here with You" and "There'll Be Another Spring." Listening to her, you feel the breath of life against your skin.

— *Nancy Franklin*

Copyright ©2002 Condé Nast Publications Inc.
Originally published in the February 4, 2002, issue of *The New Yorker*.
Reprinted by permission. All rights reserved.

Closing Comments

When you listen to Peggy Lee, you invariably feel that she is singing only to you. There is something mystical about her ability to create this illusion, if illusion it be. I prefer to think of it as a quality that only a select few have possessed, producing the same effect aurally as reading the novels of Proust or viewing a painting by Van Gogh. Listening to her definitive versions of "The Folks Who Live on the Hill," "Don't Smoke in Bed," "Fever" and any of her many classic recordings, the whole of human experience is there, distilled into three-minute masterpieces that reveal fresh nuances no matter how many times you hear them.

How lucky we are today that we live in an age where the legacies of great performers can be permanently preserved for us to enjoy long after the death of the artist. Most of Peggy Lee's recordings are available on CD now and we can listen to her impeccable artistry whenever we choose. We can hear her early days with the Goodman band, trace her development through her first Capitol tenure, revel in the freedom and innovative spirit of her Decca career and enjoy the maturity of her return to Capitol and beyond, all at the press of a button.

A sketch by Ronald Towe.

We all have our favorite Peggy Lee track, but apart from the obvious choices, the album that for me expresses the very essence of her peerless qualities is *Sea Shells*, and one track in particular, "Nine Thorny Thickets." I must have listened to this song literally hundreds of times over the past 40 years or so, and I don't suppose I shall ever get tired of it because for me it epitomizes the magic of Peggy Lee singing directly to me: ethereal, vulnerable, self-doubting, but in the end, resolute and strong. All this she achieves without recourse to any cheap pseudo-dramatic effects or vocal gymnastics. She doesn't sing the song, or act the song; she *is* the song.

— Gerry Stonestreet
Editor, *In Tune International*

Peggy Lee and Bing Crosby were always a magical combination when they sang together. The voices melded so well that they seemed to endow each other with a special ingredient in their many duets on radio. Their most prolific time together was in the late forties when Peggy was a featured guest on Bing's radio show. In her book, Peggy describes how Bing was so protective of her during their early days together, and this developed into a real friendship both musical and non-musical. They worked with each other from 1946 to 1968, which is testament indeed to their enduring relationship.

Listening to those radio duets of Bing and Peggy from the late 1940s, they still seem 'modern,' and they continue to hold the listener's attention with their charm. Just sit back and listen to the version of "So in Love" from the *Philco* show of February 23, 1949, and you'll see what I mean. But fast songs or slow songs, it didn't matter, they could make everything sound special.

— Malcolm Macfarlane
Editor of *BING* magazine,
author of *Bing Crosby: Day by Day*

Peggy Lee was a mountain of talent. She had a style all her own, and getting Walt Disney to give her a free hand to write for them was no small matter!

Never mind all the songs she wrote that we will sing forever. She will be a *star* forever and rightfully so.

— Kay Starr

Miss Peggy Lee was a one-of-a-kind artiste and will remain that way for all time. Even though she has influenced many young singers, both male and female, who never heard her in the flesh, she has remained the delectable, one and only Miss Lee. Her calm, understated, meaningful work over the years is one of the most identifiable sounds, after just a couple of words. Like all great artistes she can be aped, but her core is unattainable, her intelligence and creative spirit shined through everything she did. To me she will always remain one of the all-time jazz divas, who brought the music to millions of fans in her lifetime. A rare feat indeed. But she achieved it by being none other than, Miss Peggy Lee.

— Cleo Laine

Peggy Lee and I were friends for many years. One man, Mr. Benny Goodman, brought us both to national and international attention. We often talked about the effect he had on us; we became perfectionists about our music.

Not only was Peggy a wonderful performer and recording artist, she was a gifted and prolific songwriter. In the past year or so I have had the pleasure of writing thirty or more arrangements of her songs and loved every minute of it.

I consider her one of the most important women in American music. I was honored to work with her and know her.

— Buddy Greco

I first became aware of Peggy Lee when I heard her sing the Rodgers and Hart song "Lover." It must have been in the 1950s. I bought the record, and played that song over and over again. What a voice, and what an arrangement!

As I became older (maybe 19 or so), I went to one of her concerts here in San Francisco with the wonderful singer Mark Murphy. She totally mesmerized me with her voice, style, the way she sang unmoving, her charts. She was the BEST!

I now sing "Lover" myself. Whenever I do, I dedicate it to her, and afterwards, people clap even more than usual. Peggy Lee — a gorgeous, remarkable woman who I will never forget.

— Bobbe Norris

I enjoyed being on Peggy's radio show. That was way back in 1947.
Peggy Lee was one of the greatest singers to ever perform.

— Frankie Laine

Appendix A.
Miss Peggy Lee on CD

This list was compiled by Jarl Ingves, and edited by the author. Mr. Ingves provided the title, label, catalog number, country of release and number of tracks on each CD. The author added the song titles. Wilfred Johnson and Ivan Santiago provided additional guidance and support.

1984

Perfect Lee MCA DMCL 1794 England 16

Bauble, Bangles and Beads; I'm Glad There Is You; Ooh That Kiss; Who's Gonna Pay the Check; Sugar (That Sugar Baby of Mine); Where Flamingos Fly; That's Alright Honey; I Don't Want to Play in Your Yard; You Go to See Mamma Every Night; Street of Dreams; Be Anything (But Be Mine); I Hear the Music Now; Moonflowers; Johnny Guitar; This Is a Very Special Day; (Ah the Apple Trees) When the World Was Young

1985

Uncollected Barbour and Billy May Bands Hindsight HCD-220 USA 12

Riding High; Let There Be Love ; I Gotta Right to Sing the Blues; Oh, What a Beautiful Morning; It's a Good Day; What Is This Thing Called Love?; Love Is Just Around the Corner; 'Deed I Do; Do I Love You?; Just One of Those Things; You; I've Got the World on a String

1986

Best 22 Songs MCA 35XD-510 Japan 22

Mr. Wonderful; Black Coffee; There's a Small Hotel; You Go to My Head; I've Got You Under My Skin; You're My Thrill; It's All Right with Me; Bye Bye Blackbird; Just One of Those Things; Somebody Loves Me; Apples, Peaches and Cherries; The Siamese Cat Song; Sans Souci; Let Me Go, Lover; Johnny Guitar; Love Me or Leave Me; Love Letters; Lover; Easy Living; Swing Low, Sweet Chariot; My Heart Belongs to Daddy; La La Lu

If I Could Be with You Jasmine JSMCD 2534 Czech Republic 15

If I Could Be with You; Too Young; Clarinade (Benny Goodman instrumental); Make the Man Love Me; Toodle-Lee-Oo-Do (duet with Benny Goodman); It Never Happened to Me; Goodbye; Shanghai; A Guy Is a Guy; These Foolish Things; Just One More Chance; Dorsey Medley (duet with Tommy Dorsey); The Lady Is a Tramp; Close

1987

Best 20 Toshiba CP32-5297 Japan 20

Strangers in the Night; The Boy from Ipanema; I Could Have Dance All Night; Love; I Don't Know How to Love Him; A Hard Days Night; I Can't Stop Loving You; Heart; Unforgettable; Alright, Okay, You Win; Mack the Knife; On the Street Where You Live; One Note Samba;

The Surrey with the Fringe on Top; Fever; Hallelujah, I Love Him So; C'est Magnifique; Kansas City; Don't Smoke in Bed; Superstar

Unforgettable 15 Golden Classics
**Castle Com.   UNCD 27
England   15**

Mr. Wonderful; Lover; I Didn't Know What Time It Was; Black Coffee; Love Me or Leave Me; My Heart Belongs to Daddy; I've Got You Under My Skin; (Ah, the Apple Trees) When the World Was Young; Siamese Cat Song; He's a Tramp; Let Me Go Lover; Easy Living; Johnny Guitar; He Needs Me; Joey, Joey, Joey

1988

Best Of **EMI Capitol   7905522
Australia   16**

Mañana (Is Soon Enough for Me); Golden Earrings; It's a Good Day; Don't Smoke in Bed; Why Don't You Do Right?; Fever; The Folks Who Live on the Hill; Hallelujah I Love Him So; I'm a Woman; A Doodlin' Song; Big Spender; So What's New?; The Shinning Sea; Alright, Okay, You Win; Is That All There Is?; I'm Gonna Go Fishin'

Best of Capitol Years **Capitol Jazz
CDP 7-90522-2   UK   16**

(Same songs as the Australian version above; different artwork on the cover)

Fever **Jazz World   JW 77023   EU
16**

Fever; Golden Earrings; I Can't Give You Anything but Love; Stormy Weather; Bye, Bye Blues; Mañana (Is Soon Enough for Me); Sugar; 'Deed I Do; I'm Glad There Is You; It's a Good Day; Don't Smoke in Bed; Them There Eyes; Why Don't You Do Right?; I Don't Know Enough About You; You Go to See Mamma Every Night; I'm Gonna Meet My Sweetie Now

Sings the Blues **Music Masters
CIJD 60155F   USA   12**

See See Rider; Basin Street Blues; Squeeze Me; You Don't Know; Fine and Mellow; Baby Please Come Home; Kansas City; Birmingham Jail; Love Me; Beale Street; Tain't Nobody's Bizness; God Bless the Child

Sings with Benny Goodman
Columbia   CK 7005   USA   10

How Long Has This Been Going On; That Did It, Marie; Elmer's Tune; I Threw a Kiss in the Ocean; We'll Meet Again; My Old Flame; That's the Way It Goes; All I Need Is You; Not a Care in the World; Full Moon (Noche de Luna)

1989

Mirrors **A & M Records   CD 5268
USA   11**

Is That All There Is?; Ready to Begin Again (Manya's Song); Some Cats Know; I've Got Them Feelin' Too Good Today Blues; A Little White Ship; Tango; Professor Hauptmann's Performing Dogs; The Case of M.J.; I Remember; Say It; Longings for a Simpler Time

Seductive **US Pair   PCD-2-1194
USA   16**

Hallelujah, I Love Him So; The Best Is Yet to Come; Hey! Look Me Over; So in Love; Heart; When a Woman Loves a Man; I'll Get By; Yes Indeed; I've Got Your Number; Alright, Okay, You Win; My Man; A Doodlin' Song; I Enjoy Being a Girl; What Are You Doing the Rest of Your Life?; I Get Along Without You Very Well; Don't Smoke in Bed

1990

Portrait of a Song Stylist
Mastertone HARCD 116   UK   14

The Folks Who Live on the Hill; As Time Goes By; That Old Devil Moon; Cheek to Cheek; When a Man Loves a Woman; I Hear Music; The Party's Over; Till There Was You; I Enjoy Being a Girl; Fly Me to the Moon; Stormy Weather; Alright, Okay, You Win; Something; Is That All There Is?

All Time Greatest Hits Volume 1
Curb   D2-77379   USA   11

It's a Good Day; Is That All There Is?; Fever; I'm a Woman; Mañana (Is Soon Enough for Me); Alright, Okay, You Win; Why Don't You Do Right?; Heart; My Man; Hallelujah, I Love Him So; I Enjoy Being a Girl

An American Legend **K-tel
BCD 3741   UK   20**

Them There Eyes; Mañana (Is Soon Enough for Me); It's a Good Day; What's New; The Old

Master Painter (with Mel Torme); The Lady Is a Tramp; Why Don't You Do Right?; How Long Has This Been Going On?; That Old Magic; People Will Say We're in Love; Bye, Bye Blackbird; Let There Be Love; The Way You Look Tonight; I Get a Kick Out of You; Fools Rush In; From This Moment On; The Surrey with the Fringe on Top; Let's Do It; Waiting for the Train to Come In; Swing Low, Sweet Chariot

Best Now   Capitol Toshiba
   TOCP-9068   Japan   20

Strangers in the Night; The Boy from Ipanema; I Could Have Danced All Night; Love; I Don't Know How to Love Him; A Hard Day's Night; I Can't Stop Loving You; Heart; Unforgettable; Alright, Okay, You Win; Mack the Knife; On the Street Where You Live; One Note Samba; The Surrey with the Fringe on Top; Fever; Hallelujah, I Love Him So; C'est Magnifique; Kansa City; Don't Smoke in Bed; Superstar

Capitol Collectors Series   Capitol
   D 101796   USA   25

Waiting for the Train to Come In; I'm Glad I Waited for You; I Don't Know Enough About You; Linger in My Arms a Little Longer, Baby; It's All Over Now; It's a Good Day; Everything's Movin' Too Fast; Chi-Baba, Chi-Baba (My Bambino Go to Sleep); Sugar (That Sugar Baby o' Mine); Golden Earrings; I'll Dance at Your Wedding; Mañana (Is Soon Enough for Me); All Dressed Up with a Broken Heart; Talkin' to Myself About You; Why Don't You Do Right? (Get Me Some Money Too); 'Deed I Do; Don't Smoke in Bed; Cramba! It's the Samba; Them There Eyes; Baby, Don't Be Mad at Me; Bali Ha'i; I'm Gonna Wash That Man Right Outta My Hair; Ghost Riders in the Sky (A Cowboy Legend); The Old Master Painter (duet with Mel Torme); Show Me the Way to Get Out of This World

Christmas Carousel   Capitol
   CDP 7-94450-2   USA   17

I Like a Sleighride (Jingle Bells); The Christmas Song (Merry Christmas to You); Don't Forget to Feed the Reindeer; The Star Carol; The Christmas List; Christmas Carousel; Santa Clause Is Comin' to Town; The Christmas Waltz; The Christmas Riddle; The Tree; Deck the Halls; White Christmas; Winter Wonderland; Little Drummer Boy; Happy Holiday; The Christmas Spell; Toys for Tots

Fever & Other Hits   Cema Records
   CDL-57358   USA   10

Fever; I'm a Woman; Is That All There Is?; (You Gotta Have) Heart; My Man; A Doodlin' Song; Hallelujah, I Love Him So; Big Spender; Alright, Okay, You Win; The Alley Cat Song

Peggy Lee The Christmas Album
   EMI   7243 4 97537 2 3   UK   17

(Same as Christmas Carousel, Capitol   CDP 7-94450-2)

Sings the Blues   Jazz Heritage
   MHS 512487M   USA   12

See See Rider; Basin Street Blues; Squeeze Me; You Don't Know; Fine and Mellow; Baby Please Come Home; Kansas City; Birmingham Jail; Love Me; Beale Street; Tain't Nobody's Bizness; God Bless the Child

There'll Be Another Spring
   Music Masters   MMD 60249 K
   USA   13

Circle in the Sky; I Just Want to Dance; He's a Tramp; There'll Be Another Spring; Johnny Guitar; Fever; I'll Give It All to You; Sans Souci; Where Can I Go Without You?; Boomerang (I'll Come Back to You); Things Are Swingin'; Over the Wheel; The Shining Sea

Why Don't You Do Right?
   The Entertainers   CD 0239   UK
   25

Why Don't You Do Right?; I Don't Know Enough About You; 'Deed I Do; I'm Glad There Is You; It's a Good Day; Don't Smoke in Bed; Them There Eyes; Fever; Sugar; Baubles, Bangles and Beads; Mañana (Is Soon Enough for Me); I Can't Give You Anything but Love; Golden Earrings; You've Got to See Mamma Every Night; Johnny Guitar; That's Alright Honey; Stormy Weather; I Hear the Music Now; Bye, Bye Blackbird; What Can I Say After I'm Sorry?; He Needs Me; I'm Gonna Meet My Sweetie Now; I Never Knew; All Too Soon; If Dreams Comes True

1991

Peggy Lee   MCA UICY-1534   Japan
   22

Johnny Guitar; Autumn in Rome; Black Coffee; What's New?; Mr. Wonderful; There's a Small

Hotel; You Go to My Head; I've Got You Under My Skin; It's All Right with Me; Bye Bye Blackbird; Love Letters; My Heart Belongs to Daddy; La La Lu; Bella Notte; Somebody Loves Me; Apples, Peaches and Cherries; The Siamese Cat Song; Sans Souci; Let Me Go, Lover; Love Me or Leave Me; Swing Low, Sweet Chariot; I Don't Want to Play in Your Yard

Golden Greats   MCA   MCLD 19123   UK   16

Lover; Apples, Peaches and Cherries; Love Me or Leave Me; I Don't Enough About You; He's a Tramp; Mr. Wonderful; Black Coffee; The Siamese Cat Song; He Needs Me; My Heart Belongs to Daddy; Where Can I Go Without You?; Easy Living; I Didn't Know What Time It Was; They Can't Take Away from Me; Just One of Those Things; Love You Didn't Do Right by Me

If You Go   Capitol   TOCJ-5393   Japan   12

As Time Goes By; If You Go; Oh Love Hast Thou Forsaken Me; Say It Isn't So; I Wish I Didn't Love You So; Maybe It's Because (I Love You Too Much); I'm Gonna Laugh You Out of My Life; I Get Along Without You Very Well; (I Love Your) Gypsy Heart; When I Was a Child; Here's That Rainy Day; Smile

It's a Good Day with Bing Crosby   Parrot   PARCD 001   England   36

It's a Good Day (with Bing Crosby); He Just My Kind; Everything's Moving Too Fast (with Bing Crosby); Linger in My Arms a Little Longer, Baby; Baby You Can Count on Me (with Bing Crosby); What More Can a Women Do?; The Best Man (with Bing Crosby); For Sentimental Reasons; I Still Suits Me (with Bing Crosby); It's All Over Now; You Came a Long Way from St. Louis (with Bing Crosby); A Nightingale Can Sing the Blues; Exactly Like You (with Bing Crosby); I'll Close My Eyes; I Got Rhythm (with Bing Crosby); It Takes a Long, Long Train with a Red Caboose; A Little Bird Told Me (with Bing Crosby); Just an Old Love of Mine; On a Slow Boat to China (with Bing Crosby); Golden Earrings; Cuanta le Gusta (with Bing Crosby); Love, Your Magic Spell Is Everywhere; What Is This Thing Called Love?; Medley performed by Peggy Lee, Bing Crosby and Fred Astaire: Top Hat, White Tie and Tails/ Cheek to Cheek/ Isn't This a Lovely Day/ A Fine Romance/ They Can't Take That Away from Me/ Smoke Gets in Your Eyes/ Dearly Beloved/ White Christmas/ Catalogue Day/ Kamehameha Day; Then I'll Be Happy; I Got Lucky in the Rain; Maybe You'll Be There (with Bing Crosby). *(This material was recorded for Bing Crosby's radio program)*

Latin Ala Lee/Olé Ala Lee   Capitol Toshiba   TOCJ-5418   Japan   24

(Latin Ala Lee): Heart; On the Street Where You Live; I Am in Love; Hey There; I Could Have Danced All Night; The Surrey with the Fringe on Top; The Party's Over; Dance Only with Me; Wish You Were Here; C'est Magnifique; I Enjoy Being a Girl; Till There Was You. *(Ole Ala Lee):* Come Dance with Me; By Myself; You're So Right for Me; Just Squeeze Me; Fantastico; Love and Marriage; Non Dimenticar; From Now On; You Stepped Out of a Dream; Ole; I Can't Resist You; Together Wherever We Go

Mink Jazz   Capitol Toshiba   TOCJ-5342   Japan   12

You Stepped Out of a Dream; It's a Big Wide Wonderful World; Whisper Not; My Silent Love; The Lady Is a Tramp; Days of Wine and Roses; As Long as I Live; I Won't Dance; Cloudy Morning; I Could Write a Book; I Never Had a Chance; Close Your Eyes; Where Can I Go Without You?

My Greatest Songs   MCA   MCD 18346   Germany   14

Johnny Guitar; Lover; Street of Dreams; It's All Right with Me; You Ought to Be Mine; They Can't Take That Away from Me; I Didn't Know What Time It Was; Black Coffee; Guess I'll Go Back Home This Summer; Mr. Wonderful; Love Me or Leave Me; I've Got You Under My Skin; Something I Dreamed Last Night; There's a Small Hotel

Peggy Lee Story   Deja Vu   DVRECD 57   Italy   24

Somebody Loves Me; I Don't Know Enough About You; Big Spender; Lazy River; Fever; Moments Like This; The Best Is Yet to Come; Big, Bad Bill; It's a Good Day; Where Can I Go Without You?; I Love Being Here with You; Lonesome Road; Lover; *Medley:* The Clown Song/ Funny Man/ What Kind of Fool Am I?; The Train Blues; Then Was Then; Come Back to Me; So What's New?; On the Sunny Side of the Street; Alright, Okay, You Win; Mañana (Is

Soon Enough for Me); Making Whoopee; Unforgettable; I Can't Stop Loving You

With Dave Barbour Band Laserlight 15742 USA 14

You Can Depend on Me; I've Had My Moments; Sugar; I Should Care; Someday Sweetheart; September in the Rain; That Old Gang of Mine; Nice Work If You Can Get It; I'm Beginning to See the Light; Gone with the Wind; Don't Blame Me; Baby Won't You Please Come Home; My Last Affair; I'm Confessin'

1992

Beauty and the Beat Capitol Jazz CDP 7-98454-2 Holland 14

Do I Love You?; I Lost My Sugar in Salt Lake City; If Dreams Come True; All Too Soon; Mambo in Miami (instrumental); Isn't It Romantic?; Blue Prelude; You Came a Long Way from St. Louis; Always True in My Fashion; There Be Another Spring; Get Out of Town; Satin Doll (instrumental); Don't Ever Leave Me; Nobody's Heart

Best of Peggy Lee Fever Capitol 0777-7-80361-2-8 UK 24

Fever; Things Are Swinging; Fly Me to the Moon; I'm a Woman; Mañana (Is Soon Enough for Me); I'll Get By; Pass Me By; Till There Was You; I'm Just Wild About Harry; Sneakin' Up on You; It's a Good Day; The Folks Who Live on the Hill; Come Dance with Me; The Best Is Yet to Come; It Could Happen to You; You Deserve; Love and Marriage; Charlie, My Boy; Sugar; Sing a Rainbow; Makin' Whoopee; It's a Wonderful World; The Party's Over; Hey, Look Me Over

Dream Street MCA Decca MVCM-263 Japan 12

Street of Dreams; What's New?; You're Blasé; It's Alright with Me; My Old Flame; Dancing on the Ceiling; It Never Entered My Mind; Too Late Now; I've Grown Accustomed to His Face; Something I Dreamed Last Night; Last Night When We Were Young; So Blue

Miss Wonderful MCA Decca MVCM-262 Japan 12

Mr. Wonderful; They Can't Take That Away from Me; Where the Flamingos Fly; You've Got to See Mama Every Night; The Comeback; Take a Little Time to Smile; I Don't Know Enough About You; Joey, Joey, Joey; Crazy in the Heart; You Oughta Be Mine; We Laughed at Love; That Alright, Honey

Sea Shells MCA Decca MVCM 264 Japan 16

Sea Fever; Nine Thorny Thickets; Little Old Car; Greensleeves; Chinese Love Poems—(a) "The Fisherman" (b) "Autumn Evening"; The Happy Monk (instrumental); The White Birch and the Sycamore; Of Such Is the Kingdom of God; A Brown Bird Singing; I Don't Want to Play in Your Yard; The Maid with the Flaxen Hair (instrumental); The Wearing of the Green; Chaconde (instrumental); Chinese Love Poems—(a) "Going Rowing" (b) "Like the Moon" (c) "The Musicians"; The Riddle Song; The Golden Wedding Ring

Sings for You Avid AVC 514 England 20

You Do Something to Me; Almost Like Being in Love; Just One of Those Things; That Old Magic; Sans Souci; It's a Good Day; You're Mine, You; Between the Devil and the Deep Blue Sea; I Feel a Song Coming On; From This Moment On; Surrey with the Fringe on Top; People Will Say We're in Love; Speak Low; Bye, Bye Blackbird; I Get a Kick Out of You; Ac-Cent-Tchu-Ate the Positive; What's New?; Don't Worry About Me; It Ain't Necessarily So; Fools Rush In

Sings with Benny Goodman Sony A 13584 USA 10

My Old Flame; That's the Way It Goes; All I Need Is You; Not a Care in the World; Full Moon (Noche de Luna); How Long Has This Been Going On?; That Did It, Marie; Elmer's Tune; I Threw a Kiss in the Ocean; We'll Meet Again

Wonderful World Of Remember Records RMB 75629 Portugal 26

I Don't Know Enough About You; Golden Earrings; It's a Good Day; Mañana (Is Soon Enough for Me); Don't Smoke in Bed; Lover; Just One of Those Things; Baubles, Bangles and Beads; Let Me Go Lover; Mr. Wonderful; Fever; Alright, Okay, You Win; Hallelujah, I Love Him So; I'm a Woman; Black Coffee; I've Got You Under My Skin; It's Alright with Me; Johnny

Guitar; Love Me or Leave Me; My Heart Belongs to Daddy; Why Don't You Do Right?; Big Spender; 'Deed I Do; Them There Eyes; I Can't Give You Anything but Love; If Dreams Come True

1993

Basin Street East   Capitol Toshiba TOCJ-5439   Japan   13

Day In—Day Out; Moments Like This; Fever; The Second Time Around; Medley: One Kiss/ My Romance/ The Vagabond King Waltz; I Got a Man; Peggy Lee Bow Music; Call Me Darling, Call Me Sweetheart, Call Me Dear; I Love Being Here with You; But Beautiful; Them There Eyes; A Tribute to Ray Charles: Just for a Thrill/ Yes Indeed; Peggy Lee Bow Music

Benny Goodman Featuring Peggy Lee   Sony CK   CK 53422   USA   16

Elmer's Tune; I See a Million People; That's the Way It Goes; I Got It Bad and That Ain't Good; My Old Flame; How Deep Is the Ocean?; Shady Lady Bird; Let's Do It; Somebody Else Is Taking My Place; Somebody Nobody Loves; How Long Has This Been Going On?; That Did It, Marie; Winter Weather; Everything I Love; Not Mine; Not a Care in the World

Classics   Curb   D2-77629   USA   10

Mack the Knife; A Taste of Honey; The Shadow of Your Smile; There'll Be Some Changes Made; On the Street Where You Live; Hey, Look Me Over; The Boy from Ipanema; Surrey With the Fringe on Top; Hey, Big Spender; The Alley Cat Song

Fever 24 Great Songs   Personality PRS 23012   Portugal   24

Fever; It's All Right with Me; Hallelujah, I Love Him So; Apples, Peaches and Cherries; Mr. Wonderful; They Can't Take That Away from Me; Alright, Okay, You Win; Love Me or Leave Me; Black Coffee; Sans Souci; Lover; My Heart Belongs to Daddy; Baubles, Bangles and Beads; Is That All There Is?; Big Spender; That's What a Woman Is For; The Siamese Cat Song; Where Can I Go Without You?; Love Letters; I'm Glad There Is You; I'm a Woman; Swing Low, Sweet Chariot; He Needs Me; Guess I'll Go Back Home This Summer

Live 1947–1952   Jazzband Classic EBCD 2115-2   France   25

Introduction; The Lady from 29 Palms; I Can't Give You Anything but Love; Back Home Again in Indiana; Ask Anyone Who Knows; Cecilia; Beside the Zeiderze; Half as Much; Alone Together; Trying (vocal Johnny Desmond); It Never Happened to Me; For Me and My Girl (duet with Johnny Desmond); Just One of Those Things; Perefidia; Jump Through the Rain; Similau (See-me-lo) (vocal Desi Arnaz); Mambo Jambo; Mañana (Is Soon Enough for Me) (duet with Desi Arnaz); Accentuate the Positive; Frenisi; Bermudian Waters; That Old Black Magic (vocal Jeff Chandler); We're One; Slumming on Park Avenue (duet with Jeff Chandler); It's a Good Day

Love Held Lightly   Angel CDC 54798   USA   14

Look Who's Been Dreaming; Love Held Lightly; Buds Won't Bud; Can You Explain?; Wait'll It Happens to You; Come on, Midnight; Happy with the Blues; Bad for Each Other; Love's No Stranger to Me; I Could Be Good to You; Got to Wear You Off My Weary Mind; I Had a Love Once; Love's a Necessary Thing; My Shining Hour

Moments Like This   Chesky Records JD 84   USA   15

I Don't Know Enough About You; I'm in Love Again; Why Don't You Do Right?; Remind Me; Moments Like This; Our Love Is Here to Stay; Don't Ever Leave Me; Mañana (Is Soon Enough for Me); The Folks Who Live on the Hill; S'-Wonderful; Amazing; Do I Love You?; You're My Thrill; Always True in My Fashion; Then Was Then (And Now Is Now)

Peggy Lee   Cema Records S21-56958   USA   24

Fever; Love Letters; You Go to My Head; I Wanna Be Around; I'll Get By (As Long as I Have You); Say It Isn't So; Alright, Okay, You Win; Come Rain or Come Shine; You're Nobody 'Til Somebody Loves You; The Man I Love; Watch What Happens; If I Should Lose You; Mañana (Is Soon Enough for Me); Pass Me By; Lover; Baubles, Bangles and Beads; Mr. Wonderful; You Always Hurt the One You Love; There Is No Greater Love; Quiet Nights; My Heart Stood Still; Love Me or Leave Me; Be Anything (But Be Mine); Them There Eyes

Peggy Lee—Fever Spectrum
550-088-2 Germany 14

Misty; What I Did for Love; Every Little Movement; Mr. Wonderful; Is That All There Is?; The Folks Who Live on the Hill; Love for Sale; Fever; Mack the Knife; Sing a Rainbow; I'm Not in Love; Hungry Years; Lover; Star Sounds *1994*

Best of Peggy Lee 1952–1956 MCPS
MCCD 157 England 18

Lover; Black Coffee; My Heart Belongs to Daddy; It Ain't Necessarily So; There's a Small Hotel; A Brown Bird Sings; He's a Tramp; Mr. Wonderful; The Siamese Cat Song; Sing a Rainbow; Somebody Loves Me; I Don't Want to Play in Your Yard; Street of Dreams; It's All Right with Me; It Never Entered My Mind; Too Late Now; I've Grown Accustomed to His Face; Something I Dreamed Last Night

Best of Let There Be Love Castle
MAT CD 316 EU 20

I've Got the Right to Sing the Blues; Let There Be Love; If I Could Be with You One Hour Tonight; These Foolish Things; Shanghai; Make the Man Love Me; The Lady Is a Tramp; It's All Over Now; It Takes a Long, Long Train with a Red Caboose; Golden Earrings; I Got Lucky in the Rain; He's Just My Kind; What Is This Thing Called Love?; For Sentimental Reasons; My Last Affair; Just One More Chance; Love Is Just Around the Corner; Love, Your Magic Spell Is Everywhere; Oh, What a Beautiful Morning; Linger in My Arms a Little Longer, Baby

Best One MCA MVCM 28023
Japan 22

Johnny Guitar; Autumn in Rome; Black Coffee; What's New?; Mr. Wonderful; There's a Small Hotel; You Go to My Head; I've Got You Under My Skin; It's All Right with Me; Bye Bye Blackbird; Love Letters; My Heart Belongs to Daddy; La La Lu; Bella Notte; Somebody Loves Me; Apples, Peaches and Cherries; The Siamese Cat Song; Sans Souci; Let Me Go, Lover; Love Me or Leave Me; Swing Low, Sweet Chariot; I Don't Want to Play in Your Yard

Black Coffee/The Decca Anthology
MCA Decca MCAD2-11122 USA 46

Disc One: Lover; Be Anything (But Be Mine); You Go to My Head; Just One of Those Things; Forgive Me; I'm Glad There Is You (In This World of Ordinary People); Watermelon Weather (with Bing Crosby); Moon Flowers; River River; Sans Souci; That's Him Over There; Who's Gonna Pay the Check?; Where Can I Go Without You?; My Heart Belongs to Daddy; Easy Living; Black Coffee; Apples, Peaches, and Cherries; (Ah, the Apple Trees) When the World Was Young; Baubles, Bangles, and Beads; Johnny Guitar; Sisters; Bouquet of Blues; Love Letters; Love, You Didn't Do Right by Me. *Disc Two:* Let Me Go, Lover!; I Don't Want to Play in Your Yard; Sugar (That Sugar Baby of Mine); Somebody Loves Me; What Can I Say After I Say I'm Sorry?; Sing a Rainbow; Mr. Wonderful; He Needs Me; They Can't Take That Away from Me; You've Got to See Mama Every Night (Or You Can't See Mama at All); Joey, Joey, Joey; I Don't Know Enough About You; Guess I'll Go Back Home (This Summer); You're Blasé; It's All Right with Me; It Never Entered My Mind; Too Late Now; My Old Flame; I Still Get a Thrill (Thinking of You); Dancing on the Ceiling; Where Flamingos Fly; Street of Dreams

Fever 20 Original Classics Cedar
CD CRB 527 Germany 20

I Don't Know Enough About You; It's a Good Day; Golden Earrings; Mañana (Is Soon Enough for Me); Lover; Just One of Those Things; Do I Love You; Baubles, Bangles and Beads; Black Coffee; When the World Was Young; Johnny Guitar; Mr. Wonderful; The Folks Who Live on the Hill; Fever; Alright, Okay, You Win; Heart; Hey There; Hallelujah, I Love Him So; I'm a Woman; I've Got You Under My Skin

Legends Peggy Lee Wisepack
LECD 092 England 16

Them There Eyes; Mañana (Is Soon Enough for Me); I Can't Give You Anything but Love; Golden Earrings; Stormy Weather; You've Got to See Mama Every Night; Johnny Guitar; That's Alright Honey; Why Don't You Do Right?; I Don't Know Enough About You; It's a Good Day; I'm Glad There Is You; 'Deed I Do; Don't Smoke in Bed; Sugar; Baubles, Bangles and Beads

Very Special Castle Com.
PCD 10016 Australia 16

Johnny Guitar; You've Got to See Mama Every Night; The Siamese Cat Song; Be Anything

(But Be Mine); Lover; You Go to My Head; I'm Glad There Is You; Just One of Those Things; Little Jack Frost, Get Lost (with Bing Crosby); This Is a Very Special Day; I've Got You Under My Skin; My Heart Belongs to Daddy; When the World Was Young; A Woman Alone with the Blues; Baubles, Bangles and Beads; Black Coffee

Why Don't You Do Right?
   Charly Records   CDCD 1216   England   12

Elmer's Tune; My Old Flame; How Deep Is the Ocean?; That's the Way It Goes; I Threw a Kiss in the Ocean; We'll Meet Again; Full Moon (Noche de Luna); All I Need Is You; Why Don't You Do Right?; Not a Care in the World; How Long Has This Been Going On; That Did It Marie

1995

A Woman Alone with the Blues
   Blue Moon   BMCD 3034   Spain   18

Love, You Didn't Do Right by Me; Be Anything (But Be Mine); Black Coffee; River River; That's Him Over There; You Go to My Head; Forgive Me; Baubles, Bangles and Beads; Where Can I Go Without You?; Bouquet of Blues; I'm Glad There Is You; I Didn't Know What Time It Was; Moon Flowers; Easy Living; When the World Was Young; I've Got You Under My Skin; Johnny Guitar; A Woman Alone with the Blues

Basin Street East   Capitol Jazz
   7243-832744-2-0   USA   13

Day In — Day Out; Moments Like This; Fever; The Second Time Around; Medley: One Kiss/ My Romance/ The Vagabond King Waltz; I Got a Man; Peggy Lee Bow Music; Call Me Darling, Call Me Sweetheart, Call Me Dear; I Love Being Here with You; But Beautiful; Them There Eyes; A Tribute to Ray Charles: Just for a Thrill/ Yes Indeed; Peggy Lee Bow Music

Basin Street East   Capitol Jazz
   7243-8-32744-2-0   Holland   13

(Same as US release above)

Gold   San Juan Music   GOLD 055   EU   14

Let There Be Love; 'Deed I Do; Gone with the Wind; Oh, What a Beautiful Morning; Baby, Won't You Please Come Home; Just One of Those Things; Ridin' High; September in the Rain; What Is This Thing Called Love?; You; I've Got the World on a String; Do I Love You?; It's a Good Day; I've Got the Right to Sing the Blues

Gone with the Wind   Compilation
   705118-2   England   14

You Can Depend on Me; Sugar; Someday Sweetheart; September in the Rain; Gone with the Wind; Let There Be Love; I've Got the Right to Sing the Blues; Oh, What a Beautiful Morning; What Is This Thing Called Love?; Love Is Just Around the Corner; 'Deed I Do; Just One of Those Things; You; I've Got the World on a String

I've Got a Crush on You   Avid
   AVC 549   England   25

A Wonderful Guy; You Go to My Head; Just One of Those Things; Trouble Is a Man; Golden Earrings; Just Squeeze Me; Happiness Is Just a Thing Called Joe; It Takes a Long, Long Train with a Red Caboose; So Dear to My Heart; Louisa from Lake Louise; When You Speak with Your Eyes; Lover; You and the Night and the Music; It's Lovin' Time; Then I'll Be Happy; Linger in My Arms a Little Longer, Baby; Orange Colored Sky; I've Got a Crush on You; I'm Sweet, Shy Ophelia; A Dream Is a Wish Your Heart Makes; Bali Ha'i; Speaking of Angels; What Is This Thing Called Love?; When Is Sometime?; For Just the Chance to Love You

Lady Is a Tramp   Hallmark   300862   England   18

I'm Confessin'; September in the Rain; That Old Gang of Mine; If I Could Be with You; Baby, Please Come Home; Make the Man Love Me; These Foolish Things; Too Young; Just One More Chance; Nice Work If You Can Get It; The Lady Is a Tramp; Don't Blame Me; It Never Happened to Me; Shanghai; A Guy Is a Guy; I'm Beginning to See the Light; My Last Affair; Gone with the Wind

Let There Be Love   Kaz
   TRT CD 153   England   20

I've Got the Right to Sing the Blues; Let There Be Love; If I Could Be with You One Hour Tonight; These Foolish Things; Shanghai; Make the Man Love Me; The Lady Is a Tramp; It's All Over Now; It Takes a Long, Long Train with a Red Caboose; Golden Earrings; I Got Lucky in the Rain; He's Just My Kind; What Is This Thing Called Love?; For Sentimental Reasons; My Last Affair; Just One More Chance; Love Is Just Around the Corner; Love, Your Magic Spells Is Everywhere; Oh, What a Beautiful Morning; Linger in My Arms a Little Longer, Baby

Spotlight On (Great Ladies of Song) Capitol 7243-8-28533-2-9 USA 18

I've Got the World on a String; When a Woman Loves a Man; I'm Beginning to See the Light; There Is No Greater Love; Too Close for Comfort; Unforgettable; Close Your Eyes; If I Should Lose You; I'm Just Wild About Harry; Deep Purple; It's Been a Long, Long Time; The Man I Love; The Best Is Yet to Come; Come Rain or Come Shine; Fever; I Wanna Be Around; I Hear Music; The Folks Who Live on the Hill

These Foolish Things and Other Great Standards Hallmark 300862 England 18

I'm Confessin'; September in the Rain; That Old Gang of Mine; If I Could Be with You; Baby, Please Come Home; Make the Man Love Me; These Foolish Things; Too Young; Just One More Chance; Nice Work If You Can Get It; The Lady Is a Tramp; Don't Blame Me; It Never Happened to Me; Shanghai; A Guy Is a Guy; I'm Beginning to See the Light; My Last Affair; Gone with the Wind

Why Don't You Do Right? Vipers Nest VN-158 USA 21

Why Don't You Do Right; It's the Sentimental Thing to Do; I May Be Wrong (But I Think You're Wonderful); All of Me; I'll Dance at Your Wedding; There'll Be Some Changes Made; You Don't Have to Know the Language; The Christmas Song; I Can't Give You Anything but Love, Baby; Lone Star Moon; Mañana (Is Soon Enough for Me); But Beautiful; Golden Earrings; How Lucky You Are; The Secretary Song; Laroo, Laroo Lili Bolero; You Turned the Tables on Me; I Went Down to Virginia; Nature Boy; Baby, Don't Be Mad at Me; Wish You Were Here

1996

Fever the Best of Pulse PLSCD 144 England 17

(In Concert at the London Palladium): Love for Sale Misty; Make Believe; I'm Not in Love; Have a Good Time; Mr. Wonderful; Why Don't You Do Right?; Sing a Rainbow; You Gotta Know How; Everything Must Change; Fever; I Don't Want to Play in Your Yard; Rodgers & Hart Medley: Who Are You?/ Where or When/ Glad to Be Unhappy/ It Never Entered My Mind/ Falling in Love with Love/ Bewitched; Mack the Knife; The Folks Who Live on the Hill; Lover; Here's to You

Golden Hits Music Masters MACD 61078-2 Germany 10

Just One of Those Things; I've Got the World on a String; Oh, What a Beautiful Morning; It's a Good Day; What Is This Thing Called Love?; I'm Beginning to See the Light; Don't Blame Me; Let There Be Love; 'Deed I Do; That Old Gang of Mine

In Concert The Entertainers CD 346 AAD UK 23

(Copacabana show): Do I Hear a Waltz; By the Time I Get to Phoenix; Reason to Believe; Didn't Want to Have to Do It; Personal Property; Hand on the Plow; Until It's Time for You to Go; Something Stupid; What Is a Woman; Alright, Okay, You Win; Here's to You; Come Back to Me. *(Basin Street East show):* Day In — Day Out; Moments Like This; Fever; The Second Time Around; Medley: One Kiss/ My Romance/ The Vagabond King Waltz; I Got a Man; Peggy Lee Bow Music; Call Me Darling, Call Me Sweetheart, Call Me Dear; I Love Being Here with You; But Beautiful; Them There Eyes; A Tribute to Ray Charles: Just for a Thrill/ Yes Indeed

In the Beginning (The Legend Of) Flapper PAST CD 7801 Germany 22

On the Sunny Side of the Street; Blues in the Night; Where or When; Why Don't You Do Right?; How Deep Is the Ocean?; Everything I Love; How Long Has This Been Going On?; Let's Do It (Let's Fall in Love); Full Moon (Noche de Luna); That Did It Marie; Not Mine; My Old Flame; Winter Weather; I See a Million People (But All I Can See Is You); Shady Lady

Bird; All I Need Is You; Somebody Else Is Taking My Place; Somebody Nobody Loves; The Way You Look Tonight; I Got It Bad (And That Ain't Good); I Threw a Kiss in the Ocean; We'll Meet Again

...just one of those things Master Tone RZ4031 Holland 12

Why Don't You Do Right?; It's the Sentimental Thing to Do; I May Be Wrong (But I Think You're Wonderful); All of Me; I'll Dance at Your Wedding; The Christmas Song; Under a Long Star Moon; Mañana (Is Soon Enough for Me); How Lucky You Are; The Secretary Song; You Turned the Tables on Me; I Went Down to Virginia

Listen to the Magic President PLCD 550 England 28

It's a Good Day; I Don't Know Enough About You; As Long as I'm Dreaming; I'll Close My Eyes; For Sentimental Reasons; You and I Passing By; He's Just My Kind; Linger in My Arms a Little Longer, Baby; It's All Over Now; What More Can a Woman Do?; A Nightingale Can Sing the Blues; Ain't Cha Ever Coming Back; It Takes a Long, Long Train with a Red Caboose; Just an Old Love of Mine; Golden Earrings; Ridin' High; Let There Be Love; I've Got a Right to Sing the Blues; Oh, What a Beautiful Morning; What Is This Thing Called Love?; Love Is Just Around the Corner; 'Deed I Do; Do I Love You?; Just One of Those Things; You; I've Got the World on a String; Love Your Magic Spell Is Everywhere; I Got Lucky in the Rain

Mack the Knife Kaz TRT CD 209 England 17

(*Peggy Lee in Concert at the London Palladium*): Love for Sale; Misty; You Gotta Know How; Rodgers and Hart Medley: Who Are You?/ Where or When/ Glad to Be Unhappy/; It Never Entered My Mind/ Falling in Love with Love/ Bewitched; Have a Good Time; Mr. Wonderful; Sing a Rainbow; Make Believe; Fever; Why Don't You Do Right?; I Don't Want to Play in Your Yard; I'm Not in Love; Everything Must Change; Mack the Knife; The Folks Who Live on the Hill; Lover; Here's to You

More of the Best Laserlight 12642 USA 12

Just One of Those Things; That Old Feeling; Let There Be Love; Little Old Car; For Sentimental Reasons; Baby, You Can Count on Me (with Bing Crosby); Love You So; I Hear the Music Now; Last Night When We Were Young; I Don't Know Enough About You; I'm Beginning to See the Light; Of Such Is the Kingdom of God

Portrait Of Penny PYCD 148 England 18

September in the Rain; That Old Gang of Mine; Nice Work If You Can Get It; I'm Beginning to See the Light; Gone with the Wind; Don't Blame Me; Riding High; My Last Affair; I'm Confessing; The Lady Is a Tramp; Let There Be Love; You Can Depend on Me; These Foolish Things (Remind Me of You); Just One More Chance; A Guy Is a Guy; Shanghai; It Never Happened to Me; Make the Man Love Me

Some of the Best Laserlight 12641 USA 13

Why Don't You Do Right?; You Can Depend on Me; My Old Flame; River, River; It's a Good Day (with Bing Crosby); Golden Earrings; Maybe You'll Be There (with Bing Crosby); I Don't Want to Play in Your Yard; Take a Little Time to Smile; That's What a Woman Is For; Sans Souci; Crazy in the Heart; How Strange

Things Are Swingin'/Jump for Joy EMI Capitol 7243-8-54543-2-5 UK 24

(*Things Are Swingin'*): It's a Wonderful World; Things Are Swingin'; Alright, Okay, You Win; Ridin' High; It's Been a Long, Long Time; Lullaby in Rhythm; Alone Together; I'm Beginning to See the Light; It's a Good, Good Night; You're Getting to Be a Habit with Me; You're Mine, You; Life Is for Livin'. (*Jump for Joy*): Jump for Joy; Back in Your Own Backyard; When My Sugar Walks Down the Street; I Hear Music; Just in Time; Old Devil Moon; What a Little Moonlight Can Do; Four or Five Times; Music! Music! Music!; Cheek to Cheek; The Glory of Love; Ain't We Got Fun

Why Don't You Do Right? The Entertainers CD 239 UK 25

(*Remastered from the CD* Why Don't You Do Right, *The Entertainers CD 0239 from 1990*)

1997

A Touch of Class Disky TC 862652 Holland 16

Sneakin' Up on You; Come Dance with Me; Fever; Light of Love; Till There Was You; My Man; Hallelujah, I Love Him So; I'm a Woman; Pass Me By; Is That All There Is; Golden Earrings; Mañana (Is Soon Enough for Me); Alright, Okay, You Win; The Lady Is a Tramp; Mack the Knife; See See Rider

Bing Crosby with Ella Fitzgerald and Peggy Lee featuring Fred Astaire AVID 624   UK   52

Disc One: Bing Crosby and Ella Fitzgerald: Stay with the Happy People*; I Hadn't Anyone 'Till You; A Dreamer's Holiday*; My Happiness; Basin Street Blues (Red Nichols on trumpet)*; Can Anyone Explain?; Five Foot Two, Eyes of Blue; Silver Bells*; Medley performed by Bing Crosby and Ella Fitzgerald: Trying/ My Favorite Song/ Between the Devil and the Deep Blue Sea; I Can Dream, Can't I?; Rudolph the Red-Nosed Reindeer*; Someone to Watch Over Me; White Christmas*; Marshmallow World*; Moanin' Low; That's a Plenty*; Taking a Chance on Love; Way Back Home (plus the Mills Brothers)*; Medley performed by Bing Crosby and Ella Fitzgerald: I Hadn't Anyone 'Till You/ If You Ever Should Leave/ I Can't Give You Anything but Love; Istanbul (trumpet solo Ziggy Elman)*; Looking for a Boy; Chicago Style*; Everything I Have Is Yours; Undecided; Memphis Blues (with the Firehouse Five + Two) *Ella Fitzgerald & Bing Crosby Duets. All titles with John Scott Trotter's Orchestra except where indicated. Disc Two: Bing Crosby and Peggy Lee:* It's a Good Day*; He's Just My Kind; Everything's Moving Too Fast*; Linger in My Arms a Little Longer, Baby; Baby You Can Count on Me*; What More Can a Woman Do?; The Best Man*; For Sentimental Reasons; It Still Suits Me*; It's All Over Now; You Came a Long Way from St. Louis*; A Nightingale Can Sing the Blues; Exactly Like You*; I'll Close My Eyes; I Got Rhythm (G & I Gershwin)*; It Takes a Long, Long Train with a Red Caboose; A Little Bird Told Me*; Just an Old Love of Mine; On a Slow Boat to China*; Golden Earrings Cuanta La Gusta*; Love, Your Magic Spell Is Everywhere; What Is This Thing Called Love?; Medley performed by Peggy Lee, Bing Crosby and Fred Astaire: Top Hat, White Tie and Tails/ Cheek to Cheek/ Isn't This a Lovely Day/ A Fine Romance/ They Can't Take That Away from Me/ Smoke Gets in Your Eyes/ Dearly Beloved/ White Christmas/ Catalogue Day /Kamehameha Day' The I'll Be Happy; I Got Lucky in the Rain; Maybe You'll Be There.*
**Peggy Lee and Bing Crosby Duets. All titles with John Scott Trotter's Orchestra (CD 2 is exactly the same as the Avid 1-CD* Peggy Lee Sings for You, *which was released in 1992)*

At Her Best   Pulse   PDS CD 543   England   40

Disc One: Come Back to Me; Moments Like This; Here, Now; I'm Not in Love; I Go to Rio; Unforgettable; Alright, Okay, You Win; I Can't Stop Loving You; Big Bad Bill (Is Sweet William Now); Misty; The Train Blues; Fisherman's Wharf; St. Louis Blues; Kansas City; Goin' to Chicago Blues; Boston Beans; Basin Street Blues; New York City Blues; The Hungry Years; Switchin' Channels; Dreams of Summer; Big Spender; What I Did for Love. *Disc Two:* Love for Sale; Misty; Make Believe; I'm Not in Love; Have a Good Time; Mr. Wonderful; Why Don't You Do Right?; Sing a Rainbow; You Gotta Know How; Everything Must Change; Fever; I Don't Want to Play in Your Yard; Rodgers and Hart Medley: Who Are You?/ Where or When/ Glad to Be Unhappy/ It Never Entered My Mind/ Falling in Love with Love/ Bewitched; Mack the Knife; The Folks Who Live on the Hill; Lover; Here's to You

Best of Peggy Lee The Capitol Years   Capitol   7243-8-21204-2-1   USA   18

Why Don't You Do Right?; For Every Man There's a Woman; Fever; Alright, Okay, You Win; Blue Prelude; Hallelujah, I Love Him So; Just for a Thrill; Goin' to Chicago; I'm a Woman; See See Rider; You Don't Know; Call Me; Whisper Not; The Thrill Is Gone (From Yesterday's Kiss); Seventh Son; Please Send Me Someone to Love; Mama's Gone, Goodbye; I'm Gonna Go Fishin'

Best of Decca Years   MCA Decca   MCAD-11571   USA   16

Lover; This Is a Very Special Day; Just One of Those Things; Be Anything (But Be Mine); Black Coffee; He's a Tramp; It Must Be So (with the Mills Brothers); Where Can I Go Without You?; Somebody Loves Me; Sans Souci; The Possibility's There (with Bing Crosby); I Hear the Music Now; Johnny Guitar; The Siamese Cat Song; He Needs Me; Mr. Wonderful

Black Coffee/Best of Decca Years
MCA Half Moon   HMNCD 023   UK   23

Black Coffee; Lover; Mr. Wonderful; Johnny Guitar; You Go to My Head; I've Got You Under My Skin; Baubles, Bangles and Beads; Swing Low Sweet Chariot; I Don't Want to Play in Your Yard; Love Letters; Apples, Peaches and Cherries; Sisters; Bye Bye Blackbird; He Needs Me; Sing a Rainbow; How Bitter My Sweet; They Can't Take That Away from Me; My Heart Belongs to Daddy; Love You Didn't Do Right by Me; Sans Souci; I Never Knew; I've Grown Accustomed to His Face; What's New

Christmas   Disky   CH 877292   Holland   17

(Exact same tracks as 1990 Christmas Carousel CD.) I Like a Sleighride (Jingle Bells); The Christmas Song; Don't Forget to Feed the Reindeer; The Star Carol; The Christmas List; Christmas Carousel; Santa Claus Is Coming to Town; The Christmas Waltz; The Christmas Riddle; The Tree; Dock the Bells; White Christmas; Winter Wonderland; Little Drummer Boy; Happy Holiday; The Christmas Spell; Toys for Tots

Extra Special   Marginal   MAR 068   Belgium   31

Fever; Heart; Hey There; Dance Only with Me; Big Spender; Bewitched; You Always Hurt the One You Love; Sneakin' Up on You; Love; Call Me; A Lot of Livin' to Do; I'm a Woman; Why Don't You Do Right?; Hallelujah, I Love Him So; So What's New?; Alright, Okay, You Win; Is That All There Is?; My Man; Pass Me By; 'Deed I Do; Them There Eyes; Sweet Heart; Light of Love; Every Night; A Bucket of Tears; You Deserve; Mr. Wonderful; So Blue; Hey Look Me Over; Ain't That Love; The Boy from Ipanema

Fever   Disky   HR 883492   Holland   42

Disc One: Fever; Bewitched; Come Rain or Come Shine; I Left My Heart in San Francisco; Let's Fall in Love; Me and My Shadow; One Note Samba; Mañana (Is Soon Enough for Me); On the Street Where You Live; I've Got the World on a String; Raindrops Keep Fallin' on My Head; There's Always Something There to Remind Me; See See Rider; Big Spender. *Disc Two:* Alright, Okay, You Win; Cheek to Cheek; Hallelujah, I Love Him So; I Could Have Danced All Night; L-O-V-E; It's a Wonderful World; Something; Till There Was You; I'm Beginning to See the Light; That's All; What Are You Doing the Rest of Your Life?; I'll Get By; Pass Me By; Music Music Music. *Disc Three:* My Man; Days of Wine and Roses; You Always Hurt the One You Love; The Lady Is a Tramp; Mack the Knife; Taste of Honey; You're Nobody Till Somebody Loves You; Is That All There Is?; It's Been a Long, Long Time; When in Rome (I Do as the Romans Do); (There Is) No Greater Love; You Don't Know; I'm a Woman; The Party's Over

First Lady of Song   Samba   MTLCD 5052   England   10

I've Got the World on a String; You; Oh, What a Beautiful Morning; Riding High; Let There Be Love; It's a Good Day; I've Got a Right to Sing the Blues; Just One of Those Things; Love Is Just Around the Corner; What Is This Thing Called Love

For Sentimental Reasons   Prism   PLATCD 160   England   16

The Lady Is a Tramp; Just One More Chance; Shanghai; Let There Be Love; He's Just My Kind; I'm Confessin'; I've Got the Right to Sing the Blues; Oh, What a Beautiful Morning; Love Is Just Around the Corner; September in the Rain; I'm Beginning to See the Light; Nice Work If You Can Get It; These Foolish Things; That Old Gang of Mine; For Sentimental Reasons

Gold Collection   Retro   R2CD 40-34   Italy   40

Disc One: That Old Black Magic; People Will Say We're in Love; Up the Lazy River; It Ain't Necessarily So; On the Sunny Side of the Street; You Do Something to Me; Unforgettable; The Best Is Yet to Come; Bye Bye Blackbird; From This Moment On; I Don't Know Enough About You; Big Spender; Lover; Surrey with the Fringe on Top; Somebody Loves Me; Moments Like This; Big Bad Bill (Is Sweet William Now); It's a Good Day; Where Can I Go Without You?; I Can't Stop Loving You. *Disc Two:* Fever; Almost Like Being in Love; I Love Being Here with You; So What's New?; Between the Devil and the Deep Blue Sea; Speak Low; I Get a Kick Out of You; Ac-Cent-Tchu-Ate the Positive; Don't Worry 'Bout Me; Fools Rush In; Just One of Those Things; I Feel a Song Coming On;

Lonesome Road; The Train Blues; Then Was Then (And Now Is Now); Come Back to Me; Alright, Okay, You Win; Mañana (Is Soon Enough for Me); Making Whoopee; You're Mine You

Lady and the Tramp Walt Disney 60951-7 USA 22

(Peggy sings only La La Lu, He's a Tramp and The Siamese Cat Song.) Main Title (Bella Notte)/ The Wag of a Dog's Tail; Peace on Earth; It Has a Ribbon/ Lady to Bed/ A Few Mornings Later; Sunday/ The Rat/ Morning Paper; A New Collar/ Jock & Trusty/ It's Jim Dear; What a Day!/ Breakfast at Tony's; Warning/ Breakout/ Snob Hill/ A Wee Bairn; Countdown to B-Day; Baby's First Morning/ What Is a Baby/ La, La, Lu; Going Away/ Aunt Sarah; The Siamese Cat Song/ What's Going on Down There; The Muzzle/ Wrong Side of the Tracks; You Poor Kid/ He's Not My Dog; Through the Zoo/ A Log Puller; Footloose and Collar-Free/ Bella Notte; It's Morning/ Ever Chase Chickens/ Caught; Home Sweet Home; The Pound; What a Dog/ He's a Tramp; In the Doghouse/ The Rat Returns/ Falsely Accused/ We've Got to Stop That Wagon/ Trusty's Sacrifice; Watch the Birdie/ Visitors; Finale/ Peace on Earth

Latin Ala Lee/Olé Ala Lee EMI Capitol 7243-8-56056-2-8 UK 24

(Latin Ala Lee): Heart; On the Street Where You Live; I Am in Love; Hey There; I Could Have Danced All Night; The Surrey with the Fringe on Top; The Party's Over; Dance Only with Me; Wish You Were Here; C'est Magnifique; I Enjoy Being a Girl; Till There Was You. *(Olé Ala Lee):* Come Dance with Me; By Myself; You're So Right for Me; Just Squeeze Me; Fantastico; Love and Marriage; Non Dimenticar; From Now On; You Stepped Out of a Dream; Ole; I Can't Resist You; Together Wherever We Go

Let's Do It Delta CD 6102 UK 20

Elmer's Tune; My Old Flame; That's the Way It Goes; I Threw a Kiss in the Ocean; I Got It Bad (And That Ain't Good); Shady Lady Bird; Let's Do It; Somebody Else Is Taking My Place; We'll Meet Again; Full Moon (Noche de Luna); All I Need Is You; Why Don't You Do Right?; Not a Care in the World; How Long Has This Been Going On?; That Did It, Marie; Not Mine; These Foolish Things (Remind Me of You); The Lady Is a Tramp; Winter Weather

Let There Be Love Pulse PLS CD 214 England 20

I've Got the World on a String; Let There Be Love; If I Could Be with You; These Foolish Things; Shanghai; Make the Man Love Me; The Lady Is a Tramp; It's All Over Now; It Takes a Long, Long Train with a Red Caboose; Golden Earrings; I Got Lucky in the Rain; He's Just My Kind; What Is This Thing Called Love?; For Sentimental Reasons; My Last Affair; Just One More Chance; Love Is Just Around the Corner; Love, Your Magic Spell Is Everywhere; Oh, What a Beautiful Morning; Linger in My Arms a Little Longer, Baby

Magic Of EMI Capitol 7243-8-57013-2-0 Australia 20

As Time Goes By; Basin Street Blues; Stormy Weather; Cheek to Cheek; Come Dance with Me; Fever; Fly Me to the Moon (In Other Words); The Folks Who Live on the Hill; From Now On; Unforgettable; Hallelujah, I Love Him So; Happy Holiday; I Am in Love Again; I Could Have Danced All Night; I Hear Music; I'm a Woman; The Man I Love; The Lady Is a Tramp; Mack the Knife; On the Street Where You Live

Man I Love/If You Go EMI Capitol 7243-8-55389-2-6 UK 24

(The Man I Love): The Man I Love; Please Be Kind; Happiness Is Just a Thing Called Joe; Just One Way to Say I Love You; That's All; Something Wonderful; He's My Guy; Then I'll Be Tired of You; My Heart Stood Still; If I Should Lose You; There Is No Greater Love; The Folks Who Live on the Hill. *(If You Go):* As Time Goes By; If You Go; Oh Love Hast Thou Forsaken Me; Say It Isn't So; I Wish I Didn't Love You So; Maybe It's Because (I Love You So Much); I'm Gonna Laugh You Right Out of My Life; I Get Along Without You Very Well; (I Love Your) Gypsy Heart; When I Was a Child; Here's That Rainy Day; Smile

New Collection Carlton 30360-01222 England 21

I Love Being Here with You; As You Desire Me; Witchcraft; The Wind Beneath My Wings; So What's New?; But Beautiful; Lonesome Road; Is That All There Is?; As Time Goes By; Just for

Tonight; Medley: I Don't Know Enough About You/ It's a Good Day/ Then Was Then (And Now Is Now);/ Mañana (Is Soon Enough for Me)/ Things Are Swingin'; We Don't Cry Out Loud; Medley: The Best Is Yet to Come/ You Fascinate Me So; Touch Me in the Morning; Star Sounds; Lover

Peggy Lee   TKO Records Ltd. UAE 30712   Holland   24

Ridin' High; What Is This Thing Called Love; Why Don't You Do Right?; Let There Be Love; 'Deed I Do; You; Just One of Those Things; Lone Star Moon; Secretary Song; It's a Good Day; I Went Down to Virginia; All of Me; Do I Love You; I've Got the Right to Sing the Blues; How Deep Is the Ocean?; We'll Meet Again; All I Need Is You; That Did It, Marie; Not a Care in the World; Full Moon (Noche de Luna); I Threw a Kiss in the Ocean; It's the Sentimental Thing to Do; I May Be Wrong

Platinum Collection   MCPS   PC 617   England   40

Disc One: I've Got the Right to Sing the Blues; Let There Be Love; If I Could Be with You One Hour Tonight; These Foolish Things; Shanghai; Make the Man Love Me; The Lady Is a Tramp; It's All Over Now; It Takes a Long, Long Train with a Red Caboose; Golden Earrings; I Got Lucky in the Rain; He's Just My Kind; What Is This Thing Called Love?; For Sentimental Reasons; My Last Affair; Just One More Chance; Love Is Just Around the Corner; Love, Your Magic Spell Is Everywhere; Oh, What a Beautiful Morning; Linger in My Arms a Little Longer, Baby. *Disc Two:* Why Don't You Do Right?; It's the Sentimental Thing to Do; I Have Been Wrong (But I Think You're Wonderful); All of Me; I'll Dance at Your Wedding; There'll Be Some Changes Made; You Don't Have to Know the Language; The Christmas Song; I Can't Give You Anything but Love; Lone Star Moon; Mañana (Is Soon Enough for Me); But Beautiful; How Lucky You Are; The Secretary Song; Laroo, Laroo, Lilli Bolero; You Turned the Tables on Me; I Went Down to Virginia; Nature Boy; Baby, Don't Be Mad at Me; Wish You Were Here

Songbook   Venus Records TKCZ 36031   Japan   13

Circle in the Sky; I Just Want to Dance; He's a Tramp; There'll Be Another Spring; Johnny Guitar; Fever; I'll Give It All to You; Sans Souci; Where Can I Go Without You?; Boomerang (I'll Come Back to You); Things Are Swingin'; Over the Wheel; The Shining Sea

Why Don't You Do Right?   Living Era CD AJA 5237   England   25

Elmer's Tune; I See a Million People (But All I Can See Is You); I Got It Bad (And That Ain't Good); My Old Flame; How Deep Is the Ocean?; Somebody Else Is Taking My Place; How Long Has This Been Going On?; Winter Weather; Blues in the Night; On the Sunny Side of the Street; The Way You Look Tonight; We'll Meet Again; Full Moon (Noche de Luna); Why Don't You Do Right?; Ain't Goin No Place; That Old Feeling; What More Can a Woman Do?; You Was Right, Baby; Waitin' for the Train to Come In; I Don't Know Enough About You; Everything's Movin' Too Fast; Linger in My Arms a Little Longer, Baby; It's a Good Day; It's Lovin' Time; It's All Over Now

Peggy Lee: The Gold Collection Proper/Retro R2CD4034   EEC   40

Disc One: That Old Black Magic; People Will Say We're in Love; Lazy River; It Ain't Necessarily So; On the Sunny Side of the Street; You Do Something to Me; Unforgettable; Best Is Yet to Come; Bye Bye Blackbird; From This Moment On; I Don't Know Enough About You; Big Spender; Lover; Surrey with the Fringe on Top; Somebody Loves Me; Moments Like This; Big Bad Bill (Is Sweet William Now); It's a Good Day; Where Can I Go Without You?; I Can't Stop Loving You. *Disc Two:* Fever; Almost Like Being in Love; I Love Being Here with You; So What's New?; Between the Devil and the Deep Blue Sea; Speak Low; I Get a Kick Out of You; Ac-Cent-Tchu-Ate the Positive; Don't Worry 'Bout Me; Fools Rush In; Just One of Those Things; I Feel a Song Coming On; Lonesome Road; Train Blues; Then Was Then (And Now Is Now); Come Back to Me; Alright, Okay, You Win; Mañana (Is Soon Enough for Me); Makin' Whoopee; You're Mine, You. *(This 2-CD set has been released twice, the second time in 2001. That second version has a different cover, but everything else is the same, including the label number.)*

1998

Best of Miss Peggy Lee Capitol
7243-4-97308-2-3 USA 16

Waiting for the Train to Come In; I Don't Know Enough About You; It's All Over Now; It's a Good Day; Chi-Baba, Chi-Baba (My Bambino Go to Sleep); Golden Earrings; Why Don't You Do Right? (Get Me Some Money Too); Mañana (Is Soon Enough for Me); Riders in the Sky (A Cowboy Legend); Happiness Is a Thing Called Joe; Fever; Alright, Okay, You Win; I'm a Woman; Pass Me By; Big Spender; Is That All There Is?

Black Coffee/Sea Shells MCA Decca
MCLD 19363 England 28

(Black Coffee): Black Coffee; I've Got You Under My Skin; Easy Living; My Heart Belongs to Daddy; A Woman Alone with the Blues; I Didn't Know What Time It Was; When the World Was Young; Love Me or Leave Me; It Ain't Necessarily So; Gee Baby (Ain't I Good to You); You're My Thrill; There's a Small Hotel. *(Sea Shells):* Sea Fever; Nine Thorny Thickets; Little Old Car; Greensleeves; Chinese Love Poems—(a) "The Fisherman" (b) "Autumn Evening"; The Happy Monk (instrumental); The White Birch and the Sycamore; Of Such Is the Kingdom of God; A Brown Bird Singing; I Don't Want to Play in Your Yard; The Maid with the Flaxen Hair (instrumental); The Wearing of the Green; Chaconde (instrumental); Chinese Love Poems—(a) "Going Rowing" (b) "Like the Moon" (c) "The Musicians"; The Riddle Song; The Golden Wedding Ring

Cést Magnifique EMI Capitol
7243-4-97143-2-8 UK 45

Disc One: C'est Magnifique; Fly Me to the Moon; Always Something There to Remind Me; Big Spender; Cheek to Cheek; Love and Marriage; Makin' Whoopee; I'm a Woman; Cannonball Express; He's My Guy; Swing Low Sweet Chariot; Smile; I Can't Stop Loving You; The Man I Love; Nice 'n' Easy. *Disc Two:* The Folks Who Live on the Hill; Let's Fall in Love; When a Woman Loves a Man; The More I See You; After You've Gone; As Time Goes By; The Days of Wine and Roses; Have You Seen My Baby?; I Could Have Danced All Night; I Wish I Didn't Love You So; Till There Was You; You're Getting to Be a Habit with Me; It's a Wonderful World; I Left My Heart in San Francisco; You're Nobody Till Somebody Loves You. *Disc Three:* Fever; From Now On; Mañana (Is Soon Enough for Me); You Must Have Been a Beautiful Baby; I Can Hear the Music; I've Got You Under My Skin; Bewitched; Sing a Rainbow; I Remember You; Here's That Rainy Day; Come Dance with Me; I'm Gonna Go Fishin'; (I Love Your) Gypsy Heart; The Best Is Yet to Come; It Might as Well Be Spring

Complete Capitol Transcriptions
Mosaic MD5-184 USA 99

Disc One—June Christy: Make Love to Me; How High the Moon; Wrap Your Troubles in Dreams; Can't Help Loving That Man; Sweet Lorraine; Don't Worry About Me; I Can Believe That You're in Love with Me; June's Blues; Mean to Me; September in the Rain; You Took Advantage of Me; Stompin' at the Savoy; I Don't Stand a Ghost of a Chance; The One I Love Belongs to Someone Else; Moonglow; Get Happy; I Got a Guy; Lover Man. *Disc Two—June Christy (tracks 1–9) and Peggy Lee (tracks 10–18):* Lullaby in Rhythm; This Is Romance; Supper Time; I'm Thrilled; I Can't Give You Anything but Love; How Long Has This Been Going On; You're Blase; Prelude to a Kiss; What's New. *(Peggy Lee):* Wherever There's Me There's You; All the Cats Join In; A Nightingale Can Sing the Blues; Come Rain or Come Shine; The Best Man; If You Were the Only Boy; Love Doesn't Grow on Trees; I Guess I'll Get the Papers and Go Home; My Sugar Is So Refined. *Disc Three—Peggy Lee:* I Can Believe That You're in Love with Me; Lonesome Road; Them There Eyes; You Brought a New Kind of Love to Me; The Glory of Love; Melancholy Lullaby; Taking a Chance on Love; Cottage for Sale; Fools Rush In; Sometimes I'm Happy; The Way You Look Tonight; Love Is Just Around the Corner; Porgy; Blue Skies; I've Had My Moments; Blue Moon; Don't Be So Mean to Baby ('Cause Baby's So Good to You); Can't Help Lovin' That Man; Mean to Me; I'm Confessin'; Summertime. *Disc Four—Peggy Lee:* I Can't Give You Anything but Love; Georgia on My Mind; Rockin' Chair; Swing Low Sweet Chariot; Just Like a Gypsy; Somebody Loves Me; The Lullaby of Broadway; In My Solitude; I Get a Kick Out of You; Lover, Come Back to Me; I Don't Know Enough About You; Oh, Look at Me Now; I Got It Bad (And That Ain't Good); Someday, Sweetheart; If I Could Be with You One Hour Tonight; Dancing with Tears in My Eyes; Please Don't Talk About Me When I'm

Gone; Birth of the Blues; Careless; Then I'll Be Happy; I Only Have Eyes for You; Back in Your Own Back Yard; How Long Has This Been Going On? *Disc Five — Peggy Lee:* I Let a Song Go Out of My Heart; As Long as I'm Dreaming; Swingin' on a Star; Aren't You Glad You're You; Trav'lin' Light; Save Your Sorrow for Tomorrow; Oh! You Crazy Moon; 'S Wonderful; Imagination; This Can't Be Love; You're Driving Me Crazy; Goody Goody; I Ain't Got Nobody; Molly Malone; This Little Piggie; But Beautiful; Fine and Dandy; 'T Ain't So, Honey, 'T Ain't So; When a Woman Loves a Man

Extra Special/Somethin' Groovy!
EMI Capitol   7243-4-93065-2-3
UK   22

(Extra Special): Hey, Look Me Over; When He Makes Music; Walking Happy; Oh! You Crazy Moon; So What's New; Call Me Darling, Call Me Sweetheart, Call Me Dear; A Bucket of Tears; The Shining Sea; A Doodlin' Song; Amazing; I'm Gonna Go Fishin'. *(Somethin' Groovy!):* Somethin' Stupid; Makin' Whoopee!; You Must Have Been a Beautiful Baby; I Can Hear the Music; It Might as Well Be Spring; Two for the Road; Release Me; Sing a Rainbow; No Fool Like an Old Fool; Love Is Here to Stay; I'm Gonna Get It

Favorite Songs from Lady and the Tramp   Disney Enterprises
WDR 353812   USA   5

Bella Notte; He's a Tramp; What's a Baby?; Siamese Cat Song; La, La, Lu

Fever   Golden Options   GO 3812
Holland   22

Elmer's Tune; My Old Flame; How Deep Is the Ocean; That's the Way It Goes; I Threw a Kiss in the Ocean; I Got It Bad (And That Ain't Good; Shady Lady Bird; Let's Do It; Somebody Else Is Taking My Place; We'll Meet Again; Full Moon (Noche de Luna); All I Need Is You; Why Don't You Do Right?; Not a Care in the World; How Long Has This Been Going On?; That Did It, Marie; Not Mine; These Foolish Things; The Lady Is a Tramp; Winter Weather (with Art Lund); What Is This Thing Called Love; Fever

Fever   Spectrum   550 088-2   UK   14

Misty; What I Did for Love; Every Little Movement; Mr. Wonderful; Is That All There Is?; The Folks That Live on the Hill; Love for Sale; Fever; Mack the Knife; Sing a Rainbow; I'm Not in Love; Hungry Years; Lover; Star Sounds

Forever Classic (Original Hits)
Master Tune   MCPS 0395
Holland   18

September in the Rain; That Old Gang of Mine; Nice Work If You Can Get It; I'm Beginning to See the Light; Gone with the Wind; Don't Blame Me; Riding High; My Last Affair; I'm Confessin'; The Lady Is a Tramp; Let There Be Love; You Can Depend on Me; These Foolish Things; Just One More Chance; A Guy Is a Guy; Shanghai; It Never Happened to Me; Make the Man Love Me

Great Vocalists   Ronco   CDSR 9007
UK   18

September in the Rain; This Old Gang of Mine; Nice Work If You Can Get It; I'm Beginning to See the Light; Gone with the Wind; Don't Blame Me; Ridin' High; My Last Affair; I'm Confessin'; The Lady Is a Tramp; Let There Be Love; You Can Depend on Me; Just One More Chance; A Guy Is a Guy; Shanghai; It Never Happened to Me; Make the Man Love Me; These Foolish Things

I Like Men/Sugar 'n' Spice   EMI Capitol   7243-4-96729-2-5   UK   24

(I Like Men): Charley My Boy; Good for Nothin' Joe; I Love to Love; When a Woman Loves a Man; I Like Men!; I'm Just Wild About Harry; My Man; Bill; So in Love; Jim; It's So Nice to Have a Man Around the House; Oh Johnny, Oh Johnny, Oh! *(Sugar 'n' Spice):* Ain't That Love; The Best Is Yet to Come; I Believe in You; Embrasse Moi; See See Rider; Teach Me Tonight; When the Sun Comes Out; Tell All the World About You; I Don't Wanna Leave You Now; The Sweetest Sounds; I've Got the World on a String; Big Bad Bill (Is Sweet William Now)

Mink Jazz   Capitol Jazz
7243-4-95450-2-1   UK   17

It's a Big Wide Wonderful World; Whisper Not; My Silent Love; The Lady Is a Tramp; Days of Wine and Roses; As Long as I Live; I Won't Dance; Cloudy Morning; I Could Write a Book; I Never Had a Chance; Close Your Eyes; Where Can I Go Without You? *Bonus Tracks:* I'll Get

By; Please Don't Rush Me; I'm a Fool to Want You; I Didn't Find Love; Little Boat

Miss Peggy Lee   Capitol   97826   USA   113

Disc One: Waiting for the Train to Come In; I Don't Know Enough About You; It's All Over Now; It's a Good Day; Chi-Baba, Chi-Baba (My Bambino Go to Sleep); Golden Earrings; Why Don't You Do Right? (Get Me Some Money Too); Mañana (Is Soon Enough for Me); Don't Smoke in Bed; Bali Ha'i; Riders in the Sky (A Cowboy Legend); The Old Master Painter (with Mel Torme); Fever; Alright, Okay, You Win; My Man; Hallelujah, I Love Him So; Heart; I'm Gonna Go Fishin'; Hey, Look Me Over; I'm a Woman; The Alley Cat Song; Pass Me By; Come Back to Me; Big Spender; So What's New?; Walking Happy; I Feel It; Is That All There Is?; Meals for Millions. *Disc Two:* Them There Eyes; That Old Feeling; You Can Depend on Me; Stormy Weather; They Can't Take That Away from Me; Swing Low Sweet Chariot; Crazy He Calls Me; Lover Come Back to Me!; For Every Man There's a Woman; When Irish Eyes Are Smiling; A Nightingale Can Sing the Blues; Whee Baby; I'll Dance at Your Wedding; Where Are You?; There'll Be Some Changes Made; Happiness Is a Thing Called Joe; Somebody Loves Me; (When I Dance with You) I Get Ideas; 'Deed I Do; Baby (Is What He Calls Me); Bye Bye Blues; While We're Young; I Can't Give You Anything but Love; Show Me the Way to Get Out of This World ('Cause That's Where Everything Is); You Was (duet with Dean Martin); One Day; Three-Thirty Jump. *Disc Three:* It's a Wonderful World; My Heart Stood Still; Come Rain or Come Shine; I'm Walking Through Heaven with You; But Beautiful; Old Devil Moon; (I'm) In Love Again; Talk to Me Baby; Again; Do I Love You?; Bill; Just in Time; Happiness Is Just a Thing Called Joe; Close Your Eyes; You're Getting to Be a Habit with Me; I Believe in You; As Time Goes By; It Could Happen to You; Cheek to Cheek; I'm a Fool to Love You; Let's Fall in Love; Shangri-La; Basin Street Blues; You're Nobody Till Somebody Loves You; Oh! You Crazy Moon; That's All; Lullaby in Rhythm; There'll Be Another Spring. *Disc Four:* I Love Being Here with You; You Came a Long Way from St. Louis; Good for Nothin' Joe; Back in Your Own Backyard; The Second Time Around; I'll Get By (As Long as I Have You); Here's That Rainy Day; You Stepped Out of a Dream; Fly Me to the Moon; Just for a Thrill; Get Out of Town; Then I'll Be Tired of You; Ain't We Got Fun; The Right to Love (Reflections); Call Me Darling, Call Me Sweetheart, Call Me Dear; Watch What Happens; So in Love; Where Can I Go Without You?; Our Love Is Here to Stay; Moments Like This; When the Sun Comes Out; Say It Isn't So; Wish You Were Here; I'll Be Around; Don't Ever Leave Me; Them There Eyes; The Glory of Love; The Folks Who Live on the Hill; I'll Be Seeing You

Miss Wonderful/Dream Street   MCA   MCLD 19382   England   24

(Miss Wonderful): Mr. Wonderful; They Can't Take That Away from Me; Where Flamingos Fly; You've Got to See Mama Every Night; The Comeback; Take a Little Time to Smile; I Don't Know Enough About You; Joey, Joey, Joey; Crazy in the Heart; You Oughta Be Mine; We Laughed at Love; That Alright, Honey. *(Dream Street):* Street of Dreams; What's New; You're Blasé; It's Alright with Me; My Old Flame; Dancing on the Ceiling; It Never Entered My Mind; Too Late Now; I've Grown Accustomed to His Face; Something I Dreamed Last Night; Last Night When We Were Young; So Blue

Why Don't You Do Right   Carlton   309542   UK   11

Elmer's Tune; My Old Flame; How Deep Is the Ocean; I Threw a Kiss in the Ocean; We'll Meet Again; Full Moon (Noche de Luna); All I Need Is You; Why Don't You Do Right?; Not a Care in the World; How Long Has This Been Going On?; That Did It, Marie

1999

A Musical Marriage   Jasmine   JASCD 355   Czech Republic   22

I Let a Song Go Out of My Heart; Trav'lin' Light; Swinging on a Star; Imagination; Oh! You Crazy Moon; Aren't You Glad You're You; As Long as I'm Dreaming; Molly Malone; This Little Piggy Went to Market; But Beautiful; You're Driving Me Crazy; Goody, Goody; This Can't Be Love; I Ain't Got Nobody; When a Woman Loves a Man; Fine and Dandy; Lonesome Road; You Brought a New Kind of Love to Me; The Glory of Love; Melancholy Lullaby; Cottage for Sale; Taking a Chance on Love

A Portrait Of   Gallerie   GALE 442   England   47

Disc One: Elmer's Tune; That's the Way It Goes; My Old Flame; Shady Lady Bird; Somebody Else Is Taking My Place; I See a Million People (But All I Can See Is You); I Got It Bad (And That Ain't Good); How Deep Is the Ocean?; Let's Do It; Somebody Nobody Loves; How Long Has This Been Going On?; Winter Weather; Not Mine; That Did It Marie; Everything I Love; Not a Care in the World; What More Can a Woman Do?; Waiting for the Train to Come In; I Don't Know Enough About You; It's All Over Now; It's a Good Day; Swing Low Sweet Chariot; When Irish Eyes Are Smiling. *Disc Two:* Mañana (Is Soon Enough for Me); Chi-Baba Chi-Baba (My Bambino Go to Sleep); Golden Earrings; Why Don't You Do Right?; Don't Smoke in Bed; Them There Eyes; That Old Feeling; You Can Depend on Me; Stormy Weather; For Every Man There's a Woman; A Nightingale Can Sing the Blues; I'll Dance at Your Wedding; There'll Be Some Changes Made; Happiness Is a Thing Called Joe; Somebody Loves Me; 'Deed I Do; Bye Bye Blues; I Can't Give You Anything but Love; You Was (duet with Dean Martin); I'm Confessin'; Melancholy Lullaby; If I Could Be with You; Rockin' Chair; Summertime

All Time Greatest EMI Special 15453 USA 36

Disc One: Waiting for the Train to Come In; I Don't Know Enough About You; Linger in My Arms a Little Longer, Baby; It's All Over Now; It's a Good Day; Chi-Baba, Chi-Baba (My Bambino Go to Sleep); I'll Dance at Your Wedding; Sugar (That Sugar Baby o' Mine); Golden Earrings; Why Don't You Do Right? (Get Me Some Money Too); 'Deed I Do; Them There Eyes. *Disc Two:* Baby, Don't Be Mad at Me; Caramba! It's the Samba; Mañana (Is Soon Enough for Me); Don't Smoke in Bed; Similau; Bali Ha'i; I'm Gonna Wash That Man Right Out of My Hair; Riders in the Sky (A Cowboy Legend); The Old Master Painter; Lover Come Back to Me!; (When I Dance with You) I Get Ideas; Fever. *Disc Three:* Alright, Okay, You Win; I'm a Woman; Light of Love; Sweetheart; My Man; Hallelujah, I Love Him So; Come Rain or Come Shine; A Lot of Livin' to Do; Pass Me By; Big Spender; Call Me; Is That All There Is?

Black Coffee MCA Decca MVCJ-19194 Japan 12

Black Coffee; I've Got You Under My Skin; Easy Living; My Heart Belongs to Daddy; A Woman Alone with the Blues; I Didn't Know What Time It Was; When the World Was Young; Love Me or Leave Me; It Ain't Necessarily So; Gee Baby (Ain't I Good to You); You're My Thrill; There's a Small Hotel

Blues Cross Country Capitol Jazz 7243-5-20088-2-7 USA 14

Kansas City; Basin Street Blues; Los Angeles Blues; I Left My Sugar (In Salt Lake City); The Grain Belt Blues; New York City Blues; Goin' to Chicago Blues; San Francisco Blues; Fisherman's Wharf; Boston Beans; The Train Blues; St. Louis Blues; Hey! Look Me Over; The Shining Sea

Bewitching-Lee DCC DZS-179 USA 14

Why Don't You Do Right?; Don't Smoke in Bed; It's a Good Day; Alright, Okay, You Win; Golden Earrings; Hallelujah, I Love Him So; Fever; I Don't Know Enough About You; Them There Eyes; While We're You; My Man; You Don't Know; I'm Gonna Go Fishin'; Is That All There Is?

Complete Benny Goodman 1941–1947 Columbia C2K 65686 USA 38

Disc One: Elmer's Tune; I See a Million People (But All I Can See Is You); That's the Way It Goes; I Got It Bad (And That Ain't Good); My Old Flame; How Deep Is the Ocean; Shady Lady Bird; Let's Do It (Let's Fall in Love); Somebody Else Is Taking My Place; Somebody Nobody Knows; How Long Has This Been Going On?; That Did It, Marie; Winter Weather (with Art London); Ev'rything I Love; Not Mine; Not a Care in the World; My Old Flame; How Deep Is the Ocean. *Disc Two:* Blues in the Night; Where or When; On the Sunny Side of the Street; The Lamp of Memory (Incertidumbre); If You Build a Better Mousetrap (with Art London); When the Roses Bloom Again; My Little Cousin; The Way You Look Tonight; I Threw a Kiss in the Ocean; We'll Meet Again; Full Moon (Noche de Luna); There Won't Be a Shortage of Love; You're Easy to Dance With; All I Need Is You; Why Don't You Do Right?; Let's Say a Prayer; The Freedom Train (with Margaret Whiting, Johnny Mercer and the Pied Pipers); Keep Me in Mind; For Every Man There's a Woman

Cocktail Hour Allegro Music CRG 218010 USA 28

Disc One: Why Don't You Do Right?; Waiting for the Train to Come In; I See a Million People (But All I Can See Is You); My Old Flame; Somebody Else Is Taking My Place; Not Mine; Blues in the Night; We'll Meet Again; All I Need Is You; Ain't Going No Place; Two Silhouettes; I'm Glad I Waited for You; It's All Over Now; It's a Good Day. *Disc Two:* Mañana (Is Soon Enough for Me); Aren't You Kind of Glad We Did; You Was Right, Baby!; I Don't Know Enough About You; Linger in My Arms a Little Longer, Baby; Baby, You Can Count on Me; Talkin' to Myself About You; I'll Dance at Your Wedding; Stormy Weather; Them There Eyes; Bali Ha'i; Don't Smoke in Bed; Caramba! It's the Samba; Everything Movin' Too Fast

Dream Street   MCA Decca
MVCJ-19195   Japan   12

Street of Dreams; What's New; You're Blasé; It's Alright with Me; My Old Flame; Dancing on the Ceiling; It Never Entered My Mind; Too Late Now; I've Grown Accustomed to His Face; Something I Dreamed Last Night; Last Night When We Were Young; So Blue

In Love Again/In the Name of Love
EMI Capitol   7243-5-21096-2-3
UK   23

(In Love Again): A Lot of Livin' to Do; I've Got Your Number; Little by Little; Got That Magic; The Moment of Truth; That's My Style; I Can't Stop Loving You; Unforgettable; Once (Ils S'aimaient); (I'm) In Love Again; I Got Lost in His Arms; How Insensitive (Insensatez). *(In the Name of Love):* In the Name of Love; My Sin; The Boy from Ipanema; Shangri-La; Talk to Me Baby; There'll Be Some Changes Made; After You've Gone; The Right to Love (Reflections); Theme from 'Joy House' (Just Call Me Lovebird); Senza Fine; When in Rome (I Do as the Romans Do)

It's Lovin' Time   ABM
ABMMCD 1092   England   18

Shady Lady Bird; Somebody Else Is Taking My Place; Somebody Nobody Knows; Where or When; The Way You Look Tonight; Ain't Goin' No Place; Baby (Is What He Calls Me); What More Can a Woman Do?; I'm Glad I Waited for You; I Can See It Your Way; Two Silhouettes; Linger in My Arms a Little Longer, Baby; Baby You Can Count on Me; It's All Over Now; He's Just My Kind; Don't Be So Mean to Me Baby; It's Lovin' Time; Everything's Movin' Too Fast

Lady Is a Tramp   Janda Music
CDPLAT-078   New Zeeland   20

The Lady Is a Tramp; Too Young; If I Could Be with You; These Foolish Things; Just One More Chance; A Guy Is a Guy; Shanghai; It Never Happened to Me; Make the Man Love Me; It's All Over Now; It Takes a Long, Long Train with a Red Caboose; Golden Earrings; Love, Your Magic Spell Is Everywhere; What Is This Thing Called Love?; I Got Lucky in the Rain; He's Just My Kind; Linger in My Arms a Little Longer, Baby; For Sentimental Reasons; My Last Affair; I'm Confessin'

Lady Is Peggy Lee   Newsound
NST 026   EU   18

The Lady Is a Tramp; Let There Be Love; I'm Confessin'; September in the Rain; Nice Work If You Can Get It; Don't Blame Me; Make the Man Love Me; These Foolish Things; I'm Beginning to See the Light; My Last Affair; Just One More Chance; It Never Happened to Me; A Guy Is a Guy; That Old Gang of Mine; Gone with the Wind; You Can Depend on Me; Shanghai; Riding High

Legendary Peggy Lee   Readers Digest
7-2434-99216-2-7   USA   55

Disc One: It's a Good Day; Golden Earrings; Lover; Laroo, Laroo Lili Bolero; Linger in My Arms a Little Longer, Baby; Fever; Mr. Wonderful; Chi-Baba, Chi-Baba (My Bambino Go to Sleep); It's All Over Now; Mañana (Is Soon Enough for Me); Waiting for the Train to Come In; I'll Dance at Your Wedding; I Get Ideas; Bali Ha'i; Riders in the Sky (A Cowboy Legend); Is That All There Is? *Disc Two:* Big Spender; Sing a Rainbow; Joey, Joey, Joey; This Is a Very Special Day; My Heart Stood Still; Somebody Loves Me; Baubles, Bangles and Beads; Why Don't You Do Right; Johnny Guitar; Sugar; The Folks Who Live on the Hill; Watermelon Weather (with Bing Crosby); Do I Love You?; The Old Master Painter (with Mel Torme); For Every Man There's a Woman; You Was (duet with Dean Martin); I Love Being Here with You; But Beautiful; Fever; The Second Time Around; Yes, Indeed! *Disc Three:* Oh, What a Beautiful Morning; You Came a Long Way from St. Louis; Caramba! It's the Samba; Similau (See-Me-Lo); Heart; I Feel It; Alright, Okay, You

Win; Bubble-Loo, Bubble-Loo; Light of Love; My Man; You; I Don't Know Enough About You; Just One of Those Things; I'm a Woman; Show Me the Way to Get Out of This World; Baby, Don't Be Mad at Me; Hallelujah, I Love Him So; I'll Be Seeing You

Let's Do It   Warner Music 3984275272   Australia   20

Let's Do It; I Got It Bad (And That Ain't Good); Somebody Else Is Taking My Place; Why Don't You Do Right?; How Deep Is the Ocean?; Waiting for the Train to Come In; I'm Glad I Waited for You; I Don't Know Enough About You; Linger in My Arms a Little Longer, Baby; It's All Over Now; It's a Good Day; Chi-Baba, Chi-Baba (My Bambino Go to Sleep); Golden Earrings; I Can't Give You Anything but Love; I'll Dance at Your Wedding; Mañana (Is Soon Enough for Me); Stormy Weather; Don't Smoke in Bed; 'Deed I Do; Them There Eyes

Mañana   Castle Pie   PIESD 045   England   20

Mañana (Is Soon Enough for Me); Golden Earrings; I'll Close My Eyes; I Don't Know Enough About You; It's a Good Day; As Long as I'm Dreaming; Waitin' for the Train to Come In; What More Can a Woman Do; He's Just My Kind; That Old Feeling; Let There Be Love; Somebody Else Is Taking My Place; Caramba! It's the Samba; A Nightingale Can Sing the Blues; Them There Eyes; The Way You Look Tonight; Everything's Movin' Too Fast; Ain't Goin' No Place; You Was Right, Baby; Why Don't You Do Right?

Oh La La Lee   GVC   GVC 2006   UK   47

Disc One: Elmer's Tune; I See a Million People (But All I See Is You); How Deep Is the Ocean; That's the Way It Goes; Let's Do It (Let's Fall in Love); I Got It Bad (And That Ain't Good); My Old Flame; How Long Has This Been Going On?; That Did It, Marie; Everything I Love; Not Mine; Blues in the Night; Where or When; The Way You Look Tonight; I Threw a Kiss in the Ocean; Full Moon (Noche de Luna); All I Need Is You; Why Don't You Do Right?; I Don't Know Enough About You; It's a Good Day; Sugar; 'Deed I Do. *Disc Two:* Golden Earrings; I Should Care; I've Had My Moments; Mañana (Is Soon Enough for Me); Don't Smoke in Bed; That Old Feeling; Someday Sweetheart; September in the Rain; That Old Gang of Mine;

I'm Beginning to See the Light; Nice Work If You Can Get It; Gone with the Wind; Don't Blame Me; I'm Confessin'; My Last Affair; Baby, Won't You Please Come Home?; Let There Be Love; I've Got a Right to Sing the Blues; What Is This Thing Called Love?; Oh, What a Beautiful Morning; Just One of Those Things; I've Got the World on a String; You; Love Is Just Around the Corner; Do I Love You?

Peggy Lee Collection   EMI 7243 5 22253 2 3   UK   22

As Time Goes By; Basin Street Blues; Stormy Weather; Makin' Whoopee; Fever; Fly Me to the Moon; The Folks Who Live on the Hill; Always Something There to Remind Me; I Am in Love; The Man I Love; Mack the Knife; I Could Have Danced All Night; On the Street Where You Live; I'm a Woman; Come Dance with Me; I Hear Music; Love and Marriage; The More I See You; Let's Fall in Love; From Now On; Cheek to Cheek; Smile

Pete Kelly's Blues   MCA Decca MVCJ-19197   Japan   12

Oh Didn't He Ramble; Sugar (That Sugar Baby of Mine); Somebody Loves Me; I'm Gonna Meet My Sweety; I Never Knew/ Bye Bye Blackbird; What Can I Say After I Say I'm Sorry. *(Ella Fitzgerald):* Hard Hearted Hanna (The Vamp of Savannah); Ella Hums the Blues. *(Peggy Lee):* He Needs Me; Sing a Rainbow. *(Ella Fitzgerald):* Pete Kelly's Blues

Pretty Eyes/Guitars Ala Lee   EMI Capitol   7243-4-98883-2-6   UK   24

(Pretty Eyes): As You Desire Me; It Could Happen to You; Pretty Eyes; Moments Like This; Remind Me; You Fascinate Me So; I Wanna Be Loved; I'm Walking Through Heaven with You; I Remember You; Too Close for Comfort; In Other Words; Because I Love Him So. *(Guitars Ala Lee):* Nice 'n' Easy; Strangers in the Night; Mohair Sam; Goodbye, My Love; Think Beautiful; An Empty Glass; Good Times; Sweet Happy Life; Touch The Earth; Beautiful, Beautiful World; My Guitar; Call Me

Sea Shells   MCA Decca MVCJ-19196   Japan   16

Sea Fever; Nine Thorny Thickets; Little Old Car; Greensleeves; Chinese Love Poems—(a) "The Fisherman" (b) "Autumn Evening"; The

Happy Monk (instrumental); The White Birch and the Sycamore; Of Such Is the Kingdom of God; A Brown Bird Singing; I Don't Want to Play in Your Yard; The Maid with the Flaxen Hair (instrumental); The Wearing of the Green; Chaconde (instrumental); Chinese Love Poems—(a) "Going Rowing" (b) "Like the Moon" (c) "The Musicians"; The Riddle Song; The Golden Wedding Ring

The Wonderful   ABM   ABMMCD 1024   England   17

Why Don't You Do Right?; Elmer's Tune; On the Sunny Side of the Street; How Long Has This Been Going On?; Let's Do It (Let's Fall in Love); That Old Feeling; Full Moon (Noche de Luna); How Deep Is the Ocean?; I Don't Know Enough About You; I Got It Bad (And That Ain't Good); Blues in the Night; It's a Good Day; All I Need Is You; You Was Right, Baby; I Threw a Kiss in the Ocean; Waitin' for the Train to Come In; We'll Meet Again

There'll Be Another Spring   Jazz Heritage   515674H   USA   13

Circle in the Sky; I Just Want to Dance; He's a Tramp; There'll Be Another Spring; Johnny Guitar; Fever; I'll Give It All to You; Sans Souci; Where Can I Go Without You?; Boomerang (I'll Come Back to You); Things Are Swingin'; Over the Wheel; The Shining Sea

Peggy Lee   Magnum   UAE30712   16

I Can't Give You Anything but Love; Back Home in Indiana (instrumental by Andre Previn); Ask Anyone Who Knows; It Never Happened to Me; We're One; Slumming on Park Avenue (duet with Jeff Chandler); As Long as I'm Dreaming; Ain't Cha Ever Comin' Back; Pancho Maximillian Hernandez (Woody Herman solo); The Lady from 29 Palms (with Woody Herman); You and I Passing By; On the Sunny Side of the Street (with Woody Herman); It's a Good Day; Up a Lazy River (with Woody Herman); I Don't Know Enough About You; Cecilia (with Woody Herman)

2000

Best of Peggy Lee 1952–1956   Music Club   MCCD 426   England   18

(It appears that this CD was also released in 1994 on the Music Club label, with a catalog number *of MCCDSE 157.*) Lover; Black Coffee; My Heart Belongs to Daddy; It Ain't Necessarily So; A Brown Bird Singing; He's a Tramp; Mr. Wonderful; The Siamese Cat Song; Sing a Rainbow; Somebody Loves Me; I Don't Want to Play in Your Yard; Street of Dreams; It's All Right with Me; It Never Entered My Mind; Too Late Now; I've Grown Accustomed to His Face; Something I Dreamed Last Night

Elegant Miss Peggy Lee   Master Song   502022   Australia   17

Why Don't You Do Right?; Elmer's Tune; On the Sunny Side of the Street; How Long Has This Been Going On?; Let's Do It (Let's Fall in Love); That Old Feeling; Full Moon (Noche de Luna); How Deep Is the Ocean; I Don't Know Enough About You; I Got It Bad (And That Ain't Good); Blues in the Night; It's a Good Day; All I Need Is You; You Was Right, Baby; I Threw a Kiss in the Ocean; Waitin' for the Train to Come In; We'll Meet Again

Great Female Vocalists   Going for a Song   GFS041804   UK   24

Shady Lady Bird; My Old Flame; How Long Has This Been Going On?; I See a Million People (But All I Can See Is You); It's a Good Day; Linger in My Arms a Little Longer, Baby; It's All Over Now; Waiting for the Train to Come In; I Don't Know Enough About You; Everything's Moving Too Fast; I'm Glad I Waited for You; Chi-Baba, Chi-Baba (My Bambino Go to Sleep); Sugar; I'll Dance at Your Wedding; Golden Earrings; Mañana (Is Soon Enough for Me); Talking to Myself About You; Caramba! It's the Samba; All Dressed Up with a Broken Heart; Don't Smoke in Bed; 'Deed I Do; Them There Eyes; Why Don't You Do Right?

Great Peggy Lee   Rajon Music   RED021   Australia   48

Disc One: Elmer's Tune; I See a Million People (But All I See Is You); That's the Way It Goes; I Got It Bad (And That Ain't Good); My Old Flame; How Deep Is the Ocean?; Let's Do It; Shady Lady Bird; How Long Has This Been Going On?; Somebody Else Is Taking My Place; Somebody Nobody Loves; That Did It, Marie; Everything I Love; Winter Weather; Not a Care in the World; Not Mine. *Disc Two:* I'm Glad I Waited for You; Waiting for the Train to Come In; I Don't Know Enough About You; Linger in My Arms a Little Longer, Baby; It's a Good Day;

It's All Over Now; Everything's Movin' Too Fast; I'm Confessin'; Rocking Chair; Summertime; You Can Depend on Me; Chi-Baba, Chi-Baba (My Bambino Go to Sleep); I'll Dance at Your Wedding; Golden Earrings; 'Deed I Do; Somebody Loves Me. *Disc Three:* That Old Feeling; Why Don't You Do Right? (Get Me Some Money Too); Sugar (That Sugar Baby o' Mine); Mañana (Is Soon Enough for Me); Talking To Myself About You; All Dressed Up with a Broken Heart; Baby, Don't Be Mad at Me; Caramba! It's the Samba; Bye Bye Blues; Don't Smoke in Bed; For Every Man There's a Woman; I Can't Give You Anything but Love; If I Could Be with You One Hour Tonight; Stormy Weather; Them There Eyes; There'll Be Some Changes Made

In Love with Peggy Lee Metrodome Metro 331 England 22

Baby Don't Be Mad at Me; Winter Weather; Caramba! It's the Samba; Chi-Baba, Chi-Baba (My Bambino Go to Sleep); Don't Smoke in Bed; For Every Man There Is a Woman; Golden Earrings; Gone with the Wind; I Don't Know Enough About You; I'll Dance at Your Wedding; Full Moon (Noche de Luna); I'm Glad I Waited for You; I've Got the World on a String; It's a Good Day; It's All Over Now; Just One of Those Things; Linger in My Arms a Little Longer, Baby; September in the Rain; Waitin' for the Train to Come In; Everything Moving Too Fast; Mañana (Is Soon Enough for Me); My Old Flame

Lady Is a Tramp Bianco Music BIR4014 England 24

Let There Be Love; He's Just My Kind; What Is This Thing Called Love?; The Lady Is a Tramp; These Foolish Things; I've Got the Right to Sing the Blues; Oh, What a Beautiful Morning; Just One More Change; I'll Dance at Your Wedding; Love, Your Magic Spell Is Everywhere; Linger in My Arms a Little Longer, Baby; Love Is Just Around the Corner; September in the Rain; Nice Work If You Can Get It; If I Could Be with You One Hour Tonight; That Old Gang of Mine; All of Me; A Guy Is a Guy; The Secretary Song; Wish You Were There; Let's Do It (Let's Fall in Love); How Long Has This Been Going On?; Mañana (Is Soon Enough for Me); We'll Meet Again

Latin Ala Lee DCC DZS-181 USA 15

Heart; On the Street Where You Live; Till There Was You; I Am in Love; Hey There; I Could Have Danced All Night; The Surrey with the Fringe on Top; The Party's Over; Dance Only with Me; Wish You Were Here; C'est Magnifique; I Enjoy Being a Girl; Senza Fine; Ole; Mañana (Is Soon Enough for Me)

Let's Do It Golden Options GO 3812 Germany 20

Elmer's Tune; My Old Flame; How Deep Is the Ocean?; That's the Way It Goes; I Threw a Kiss in the Ocean; I Got It Bad (And That Ain't Good); Shady Lady Bird; Let's Do It; Somebody Else Is Taking My Place; We'll Meet Again; Full Moon (Noche de Luna); All I Need Is You; Why Don't You Do Right?; Not a Care in the World; How Long Has This Been Going On?; That Did It, Marie; Not Mine; These Foolish Things; The Lady Is a Tramp; Winter Weather (with Art Lund)

Let There Be Love MCPS PLM 1027 Germany 20

Let There Be Love; I Don't Know Enough About You; Mañana (Is Soon Enough for Me); That Old Feeling; What More Can a Woman Do?; Elmer's Tune; How Deep Is the Ocean?; You Brought a New Kind of Love to Me; All I Need Is You; Not a Care in the World; Them There Eyes; How Long Has This Been Going On?; My Old Flame; It's a Good Day; Golden Earrings; Full Moon (Noche de Luna); Why Don't You Do Right?; The Way You Look Tonight; Caramba! It's the Samba; We'll Meet Again

Linger Snapper Music SMDCD 304 UK 48

Disc One: Let There Be Love; He's Just My Kind (live); What Is This Thing Called Love? (live); I've Got the Right to Sing the Blues (live); Just One More Change; Shanghai (live); Linger in My Arms a Little Longer, Baby (live); If I Could Be with You One Hour Tonight (live); That Old Gang of Mine; It Never Happened to Me (live); A Guy Is a Guy; The Man I Love (live); My Last Affair; Golden Earrings (live); I Got Lucky in the Rain (live); It's All Over Now (live); I Can't Give You Anything but Love, Baby (live); The Secretary Song (live); Baby, Don't Be Mad at Me (live); Wish You Were Here (live); Let's Do It (Let's Fall in Love); How Deep Is the Ocean?; How Long Has This Been Going On?; Where or When. *Disc Two:* The Lady Is a Tramp; These

Foolish Things; I'll Dance at Your Wedding (live); Oh, What a Beautiful Morning; Love, Your Magic Spell Is Everywhere (live); It Takes a Long, Long Train with a Red Caboose (live); Why Don't You Do Right? (live); It's the Sentimental Thing to Do (live); Love Is Just Around the Corner; For Sentimental Reasons; September in the Rain; Baby Please Come Home; Don't Blame Me; Nice Work If You Can Get It; I'm Beginning to See the Light; Gone with the Wind; There'll Be Some Changes Made (live); You Don't Have to Know the Language (live); All of Me (live); Mañana (Is Soon Enough for Me) (live); Blues in the Night; On the Sunny Side of the Street; Full Moon (Noche De Luna); We'll Meet Again

Peggy Lee Christmas EMI Capitol 7243-5-26239-2-1 USA 11

Winter Wonderland; I Like a Sleighride (Jingle Bells); Christmas Carousel; Santa Claus Is Coming to Town; Don't Forget to Feed the Reindeer; The Star Carol; The Little Drummer Boy; White Christmas; The Christmas Waltz; The Christmas Song (Merry Christmas to You); Happy Holiday

Rare Gems and Hidden Treasures Capitol 7243-5-27564-2-1 USA 19

Every Night; Please Don't Rush Me; Light of Love; Ain't Doin' Bad Doin' Nothin'; Eight, Nine and Ten; Baby, Come Home; The Way You're Breaking My Heart; Why Shouldn't I Cry Over You?; Bubble-Loo Bubble-Loo; Blum Blum, I Wonder Who I Am; Similau (See-Me-Lo); Laroo, Laroo, Lili Bolero; Hold Me; (I'm Not Gonna) Let It Bother Me; It's the Bluest Kind of Blue; While We're Young; Foolin' Nobody but Me; All Cats Join In; Farewell to Arms

Rendezvous with Peggy Lee Vocalion CDUS 3008 England 26

I Can't Give You Anything but Love; Why Don't You Do Right?; Stormy Weather; Them There Eyes; 'Deed I Do; Don't Smoke in Bed; There'll Be Some Changes Made; A Nightingale Can Sing the Blues; Everything's Moving Too Fast; It's Lovin' Time; Swing Low Sweet Chariot; Linger in My Arms a Little Longer, Baby; Laroo, Laroo Lili Bolero; Aren't You Kind of Glad We Did?; Caramba! It's the Samba; Bubble-Loo, Bubble-Loo; It's All Over Now; Please Love Me Tonight; Riders in the Sky (A Cowboy Legend); Love, Your Spell Is Everywhere; She Didn't Say Yes; I'll Dance at Your Wedding; Golden Earrings; Everybody Loves Somebody; It Takes a Long, Long Train with a Red Caboose; Just An Old Love of Mine

Very Best Of EMI Capitol 7243-5-27818-2-9 England 24

Fever; He's a Tramp; Things Are Swingin'; Alright, Okay, You Win; Caramba! It's the Samba; I Enjoy Being a Girl; Mañana (Is Soon Enough for Me); Siamese Cat Song; Big Spender; I'm a Woman; Black Coffee; Don't Smoke in Bed; The Folks Who Live on the Hill; Till There Was You; Why Don't You Do Right? (Get Me Some Money Too); Golden Earrings; I Go to Sleep; I Feel It; I Get Ideas; Bali Ha'i; So What's New?; You'll Remember Me; Walking Happy; Pass Me By

Very Best Of First Budget FBS070 EU 21

Elmer's Tune; My Old Flame; How Deep Is the Ocean?; That's the Way It Goes; I Threw a Kiss in the Ocean; I Got It Bad (And That Ain't Good); Shady Lady Bird; Let's Do It; Somebody Else Is Taking My Place; We'll Meet Again; Full Moon (Noche de Luna); All I Need Is You; Why Don't You Do Right?; Not a Care in the World; How Long Has This Been Going On?; That Did It, Marie; Not Mine; These Foolish Things; The Lady Is a Tramp; Winter Weather; What Is This Thing Called Love?

Trav'lin' Light Capitol Jazz 7243-5-23567-2-0 USA 15

I Let a Song Go Out of My Heart; Aren't You Glad You're You; As Long as I'm Dreaming; Somebody Loves Me; Trav'lin' Light; I Ain't Got Nobody; Oh! You Crazy Moon; Goody Goody; Imagination; You're Driving Me Crazy; Save Your Sorrow for Tomorrow; But Beautiful; Fine and Dandy; When a Woman Loves a Man; 'T'ain't So, Honey, 'T'ain't So

Why Don't You Do Right? Hallmark 309542 Germany 11

Elmer's Tune; My Old Flame; How Deep Is the Ocean?; I Threw a Kiss in the Ocean; We'll Meet Again; Full Moon (Noche de Luna); All I Need Is You; Why Don't You Do Right?; Not a Care in the World; How Long Has This Been Going On?; That Did It, Marie

In Love with Peggy Lee Metrodome
METRO331   22

Baby Don't Be Mad at Me; Winter Weather; Caramba! It's the Samba; Chi-Baba, Chi-Baba (My Bambino Go to Sleep); Don't Smoke in Bed; For Every Man There's a Woman; Golden Earrings; Gone with the Wind; I Don't Know Enough About You; I'll Dance at Your Wedding; Full Moon (Noche de Luna); I'm Glad I Waited for You; I've Got the World on a String; It's a Good Day; It's All Over Now; Just One of Those Things; Linger in My Arms a Little Longer, Baby; September in the Rain; Waitin' for the Train to Come In; Everything's Moving Too Fast; Mañana (Is Soon Enough for Me); My Old Flame

2001

Best Of Pegasus   PEG CD 346
    Germany   20

All I Need Is You; Let's Do It; Not a Care in the World; These Foolish Things; Full Moon (Noche de Luna); Why Don't You Do Right?; That's the Way It Goes; The Lady Is a Tramp; My Old Flame; Not Mine; Somebody Else Is Taking My Place; How Long Has This Been Going On?; Winter Weather; How Deep Is the Ocean?; I Threw a Kiss in the Ocean; I Got It Bad (And That Ain't Good); Shady Lady Bird; Elmer's Tune; Up a Lazy River; That Did It, Marie

The Fever of Peggy Lee Going for a Song
    GFS241   UK   24

Shady Lady Bird; My Old Flame; How Long Has This Been Going On?; I See a Million People (But All I Can See Is You); It's a Good Day; Linger in My Arms a Little Longer, Baby; It's All Over Now; Waiting for the Train to Come In; I Don't Know Enough About You; Everything's Movin' Too Fast; I'm Glad I Waited for You; Chi-Baba, Chi-Baba (My Bambino Go to Sleep); Sugar; I'll Dance at Your Wedding; Golden Earrings; Mañana (Is Soon Enough for Me); Talking to Myself About You; Caramba! It's the Samba; All Dressed Up with a Broken Heart; Don't Smoke in Bed; Baby, Don't Be Mad at Me; 'Deed I Do; Them There Eyes; Why Don't You Do Right

Best of Mañana   Rajon Music
    RMGR 0423   Australia   25

Riders in the Sky (A Cowboy Legend); The Old Master Painter (with Mel Torme); Show Me the Way to Get Out of This World; Bali Ha'i; Baby, Don't Be Mad at Me; Caramba! It's the Samba; Don't Smoke in Bed; Talking to Myself About You; For Every Man There's a Woman; All Dressed Up with a Broken Heart; Mañana (Is Soon Enough for Me); I'll Dance at Your Wedding; Golden Earrings; Chi-Baba, Chi-Baba (My Bambino Go to Sleep); I Can't Give You Anything but Love; Everything's Movin' Too Fast; It's a Good Day; Stormy Weather; There'll Be Some Changes Made; It's All Over Now; Linger in My Arms a Little Longer, Baby; I Don't Know Enough About You; I'm Glad I Waited for You; Waitin' for the Train to Come In; Why Don't You Do Right?

Black Coffee   Tim International
    205797-203   Germany   21

Aren't You Glad You're You; Somebody Loves Me; I Let a Song Go Out of My Heart; Goody Goody; Save Your Sorrow for Tomorrow; Trav'lin' Light; I Ain't Got Nobody; You're Driving Me Crazy; Be Anything (But Be Mine); Black Coffee; I've Got You Under My Skin; You Go to My Head; I'm Glad There Is You; River River; Forgive Me; I Didn't Know What Time It Was; Easy Living; When the World Was Young; My Heart Belongs to Daddy; Lover; A Woman Alone with the Blues

Complete Capitol Small Groups
    Transcription   Jazz Factory
    JFCD 22822   Spain   61

Disc One: I Can't Believe That You're in Love with Me; Lonesome Road; Them There Eyes; You Brought a New Kind of Love to Me; The Glory of Love; Melancholy Lullaby; Taking a Chance on Love; Cottage for Sale; Fools Rush In; Sometimes I'm Happy; The Way You Look Tonight; Love Is Just Around the Corner; Porgy; Blue Skies; I've Had My Moments; Blue Moon; Can't Help Lovin' That Man; Mean to Me; I'm Confessin'; Summertime. *Disc Two:* I Can't Give You Anything but Love; Georgia on My Mind; Rockin' Chair; Swing Low Sweet Chariot; Just Like a Gypsy; Somebody Loves Me; The Lullaby of Broadway; Solitude; I Get a Kick Out of You; Lover, Come Back to Me; I Don't Know Enough About You; Oh, Look at Me Now; It Got It Bad (And That Ain't Good); Someday, Sweetheart; If I Could Be with You One Hour Tonight; Dancing with Tears in My Eyes; Please Don't Talk About Me When I'm

Gone; Birth of the Blues; Careless; Then I'll Be Happy; I Only Have Eyes for You. *Disc Three:* Back In Your Own Backyard; How Long Has This Been Going On?; I Let a Song Go Out of My Heart; As Long as I'm Dreaming; Swingin' on a Star; Aren't You Glad You're You; Trav'lin' Light; Save Your Sorrow for Tomorrow; Oh! You Crazy Moon; 'S Wonderful; Imagination; This Can't Be Love; You're Driving Me Crazy; Goody Goody; I Ain't Got Nobody; Molly Malone; This Little Piggie; But Beautiful; Fine and Dandy; When a Woman Loves a Man

Forever Gold Solo Music FG080 UK 15

Mañana (Is Soon Enough for Me); Let There Be Love; 'Deed I Do; Gone with the Wind; Oh, What a Beautiful Morning; Baby Won't You Please Come Home; Just One of Those Things; Ridin' High; September in the Rain; What Is This Thing Called Love?; You; I've Got the World on a String; Do I Love You?; It's a Good Day; I've Got a Right to Sing the Blues

Golden Earrings Warner Music 857387082 Australia 20

Riders in the Sky (A Cowboy Legend); The Old Master Painter (with Mel Torme); Bali Ha'i; Baby, Don't Be Mad at Me; Caramba! It's the Samba; Don't Smoke in Bed; Talkin' to Myself About You; For Every Man There Is a Woman; All Dressed Up with a Broken Heart; Mañana (Is Soon Enough for Me); Golden Earrings; There'll Be Some Changes Made; Everything's Movin' Too Fast; Just an Old Love of Mine; Sugar (That Sugar Baby o' Mine); I Don't Know Enough About You; I'm Confessin'; Waiting for the Train to Come In; Why Don't You Do Right?; Somebody Else Is Taking My Place

Golden Earrings Godly GLD 25438 Portugal 42

Disc One: I Got It Bad (And That Ain't Good); Winter Weather (with Art Lund); Blues in the Night; Somebody Else Is Taking My Place; My Little Cousin; We'll Meet Again; Full Moon (Noche de Luna); The Way You Look Tonight; Why Don't You Do Right?; My Old Flame; How Deep Is the Ocean?; Let's Do It (Let's Fall in Love); Where or When; On the Sunny Side of the Street. *Disc Two:* Waiting for the Train to Come In; I Don't Know Enough About You; It's All Over Now; It's a Good Day; Chi-Baba, Chi-Baba (My Bambino Go to Sleep); Golden Earrings; I'll Dance at Your Wedding; Mañana (Is Soon Enough for Me); For Every Man There Is a Woman; Don't Smoke in Bed; Bali Ha'i; Riders in the Sky (A Cowboy Legend); The Old Master Painter (with Mel Torme); Them There Eyes. *Disc Three:* Swing Low Sweet Chariot; Crazy He Calls Me; Lover Come Back to Me; Stormy Weather; A Nightingale Can Sing the Blues; Where Are You?; There'll Be Some Changes Made; Somebody Loves Me; 'Deed I Do; Baby (Is What He Calls Me); While We're Young; I Can't Give You Anything but Love; You Was (duet with Dean Martin); Why Don't You Do Right? (alternate version)

Greatest Hits Musicbank APWCD 1183 Czechoslov 20

Big Spender; On the Sunny Side of the Street; Somebody Loves Me; That Old Magic; So What's New?; Fools Rush In; It's a Good Day; You Do Something to Me; The Best Is Yet to Come; Then Was Then (And Now Is Now); Lover; Fever; Big Bad Bill (Is Sweet William Now); Come Back to Me; From This Moment On; Speak Low; The Train Blues; Moments Like This; Lonesome Road; Up the Lazy River

It's Lovin' Time Hallmark HALMCD 1320 England 18

Shady Lady Bird; Somebody Else Is Taking My Place; Somebody Nobody Loves; Where or When; The Way You Look Tonight; Ain't Going No Place; Baby (Is What He Calls Me); What More Can a Woman Do?; I'm Glad I Waited for You; I Can See It Your Way; Two Silhouettes; Linger in My Arms a Little Longer, Baby; Baby You Can Count on Me; It's All Over Now; He's Just My Kind; Don't Be So Mean to Me, Baby; It's Lovin' Time; Everything's Movin' Too Fast

Mirrors Universal UICY-3333 Japan 11

Is That All There Is?; Ready to Begin Again (Manya's Song); Some Cats Know; I've Got Them Feelin' Too Good Today Blues; A Little White Ship; Tango; Professor Hauptmann's Performing Dogs; The Case of M.J.; I Remember; Say It; Longings for a Simpler Time

Pass Me By/Big Spender EMI Capitol 7243-5-35210-2-8 UK 22

(Pass Me By): Sneakin' Up on You; Pass Me By; I Wanna Be Around; Bewitched; My Love,

Forgive Me; You Always Hurt the One You Love; A Hard Days Night; Love; Dear Heart; Quiet Nights; That's What It Takes. *(Big Spender):* Come Back to Me; You've Got Possibilities; It's a Wonderful World; I'll Only Miss Him When I Think of Him; Big Spender; I Must Know; Alright, Okay, You Win; Watch What Happens; You Don't Know; Let's Fall in Love; Gotta Travel On

Star Power   Direct Source
PST 14652   Canada   12

I Can't Give You Anything but Love, Baby; Just One of Those Things; Ask Anyone Who Knows; It Never Happened to Me; We're One; Slumming on Park Avenue; As Long as I'm Dreaming; Ain't Cha Ever Coming Back; On the Sunny Side of the Street; Up a Lazy River; Somebody Loves Me; Ac-Cent-Tchu-Ate the Positive

Sugar 'n' Spice   Capitol Jazz
7243-5-25249-2-1   UK   15

Ain't That Love; The Best Is Yet to Come; I Believe in You; Embrasse Moi; See See Rider; Teach Me Tonight; When the Sun Comes Out; Tell All the World About You; I Don't Wanna Leave You Now; The Sweetest Sound; I've Got the World on a String; Big Bad Bill (Is Sweet William Now); I'll Be Around; Loads of Love; Amazing

Sings the Standards   EMI Capitol
7243-5-32580-2-3   UK   22

Cheek to Cheek; Fly Me to the Moon; You're Getting to Be a Habit with Me; I Could Have Danced All Night; I'll Be Around; Oh! You Crazy Moon; The Old Devil Moon; The Folks Who Live on the Hill; Basin St. Blues; When a Woman Loves a Man; Then Was Then (And Now Is Now); I've Got Your Number; Just for a Thrill; L-O-V-E; Release Me; Smile; As Time Goes By; Unforgettable; I Left My Heart in San Francisco; Strangers in the Night; Something; Bridge Over Troubled Water

That Old Feeling/You Go to My Head
Tim International   205422-304
Germany   40

Disc One—That Old Feeling: Ain't Go No Place; That Old Feeling; Waiting for the Train to Come In; I'm Glad I Waited for You; I Don't Know Enough About You; Somebody Loves Me; It's All Over Now; Linger in My Arms a Little Longer, Baby; Everything's Movin' Too Fast; It's a Good Day; Chi-Baba, Chi-Baba (My Bambino Go to Sleep); Sugar; I'll Dance at Your Wedding; Golden Earrings; Talkin' to Myself About You; 'Deed I Do; Why Don't You Do Right?; Baby, Don't Be Mad at Me; Them There Eyes; Mañana (Is Soon Enough for Me). *Disc Two — You Go to My Head:* Caramba! It's the Samba; All Dressed Up with a Broken Heart; Don't Smoke in Bed; Fine and Dandy; As Long as I'm Dreaming; I Let a Song Go Out of My Heart; Imagination; You're Driving Me Crazy; Aren't You Glad You Are You?; But Beautiful; When a Woman Loves a Man; Save Your Sorrow for Tomorrow; T'ain't So, Honey; I'm Glad There Is You; Be Anything (But Be Mine); River River; Easy Living; I've Got You Under My Skin; Black Coffee; You Go to My Head

The Way You Look Tonight
Brisa Ent.   48036-2BD   UK   14

On the Sunny Side of the Street; Elmer's Tune; Full Moon (Noche de Luna); Why Don't You Do Right?; Linger in My Arms a Little Longer, Baby; I See a Million People (But All I Can See Is You); I Got It Bad (And That Ain't Good); How Deep Is the Ocean?; How Long Has This Been Going On?; Winter Weather; Blues in the Night; The Way You Look Tonight; We'll Meet Again; That Old Feeling

Why Don't You Do Right?   Magic
DAWE102   England   15

Somebody Loves Me; As Long as I'm Dreaming; When the Red Red Robin Comes Bob-Bob-Bobbin' Along (with Woody Herman); Go Away (with Woody Herman and Eddie Bracken); Ain'tcha Ever Coming Back; Pancho Maximillian Hernandez (with Woody Herman); It Takes a Long, Long Train with a Red Caboose; I Don't Know Enough About You; The Lady from 29 Palms (with Woody Herman); You and I Passing By; On the Sunny Side of the Street; It's a Good Day; Up a Lazy River (with Woody Herman); Why Don't You Do Right?; I Love a Piano (with Benny Goodman)

2002

Fever   Green Hill/EMI
72435-39935-2 8   USA   14

Fever; Too Close for Comfort; Come Rain or Come Shine; Unforgettable; Hallelujah, I Love Him So; There Is No Greater Love; Big

Spender; Deep Purple; Why Don't You Do Right?; The Man I Love; Alright, Okay, You Win; The Folks Who Live on the Hill; It's a Good Day; Everybody Loves Somebody

It's a Good Day Naxos Jazz Legends
   8120642   UK   20

Why Don't You Do Right?; My Old Flame; Blues in the Night; My Little Cousin; Ain't Goin' No Place; That Old Feeling; You Was Right Baby; Waitin' for My Train to Come In; I Don't Know Enough About You; Baby You Can Count on Me; Linger in My Arms a Little Longer, Baby; It's a Good Day; Two Silhouettes; I'll Dance at Your Wedding; Golden Earrings; Mañana (Is Soon Enough for Me); Bali Ha'i; Caramba! It's the Samba; Don't Smoke in Bed; Show Me the Way to Get Out of This World

A Nightingale Can Sing the Blues
   Tim International   2208401-202
   Germany 99

Disc One — The Way You Look Tonight: Shady Lady Bird; How Deep Is the Ocean?; Let's Do It; Somebody Else Is Taking My Place; Somebody Nobody Knows; How Long Has This Been Going On?; That Did It, Marie; Winter Weather; Everything I Love; Not Mine; Not a Care in the World; Blues in the Night; Where or When; The Way You Look Tonight; I Threw a Kiss in the Ocean; We'll Meet Again; Full Moon (Noche de Luna); There Won't Be a Shortage of Love; You're Easy to Dance With; All I Need Is You. *Disc Two — Sugar:* Ain't Going No Place; That Old Feeling; Baby (Is What He Calls Me); Waiting for the Train to Come In; I'm Glad I Waited for You; I Don't Know Enough About You; Somebody Loves Me; It's All Over Now; You Can Depend on Me; A Nightingale Can Sing the Blues; The Freedom Train; When Irish Eyes Are Smiling; Linger in My Arms a Little Longer, Baby; Everything's Movin' Too Fast; It's a Good Day; Chi-Baba, Chi-Baba (My Bambino Go to Sleep); Swing Low Sweet Chariot; Somebody Loves Me *(different version)*; There'll Be Some Changes Made; Sugar. *Disc Three — Keep Me in Mind:* I'll Dance at Your Wedding; Golden Earrings; Talking to Myself About You; Stormy Weather; I Can't Give You Anything but Love; Happiness Is a Thing Called Joe; Them There Eyes; 'Deed I Do; Why Don't You Do Right?; Baby, Don't Be Mad at Me; Them There Eyes (Same Version as No. 7); Mañana (Is Soon Enough for Me); Caramba! It's the Samba; All Dressed Up with a Broken Heart; While We're Young; Don't Smoke in Bed; Keep Me in Mind; For Every Man There Is a Woman; Bye, Bye Blues; You Was. *Disc Four — Oh, You Crazy Moon:* Bali Ha'i; Crazy He Calls Me; One Day; I Let a Song Go Out of My Heart; Aren't You Glad You're You; As Long as I'm Dreaming; Somebody Loves Me *(different version)*; Trav'-lin' Light; I Ain't Got Nobody; Oh, You Crazy Moon; Goody Goody; Imagination; You're Driving Me Crazy; Save Your Sorrow for Tomorrow; But Beautiful; Fine and Dandy; When a Woman Loves a Man; 'T Ain't So, Honey, 'T Ain't So; They Can't Take That Away from Me; Lover Come Back to Me. *Disc Five — Moon Flowers:* Show Me the Way to Go Out of This World; Where Are You?; (When I Dance with You) I Get Ideas; Whee Baby; I'm Glad There Is You; You Go to My Head; Forgive Me; Be Anything (But Be Mine); Just One of Those Things; Lover; I Didn't Know What Time It Was; Easy Living; (Ah, the Apple Trees) When the World Was Young; Watermelon Weather; Moon Flowers; River River; That's Him Over There; Who Gonna Pay That Check?; A Woman Alone with the Blues. *(This collection is missing song no. 17 on disc five; they had planned 100 songs, with 20 songs on each CD.)*

Basin Street East (Unreleased Show)
   Collectors Choice
   72435-39997-2-8 USA   14

Overture; Day In — Day Out; Call Me Darling, Call Me Sweetheart, Call Me Dear; Medley: One Kiss/ My Romance/ The Most Beautiful Man in the World; Medley: But Beautiful/ The Second Time Around; Fever; I'm Gonna Go Fishin'; I Love Being Here with You; By Myself; Heart; I've Never Left Your Arms; Ray Charles Tribute: Hallelujah, I Love Him So/ I Got a Man/ You Won't Let Me Go/ Just for a Thrill/ Yes Indeed!; Peggy Lee Bow Music; Medley: I Don't Know Enough About You/ Mañana (Is Soon Enough for Me)/ Why Don't You Do Right (Get Me Some Money Too)/ Lover/ It's a Good Day

Best of 20th Century Masters   MCA
   USA   12

Lover; Be Anything (But Be Mine); Just One of Those Things; Sans Souci; Black Coffee; Somebody Loves Me; Let Me Go, Lover; The Siamese Cat Song; Johnny Guitar; Mr. Wonderful; He Needs Me; I Don't Know Enough About You

Close Enough for Love DRG 91471 USA 10

You; Easy Does It; Close Enough for Love; A Robinsong; Just One of Those Things; I Can't Resist You; Come in from the Rain; In the Days of Our Love; Through the Eyes of Love; Rain Sometimes

El Rancho Grande (with Bing Crosby) Sunflower SUN 2108 England 23

It Takes a Long, Long Train with a Red Caboose; El Rancho Grande (with Bing Crosby and Gary Cooper); Just an Old Love of Mine; Love, Your Magic Spell Is Everywhere; You Came a Long Way from St. Louis (with Bing Crosby); What Is This Thing Called Love; Exactly Like You (with Bing Crosby); They Can't Take That Away from Me (with Bing Crosby); On a Slow Boat to China (with Bing Crosby); A Little Bird Told Me (with Bing Crosby); I Want to Go Where You Go (with Bing Crosby); Cuanto le Gusta (with Bing Crosby); I Got Lucky in the Rain; Maybe You'll Be There (with Bing Crosby); Trouble Is a Man; So in Love (with Bing Crosby); When a Man Is a Man (with Bing Crosby); When Is Sometimes; Once and for Always (with Bing Crosby); Easter Parade (with Bing Crosby); Bebop Spoken Here (with Bing Crosby); How It Lies (with Bing Crosby); Bali Ha'i

Fever Prism PLATCD 716 England 24

Fever; Mañana (Is Soon Enough for Me); Let's Do It (Let's Fall in Love); Stormy Weather; Summertime; Them There Eyes; That Old Feeling; Golden Earrings; There'll Be Some Changes Made; Somebody Loves Me; If I Could Be with You One Hour Tonight; Where or When; On the Sunny Side of the Street; Happiness Is a Thing Called Love; 'Deed I Do; The Way You Look Tonight; Why Don't You Do Right?; My Old Flame; It's All Over Now; You Can Depend on Me; You Was (with Dean Martin); Everything I Love; Bye Bye Blues; Chi-Baba, Chi-Baba

Golden Greats Disky MP 905191 Holland 75

Disc One: Mañana (Is Soon Enough for Me); Caramba! It's the Samba; Chi-Baba Chi-Baba (My Bambino Go to Sleep); Golden Earrings; Full Moon (Noche de Luna); I Don't Know Enough About You; Let's Do It (Let's Fall in Love); I Got It Bad (And That Ain't Good); My Old Flame; I Threw a Kiss in the Ocean; Blues in the Night; On the Sunny Side of the Street; What More Can a Woman Do?; If I Could Be with You; It's All Over Now; Stormy Weather; There'll Be Some Changes Made; Bye Bye Blues; September in the Rain; Somebody Loves Me; That Old Feeling; Winter Weather (with Art Lund); You Was (with Dean Martin); Where or When; We'll Meet Again. *Disc Two:* Why Don't You Do Right?; Don't Smoke in Bed; Waiting for the Train to Come In; Them There Eyes; It's a Good Day; Happiness Is a Thing Called Joe; That Did It, Marie; How Deep Is the Ocean?; I See a Million People; Everything I Love; Just One of Those Things; The Glory of Love; Trav'lin' Light; You Can Depend on Me; 'Deed I Do; All I Need Is You; Somebody Else Is Taking My Place; I've Had My Moments; This Can't Be Love; Rockin' Chair; Elmer's Tune; Not Mine; I Should Care; I Can't Give You Anything but Love; That's the Way It Goes. *Disc Three:* I'll Dance at Your Wedding; For Every Man There's a Woman; Let There Be Love; The Way You Look Tonight; A Nightingale Can Sing the Blues; Swinging on a Star; My Last Affair; Shady Lady Bird; Not a Care in the World; Somebody Nobody Loves; Melancholy Lullaby; I'm Confessin'; Love Is Just Around the Corner; Yeah, Yeah, Yeah; I Let a Song Go Out of My Heart; Summertime; How Long Has This Been Going On?; Somebody Sweetheart; Swing Low Sweet Chariot; I Ain't Got Nobody; You; Nice Work If You Can Get It; Don't Blame Me; Cottage for Sale; You Brought a New Kind of Love to Me (with Frank Sinatra)

It's a Good Day Living Era CD AJS 256 England 50

Disc One: Elmer's Tune; I See a Million People; I Got It Bad (And That Ain't Good); My Old Flame; How Deep Is the Ocean?; Shady Lady Bird; Let's Do It; Somebody Else Is Taking My Place; How Long Has This Been Going On?; Winter Weather (with Art Lund); Blues in the Night; Where or When?; On the Sunny Side of the Street; My Little Cousin; The Way You Look Tonight; We'll Meet Again; Full Moon (Noche de Luna); All I Need Is You; Why Don't You Do Right?; Ain't Going No Place; That Old Feeling; What More Can a Woman Do?; You Was Right, Baby; Waiting for the Train to Come In; I Don't Know Enough About You. *Disc Two:* It's a Good Day; Linger in My Arms a Little Longer, Baby;

A Nightingale Can Sing the Blues; It's All Over Now; Everything's Movin' Too Fast; Chi-Baba, Chi-Baba (My Bambino Go to Sleep); There'll Be Some Changes Made; I'll Dance at Your Wedding; Sugar; Golden Earrings; 'Deed I Do; Them There Eyes; Baby, Don't Be Mad at Me; Caramba! It's the Samba; Laroo, Laroo, Lili Bolero; Mañana (Is Soon Enough for Me); For Every Man There's a Woman; Don't Smoke in Bed; Bali Ha'i; I'm Gonna Wash That Man Right Outta My Hair; Ghost Riders in the Sky; The Old Master Painter (with Mel Torme); Climb Up the Mountain; (When I Dance with You) I Get Ideas; Aren't You Kind of Glad We Did?

It's a Good Day   Rajon Music RMGSN 2029   UK   36

Disc One: Golden Earrings; Waitin' for the Train to Come In; I Don't Know Enough About You; The Old Master Painter (with Mel Torme); Linger in My Arms a Little Longer, Baby; It's a Good Day; Caramba! It's the Samba; For Every Man There's a Woman; Talking to Myself About You; Them There Eyes; 'Deed I Do; Somebody Loves Me; I'm Confessin'; Summertime; Baby, Don't Be Mad at Me; Laroo, Laroo, Lili Bolero; Blum, Blum (I Wonder Who I Am); Bye Bye Blues. *Disc 2:* Mañana (Is Soon Enough for Me); Why Don't You Do Right?; Chi-Baba, Chi-Baba (My Bambino Go to Sleep); Riders in the Sky (A Cowboy Legend); It's All Over Now; I'll Dance at Your Wedding; Bali Ha'i; Sugar; All Dressed Up with a Broken Heart; Don't Smoke in Bed; Everything's Movin' Too Fast; I'm Glad I Waited for You; Rockin' Chair; You Can Depend on Me; That Old Feeling; I Can't Give You Anything but Love; Similau; Show Me The Way to Go Out of This World ('Cause That's Where Everything Is)

Just the Way You Are (with Bing Crosby)   Sunflower Records Sun 2110   England   20

Louisa from Lake Louise; Maybe It's Because (with Bing Crosby); You're in Love with Someone (with Bing Crosby); A Wonderful Guy; I've Got a Crush on You (with Bing Crosby); Again (with Bing Crosby); I Got the Right to Sing the Blues; A Thousand Violins (with Bing Crosby); Way Back Home (with Bing Crosby); Stay Well (with Bing Crosby); Mañana (with Bing Crosby); Little Jack Frost Get Lost (with Bing Crosby); When You Speak with Your Eyes; Sunshine Cake (with Bing Crosby); I'm Coming Virginia; A Dream Is a Wish Your Heart Makes; Bushel and a Peck (with Bing Crosby); Orange-colored Sky; Just the Way You Are (with Bing Crosby); Would I Love You

Let's Do It   Rajon Music RMGS 1048   UK   20

Let's Do It (Let's Fall in Love); I Got It Bad (And That Ain't Good); Somebody Else Is Taking My Place; Everything I Love; I'm Glad I Waited for You; Waitin' for the Train to Come In; I Don't Know Enough About You; It's All Over Now; I'm Confessin' (That I Love You); Rockin' Chair; Summertime; You Can Depend on Me; I'll Dance at Your Wedding; Somebody Loves Me; Bye Bye Blues; Don't Smoke in Bed; I Can't Give You Anything but Love; Stormy Weather; Them There Eyes; There'll Be Some Changes Made

Let There Be Love   Sunflower Records SUN 2089   UK   20

Linger in My Arms a Little Longer, Baby; Oh, What a Beautiful Morning; Love, Your Magic Spell Is Everywhere; Love Is Just Around the Corner; Just One More Change/ My Last Affair/ For Sentimental Reasons/ What Is This Thing Called Love?; He's Just My Kind/ I Got Lucky in the Rain/ Golden Earrings; It Takes a Long, Long Train with a Red Caboose; It's All Over Now; The Lady Is a Tramp; Make the Man Love Me; Shanghai; These Foolish Things; If I Could Be with You One Hour Tonight; Let There Be Love; I've Got the Right to Sing the Blues

Marvelous Miss Lee   North Star 72435-40699-2-5   USA   14

Fever; I Don't Know Enough About You; It's All Over Now; Why Don't You Do Right? (Get Me Some Money Too); Golden Earrings; Waitin' for the Train to Come In; I'll Dance at Your Wedding; Unforgettable; As Time Goes By; Cheek to Cheek; Fly Me to the Moon; Kansas City; See See Rider; Is That All There Is?

40 Outstanding Performances   Prism PLATBX 2232   England   40

Disc One: Fever; Mañana (Is Soon Enough for Me); Let's Do It (Let's Fall in Love); Stormy Weather; Summertime; Them There Eyes; That Old Feeling; Golden Earrings; There'll Be Some Changes Made; Somebody Loves Me; If I Could Be with You One Hour Tonight; Where or

When; On the Sunny Side of the Street; Happiness Is a Thing Called Love; 'Deed I Do; The Way You Look Tonight; Why Don't You Do Right?; My Old Flame; It's All Over Now; You Can Depend on Me; You Was; Everything I Love; Bye Bye Blues; Chi-Baba, Chi-Baba (My Bambino Go to Sleep). *Disc Two:* The Lady Is a Tramp; Too Young; Just One More Change; Shanghai; Let There Be Love; He's Just My Kind; I'm Confessin'; I've Got the Right to Sing the Blues; Oh, What a Beautiful Morning; Love Is Just Around the Corner; September in the Rain; I'm Beginning to See the Light; Nice Work If You Can Get It; These Foolish Things; That Old Gang of Mine; For Sentimental Reasons

Peggy Lee Signature SIGNCD2132 England 20

Elmer's Tune; Lets Do It (Let's Fall in Love); How Deep Is the Ocean?; I Got It Bad (And That Ain't Good); Shady Lady Bird; How Long Has This Been Going On?; Blues in the Night; My Little Cousin; Why Don't You Do Right?; That Old Feeling; I Get the Blues When It Rains; Golden Earrings; Them There Eyes; For Every Man There Is a Woman; Keep Me in Mind; It's a Good Day; Waiting for the Train to Come In; I Don't Know Enough About You; You Was Right, Baby; Mañana (Is Soon Enough for Me)

Peggy Lee Story Proper Music P1277-80 England 95

Disc One — Why Don't You Do Right?: Elmer's Tune; I Can See a Million People (But All I Can See Is You); I Got It Bad (And That Ain't Good); My Old Flame; How Deep Is the Ocean; Let's Do It (Let's Fall in Love); Somebody Else Is Taking My Place; Somebody Nobody Knows; Winter Weather; Everything I Love; Not Mine; Where or When; On the Sunny Side of the Street; Why Don't You Do Right?; Ain't Goin' No Place; That Old Feeling; Baby (Is What He Calls Me); Waitin' for the Train to Come In; I'm Glad I Waited for You; I Don't Know Enough About You; Linger in My Arms a Little Longer, Baby; It's a Good Day; A Nightingale Can Sing the Blues. *Disc Two — Sugar:* It's All Over Now; Aren't You Kind of Glad We Did?; She Didn't Say Yes; Birmingham Jail; It's Lovin' Time; Everything's Movin' Too Fast; Swing Low Sweet Chariot; Somebody Loves Me; Chi-Baba, Chi-Baba (My Bambino Go to Sleep); It Takes a Long, Long Train with a Red Caboose; Just an Old Love of Mine; There'll Be Some Changes Made; I'll Dance at Your Wedding; Sugar (That Sugar Baby o' Mine); Golden Earrings; I Can't Give You Anything but Love; Talkin' to Myself About You; Why Don't You Do Right?; 'Deed I Do; Hold Me; Them There Eyes; Baby, Don't Be Mad at Me; Everybody Loves Somebody. *Disc Three — Mañana:* Laroo, Laroo Lili Bolero; Caramba! It's the Samba; Mañana (Is Soon Enough for Me); All Dressed Up with a Broken Heart; While We're Young; For Every Man There's a Woman; Just a Shade on the Blue Side; Bubble-Loo, Bubble-Loo; Don't Smoke in Bed; Please Love Me Tonight; Bali Ha'i; I'm Gonna Wash That Man Right Outta My Hair; Riders in the Sky (A Cowboy Legend); Crazy, He Calls Me; Coney Island; Got the Gate on the Golden Gate; The Old Master Painter (with Mel Torme); Cannonball Express; Show Me the Way to Get Out of This World; Lover Come Back to Me; Where Are You?; (When I Dance with You) I Get Ideas; Don't Fan the Flame (with Mel Torme). *Disc Four — The Radio Years:* You Brought a New Kind of Love to Me; Lonesome Road; I Can Believe That You're in Love with Me; A Cottage for Sale; Porgy; Summertime; Solitude; My Sugar Is So Refined; I Guess I'll Get the Papers and Go Home; All of Me; But Beautiful; You Turned the Tables on Me; I May Be Wrong (But I Think You're Wonderful); Nature Boy; You Came a Long Way from St. Louis; On a Slow Boat to China; Cuanto la Gusta; As Long as I'm Dreaming; Oh! You Crazy Moon; Trav'lin' Light; 'S Wonderful; I Let a Song Go Out of My Heart; This Can't Be Love; You're Driving Me Crazy; Fine and Dandy; When a Woman Loves a Man

Singles Collection EMI Capitol 7243-5-39756-2-3 England 105

Disc One: Columbia Records (with the Benny Goodman Orchestra); Let's Do It; Somebody Nobody Loves; Why Don't You Do Right? *ARA Records:* On the Atchison, Topeka, and the Santa Fe (with Bob Crosby); It's Anybody's Spring. *Capitol Records (First Period):* What More Can a Woman Do?; You Was Right, Baby; Waiting for the Train to Come In; I Don't Know Enough About You; I Can See It Your Way; It's a Good Day; A Nightingale Can Sing the Blues; He's Just My Kind; She Didn't Say Yes; Birmingham Jail; Don't Be So Mean to Baby; Bluest Kind of Blue (Nuages); Everything's Movin' Too Fast; Speaking of Angels; Chi-Baba, Chi-

Baba (My Bambino Go to Sleep); Just an Old Love of Mine; Sugar (That Sugar Baby of Mine); Golden Earrings; Why Don't You Do Right?; Hold Me; Them There Eyes. *Disc Two:* Everybody Loves Somebody; Caramba! It's the Samba; Mañana (Is Soon Enough for Me); So Dear to My Heart; While We're Young; Don't Smoke in Bed; Just a Shade on the Blue Side; You Was (with Dean Martin); Someone Like You; Please, Love Me Tonight; If You Could See Me Now; Similau (See-me-lo); You Can Have Him; At the Café Rendezvous; Goodbye John; Through a Long and Sleepless Night; Save Your Sorrow for Tomorrow; The Old Master Painter (with Mel Torme); Bless You (For the Good That's in You) (with Mel Torme); When You Speak with Your Eyes; My Small Senor (With the Sonriente Eyes); Cry, Cry, Cry; Once Around the Moon; Helpless; They Can't Take That Away from Me; Happy Music; Life Is So Peculiar. *Disc Three:* Where Are You?; Once in a Lifetime; The Mill on the Floss; Yeah! Yeah! Yeah!; Rock Me to Sleep; He's Only Wonderful; Wandering Swallow; I Love You but I Don't Like You; Tonight You Belong to Me; Don't Fan the Flame (with Mel Torme); Would You Dance with a Stranger?; Everytime; Whee, Baby; Louisville Lou; Let's Call It a Day. *Decca Records:* Lover; Sugar (That Sugar Baby of Mine); You've Got to See Mama Every Night; Mr. Wonderful. *Capitol Records (Second Period):* The Folks Who Live on the Hill; Listen to the Mocking Bird; Uninvited Dream; Fever; Alright, Okay, You Win; Hallelujah, I Love Him So; I'm Lookin' Out the Window; You Deserve; Heart; I'm Gonna Go Fishin'; My Gentle Young Johnny; Moments Like This; I Love Being Here with You; I'm a Woman; Sneakin' Up on You; Pass Me By; Stop Living in the Past; Big Spender; Come Back to Me; Walking Happy; Didn't Want to Have to Do It; Misty Roses; It'll Never Happen Again; Spinning Wheel; Is That All There Is?; Something; You'll Remember Me; Pieces of Dreams; Where Did They Go?; Love Song. *A&M Records:* Some Cats Know. *Capitol/Toshiba — EMI Records:* Senza Fine. *Bonus tracks of studio talk:* False start on 'Caramba! It's the Samba'; False start on 'Mañana'; 'It Jumps' about 'Helpless'; 'Sonriente' practice; 'Thank you very much' break 'Lookin'/Window'

Fever Green Hill Records GHD 5318 14

Fever; Too Close for Comfort; Come Rain or Come Shine; Unforgettable; Hallelujah, I Love Him So; There Is No Greater Love; Big Spender; Deep Purple; Why Don't You Do Right?; The Man I Love; Alright, Okay, You Win; The Folks Who Live on the Hill; It's a Good Day; Everybody Loves Somebody

2003

Bewitching-Lee! S&P SPR-709 USA 15

Why Don't You Do Right?; Don't Smoke in Bed; It's a Good Day; Alright, Okay, You Win; Golden Earrings; Hallelujah, I Love Him So; Fever; I Don't Know Enough About You; Them There Eyes; While We're Young; Mañana (Is Soon Enough for Me); My Man; Unforgettable; You Don't Know; I'm a Woman

Beauty and the Beat Blue Note Records 7243-5-42308-2-0 EU 14

Do I Love You?; I Lost My Sugar in Salt Lake City; If Dreams Come True; All Too Soon; Mambo in Miami (instrumental); Isn't It Romantic?; Blue Prelude; You Came Along Way from St. Louis; Always True in My Fashion; There Be Another Spring; Get Out of Town; Satin Doll (instrumental); Don't Ever Leave Me; Nobody's Heart

Best of Singles Collection Capitol 72435-82680-2-7 USA 22

You Was Right, Baby; It's a Good Day; Birmingham Jail; Don't Smoke in Bed; If You Could See Me Now; At the Cafe Rendezvous; Once Around the Moon; Life Is So Peculiar; Yeah! Yeah! Yeah!; Fever; I'm Lookin' Out the Window; I'm Gonna Go Fishin'; My Gentle Young Johnny; The Folks Who Live on the Hill; I Love Being Here with You; Moments Like This; Senza Fine; Come Back to Me; Something; Is That All There Is?; Let's Call It a Day; Fever (Gabin Remix)

Classics and Collectibles Universal 1130342 EU 52

Disc One: Mr. Wonderful; He's a Tramp; Black Coffee; Lover; Where Can I Go Without You?; This Is a Very Special Day; Sing a Rainbow; Just One of Those Things; Johnny Guitar; The Siamese Cat Song; The Moon Came Up with a Great Idea Last Night (with Bing Crosby); Apples, Peaches and Cherries; (Sorry Baby) You

Let My Love Get Cold; Sans Souci; La La Lu; I Hear the Music Now; Oh! No! Please Don't Go; How Bitter, My Sweet; I Don't Know Enough About You; It Never Entered My Mind; Ooh, That Kiss; Bella Notte; I'm Gonna Meet My Sweetie Now; Sisters; I've Grown Accustomed to His Face; Peace on Earth/ Silent Night. *Disc Two:* I Still Get a Thrill (Thinking of You); The Tavern; It Must Be So (with the Mills Brothers); That's What a Woman Is For; Wrong, Wrong, Wrong; Never Mind; Me; How Strange; Merry Go Runaround (with Bing Crosby and Bob Hope); Wrong Joe; The Night Holds No Fear for the Lover; Summer Vacation; Go You Where You Go; Straight Ahead (with the Mills Brothers); The Gypsy with Fire in His Shoes; Pablo Pasablo; Little Jack Frost Get Lost (with Bing Crosby); I Belong to You; It's Because We're in Love (with Jimmy Rowles); Singing ('Cause He Wants to Sing); That Fellow's a Friend of Man; Old Trusty; Jim Dear; What Is a Baby?; Mister Magoo Does the Cha-Cha-Cha; Three Cheers for Mister Magoo

Classics and Collectibles
Polydor/Universal   Promotional   England   48

(This CD was for promotional use only and not for resale. It is a rarity.) Disc One: Mr. Wonderful; He's a Tramp; Black Coffee; Lover; Where Can I Go Without You?; This Is a Very Special Day; Sing a Rainbow; Just One of Those Things; Johnny Guitar; The Siamese Cat Song; The Moon Came Up with a Great Idea Last Night (with Bing Crosby); Apples, Peaches and Cherries; (Sorry Baby) You Let My Love Get Cold; Sans Souci; La La Lu; I Hear the Music Now; Oh! No! Please Don't Go; How Bitter, My Sweet; I Don't Know Enough About You; It Never Entered My Mind; Ooh, That Kiss; Bella Notte; I'm Gonna Meet My Sweetie Now; Sisters. *Disc Two:* I Still Get a Thrill (Thinking of You); The Tavern; It Must Be So (with the Mills Brothers); That's Was a Woman Is For; Wrong, Wrong, Wrong; Never Mind; Me; How Strange; Merry Go Runaround (with Bing Crosby and Bob Hope); Wrong Joe; The Night Holds No Fear for the Lover; Summer Vacation; Go You Were You Go; Straight Ahead (with the Mills Brothers); The Gypsy with Fire in His Shoes; Pablo Pasablo; Little Jack Frost Get Lost (with Bing Crosby); I Belong to You; It's Because We're in Love (with Jimmy Rowles); Singing ('Cause He Wants to Sing); That Fellow's a Friend of Man; Old Trusty; Jim Dear; What Is a Baby?

Fever and Other Hits Collectables
COL CD-9321   USA   10

Fever; I'm a Woman; Is That All There Is?; (You Gotta Have) Heart; My Man; A Doddlin' Song; Hallelujah, I Love Him So; Big Spender; Alright, Okay, You Win; The Alley Cat Song

Fever Single Remix   Capitol Records
70876-17990-2-6   USA   3

Fever, The Original Version with Peggy Lee Playing time 3:20; Fever, The Thomas Gabin & Gary Calamar Remix, Album Edit 4:20; Fever, The Thomas Gabin and Gary Calamar Remix, Long Version 5:52. (The album edit was released on the CD *The Best of the Singles Collection,* Capitol, 2003.)

Love Songs   MCA Decca
088 113 100-2   USA   14

I've Got You Under My Skin; You Go to My Head; Crazy in the Heart; Autumn in Rome; I've Grown Accustomed to His Face; Do I Love You?; I Never Knew; Love You So; Sugar (That Sugar Baby o' Mine); You're My Thrill; Me; I Belong to You; The Night Holds No Fear (For the Lover); Love Letters

My Old Flame   Legends of Jazz
18020-2   Denmark   18

My Old Flame; That's the Way It Goes; All I Need Is You; Not a Care in the World; Full Moon (Noche de Luna); How Long Has This Been Going On?; That Did It, Marie; Elmer's Tune; I Threw a Kiss in the Ocean; We'll Meet Again

Latin Ala Lee!   S&P SPR-712   US   15

Heart; On the Street Where You Live; Till There Was You; I Am in Love; Hey There; I Could Have Danced All Night; The Surrey with the Fringe on Top; The Party's Over; Dance Only with Me; Wish You Were Here; C'est Magnifique; I Enjoy Being a Girl; From Now On; Sweet Happy Life

A Natural Woman/Is That All There Is?

(A Natural Woman): (All of a Sudden) My Heart Sings; Don't Explain; Can I Change My Mind?; Lean on Me; (Sit-in' on) The Dock of the Bay; (You Make Me Feel Like) A Natural Woman; Everyday People; Please Send Me

Someone to Love; Spinning Wheel; Living Is Dying Without You; I Think It's Gonna Rain Today. *(Is That All There Is?):* Is That All There Is?; Love Story; Me and My Shadow; Sing a Rainbow; My Old Flame; I'm a Woman; Somethin' Stupid; Brother Love's Travelling Salvation Show; Something; Whistle for Happiness; Johnny (Linda); I Can Hear Music; Don't Smoke in Bed

Peggy Lee CDs Without a Release Date

A Portrait of 1941–1942   Sony CBS 32DP 563   Japan   16

(Only mono recordings — probably released before 1990.) Elmer's Tune; That's the Way It Goes; I Got It Bad (And That Ain't Good); My Old Flame; Let's Do It (Let's Fall in Love); Somebody Else Is Talking My Place; How Long Has This Been Going On?; That Did It, Marie; Winter Weather; Blues in the Night; Where or When; On the Sunny Side of the Street; The Way You Look Tonight; We'll Meet Again; Why Don't You Do Right?

Close Enough for Love   DRG

(Released in 1991 or 1992.) You; Easy Does It; Close Enough for Love; A Robinsong; Just One of Those Things; I Can't Resist You; Come in from the Rain; In the Days of Our Love; Through the Eyes of Love; Rain Sometimes

Close Enough for Love   Truing Music   JHD 067   EEC   10

(Same as above — probably released in 1992.)

Everything I Love   History Music 20.3046-H1   Germany   35

(Probably released in 1997 or 1998.) Disc One: Shady Lady Bird; My Old Flame; How Long Has This Been Going On?; I See a Million People; I Got Bad (And That Ain't Good); Let's Do It; Everything I Love; That's the Way It Goes; That Did It, Marie; How Deep Is the Ocean?; Somebody Else Is Taking My Place; Not a Care in the World; Not Mine; Somebody Nobody Loves. *Disc Two:* It's a Good Day; Linger in My Arms a Little Longer, Baby; It's All Over Now; Waiting for the Train to Come In; I Don't Know Enough About You; Everything's Movin' Too Fast; I'm Glad I Waited for You; Chi-Baba, Chi-Baba (My Bambino Go to Sleep); Sugar (That Sugar Baby o' Mine); I'll Dance at Your Wedding; Golden Earrings; Mañana (Is Soon Enough for Me); Talkin' to Myself About You; Caramba! It's the Samba; All Dressed Up with a Broken Heart; Don't Smoke in Bed; Baby, Don't Be Mad at Me; 'Deed I Do; Them There Eyes; Why Don't You Do Right?

The Fever of   Cedar   GFS 241   UK   24

(Probably released in 1998 or 1999.) Shady Lady Bird; My Old Flame; How Long Has This Been Going On?; I See a Million People (But All I Can See Is You); It's a Good Day; Linger in My Arms a Little Longer, Baby; It's All Over Now; Waiting for the Train to Come In; I Don't Know Enough About You; Everything's Movin' Too Fast; I'm Glad I Waited for You; Chi-Baba, Chi-Baba (My Bambino Go to Sleep); Sugar; I'll Dance at Your Wedding; Golden Earrings; Mañana (Is Soon Enough for Me); Talking to Myself About You; Caramba! It's the Samba; All Dressed Up with a Broken Heart; Don't Smoke in Bed; Baby Don't Be Mad at Me; 'Deed I Do; Them There Eyes; Why Don't You Do Right?

Old Favorites   Music International P 6002   USA   13

(Release date prior to 1995.) Just One of Those Things; You; I've Got the World on a String; Oh, What a Beautiful Morning; It's a Good Day; What Is This Thing Called Love?; I'm Beginning to See the Light; Gone with the Wind; Don't Blame Me; Baby, Won't You Please Come Home; September in the Rain; That Old Gang of Mine; Night Life

Why Don't You Do Right? Tim International   204329-203 Germany   17

(Released in 2001 or 2002.) It's a Good Day; Linger in My Arms a Little Longer, Baby; It's All Over Now; Waiting for the Train to Come In; I Don't Know Enough About You; Everything's Movin' Too Fast; Chi-Baba, Chi-Baba (My Bambino Go to Sleep); Sugar (That Sugar Baby o' Mine); I'll Dance at Your Wedding; Golden Earrings; Talking to Myself About You; Caramba! It's the Samba; All Dressed Up with a Broken Heart; Don't Smoke in Bed; Baby Don't Be Mad at Me; Them There Eyes; Why Don't You Do Right?

Fever Delta ASIN: B0000071JJ CPRS23012

Fever; It's All Right with Me; Hallelujah, I Love Him So; Apples, Peaches and Cherries; Mr. Wonderful; They Can't Take That Away from Me; Alright, Okay, You Win; Love Me or Leave Me; Black Coffee; Sans Souci; Lover; My Heart Belongs to Daddy; Baubles, Bangles and Beads; Is That All There Is?; Big Spender; That's What a Woman Is For; The Siamese Cat Song; Where Can I Go Without You?; Love Letters; I'm Glad There Is You; I'm a Woman; Swing Low Sweet Chariot; He Needs Me; Guess I'll Go Back Home

Appendix B.
Songs Written by Miss Peggy Lee

The following is a complete list of Peggy Lee's published compositions, listed chronologically by the year in which they were published.

1941

Little Fool

1945

You Was Right, Baby
What More Can a Woman Do?

1946

Don't Be So Mean to Baby
I Don't Know Enough About You
It's a Good Day

1947

Everything's Movin' Too Fast
Lonesome for Love
Just an Old Love of Mine

1948

Let It Bother Me
Mañana (Is Soon Enough for Me)
If I Can Live My Life with You
North Dakota
Confusion Says
Lullaby for a Wee One
Nice to be Small
Take a Little Time to Smile
Could You Love Somebody Like Me

1949

Blum, Blum (I Wonder Who I Am)
Neon Signs (Gonna Shine Like Neon, Too)
My Small Senor
Bless You (For the Good That's in You)

1950

When You Speak with Your Eyes
Happy Music
I'm in the Mood for Music
Please Treat Her Nicer
When It Rains, It Pours

1951

If I Had a Chance with You
That Ol' Devil (Won't Get Me)
I Gotta Do Something Fast
Wife, Go Home and Mind Your Cleanin'
The White Birch and the Sycamore
A Straw Hat Full of Lilacs
I Love You but I Don't Like You

1952

How Strange (Victor Young)
Sans Souci (Sonny Burke)
Goodbye My Love

1953

This Is a Very Special Day
Who's Gonna Pay the Check?
Don't Make Believe
O, Baby, Come Home
New York City Ghost
Whee, Baby

1954

The Joy of Easter
Your Last Adios
Funny Little Ole Bluebird
With Joy Shall Ye Drink
It's Because We're in Love
The Gypsy with the Fire in His Shoes
Where Can I Go Without You?
Johnny Guitar
I Love You So
(I Love Your) Gypsy Heart
I Don't Want to Walk in the Dark
This Is a Brand New Day

1955

Peace on Earth
Bella Notte
What Is a Baby?
The Siamese Cat Song
La La Lu
He's a Tramp
That Fellow's a Friend of Man
Old Trusty
Jim Dear
Singin' ('Cause He Wants to Sing)
Straight Ahead
It Must Be So
It's a Funny Old World
Mr. Magoo Does the Cha Cha Cha
We
The Gold Wedding Ring
Little Old Car
The Happy Monks

1956

(Theme from) Johnny Trouble
1957 It's a Good, Good Night

1958

From Tom Thumb
One for You and One for Me
Tom Thumb's Tune
Are You a Dream?
I'm About My Father's Business
Things Are Swingin'
The River of Life
I Like Men
Goin' Down the Road
You Gotta Keep Singing
The Walk to the Ring

1959

I'm Gonna Go Fishin'

The Tree
The Christmas List
How Can You Erase a Memory?
There'll Be Another Spring

1960

El Toro
I Love Being Here with You
The Christmas Riddle
Christmas Carousel
Don't Forget to Feed the Reindeer
Because I Love Him So
Latin a la Lee
Ole

1961

Embrasse Moi
France Theme
London Theme
Happy with the Blues

1962

All For You
Fisherman's Wharf
San Francisco Blues
The Grain Belt Blues
Los Angeles Blues
The Train Blues
New York City Blues
Boston Beans
Cross Country Blues

1963

Got That Magic
My Star
Never Depend on a Man
Politics
Because I Love You
I'm Your Girl
Today
I Don't Wanna Leave You Now
I'm Saving My Tears for Tomorrow

1964

That's My Style
(I'm) In Love Again
I'll Follow You
Since You've Gone
I Wanna Jump
I Walked by Her Door
A Great Big Love

Just Call Me Love Bird
That's What It Takes

1965

Then Was Then (And Now Is Now)
That Big Pink Cloud
But Only for You

1966

That Man
The Shining Sea
Happy Feet
Stay with Me
So What's New?

1967

Christmas Lullaby
Here's to You
I Wound It Up
I'm Gonna Get It

1968

I Want Some Men
The Heart Is a Lonely Hunter
Lean on Me

1971

Passenger of the Rain (from the film *Rider on the Rain*)

1972

Sugar, Don't You Know?

1974

The Nickel Ride (from the film *The Nickel Ride*)

1975

Mon Amor (My Love)

1977

Courage, Madame
Dreams of Summer

1978

Los Angeles Forevermore

1979

Easy Does It
In the Days of Our Love

1983

from Peg
Soul
Daddy Was a Railroad Man
Mama
That Old Piano
One Beating a Day
That's How I Learned to Sing the Blues
Sometimes You're Up
He'll Make Me Believe That He's Mine
The Other Part of Me
Angels On Your Pillow
What Did They Do to My Goil?
No More Rainbows
Flowers and Flowers
There Is More

Unused from Peg
Just Because the Years Go By
The Folks Back Home
Mr. Clown
Honey
My Little Girl Has Gone Away
Clown Party
Petit Chason de Reves
Mirrors and Marble
Get Off Your Knees

1984

Blues for Basie

1985

I'll Give It All to You
Butterfly
Let's Fall a Little Bit in Love

1986

Let It Go (Over the Wheel)
I Just Want to Dance All Night

Bibliography

The primary source for this book was the Peggy Lee scrapbook compiled by the late Ronald Towe.

For more than thirty years Ron collected everything he could find on Peggy Lee: interviews, concert reviews, record reviews, sheet music and photos. His scrapbook is over 2,400 pages and stands six feet high.

Without Ron this book would not have been possible.

Other Sources

Balliet, Whitney. *American Singers: 27 Portraits in Song*. New York: Oxford University Press, 1990.

Carr, Roy. *Jazz Singers*. London: Octopus, 1999.

Dahl, Linda. *Stormy Weather*. New York: Pantheon, 1984.

Feather, Leonard. *The Encyclopedia of Jazz*. New York: Da Capo, 1985.

Friedwald, Will. *Jazz Singing*. New York: Da Capo Press, 1992.

Lee, Peggy. *Miss Peggy Lee*. London: Bloomsbury, 1990.

Lees, Gene. *Singers and the Song*. New York: Oxford University Press, 1987.

_____. *Singers and the Song II*. New York: Oxford University Press, 1998.

Pleasants, Henry. *The Great American Popular Singers*. New York: Fireside, 1985.

Simon, George T. *The Big Bands*. New York: Macmillan, 1971.

CD Liner Notes

Peggy Lee — Black Coffee and Other Delights: The Decca Anthology. Liner notes by Jim Lowe (1994).

Miss Peggy Lee. Capitol. Four compact discs. Liner notes by Gene Lees (1998).

Periodicals

Billboard
Cosmopolitan
Downbeat
Interview
Life
Look
Metronome
Newsweek
Time
Variety

I am also indebted to the creator of peggylee.com.

Index

Numbers in *italics* have photographs. Songs written by Peggy Lee are followed by an asterisk. Peggy Lee's original album titles are listed in **boldface**.

A & M Records 177
Abbott, George 194
About Mrs. Leslie (film) 60
Academy Awards 74
The Adventures of Tom Thumb (film) 41
The Advocate 186
After Dark (magazine) 166
"After You've Gone" 114
Aggie Award 207–*208*
"Ain't Goin' No Place" 31, 85
"Ain't Nobody's Business" 218
"Ain't We Got Fun" 63
"Ain't'cha Ever Comin' Back" 40
Albers, Hans 180
Albert, Eddie 101
Albertson, Chris 220
Alf (TV) 223
"Alfie" 127
"All Alone" 123
"All Dressed Up with a Broken Heart" 42
"All I Need Is You" 25, 152
"All I Want" 148
"All of Me" 37, 42
All That Jazz (Ella Fitzgerald CD) 229
"All the Way" 102
"All Too Soon" 61, 86
"Alla en el Rancho Grande" 37
Allen, Fred 48
Allen, Peter 180
Allen, Steve 77, *79*, 87–88, 178, 188
"The Alley Cat Song" 111
Almeida, Laurindo 39
"Almost Like Being in Love" 141
"Alone Together" 115
"Alright, Okay, You Win" 82, 84, 88, 93, 117, 126, 187, 223, 239
"Always" 167–168, 171
"Always True to You in My Fashion" 86, 234
"Amazing" 235
Ambassador East and West (Chicago hotels) 16–17, 178
Ameling, Elly 203
America Salutes Richard Rodgers: The Sound of His Music 179, 184–185
American Singers — 27 Portraits in Song 3, 204–205
American Weekly (magazine) 94
Americana Hotel (New York) 114
America's No. One Female Singer of the Year 50
Anderson, Ivie 31
Andrews, Julie 81, 159, 163
Andrews, Patti 207
Andy (TV) 179
Andy Warhol's Interview (magazine) 26, 202, 229
"Any State in the Forty-Eight Is Great" 45
"Anything You Say Is True" 78
Arceri, Gene 177
"Are You a Dream?"* 82
Arlen, Harold 22, 24, 102, *105*, 237–238
Armstrong, Lil Hardin 234
Armstrong, Louis 5, 22, 70, 86, 142, 148–149, 159, 164, 198, 206, 218
Armstrong, Lucille 159
Arnold, Eddy 81
Arthur, Bea 239
"As Long as I'm Dreaming" 40
"As Time Goes By" 28, 100, 214
"As You Desire Me" 88, 121
ASCAP in Action (magazine) 211
The Asphalt Jungle (film) 57
Astaire, Fred 25, 45, 142, 174
Audie Award 75
"Autumn in Rome" 178
Avalon, Frankie 93
Avedon, Richard 171
Aznavour, Charles 182, 184

"Baby, Baby All the Time" 87–88, 91
"Baby, Baby Wait for Me" 78
"Baby, Don't Be Mad at Me" 46
"Baby, It's Cold Outside" 163
"Baby Won't You Please Come Home" 56, 222
"Baby, You Can Count On Me" 36
Bacall, Lauren 171
Bacharach, Burt 127, 140, 143, 147–148
Bachmen, Martyne 15
"Back in Your Own Back Yard" 81
Bailey, Mildred 5, 14, 20, 85–86, 91, 164, 169
Bailey, Pearl 147, 174, 185
Baker, Chet 192
Baker, Janet 203
"Bali H'ai" 47
Ball, Lucille 45
Balliett, Whitney 3, 204–206, 242
The Ballroom (New York nightclub) 204–205, 209–210, 215–216, 221, 226–227
Band Leaders (magazine) 30
Banjo Eyes (Broadway musical) 21

287

Bankhead, Tallulah 44, 49
Banquet of Melody 33, 40
Barbour, David 26–28, 29–30, 32, 35–36, 38, 40, 41, 44–45, 47, 48, 50, 51–52, 60, 63, 118, 159, 174, 193–194, 198, 233
Barbour, Nicki Lee 30–31, 35, 37–38, 51, 60, 73, 98, 159
Barcus, Alan 210
Barnes, Ken 61, 74, 180–182
Basie, Count 9, 22, 89, 153, 159, 184, 187, 199, 210, 238
"Basin Street Blues" 89, 222
Basin Street East (New York nightclub) 89, 91–92, 94, 95–100, 103, 108–111, 115, 117
Basin Street East—Proudly Presents Miss Peggy Lee 102
Bassey, Shirley 180
Batman (TV) 121
"Baubles, Bangles, and Beads" 62–64, 86
"Be Anything (But Be Mine)" 55
"Beale Street" 222
The Beatles 39, 115, 145
Beauty and the Beat! 86
"Be-Bop Spoken Here" 47
"Because I Love Him So"* 88
"Beer Barrel Polka" 139
"Bella Notte"* 65–66
The Belle of the Nineties (film) 20
Bennett, Max 83
Bennett, Tony 78–79, 109, 121–122, 148, 161, 174, 190–192, 199, 227, 240
Benny, Jack 14, 74, 158
Benson, George 184
Berg, George 23
Bergen, Candice 161
Bergen, Frances 239
Bergen, Polly 239
Bergman, Marilyn and Alan 147
Berlin, Irving 20, 25, 171, 229
Best Female Singer (1946) 32
"The Best Is Yet to Come" 106, 109, 121
"The Best Man" 37
Best of the Music Makers (book) 170
Beverly Hilton 236, 239
"Bewitched" 115
Bewitched (TV) 115
"Bewitched (Bothered and Bewildered)" 179
Bewitching-Lee! 104, 108
The Big Bands Songbook 18
Big Night Out (British TV) 101
The Big Party by Revelon (TV) 88
The Big Sky 74

Big Spender 118, 123
"Big Spender" 118, 123, 126, 132, 144, 154
"Bill" 83
Billboard (magazine) 97
Bing Crosby: Day by Day (book) 245
Bing Crosby General Electric Theatre 61, 63
"Bird in a Gilded Cage" 121
Birmingham Theatre (Michigan) 188
"The Birth of the Blues" 70
Bishop, Joey 174
Black & White (ad) 155
Black Coffee 61–62, 75, 102, 110, 113, 155, 219
"Black Coffee" 102
Blackglama Mink 171
Block, Martin 32
"Blue Hawaii" 47
Blue Room (Fairmont Hotel, New Orleans) 170, 188
Blues Cross Country 1, 98
"Blues Cross Country Suite" 98
"Blues in the Night" 22–23, 24–25, 27, 81
"Bluesette" 126
"Blum, Blum (I Wonder Who I Am)"* 47
"Body and Soul" 228
"Boise, Idaho" 43
"Boomerang"* 226
Booze, Wee Bea 210
Borge, Victor 138
"Boston Beans"* 102
Boston Pops Orchestra 167
"The Boy from Ipanema" 114, 116
Boy George 228
Boyer, Charles 44
Brenner, David 174, 178
Bridge Over Troubled Water 140, 142
"Bridge Over Troubled Water" 141
Broadway Ala Lee 133
Brooks, Jack 14
"Brother Love's Travelling Salvation Show" 134
Brown, Ruth 239
Brunner, Charlotte 15
"Bubble-Loo, Bubble-Loo" 46
Bufman, Zev 193, 197
The Bullfighter and the Lady (film) 60
Burke, Johnny 43, 45
Burke, Sonny 53–54, 66, 214, 229, 234
Burnett, Carol 141, 153, 158–160
Burns, George 211–214
Burrows, Abe 47–48, 88, 91

Burt, Al 229
"Bury Me Not on the Lone Praire" 13
"A Bushel and a Peck" 48
Bushkin, Joe 86
"But Beautiful" 43, 45, 97, 108, 145, 191
The Buttery 178
"By Myself" 97
Byfield, Ernie 16–17

Caesar's Palace (Las Vegas) 158, 178, 211, 213–214
Café Cristal (Diplomat Hotel, Florida) 121, 125, 129, 173, 190
Cagney, James 14
Cahn, Sammy 199, 207, 229
Calhoun, Bob 68
"California" 47
"California Dreamin'" 138
"California Soul" 138
"Call Me" 124
"Call Me Darling, Call Me Sweetheart, Call Me Dear" 97
Campbell, Glen 140–141, 145
"Can You Explain?" 237
Candido, Candy 43
Candoli, Pete 62
"Can't Think Straight" 232
Cantor, Eddie 21
Capitol Reunion Concert 194
Capote, Truman 237
"Caramba, It's the Samba" 46
Carmichael, Hoagy 153
Carnegie Hall (New York) 239
Carney, Art 115
The Carpenters 146
Carroll, Diahann 81, 184
Carson, Johnny 160, 171, 173–174, 176, 178, 182, 184
Carter, Benny 1, 99, 106, 108, 110–111, 207, 241
Casablanca (film) 100
"The Case of M.J." 176
Cash, Johnny 139, 145, 164
Castellucci, Stella 207
"Catalog Day" 45
The Catholic League of Decency 55
CD Review (magazine) 228
Celebrity Art (film) 161
The Chad Mitchell Trio 91
Chamberlain, Richard 158
Champion, Marge and Gower 51
Channing, Carol 81, 88
Charisse, Cyd 239
Charles, Ray 97–98, 111, 130, 134, 142, 159, 198, 202, 234
"Charley, My Boy" 83
"Cheek to Cheek" 45, 81

Index

Chesky Records 235
Chesterfield Presents Bing Crosby 47–49, 58
The Chesterfield Supper Club 40
The Chevy Show 94
"Chi-Baba, Chi-Baba (My Bambino, Go to Sleep)" 37
Chicago Daily News 152
Chicago Sun-Times 171, 217
Chicago Tribune 157, 171, 178, 196, 203–204, 217, 237
Chiodini, John 226–229
Chopin, Frederic 35
A Chorus Line (Broadway musical) 180
Christian Science Monitor (magazine) 138, 175
Christmas Carousel 93
"The Christmas Song" ("Chestnuts Roasting on an Open Fire") 42
"Christmas Time in Harlem" 91
"The Christmas Waltz" 229
Christy, George 26, 202–203
"Circle in the Sky"* 226, 228
Circle Star Theatre (San Carlos, California) 236
Ciro's (Hollywood nightclub) 58, 94
Clair de Lune (book) 158
"Clarinade" 52
Clark, Petula 136, 146
Clayton, Peter 143
Clayton-Thomas, David 135
Click (magazine) 28
Clooney, Rosemary 5, 65, 86, 174, 199, 239
Close Enough for Love 186–187, 217
"Close Enough for Love" 187
"Close Your Eyes" 109–110
"Clouds" 163, 167–168
"Cloudy Morning" 110
Club 53 (Hilton Hotel, New York) 231–232, 234–235
Club Pigalle (London nightclub) 101–102
Coburn, Charles 51
Cocoanut Grove (Los Angeles nightclub) 74, 189
Colbert, Claudette 171
Cole, Nat King 1, 5, 31, 45, 56, 64, 81, 86, 113, 182, 194
Cole, Natalie 239
Cole en Espanol (Nat King Cole LP) 86
Colegate Comedy Hour (TV) 55, 62, 64, 70
Colegate Variety Hour (TV) 71
Coleman, Cy 88, 111, 114, 117, 145, 199, 211, 227

Coles, Charles "Honi" 197
The College Inn 18
Collingwood, Charles 94, 96
Collins, Judy 191
Collins, Lloyd 13, *15*, *50*
"Come Back to Me" 118, 123, 126, 129
"Come in from the Rain" 187
"Come Rain or Come Shine" 70, 102, 105, 109
Como, Perry 5, 32, 64
Complete Directory to Prime-Time Network and Cable TV Shows 36
Concord Jazz Festival 238
Concord Pavilion 238
Connor, Chris
Cooley, Eddie 83
Cooper, Gary 37, 44
Copa Room (Sands Hotel, Las Vegas) 76
Copacabana (New York nightclub) 81, 125, 118–120, 127, 129, 132
Copland, Aaron 187
Cosmopolitan (magazine) 65, 150
Costello, Elvis 228
"Cow-Cow Boogie" 27
Cowan, Irv 193, 197
Coward, Noel 242
Crawford, Joan 60, 63
Crescendo (TV) 81
Crescendo International (UK magazine) 196, 199
Crosby, Bing 5, 25, 33, 35–37, 40, 42–49, *51*, 52, 58, 60, 63–64, 86–87, 101–102, 129–130, *131*, 229, 245
Crosby, Bob 40, 46
Cue (magazine) 135, 138, 144
"Cunta la Gusta" 46
Curtiz, Michael 54–55, 59–60

"Daddy" 19
Daily Express (UK newspaper) 163, 180
Daily Mail (UK newspaper) 225
Daily Mirror (UK newspaper) 189
Daily Telegraph (UK newspaper) 143
Dalai Llama 110
Dallas Times Herald 166
Damone, Vic *105*, 179, 184–*185*, 199
Dankworth, John 239
Darin, Bobby 160–*161*
Davenport, John 83
Davis, Bette 171
Davis, Miles 183

Davis, Sammy, Jr. 130, 142, 159, 184, 217
Day, Dennis 14, 27
Day, Doris 58
"Day In — Day Out" 97, 111
Dayan, Moshe 136
"The Days of Wine and Roses" 108, 110
Dearie, Blossom 194
"Dearie, Do You Remember?" 111
"Dearly Beloved" 45
Debussy, Claude 26, 161
Del Rio, Jack 113–*114*
DeLuise, Dom 229
The Desperate Hours (film) 75
De Sylva, Buddy 30–31
Devine, Andy 69
Devor, Sy 30
Dexter, Brad 57, 60, 63
Dexter, Dave 17, 31, 146, 190
Diamond, Neil 134
"Didn't We" 132
Dietrich, Marlene 38, 46, 150, 171
Diplomat Hotel (Florida) *see* Café Cristal
DISCoveries (magazine) 218
Disney, Walt 58, 62, 65–66, 227, 242, 245
"Do I Hear a Waltz" 129, 131
"Do I Love You?" 85
Doctor of Music (bestowed upon Miss Lee by North Dakota State University) 173
Dodds, Baby 17
The Doll House 14, 16
"Don't Blame Me" 41
"Don't Ever Leave Me" 235, 243
"Don't Explain" 134, 142, 145
"Don't Get Around Much Anymore" 27, 29, 81
"Don't Let Me Be Lonely Tonight" 167
"Don't Smoke in Bed" 46, 102, 134, 244
"A Doodlin' Song" 111
Dooley, Thomas 110
Dorothy Chandler Pavilion (Los Angeles theatre) 183, 190
Dorsey, Jimmy 93
Dorsey, Tommy 23, 53, 93
"Down the Old Ox Road" 47
DownBeat (magazine) 10, 17, 32, *34*, 58, 60–64, 66, 77, 85, 89, 140, 147, 227
Dragonfly Summer (Michael Franks CD) 232, 238
Drama-Logue (magazine) 184, 200, 209

"A Dream Is a Wish Your Heart Makes" 48
Dream Street 3, 76
Dreamgirls (Broadway musical) 197
"Dreams of Summer"* 178–179, 181
DRG Records 186
Drury Lane (Chicago theatre) 178, 203–204
Duchin, Eddie 33
Duke, Doris 115
Duke, Vernon 21
Duncan, Sandy 173, 184
Dunnock, Mildred 55
Durante, Jimmy 35, 37, 39–40, 42–46, 97, 98

East of Eden (film) 74
"Easter Parade" 44, 47
Easter Seals 184
"Easy Does It"* 187
"Easy Living" 61
Ebb, Fred 199
Eckstine, Billy 159, 194
Edwards, Ralph 159
Egstrom, Clair (brother) 6, 159
Egstrom, Della (sister) 6
Egstrom, Jean (sister) 6
Egstrom, Leonard (brother) 6
Egstrom, Marianne (sister) 6, 30
Egstrom, Marvin Olaf (father) 6
Egstrom, Milford (brother) 6, 49
Egstrom, Selma Emele Anderson (mother) 5
Eisenhower, Mamie 66
"El Toro" (My Matador)"* 88
The Electric Hour 40
Eliot, T.S. 216
Ella Lifetime Achievement Award 208, 239
Ella Sings Gershwin (Ella Fitzgerald LP) 61
Ellington, Duke 10, 20–22, 86, 89, 93, 115, 142, 159, 161, 170, 188, 223, 225
Elman, Ziggy 46
"Elmer's Tune" 18–19, 152
Elmwood Casino (Windsor, Ontario, Canada) 154
"Embrasse Moi"* 106
Emerson, Ralph Waldo 93, 199
Empire Room (Waldorf-Astoria, New York) 135, 160, 146, 174, 179
"An Empty Glass" 123, 125, 132
Engstead, John 99, 104, 151
Esquire (magazine) 130
Essex Hotel (New York) 230

Evans, Gil 183
Evans, Ray 37
"Every Day People" 134
"Every Night" 78
Everybody Comes to Rick's [aka *Everyone Comes to Peggy's*] (TV) 62–63
"Everybody Needs a Santa Claus"* 229
"Everything Must Change" 178, 186, 191
"Everything's Movin' Too Fast"* 36, 37
Evita (Broadway musical) 199
"Ev'rything I Love" 21–22, 24
"Exactly Like You" 46, 63, 126

Faith, Percy 93
Faithful, Marianne 217
Falzarano, Gino 218
Family Weekly 136
"Faraway Places" 47
Father Goose (film) 115
Feather, Jane (nee Jane Leslie Larrabee) 14–*15*, 17–18, *28*, 205
Feather, Leonard 14, 61–62, 101, 130, 132, 140, 158, 183, 189, 191–192, 200, 209, 212, 231, 236, 240
Feller, Sid 117
Ferrer, Mel 60
Festival Hall (UK Theatre) 199
"Fever" 81–84, 97, 104, 109, 115–116, 126, 144, 154, 171, 178, 182, 191, 203, 210, 222, 234–235, 237, 239, 244
"Fever"* (1990) 226, 229
Fibber McGee and Molly (radio) 40
Fiedler, Arthur 167–*168*
Fields, Dorothy 22, 25, 41, 211, 234
Fine, Donald I. 218, 221
"A Fine Romance" 45
"Fire and Rain" 153–154, 160
Firestone, Russ 19
Fischer, Muriel 59
Fisher, Eddie 64, 82, 197
The Fitch Bandwagon (radio) 20
Fitzgerald, Ella 1, 5, 61, 71 72, 84–85, 88, 93, 106, 108, 115, 130, 148, 169, 187–188, 191, 203, 227, 229, 239
Flack, Roberta 142, 159
Flamingo Hotel, Las Vegas 174
The Flattering World (TV one-act play) 74
The Fleet's In (film) 21
"Fly Me to the Moon" 115; *see also* "In Other Words"
"Flying Through the Sky" 236

FM Guide (magazine) 117, 220, 134
"The Folks Who Live On the Hill" 78, 101, 181–182, 184, 201, 235, 240, 244
Fonda, Henry 161, 187
Fonda, Jane 114
"For Every Man There's a Woman" 43
"For Just the Chance to Love You" 49
"For Sentimental Reasons" 37
"For the Good Times" 145, 147
"For You" 126
Ford, Mary 52
Ford, Tennessee Ernie 77, *79*
Fordin, Hugh 186
Forrest, Helen 17–18, 239
The Four Freshmen 194
Franchi, Sergio 127
Franklin, Aretha 130, 134, 136, 159, 163, 167
Franklin, Nancy 243
Franks, Michael 232, 235, 238
"Free Spirits" 118
Friedwald, Will 18, 240
Frontier Hotel (Las Vegas) 130, 147
Frost, David 145
"Full Moon (Noche De Luna)" 25
"Funny Man" 121

Gabin, Jean 54
Gabler, Milt 54
Garden State Arts Center (Holmdel, New Jersey) 191
Garland, Judy 5, 109, 113, 164–165, 171, 194
Garner, Erroll 186
Garson, Greer 44
Gastel, Carlos 32, 44
Gates, David 143, 163
"Gee, Baby, Ain't I Good to You" 75
General Electric Theatre 89–90
"The Gentleman Is a Dope" 42
"Georgia on My Mind" 91
Gershwin, George 21, 61, 234
Gershwin, Ira 21, 61, 234
"Get Out of Town" 86
Giant (film) 75
Giddins, Gary 1, 169, 233–234
Gielgud, John 88
The Gift of Music (TV) 191
Gillespie, Dizzy 148–*149*
The Girl from U.N.C.L.E. 126
"Girl Talk" 158
Gish, Lillian 194
"Glad to Be Unhappy" 179
The Gladstone Hotel 6, 10, 202
Gleason, Jackie 78

Gleason, Ralph J. 64
Glenn, Tyree *149*
"The Glory of Love" 85
Gobel, George 83, 93, 108
"Goin' to Chicago Blues" 98, 111
"Golden Earrings" 37–38, 42–43, 46
"Golden Wedding Ring" 74
Golson, Benny 143, 196, 236
"Good-Bye" 52, 144, 146
"Good Mornin'" 124
Good Morning America (TV) 179
"Good Morning Heartache" 61
Goodman, Benny 17–23, 25–*29*, 31–32, 35, 52, 73, 81, 84–85, 88–89, 93, 117, 136, 144, 152, 157, 170, 191, 194–196, 205–206, 227, 231–233, 238, 241, 244, 246
Goodman, Mrs. Benny 178
Goodman, Ekert 62
Goodman, Freddie 23
"Got That Magic"* 112
Graham, Martha 187
Grammy Awards 140–141
Grant, Cary 115, 123, 153, 158, 223
Grant, Earl 91
Grant, Lee 158
The Great American Popular Singers (book) 78, 164
"Great Day" 153
Greco, Buddy 246
Green, Lil 26, 191, 210, 222, 234
Greene, Shecky 184
"Greensleeves" 126
Griffin, Merv 133, 148, 174, 200
Gruber, Steve 228
Grusin, Dave 167
Guardian (UK newspaper) 143
Guideposts (magazine) 224
Guitars Ala Lee 86, 123, 125
Gunsmoke (radio) 40
"A Guy Is a Guy" 53
Guys and Dolls (Broadway musical) 48
Gypsy (Broadway musical) 191
"Gypsy in My Soul" 91

Hackett, Bobby 148–*149*
Hackett, Buddy 123
Haines, Doc 10
Haley, Jack, Jr. 166
"Hallelujah, I Love Him So" 86, 104, 130
Hamilton, Arthur 187, 214
Hamlisch, Marvin 187
Hammerstein, Oscar 78, 243
Hammond, John 18
Hampton, Lionel 84

"Hand on the Plow" 130
"Happiness Is a Thing Called Joe" 37
"Happy Feet"* 123
"Happy, Happy Days" 47
Happy Holidays 117
"Happy Holidays" 117
"Happy New Year" 153
"Happy with the Blues"* 105, 237–238
Happy with the Blues (TV) 102, 105
Harbach, Otto 213
"A Hard Day's Night" 115
Harrison, George 134, 145, 147, 154
Harrison, Noel 126
Harrison, Rex 81
Hart, Lorenz 22, 53, 58–59, 81, 179, 182, 184, 246
"Have a Good Time" 178
"Have Yourself a Merry Little Christmas" 163
Hayes, Peter Lind 56
Hayloft Jamboree 10
Hayworth, Rita 142, 171
Hazard, Dick 184, 187
"He Is the One" 167
"He Needs Me" 68, 214
"Heart" 74, 97, 200
"The Heart Is a Lonely Hunter"* 167
Heatherton, Joey 126
Hefner, Hugh 239
Hefti, Neal 101, 207
"Help Me Make It Through the Night" 147, 151, 201
Henry, Buck 174
"Here Comes Santa Claus" 48
"Here's That Rainy Day" 87–88, 100, 125
"Here's to Life" 212–213
"Here's to You"* 129, 181, 239
Herman, Woody 40
"He's a Tramp"* 65–66, 226
"He's Got the Whole World in His Hands" 145
"He's Just My Kind" 36
"He's My Guy" 81
"Hey, Look Me Over" 101–102
Hi-Fi/Stereo Review (magazine) 125
High Fidelity Magazine 123, 132, 134
Hildebrand, Lee 237–238
Hines, Earl "Fatha" 10, 148–*149*
Hinton, Milt 148–*149*
Hirt, Al 124
"Hit the Road Jack" 234
The Hits of Peggy Lee 133
Hodges, Johnny 143
Hoefer, George 85

"Hold On" 91
Holiday, Billie 5, 14, 97, 98, 102, 134, 152, 164, 169, 191, 205, 215, 233, 237, 243
Holiday Inn (film) 25
Holliday, Jennifer 220
Holly, Hal 58
Hollywood Bowl (Los Angeles) 231, 240
Hollywood Palace (TV) 129, 131
Hollywood Palladium 188
Hollywood Reporter 230–231
Holmes, Dr. Ernest 38–39, 57, 186, 203, 213, 233
Hope, Bob 33, 40, 42, 46, 197, 239
Hope, Deloris 239
Horne, Lena 5, 62, 130, 179, 184–*185*, 188, 227
Horner, Paul 192, 200
"Hound Dog" 109
Hour Glass (TV) 36
"How Deep Is the Ocean" 19–20
"How Do You Do with Me?" 24
"How Do You Erase a Memory"* 87–88
"How Insensitive" 112–113
"How It Lies, How It Lies, How It Lies" 47–48
"How Long Has This Been Going On" 21–22, 24, 118
"How Lucky You Are" 43
"How Strange" 60
Howard, Bart 88
Humes, Helen 31
"The Hungry Years" 180
Hunter, Tab *72*
Hussey, Ruth 51
Hutton, Betty 194

"I Ain't Mad at You" 56
"I Believe in Music" 159
"I Believe in You" 106
"I Can't Give You Anything but Love, Baby" 42, 117, 148, 163
"I Can't Stop Loving You" 126
"I Close My Eyes" 37
"I Could Write a Book" 191
"I Couldn't Sleep a Wink Last Night" 124
"I Don't Believe in Rumors" 29
"I Don't Know Enough About You"* 32–33, 36, 40, 45, 75, 97, 159–160, 235
"I Don't Know How to Love Him" 147
"I Don't Wanna Leave You Now"* 106
"I Don't Want to Play in Your Yard" 181
"I Don't Want to Set the World on Fire" 20

Index

"I Feel It" 126–127
"I Feel the Earth Move (Under My Feet)" 154
"I Get Along Without You Very Well" 87–88, 100
"I Get Ideas (When I Dance with You)" 49
"I Go to Rio" 180
"I Go to Sleep" 117
"I Got It Bad (And That Ain't Good)" 20–21, 152, 190, 201
"I Got Lost in His Arms" 112
"I Got Lucky in the Rain" 46–47
"I Got Rhythm" 43, 46, 63, 139
"I Had a Love Once" 237
"I Had the Craziest Dream" 27
"I Hear Music" 81
"I Hear the Music Now" 55
"I Just Want to Dance All Night"* 226–228
"I Left My Heart in San Francisco" 109
I Like Men! 82–83
"I Like Men"* 93, 113
"I Lost My Sugar in Salt Lake City" 27
"I Love a Piano" 29
"I Love Being Here with You"* 94, 97, 101–102, 118, 141, 154, 190–191, 201, 243
"I Love You" 182
"I Love You (Just One Way to Say)" 115
"(I Love Your) Gypsy Heart" 100
"I May Be Wrong" 45
"I Never Left Your Arms" 97
"I See a Million People (But All I Can See Is You)" 19–20
"I See You" (final recording) 241
"I Talk to the Trees" 163
"I Think It's Going to Rain Today" 134
"I Threw a Kiss in the Ocean" 25
"(I Want to Go Where You Go) Then I'll Be Happy" 46–47, 126
"I Was Born in Love with You" 147
"I Went Down to Virginia" 45
"I Won't Dance" 213
"If" 148, 152
"If I Could Be with You One Hour Tonight" 52
"If I Could Swing with a Band" 8
"If You Build a Better Mousetrap" 24
If You Go 1, 100, 104

"If You Go" 77, 100
"I'll Be Seeing You" 155, 163, 167, 179, 186, 209, 230
"I'll Dance at Your Wedding" 42
"I'll Get By" 106, 163
"I'll Give It All to You" 226
"I'll Never Smile Again" 53
"I'll Only Miss Him When I Think of Him" 118
"(I'll Take) Manhattan" 109
I'm a Woman 109–110
"I'm a Woman" 109, 111–112, 134, 145–146, 171, 173, 190–191, 240
"(I'm Afraid) The Masquerade Is Over" 117
"I'm Glad I Waited for You" 33
"I'm Glad There Is You" 145
"I'm Gonna Go Fishin'"* 97, 159–160
"I'm Just Wild About Harry" 83, 85
"I'm Sweet, Shy Ophelia" 47
"I'm Walkin'" 109
"I'm-a Comin' Courtin' Corabelle" 43
In Love Again! 112–113
"In Love Again (I'm)"* 112, 235
"In Other Words (Fly Me to the Moon)" 88, 94, 102, 201
"In the Days of Our Love" 187
"In the Name of Love" 114
In the Name of Love 114
In the Wee Small Hours (Frank Sinatra LP) 61
In Touch (magazine) 171
Inner View (magazine) 177
"Is It True What They Say About Dixie?" 163
Is That All There Is? 134–135, 139
"Is That All There Is?" 133–136, 139–142, 146–147, 154, 166, 173, 175, 182, 192, 200, 202, 206, 211, 216, 222, 231
"Isn't This a Lovely Day" 45
"It Ain't Necessarily So" 75
"It Amazes Me" 111
"It Means That We Are" 47
"It Might as Well Be Spring" 109
"It Must Be So"* 64–65
"It Never Entered My Mind" 179
"It Never Happened to Me" 52
"It Still Suits Me" 37
"It Takes a Long, Long Train with a Red Caboose (To Carry My Blues Away)" 37, 40

"It's a Good Day"* 30, 36–37, 40–42, 45, 97, 113, 118, 121, 141, 160, 243
"It's a Good, Good Night"* 82
"It's a Grand Night for Singing" 118, 121
"It's a Lovely Day Today" 121
"It's a Wonderful World" 118, 159
"It's About Time I Wrote the Folks in Terre Haute" 43
"It's All Over Now" 36
"It's All Right with Me" 87, 91
"It's Been a Long, Long Time" 82
"It's Lovin' Time" 36
"It's More Fun Than a Picnic" 48
"It's So Peaceful in the Country" 20, 91
"It's the Sentimental Thing to Do" 45
"I've Got a Crush on You" 43, 48, 63, 167–168
"I've Got the Right to Sing the Blues" 48, 70
"I've Got You Under My Skin" 121
"I've Got Your Number" 112
"I've Grown Accustomed to His Face" 87–88
Ives, Burl 37

Jackson, Mahalia 81, 164
The Jade (Hollywood nightclub) 13
James, Harry 18, 188
Jasper's in a Jam (film) 41
Jazz Ball (video) 42
Jazz Journal (UK magazine) 102
Jazz Portraits — The Lives and Music of the Jazz Masters (book) 9
The Jazz Singer (film) 54, 55–57, 58, 59–60
Jazz Times (magazine) 215, 220
"Jeepers Creepers" 91
Jenkins, Gordon 54
"Jim" 83
Jimmy Durante — I Say It with Music (CD) 43
Jobim, Antonio Carlos 115
Joel, Billy 182–184, 186
"Joey, Joey, Joey" 75
John, Little Willie 83, 234
"Johnny (Linda)" 134
"Johnny Guitar"* 60, 63, 178, 215, 226
Johnny Guitar (film) 63
Johnson, Budd 148–*149*
Johnson, Pete 31
Johnson, Van 44, *128*

Jones, Jack 117, *124*, 207
Jones, Max 182
Jones, Quincy 1, 98, 102, 123–124, 159, 184
Joy House (film) 114
The Judds 223
Jump for Joy 1, 81–82
Jurgens, Dick 19
"Just an Old Love of Mine" 36–37
"Just Call Me Love Bird"* 114
"Just for a Thrill" 97, 155, 171, 234
"Just for Tonight" 180
"Just Friends" 160
"Just in Time" 81, 154, 163
"Just Keep Holdin' On" 210–211
"Just One More Chance" 53
"Just One of Those Things" 55, 58, 187
"Just Squeeze Me" 94
"Just the Blues" 22
"Just the Way You Are" 49
"Just the Way You Are" (B. Joel) 182, 184, 186
"Just You, Just Me" 126
JVC Jazz Festival 239

Kahn, Chaka 239
"Kamehameha Day" 45
Kander, John 199
"Kansas City" 98, 111, 184, 220
Kaye, Danny 37, 64, 125
Kaye, Stubby 81
Kazan, Lainie 207
Keagle Street (UK musical) 210
Kelly, Gene 184, 194
Kelly, George 74
Kennedy, John F. 106–107
Kennedy, Ken 10, 13–14, 159, 203
Kennedy Arts Center (Washington, D.C.) 150, 187, 194–195
Kenton, Stan 71
Kern, Jerome 25, 234, 243
Kilgallen, Dorothy 88
King, Alan 158–159
King, B.B. 142, 163
King, Carole 154
King, Larry 150
Kirsten, Dorothy 51
Kitt, Eartha 197
Klugman, Jack 184
Kokakura, Utakaka 178
Koransky, Jason 3
Korman, Harvey 158
Kossoff, David 101
KOVC (radio) 10
Kraft Music Hall 33, 139, 144
Kristofferson, Kris 126, 147
KRMC (radio) 6
Kuralt, Charles 148–*149*

L.A. Gay and Lesbian Community Service Center 210
"La La Lu"* 66
LaBelle, Patti 220
The Lady and the Tramp (film) 65–67, 70, 214, 219, 224, 229–230, 234, 242
"The Lady from 29 Palms" 40
"The Lady Is a Tramp" 53, 55
"The Lady Who Didn't Believe in Love" 26
Laine, Cleo 180, 239, 246
Laine, Frankie 246
Lake Geneva Playboy Club 157
"The Lamp of Memory" 24–25
LaMure, Pierre 159
Lanchester, Elsa 74
The Land of the Pharaohs (film) 74
Landis, Carole 26
Lane, Burton 199, 227
lang, k.d. 225, 228, 239
"Language of Love" 115
"Laroo, Laroo, Lili Bolero" 44–45
LaRosa, Julius 81
Larrabee, Jane Leslie (see Jane Feather)
Las Vegas (film) 57
"Last Night When We Were Young" 76
Latin Ala Lee! 86, 88, 91, 94, 133, 169
Latin Casino (New Jersey nightclub) 110, 148
Laughing Song 39–40
Laurel Award 75
Lawford, Peter 101
Lawrence, Steve 109
Leadbelly 238
"Lean on Me"* 136
"Leaving on a Jet Plane" 145
Lee, Peggy (photo index) *5, 9, 11, 12, 15, 27, 28, 29, 30, 33–34, 41, 43, 49–51, 55–57, 67–72, 78, 79, 80, 87, 90, 92, 95–96, 99–100, 102–103, 107, 114, 119–122, 124, 131, 137–139, 141, 145, 149, 151- 152, 161, 168–169, 172, 187, 195, 208*
Lees, Gene 8, 115, 132, 214
Legrand, Michel 118, 147
Lehar, Franz 59
Leiber, Jerry 109, 133, 136, 173–174, 190, 200, 207, 216, 240
Leigh, Carolyn 88, 111, 211
Lemmon, Jack 74
Lennon, John 126, 134
"Let It All Begin" 186
"Let Me Go, Lover" 64
"Let Me Love You" 115

"Let's Do It (Let's Fall in Love)" 20–21, 191
Let's Face It (Broadway show) 21
"Let's Get Lost in Now" 143, 146
"Let's Keep Dancin'" 192
Let's Love 167, 171
"Let's Say a Prayer" 27
The Letters of the Scattered Brotherhood (book) 203
Levant, Oscar 43, 46
Levy, Lou 75–76, 106, 114, 147, 207
Lewis, Jerry 174
Lewis, Shari 117
Lewisham Festival of Jazz 203
Life (magazine) 44, 150
The Life and Teachings of the Masters of the Far East (book) 233
"Life Is Just a Bowl of Cherries" 53
"Life Is So Peculiar" 52
"Light of Love" 84
Lights Out (radio) 40
"Like Someone in Love" 109
Lillie, Beatrice 36
Lincoln Center (New York theatre) 197
"Linger in My Arms a Little Longer, Baby" 36
Lins, Ivan 210
"Listen to the Rockin' Bird" 78, 81
Little, Rich 176
"A Little Bird Told Me" 46
"The Little Drummer Boy" 117
The Little Foxes (Broadway drama) 193
"Little Jack Frost, Get Lost" 48
"Little Old Car"* 74
The Lively Ones 108
Livingston, Jay 37
London, Julie 192
London Palladium 180, 189
London Times (UK newspaper) 143, 180, 200, 219
"Lone Star Moon" 42
"Lonesome Road" 126–127
"Long Ago and Far Away" 70, 160
"The Long and Winding Road" 143
Look (magazine) 67, 150
Loomis, Terry 89
"The Lord's Prayer" 148, 218
Lorre, Peter 14
Los Angeles (magazine) 197
Los Angeles Daily News 230
"Los Angeles Forevermore"* 184

Los Angeles Herald Examiner 200
Los Angeles Times 69, 117, 137, 158, 175, 182, 190–191, 200, 207, 209, 212, 229, 231, 239–240
"Losing My Mind" 147
"Lost in the Stars" 145
"A Lot of Living to Do" 112
"Louisa from Lake Louise" 48
"Love Dance" 210–211
"Love for Sale" 179, 186
Love Held Lightly (Rare Songs by Harold Arlen) 218, 236–237
"Love Is Just Around the Corner" 159
Love Me Tonight (film) 53
"Love Story" 134, 145
"Love, You Didn't Do Right By Me" 64–65
"Love, Your Spell Is Everywhere" 46
"Lover" 53–55, 57–59, 64, 94, 97, 109, 115, 126, 180–181, 246
Lowe, Mundell 136
"Lullaby in Rhythm" 82
"Lullaby of Broadway" 81
Lund, Art (aka Art London) 21, 23
Lupino, Ida 159
Lyons, Len 9

Macao (film) 57
Macfarlane, Malcolm (Editor, BING magazine) 245
"Mack the Knife" 109, 111, 181
MacLeod, Gavin 89–90
MacRae, Carmen 135, 194
MacRae, Gordon 70, 194
MacRae, Sheila 158
Madison Square Garden 107, 199
Madonna 234–235
Make It with You 143–144, 146, 196
"Make It with You" 159
"Make Someone Happy" 159
"Make the Man Love Me" 52, 105
"Makin' Records" 81
"Makin' Whoopee" 81, 126
Maltin, Leonard 214
A Man and a Woman (TV) 145
The Man I Love 1, 77, 78, 80–81, 100, 181, 215, 242
"The Man I Love" 13, 21, 26, 78, 102
"Manana (Is Soon Enough for Me)"* 35, 39, 42–45, 48, 76, 93, 97, 109, 118, 126, 141, 154, 159–160, 235

Manchester, Melissa 167, 169, 173, 187–188
Mancini, Henry 167, 207
Mandate (magazine) 174–175, 198
Mandel, Freddie and Lois 16
Mandel, Johnny 122, 145, 176, 234
"Mandy Is Two" 25
The Manhattan Transfer 192, 239
Manilow, Barry 188
Mann, Thomas 142
Mansfield, Jayne 71
March, Fredric 74
March, Hal 13
"Marie" 53
Marine's Memorial Theatre (San Francisco) 211
Mark Taper Forum 137
Marshall, Jack 82–83
Martin, Dean 5, 117–118, *121*, 123, 126–129, *128*, 139, 141, 147
Martin, Dewey 74–*75*
Martin, Dick 123, 158
Martin, Tony 76, 239
Marx, Groucho 48, 51
Matinee at the Meadowbrook 20
Matthau, Walter 158
"Maxwell's Silver Hammer" 140
May, Billy 1, 88, 207
"Maybe It's Because (I Love You Too Much)" 47, 115
"Maybe You'll Be There" 46
Mayfield, Percy 134
McCall's (magazine) 82
McCartney, Paul 126, 140, 143, 167, 169
McGarrity, Lou 23
McHugh, Jimmy 22, 41
McKay, Hats 39
McPartland, Marian 187, 239
"Me and My Shadow" 134, 145
Meals for Millions 100–101, 110, 137
Melody Maker (UK magazine) 72, 83, 93, 98, 101, 106, 132, 158, 181–182
"Melody of Love" 8
Melville, Lee 184, 209
Melvoin, Mike 134, 136
The Men in My Life (Lena Horne LP) 222
Mercer, Johnny 21–22, 24, 30–32, 113, 174, 180, 203, 207, 237
Mercer, Mabel 183, 217, 238
Merman, Ethel 164–165
Metronome (magazine) 29, 32
Midnight Serenade (film) 41–42
Miles, Lizzie 222
Mill Run Playhouse (Chicago theatre) 152, 188

Milland, Ray 46
Miller, Eddie 31
Miller, Glenn 19, 93
The Mills Brothers 32, 46, 64–*65*, 178
Milwaukee Sentinel 161
Mink Jazz 1, 105, 110–111, 241
Minnelli, Liza 234
Miranda, Carmen 39
Mirrors 173–178
Miss Peggy Lee (Harmony label) 152
Miss Peggy Lee (Lee's autobiography) 6, 221, 225
Miss Peggy Lee Sings the Blues 217, 218–221, 222, 225
Miss Wonderful 75
"Mr. Five by Five" 27
Mr. Music (film) 51–52
"Mr. Wonderful" 74, 181, 191, 207
"Misty" 186
"Mohair Sam" 123
Moments Like This 235
"Moments Like This" 88, 97, 102, 121
Monroe, Marilyn 89, 106–107
Montalbon, Ricardo 174, 178
"Mood Indigo" 223
"The Moon Came Up with a Great Idea Last Night" 58
"Moon River" 108
"Moonglow" 10
Moore, Peter 180–182
Moore, Victor 43
"The More I See You" 126–127, 167–168, 184
"More Than You Know" 21
Morrison, Richard 11–12
Morse, Ella Mae 31, 194
"The Most Beautiful Man in the World" 97
Moulin Rouge (book) 159
Moulin Rouge (Fairmont Hotel, Chicago) 217
Moulin Rouge (Hollywood nightclub) 84
"Mountain Greenery" 109
Murphy, George 26
Murphy, Mark 246
Music '55 (TV) 71
Music Week (magazine) 189
Musto, Michael 224
"My Blue Heaven" 115
"My Father" 191
"My Funny Valentine" 192
"My Heart Stood Still" 81
"My Little Cousin" 24–25
"My Man (Mon Homme)" 83–84, 104
"My Old Flame" 19–20, 76, 152
"My Rock and Foundation" 147

Index

"My Romance" 98
"My Silent Love" 110
"My Song" 53
"My Sweet Lord" 147, 154

N.E.T.'s the World of Peggy Lee 137–138
Namath, Joe 125
National Ballet of Canada 218
National Educational Television 110
National Geographic (TV) 223
A Natural Woman 134–135
"Natural Woman (You Make Me Feel Like a)" 134, 136
"Nature Boy" 45
"Netty Co-ed" 63
New York-American Journal 89, 91
"New York City Blues"* 98–99, 106
New York Daily News 93, 108, 133, 135, 139, 141, 153, 160, 203, 216, 221, 226, 231–233
New York Film Critics Award 74
New York Mirror 83, 106, 148
New York Newsday 204, 215, 225, 240
New York Observer 222
New York Post 59, 111, 115, 136, 154, 169, 209, 216, 218, 220, 225, 231–232, 240
New York Times 70, 73, 97, 104, 114, 139, 141, 145, 147, 151, 158, 179, 186, 191, 193, 198, 201, 210, 215, 217, 221, 227, 232, 239
New York Times Book Review 214, 222, 225
New York World Telegram 59, 73, 81
The New Yorker (magazine) 97, 136, 153, 167, 204, 243
Newman, Randy 126, 132, 134, 136, 145
The News (Dallas newspaper) 203
Newsweek (magazine) 91, 116–117, 161
"Nice N' Easy" 109, 123–125
Nichols, Red 46
"A Nightingale Can Sing the Blues" 37
"Nine Thorny Thickets" 244
Niven, David 173
"Non Dimenticar" 98
Norma Deloris Egstrom from Jamestown, North Dakota 154–155, 157, 160, 163
Norris, Bobbe 246
North Dakota Sun 235

North West Airlines (in-flight magazine) 212
"Not a Care in the World" 21, 152
"Not Mine" 21, 25
Nova (TV) 223
Novak, Kim 161
Novarro, Ramon 176
The Nugget (Reno, Nevada) 121

O'Brien, Edmond 68
The Observer (UK newspaper) O'Connor, Carroll 160, 173
O'Day, Anita 169
"Oh, Johnny, Oh, Johnny, Oh" 83
O'Keefe Center (Toronto, Canada) 164
"Okay, Denmark, Okay" 48
"Ol' Rockin' Chair" 91
"Old Buttermilk Sky" 14
"Old Devil Moon" 81
"Old Man Mose" 41
"Ole"* 93
Ole Ala Lee! 86, 93, 133
Oliver! (Broadway musical) 159
Olson, Sev 14
"On a Slow Boat to China" 46
"On a Wonderful Day Like Today" 121
"On the Sunny Side of the Street" 21–22, 40, 73
"Once and for Always" 47
"One Beating a Day" 6, 198
"One for You and One for Me"* 81
"One Kiss" 98
"One More Ride On the Merry-Go-Round" 145, 147
Only the Lonely (Frank Sinatra LP) 61
"Orange Colored Sky" 48
Ormandy, Eugene 194
Osbourne, Will 14
O'Sullivan, Gilbert 232, 235
"Our Love Is Here to Stay" 186, 234–235
"Over the Wheel"* 226, 228
Owen Marshall, Counselor at Law (TV) 153
Owens, Garry 239

Paar, Jack 116
Pacino, Al 234
Pal, George 41
Palace Theatre 199
Palame, Emil (Emilio) 226, 228
Palitz, Morty 54
Palmer House (Chicago hotel) 146
Palmer House (Chicago nightclub) 162, 171

Pan, Hermes 142
"Pancho Maximillian Hernandez" 40
Paris (Cole Porter musical) 20
Pasadena Playhouse (theatre) 212
Pass Me By 115, 117
"Pass Me By" 115–116
"Passenger of the Rain (Le Passager De La Pluie)"* 144
Paul, Les 37, 52, 54
Paul Whiteman — A Tribute 91
Pavarotti, Luciano 197
"Peace on Earth"* 66
Peg (Broadway musical) 6, 40, 192–194, 196–202, 204, 222
Peggy 180, 182
Peggy E. Lee (boat) 109–110
Peggy Lee & Benny Goodman — The Complete Recordings 19–20, 25, 27
Peggy Lee — Black Coffee & Other Delights — The Decca Anthology 5
Peggy Lee — Capitol Collecters Series 32
Peggy Lee Entertains (UK TV) 191
Peggy Lee — Live in London 180–181
Peggy Lee — Peggy at Basin Street East 97
The Peggy Lee Rose 196
The Peggy Lee Songbook — There'll Be Another Spring 225–226, 228–229
Peggy Lee — Songs for Singers (music portfolio) 125
Peggy Lee's Fiftieth Anniversary in Show Business 215
Peggy Lee's Final Recording 241
People (magazine) 166, 186, 198, 219, 230
Perlo, Don 9
Person to Person (TV) 94–96
Pete Kelly's Blues (film) 67, 69–73, 153, 155, 181, 214, 233
Petula (TV) 146
The Philadelphia Inquirer 210, 214
Philco Radio Time 36–37, 43–47
Pied Piper (ASCAP award) 208, 227
The Pied Pipers 194
Pierce, Nat 190
Pisano, John 124–125, 190
Playback (book) 17, 31, 146
Playboy (magazine) 144
Pleasants, Henry 78, 152, 164–165
"Please Send Me Someone to Love" 134

Pleshette, Suzanne 182
Porter, Cole 20–21, 55, 85, 121, 187, 234
Powell, Mel 18–19, 23–24, 192, 206
Powers, Stefanie 126
The Powers Girl (film) 26–27
Powers Hotel and Coffee Shop 13, 50
"Praise the Lord and Pass the Ammunition" 27
President's Award (Songwriter's Guild of America) 209
Presley, Elvis 109, 164
Preston, Robert 57
Pretty Eyes 1, 88
Previn, Andre 84
Price, Vincent 158
Prima, Louis 1
Princess Grace of Monaco 101
"Professor Hauptmann's Performing Dogs" 176
Proust, Marcel 244
Provine, Dorothy 123
Prowitt, David 137
Pulse (magazine) 227–228, 240
Punch (UK newspaper) 101, 163
"Put the Blame on Mame" 124

"Quiet Nights (Corcavado)" 115
Quinn, Anthony 144–145
The Quintessential Peggy Lee 201
QW (magazine) 234

Racquet Club (Sheraton-Hyannis Hotel) 148
Radio City Music Hall (New York theatre) 186, 217
"Rain Sometimes" 187
Rainbow's End: The Judy Garland Show (book) 113
"Raindrops Keep Falling on My Head" 140–141, 144, 147
Rainey, Ma 221–222
Ralston, Matthew 202
Randall, Tony 197
Rare Songs by Harold Arlen see *Love Held Lightly*
Rasmussen, Gladys 11–12
Ravel, Maurice 26
Rawls, Lou 130
Ray, Johnnie 78
Raymond Theatre (Pasadena, California) 230
"Razor (Love Me as I Am)" 155
Reagan, Ronald 89–90
Record Whirl (magazine) 72
Record World (magazine) 175
Redbook (magazine) 66
Redding, Otis 134
Reddy, Helen 167

Reed, Rex 126, 129, 164, 179, 192, 222
Reese, Della 140–*141*, 173, 185
Reilly, Peter 125, 154, 163, 177, 187, 192
Reiner, Carl 158
"Remember Me" 144
"Remind Me" 234–235
Renzi, Mike 204, 234
Resorts International Casino Hotel (Atlantic City) 201
Revlon Presents: Night Clubs, New York 91
Revlon Presents: 76 Men and Peggy Lee 91
The Revlon Review (TV) 89
Reynolds, Burt 192
"The Rhythm of Life" 158
Rich, Buddy *149*, 188
Rickles, Don 184
Riddle, Nelson 1, 77–78, 81, 194, 223, 242
Rider on the Rain (film) 144
"Riders in the Sky (A Cowboy Legend)" 47
"Ridin' High" 74
Righteous Brothers 118
Ritz-Carlton (Washington, D.C.) 213
"River, River" 59
Rivers, Joan 158, 174, 201, 210
Riviera Hotel (Las Vegas) 111, 113
The Road to Rio (film) 42–43, 45
Robinson, Jessie Mae 60
Robison, Willard 85
"Rock-a-bye Your Baby with a Dixie Melody" 63
Rodgers, Richard 22, 53, 58–59, 78, 81, 109, 179, 182, 184, 246
Rogers, Ginger 25
Rogers St. Johns, Adela 113, 213, 218
Rolling Stone (magazine) 224
Romanza 154
Ronstadt, Linda 216, 223
Roostertail (Detroit nightclub) 127
Ross, Diana 181
"Row, Row, Row" 163
Rowan, Dan 123
Rowels, Jimmy 62
Royal Albert Hall (UK) 142
Royal Box (New York nightclub) 114
Royal York Theatre (Toronto) 209
Rucker, Laura 17, 191
Russell, Andy 194
Russell, Leon 158, 173
The Russians Are Coming, the

Russians Are Coming (film) 122

"S'Wonderful" 43, 194, 201, 232, 234–235, 239
Sade 216, 223
Sager, Carol Bayer 183, 187–188
St. Johns, Elaine 213
"St. Louis Blues" 98, 111
St. Louis Post-Dispatch 160
"St. Louis Woman" 77, 79
St. Vincent Millay, Edna 166
Salk, Jonas 136
San Diego Union 188
The San Francisco Chronicle 64, 109, 176, 179, 182, 202, 211, 214, 237
The San Francisco Examiner 188, 190, 202, 214, 223, 236, 238
San Francisco Sentinel 223
San Francisco Symphony 185
Sandberg, Carl 154
Sanders, Felicia 91
"Sans Souci"* 226
Sarandon, Susan 174
Saturday Evening Post (magazine) 115
Sauter, Eddie 19–20
Savory, Bill 19
Sawyer, Bill 10
Scaggs, Boz 186
Schaefer Festival (Wollman Rink, Central Park, NYC) 144, 148, 157
Schifrin, Lalo 114
Schurr, Diane 220
Schweitzer, Albert 95, 101
Science of Mind (book) 233
Science of Mind (church) 186
Science of Mind Institute 38
Science of Mind Magazine 38–39, 213
Sea Shells 61, 74, 207, 244
Seattle World's Fair 106
Second Annual People's Choice Command Performance (TV) 182
"The Second Time Around" 132
"The Secretary Song" 43
Sedaka, Neil 180
See America with Ed Sullivan (TV) 94
"See See Rider" 106, 221, 230, 238
Selections from White Christmas 64
"Send a Little Love My Way" 176
"Send in the Clowns" 184
The Sentinel (San Francisco newspaper) 211

"Senza Fine" 114
Seven Days (magazine) 222
"Seventh Son" 117
"The Shadow of Your Smile" 117, 121
"Shady Lady Bird" 20
"Shanghai" 52, 114
SHARE 110
Sharky's Machine (film) 192
Shaughnessy, Ed 62
Shaw, Artie 17
Shearing, George 85–86, 240, 243
Sheldon, Jack 110, 200
Sherman House (Chicago hotel)
"The Shining Sea" 122, 123, 228
Shirley, Anne 26
Shore, Dinah 32, 40, 56, 77, 84–85, 161, 171, 173
Shoreham Hotel (Florida) 123
Shoreham Hotel (Washington, D.C.) 123, 147
"Show Me the Way to Got Out of This World ('Cause That's Where Everything Is)" 48
Shower of Stars (TV) 74
"The Shrine of St. Cecilia" 20
"The Siamese Cat Song"* 66, 163
Side by Side by Sondheim (musical review) 188
Sigman, Carl 86
"Silent Night" 66
Silk Cut Festival of Jazz (UK) 194
"Silver Bells" 48
"Similau" 47
Simon, Carly 160, 183
Simon, George T. 18, 22, 35, 104, 170
Simon, Paul 140
Simon Says (book) 35
Sinatra, Frank 1, 5, 14, 23–24, 61, 76–78, 80, 81, 86, 88, 100, 115, 123, 132, 134, 162, 164, 183, 194, 203, 205, 207, 216, 227, 231, 239–240, 242
Sinatra, Nancy 127
"Sing" 146, 148, 159
"Sing a Rainbow" 69, 131, 153–154, 181–182, 214
Singers and the Song (book) 214
"(Sittin' on) The Dock of the Bay" 134
60 Minutes (TV) 223
Skelton, Red 161
Skolsky, Sidney 59
Skylar, Sunny 32
"Skylark" 24, 160
"Slender, Tender and Tall" 29
"Smack Dab in the Middle" 87, 124

"Smile" 100
Smith, Bessie 164, 169, 222
Smith, Keely 1–2, 5, 194
Smith, Paul 86
"Smoke Gets in Your Eyes" 20, 45, 76
The Snader Telescriptions 45
Snyder, Tom 190
So Deadly, So Evil (TV) 88, 90
"So Dear to My Heart" 47
"So in Love" 47, 245
"So What's New"* 124–126, 129, 131, 160
The Society of Singers 207, 239
"Soft as Spring" 20
Softly, with Feeling (a book of Lee's poetry) 59, 72
Soho Weekly News 169
Some Are Born Great (book) 113
"Some Cats Know" 176
"Somebody Else Is Taking My Place" 21–22, 24–25, 46
"Somebody Loves Me" 40, 69
"Somebody Nobody Knows" 21, 25
"Someone Who Cares" 155, 159–160, 163
Somethin' Groovy 126
"Somethin' Stupid" 127, 129, 131
"Something" 134, 140, 145
"Something I Dreamed Last Night" 76
Something Special 126
Something Special with Peggy Lee (TV) 121
"Something to Remember You By" 160
"Something Wonderful" 78
"Something's Coming" 153
"Sometimes" 167
"Sometimes I Feel Like a Motherless Child" 114
Sondheim, Stephen 147
"A Song for You" 158
A Song Is Born (film) 206
"Song of India" 53
Songs from Pete Kelly's Blues 72
Songwriter's Guild of America 207–208
Songwriter's Hall of Fame 208
Sounds of the Loop (Gilbert O'Sullivan CD) 232
Sounds of the Seventies 146
South Pacific 47
Spaeth, Dr. Sigmund 40, 59
Spalding, Baird T. 233
"Speaking of Angels" 37
"Spinning Wheel" 132, 134–136, 138
"Spring Is Here" 160
"Squeeze Me" 37

Stack, Robert 51
Stafford, Jo 38, 42, 111
The Stage (UK magazine) 189
Stage Door Canteen (film) 26
"The Star Carol" 229
"Star Sounds" 180
The Star-Ledger 194
Starr, Kay 1, 5, 245
Staten Island Advance 221
"Stay Well" 48, 126
"Stay with Me"* 123–124
Stereo Review (magazine) 117, 129, 140, 154, 163, 167, 174, 177, 187, 192, 220
The Steven Allen Show 77
Stevenson, McLean 176
Stoller, Mike 109, 133, 136, 173–174, 190, 200, 207, 216, 240
Stonestreet, Gerry (editor, *In Tune International* magazine) 245
"Straight Ahead"* 64–65
"Strangers in the Night" 123
Strauss, Johann 59
Stravinsky, Igor 35
"Street of Dreams" 76
Streisand, Barbra 137, 166–167
Strom, Lana v
Strong, Mary 203
Studio One 171
Styne, Jule 199
"Sugar (That Sugar Baby of Mine)" 68
Sugar 'n' Spice 105, 108
Sullivan, Ed 53, 94, 98, 106, 109, 118, 124–125, 127, 136, 139
Sullivan, Maxine 14, 169, 191, 215, 222
Summer on Ice (TV) 101
"Summertime" 43
Sundome Center (Phoenix, Arizona) 203
"Sunshine Cake" 48
Sweet Charity (Broadway musical and film) 118
"Sweet Lov'liness" 167
"The Sweetest Sounds" 106
"Sweetheart" 84
Swing Into Spring (TV) 84
Swing Time (film) 25
"Swingin' on a Star" 163
Syms, Sylvia 205, 227

"Talking to Myself About You" 45
"Tango" 176
"A Taste of Honey" 109
Tate, Grady 147, 204, 210
Taylor, Elizabeth (Liz) 169, 193
Taylor, James 154, 160, 169, 173
"Teach Me Tonight" 106
Teagarden, Jack 91

Templeton, Alec 47
Tennyson, Alfred 224
Terrace Room (Hotel New Yorker, New York) 22–23
"Thank Your Mother" 53
"That Did It, Marie" 21, 25
"That Man"* 121
"That Old Feeling" 31–32, 76, 79
"That Old Master Painter" 48
"That Old Piano" 8
"That Solider of Mine" 27
"That's Amore" 14, 63
"That's Aplenty" 61
"That's My Style"* 112
"That's the Way It Goes" 19–20
"That's What It Takes"* 115
"That's What Living's About" 143
Theatre Arts (magazine) 59
"Them There Eyes" 76, 91, 108, 218
Then Was Then and Now Is Now 117
"Then Was Then (and Now Is Now)"* 117, 126, 235
"There Ain't No Sweet Man That's Worth the Salt of My Tears" 109
"There Won't Be a Shortage of Love" 25
"There'll Be Another Spring"* 86, 228, 243
"There'll Be Some Changes Made" 42
"There's a Small Hotel" 75
"There's Always Something There to Remind Me" 140
"These Foolish Things" 10, 18, 53
"These Lush Moments" 43
"They Can't Take That Away from Me" 43, 46, 63, 77
Thielemans, Toots 126
The Thing (film) 74
"Things" 148
Things Are Swingin' 82, 84
"Things Are Swingin'"* 82, 126
"This Is a Very Special Day" 55
"This Is the Mrs." 53
This Is Your Life (TV) 159
"This Love of Mine" 53
Thomas, Danny 55–56, 58, 59, 138, 207
The Thomas Dooley Foundation 137
"A Thousand Violins" 48
"Three Little Fishes" 126
"Through the Eyes of Love" 187
"Till There Was You" 102, 169
Time (magazine) 57, 127, 219, 228

"Together Again" 147
Tom Thumb (film) 81
"Tom Thumb's Tune"* 82
The Tomorrow Show 190–191
The Tonight Show 145
"Too Young" 52
"Toodle-Lee-Oo-Do" 52
Top Money-Making Female Artist 50
Torme, Mel 42, 48, 91, 93, 113, 169, 182, 188, 199, 203, 229, 231, 238–240
Toronto Sun 164
"Touch Me in the Morning" 166, 176, 181, 186
Touch of Tabasco, a (Rosemary Clooney LP) 86
Towe, Ronald v, 55, 100, 111, 117, 220, 244
Tree of Life (Salk Foundation) 136
Troup, Bobby 207
Tucker, Sophie 196
Turner, Tina 216
TV Guide 167
TV Magazine 60
"Two Ladies in the Shade of the Banana Tree" 105
Two Shows Nightly 130
Tyree, Glenn 148–149

Uggams, Leslie 133, 142
The Umbrellas of Cherbourg (film) 118
"Unforgettable" 113, 126
"Uninvited Dream" 78
"Until It's Time for You to Go" 145
"Up a Lazy River" 40, 91
"Up, Up and Away" 159
Ustinov, Peter 163

"The Vagabond King Waltz" 98
Vallee, Rudy 53
Van Gogh, Vincent 244
Van Heusen, James 43, 45
Variety 53 , 63, 64, 70, 71, 74, 76, 78–79, 81–82, 87–89, 91, 94, 102–103, 110–111, 113, 115, 118, 121–122, 125–126, 130, 135–137, 139, 141, 143–144, 146–147, 154, 159–161, 173–175, 185–186, 188, 190, 198, 201, 204, 206–207, 209–210, 212–213, 217
"The Varsity Drag" 63
Vaughan, Sarah 93, 159, 189, 192, 194, 203
Venetian Room (Fairmont Hotel, Dallas) 151, 166, 203
Venetian Room (Fairmont Hotel, San Francisco) 64, 82,
177, 179, 182–183, 188, 190, 202, 214, 223
Venuti, Joe 43, 46
"The Very Thought of You" 126
Video Review (magazine) 214
"La Vie en Rose" 182
La Vie en Rose (New York nightclub) 61
Vilanch, Bruce 157
Village Voice 169, 224, 233

"Wait Till You See Her (Him)" 167–168
"Waiting for the Train to Come In" 32
Walk Don't Run (film) 123
"Walking Happy" 124–126
Wallace, Mike 91
Wallichs, Glenn 30–31, 133
Walt Disney Productions 219
Walt Disney's Cavalcade of Song (TV) 66–67
Warden, Jack 176
Warhol, Andy 26
Warner, Jack 72
Warren Star Theatre 213
Warwick, Dionne 140
Washington, Dinah 81
Washington Post 213
Washington Times 212
"Watch What Happens" 118, 141
"Watermelon Weather" 58
"Way Back Home" 48
"The Way We Were" 165
"The Way You Look Tonight" 25–26, 152
Wayne, John 117, 184
Wayne, Max 62
WDAY 10, 11, 13, 197
"The We Are Siamese"* *see* "Siamese Cat Song"
"We Be Friends" 229
"We Love the Canadian Rockies" 47
Weatherwax, Frank 44
Webb, Jack 67, 69, 70–71, 145, 214
Webb, Jimmy 132
"Wedding Bell Blues" 146
Weiss, George David 207
Weiss, Sid 23
"We'll Meet Again" 24–25, 152
Wells, Bob 42, 229
West, Mae 20, 126, 239
Westbury Music Fair 155, 210
Westwood Playhouse (West Hollywood theatre) 200, 207
"What Are You Doing the Rest of Your Life" 140, 144, 146
"What Did They Do to My Goil?" 40
"What I Did for Love" 180, 182

Index

"What Is a Women?" 129, 145
"What Is This Thing Called Love" 46, 63
"What Kind of Fool Am I?" 121–122
"What More Can a Woman Do?"* 30, 32, 45
What's My Line? (TV) 78, 125
"What's New" 61
"When a Woman Loves a Man" 85
"When I Found You" 160, 167–168
"When I Need You" 182
"When in Rome" 114
"When Johnny Comes Marching Home" 146
"When the Red, Red Robin Comes Bob-Bob-Bobbin' Along" 40
"When the Roses Bloom Again" 24
"When the Saints Go Marching In" 89
"When the Sun Comes Out" 20, 106, 108
"When the World Was Young (Ah, the Apple Trees)" 84, 113, 118
"When You Speak with Your Eyes"* 48
"When You're in Love with the Lover You Love" 47
Where (magazine) 216
"Where Can I Go Without You"* 60, 63, 110, 160, 228
Where Did They Go? 147
"Where Did They Go?" 147–148
"Where Has My Little Dog Gone" 163
"Where or When" 22, 26, 55, 117, 194–195
"While We're Young" 206
"Whisper Not" 110
"Whistle for Happiness" 134
Whitcomb, John 65
White, George 53

"The White Birch and the Sycamore"* 74
"White Christmas" 45, 93, 229
Whiteman, Paul 20, 53, 91
Whiting, Margaret 31, 194, 227
"Who Will Buy" 159
"Who's Gonna Pay the Check"* 60, 62
"Why Don't We Do This More Often?" 21
"Why Don't You Do Right?" 25–31, 46, 67, 73, 84–85, 97, 109, 111, 126, 152, 154, 233–234, 240
Wilder, Alec 19–20, 114, 206
Wiley, Lee 5, 14, 31, 152
Williams, Andy 108, 111, 115–116, 121–*122*, *124*, 137, 179
Williams, Hank 164
Williams, Joe 5, 159, 187–188, 192, 194, 199, 203, 239
Williams, Paul 188
Williams, Tennessee 187
Wilson, Earl 109, 115, 132, 153
Wilson, John S. 147, 158, 179, 186, 190, 210, 217, 221, 225
Wilson, Nancy 129
Wilson, Teddy 22
Winchell, Walter 76
"The Wind Beneath My Wings" 201
"Windmills of Your Mind" 132
"Winter Weather" 21, 23
"Winter Wonderland" 117
WNEW 199
Wogan (UK TV) 225
"A Woman Alone with the Blues" 85
Wonder, Stevie 142, 173
"A Wonderful Guy" 48
Wood, Natalie *72*
World Tribune 125
"Would You Dance with a Stranger" 93

The Yale Glee Club 91
"Yes, Indeed" 94, 97, 118, 234

"You and I Passing By" 40
"You and the Night and the Music" 63
"You Are My Sunshine" 108
"You Came a Long Way from St. Louis" 46
"You Don't Have to Know the Language" 42
"You Don't Know" 118, 240
"You Fascinate Me So" 88, 126
"You Go to My Head" 58
"You Let My Love Get Cold" 60
"You Must Have Been a Beautiful Baby" 126
"You Stepped Out of a Dream" 94
"You Turned the Tables on Me" 45
"You Was" 47, 118
"You Was Right, Baby"* 32, 45
"You Were Meant for Me" 232, 238
"You'll Remember Me" 141, 146
Young, Lester 233
Young, Snooky 153
Young, Victor 37, 60, 63, 66, 76, 234
The Youngstown Daily Vindicator 193
"You're Driving Me Crazy" 126
"You're Easy to Dance With" 25
"You're in Love with Someone" 48
"You're Mine You" 82
"You're My Thrill" 75
"You've Got Possibilities" 118, 123
"You've Got to See Mama Every Night (Or You Can't See Mama at All)" 115

"Zing a Little Zong" 58
"Zip-a-dee-doo-dah" 139
Zoo World 167

www.ingramcontent.com/pod-product-compliance
Lightning Source LLC
Chambersburg PA
CBHW080935020526
44116CB00034B/2704